The Korean Economy at the Crossroads

For many years, Korea was widely seen in economic and financial circles as something of a miracle. The financial crisis that Korea experienced in 1997 did much to setback its economy, but by 2001 it was still the thirteenth largest economy in terms of GDP in the world.

This enticing collection, with contributions from experts with an impressive knowledge of Korea and its economy, charts not only the well-documented causes of the crisis, but more importantly, its response and recovery from it. With an admirable scholarly rigour, the book covers such topics as:

- the origin and evolution of the Korean economic system and its special factors, including *chaebols*
- Korean industries since the crisis
- what happened to the money after the capital flight of the crisis and did the USA benefit?

The Korean Economy at the Crossroads is intended and recommended not only for students and academics involved in international finance, economics and Asian studies, but also for the business leaders and policy makers who can draw lessons from the important analyses presented.

MoonJoong Tcha is Senior Lecturer in Economics and Associate Director of the Economic Research Centre at the University of Western Australia.

Chung-Sok Suh is Director of the Korea-Australasia Research Centre, the University of New South Wales, Australia.

Routledge studies in the growth economies of Asia

1 **The Changing Capital Markets of East Asia**
Edited by Ky Cao

2 **Financial Reform in China**
Edited by On Kit Tam

3 **Women and Industrialization in Asia**
Edited by Susan Horton

4 **Japan's Trade Policy**
Action or reaction?
Yumiko Mikanagi

5 **The Japanese Election System**
Three analaytical perspectives
Junichiro Wada

6 **The Economics of the Latecomers**
Catching-up, technology transfer and institutions in Germany, Japan and South Korea
Jang-Sup Shin

7 **Industrialization in Malaysia**
Import substitution and infant industry performance
Rokiah Alavi

8 **Economic Development in Twentieth-Century East Asia**
The international context
Edited by Aiko Ikeo

9 **The Politics of Economic Development in Indonesia**
Contending perspectives
Edited by Ian Chalmers and Vedi Hadiz

10 **Studies in the Economic History of the Pacific Rim**
Edited by Sally M. Miller, A. J. H. Latham and Dennis O. Flynn

11 **Workers and the State in New Order Indonesia**
Vedi R. Hadiz

12 **The Japanese Foreign Exchange Market**
Beate Reszat

13 **Exchange Rate Policies in Emerging Asian Countries**
Edited by Stefan Collignon, Jean Pisani-Ferry and Yung Chul Park

14 **Chinese Firms and Technology in the Reform Era**
Yizheng Shi

15 **Japanese Views on Economic Development**
Diverse paths to the market
Kenichi Ohno and Izumi Ohno

16 **Technological Capabilities and Export Success in Asia**
Edited by Dieter Ernst, Tom Ganiatsos and Lynn Mytelka

17 **Trade and Investment in China**
The European experience
Edited by Roger Strange, Jim Slater and Limin Wang

18 **Technology and Innovation in Japan**
Policy and management for the 21st Century
Edited by Martin Hemmert and Christian Oberländer

19 **Trade Policy Issues in Asian Development**
Prema-chandra Athukorala

20 **Economic Integration in the Asia Pacific Region**
Ippei Yamazawa

21 **Japan's War Economy**
Edited by Erich Pauer

22 **Industrial Technology Development in Malaysia**
Industry and firm studies
Edited by K. S. Jomo, Greg Felker and Rajah Rasiah

23 **Technology, Competitiveness and the State**
Malaysia's industrial technology policies
Edited by K. S. Jomo and Greg Felker

24 **Corporatism and Korean Capitalism**
Edited by Dennis L. McNamara

25 **Japanese Science**
Samuel Coleman

26 **Capital and Labour in Japan**
The functions of two factor markets
Toshiaki Tachibanaki and Atsuhiro Taki

27 **Asia Pacific Dynamism 1550–2000**
Edited by A. J. H. Latham and Heita Kawakatsu

28 **The Political Economy of Development and Environment in Korea**
Jae-Yong Chung and Richard J. Kirkby

29 **Japanese Economics and Economists since 1945**
Edited by Aiko Ikeo

30 **China's Entry into the World Trade Organisation**
Edited by Peter Drysdale and Ligang Song

31 **Hong Kong as an International Financial Centre**
Emergence and development 1945–1965
Catherine R. Schenk

32 **Impediments to Trade in Services: Measurement and Policy Implication**
Edited by Christoper Findlay and Tony Warren

33 **The Japanese Industrial Economy**
Late development and cultural causation
Ian Inkster

34 **China and the Long March to Global Trade**
The accession of China to the World Trade Organization
Edited by Alan S. Alexandroff, Sylvia Ostry and Rafael Gomez

35 **Capitalist Development and Economism in East Asia**
The rise of Hong Kong, Singapore, Taiwan, and South Korea
Kui-Wai Li

36 **Women and Work in Globalizing Asia**
Edited by Dong-Sook S. Gills and Nicola Piper

37 **Financial Markets and Policies in East Asia**
Gordon de Brouwer

38 **Developmentalism and Dependency in Southeast Asia**
The case of the automotive industry
Jason P. Abbott

39 **Law and Labour Market Regulation in East Asia**
Edited by Sean Cooney, Tim Lindsey, Richard Mitchell and Ying Zhu

40 **The Economy of the Philippines**
Elites, inequalities and economic restructuring
Peter Krinks

41 **Private Enterprise in China**
Edited by Ross Garnaut and Ligang Song

42 **The Vietnamese Economy**
Awakening the dormant dragon
Edited by Binh Tran-Nam and Chi Do Pham

43 **Restructuring Korea Inc.**
Jang-Sup Shin and Ha-Joon Chang

44 **Development and Structural Change in the Asia-Pacific**
Globalising miracles or end of a model?
Edited by Martin Andersson and Christer Gunnarsson

45 **State Collaboration and Development Strategies in China**
Alexius Pereira

46 **Capital and Knowledge in Asia**
Changing power relations
Edited by Heidi Dahles and Otto van den Muijzenberg

47 **Southeast Asian Paper Tigers?**
From miracle to debacle and beyond
Edited by Jomo K. S.

48 **Manufacturing Competitiveness in Asia**
How internationally competitive national firms and industries developed in East Asia
Edited by Jomo K. S.

49 **The Korean Economy at the Crossroads**
Edited by MoonJoong Tcha and Chung-Sok Suh

The Korean Economy at the Crossroads

Edited by
MoonJoong Tcha and
Chung-Sok Suh

Routledge
Taylor & Francis Group
LONDON AND NEW YORK

First published 2003
by RoutledgeCurzon

Published 2013 by
Routledge
2 Park Square, Milton Park, Abingdon, Oxfordshire OX14 4RN

Simultaneously published in the USA and Canada
by Routledge
711 Third Avenue, New York, NY 10017

First issued in paperback 2014

Routledge is an imprint of the Taylor & Francis Group, an informa business

Typeset in Baskerville by
Newgen Imaging Systems (P) Ltd, Chennai, India

British Library Cataloguing in Publication Data
A catalogue record for this book is available from the British Library

Library of Congress Cataloging in Publication Data
A catalog record for this book has been requested

ISBN 13: 978-0-415-31602-6 (hbk)
ISBN 13: 978-1-138-81068-6 (pbk)

Father, I miss you. Mother, I love you

MoonJoong Tcha

To Hea-Kyong, Laura (Haun) and Joshua (Jinwon)
who make my life worth living

Chung-Sok Suh

Contents

Figures

Tables

Contributors

Inkyo Cheong: Research Division of Southeast and South Asia, Korea Institute for International Economic Policy.

Sang-Moon Hahm: School of Public Policy and Management, Korea Development Institute.

John Hawkins: Bank of International Settlement.

Sunseop Jung: School of Law, University of Melbourne.

David Deok-Ki Kim: Department of Economics, the University of Sydney.

Euysung Kim: Graduate School of International Studies, Yonsei University.

Hyung-Min Kim: School of Asian Languages and Studies, Monash University.

Jinu Kim: School of the Built Environment, the University of New South Wales.

Youngok Kim: School of International Business, the University of New South Wales.

Seung-Ho Kwon: Korea-Australasia Research Centre, School of International Business, the University of New South Wales.

Hyun-Hoon Lee: Department of Economics, Kangwon University.

Minsoo Lee: Division of Commerce, Lincoln University.

Sang-Young Lee: Construction and Economy Research Institute of Korea.

Wonhyuk Lim: Korea Development Institute.

Denny McGeorge: School of the Built Environment, the University of New South Wales.

John McKay: Monash Asian Institute, Monash University.

Byung S. Min: School of International Business and Asian Studies, Griffith University.

Kwang Soo Park: POSCO Research Institute (POSRI).

Jung-Soo Seo: School of Economics and Management, the University of New South Wales.

Chung-Sok Suh: Korea-Australasia Research Centre, School of International Business, the University of New South Wales.

MoonJoong Tcha: Department of Economics, Business School, the University of Western Australia.

Eric van Wincoop: Federal Reserve Bank, New York.

Kei-Mu Yi: Federal Reserve Bank, New York.

Foreword

Just as the growth of the Korean economy since the early 1960s has been incomparably dramatic and dynamic, the depth of the economic crisis that struck the economy in 1997 was so great that it threatened to become terminally destabilizing. The seriousness of the economic setback was reflected in the 10 per cent negative growth in 1998 and was accompanied by a sense of enormous frustration of the Korean people. Therefore the road to economic recovery in Korea has been as impressive, if not more, as the path leading to its earlier success during the previous forty years. Korea was the only country where people sold their personal gold possessions to rescue the economy from the crisis, which on a scale is matched only by a similar occurrence in the early part of the twentieth century (*Mulsan Jangryu Woondong*). Moreover, the restructuring of the entire economy was more comprehensive and was carried out at a faster pace than in other Asian countries and explains why this economy achieved a 'V-shaped' recovery, a sharp contraction of the economy followed by a sharp recovery. Owing to the quick passage of time, some people may regard this story of crisis and recovery as a part of history. Nevertheless, strenuous effort needs to be made to understand the causes of the collapse as well as the effects of the crisis. This process will help Korea avoid further crises and prevent a W-shaped or an inversed N-shaped recovery curve in the future.

While this volume reveals numerous interesting and constructive findings, two significant contributions to the discussion on crisis and sustainable recovery stand out. First, this book maintains consistency despite a variety of topics and issues. While most collections on the Korean economic crisis investigate certain aspects of the crisis, the articles in this book analyse the origins and evolution of the crisis, and discuss potential problems confronting the economy through an examination of the performance of the industrial and financial sectors, the operation of conglomerates and financial institutions, as well as legal aspects of the economy. In addition, selected chapters discuss the difficulties surrounding attempts to restructure the economy following the crisis and place the effects of the crises and subsequent restructuring in an international context. This kind of integrated and holistic approach is not easily found elsewhere. Second, the chapters in this book are written by scholars based in four different continents: Asia, Australia, America and Europe. Scholars who have been actively engaged in research in both Korea and abroad provide diverse perspectives and balanced assessments on a variety of issues, and, accordingly, the book gains a very rare achievement; it manages to see both the forest and the trees.

While the methodologies adopted in some chapters are rather rigorous and technical, I found that most chapters are easily comprehensible to those who have studied economics or related fields at the university level for two or three years, and to those who may not have majored in economics but are nonetheless interested in the issues discussed. There is no doubt this book provides invaluable lessons for policy makers and those professionals who are interested in Korea and the Korean economy. Not only do I recognize the important intellectual contributions made by this work, but in particular, this book has great sentimental value to me as it is edited by two of my previous students, Chung-Sok Suh and MoonJoong Tcha, who are currently working in Australia as Director of the Korea-Australasia Research Centre at the University of New South Wales and Associate Director of the Economic Research Centre at the University of Western Australia, respectively. I hope and trust this work is a significant bridge that helps to forge stronger links between Korea and Australia.

Un-Chan Chung
Seoul National University

Acknowledgements

This volume contains papers presented at the Korean Studies Association Conference held in Sydney, Australia in 2000, and at the 2002 Korea and the World Economy Conference, held in Seoul. We are indebted to the members of the programme committee who organized the two conferences, and to the participants for their comments.

We are also indebted to the *Journal of Construction Research* and *FRBNY Economic Policy Review* for their generous granting of permission to reproduce papers for Chapters 14 and 15 in this volume respectively.

We greatly appreciate the contribution made by Professor Un-Chan Chung, one of the most respected and influential economists in Korea, who managed in spite of his heavy workload to provide an invaluable foreword for this book. He was our teacher, and we firmly believe that if there is anything good in us, it is due to the wonderful training we received from those teachers like Professor Chung, who never lost enthusiasm or excitement in teaching us.

Professor Ken Clements of the Department of Economics, University of Western Australia encouraged us to complete this project, and the Korea Research Foundation and the Korea-Australasia Research Centre at the University of New South Wales generously provided financial support. We are grateful to them. Mr Robert Langham and Mr Terry Clague at Routledge were consistently helpful, patient and professional. We greatly enjoyed talking with them about soccer, as well as economics. Ms Patricia Wang has provided valuable assistance with our research and we would like to thank K. Andrew Semmens for his excellent and extensive editorial assistance. Without their support and help, this volume would not have been completed. Therefore, we thank them.

1 The Korean economy

Triumphs, difficulties, and triumphs again?

MoonJoong Tcha, Minsoo Lee, and Chung-Sok Suh

1.1 Prologue

Why is it that the Korean economy is so interesting to observe, investigate, and analyse? One of the first images of Korea frequently encountered by foreigners might be those images that they see frequently in newspapers or on TV; involving workers and university students wearing face masks violently demonstrating on the street, throwing Molotov cocktails, or, just as likely, of images depicting riot police even more violently subjugating the demonstrators. However, another common image of Korea, which makes it particularly interesting, reflects the widespread perception that it is one of the few countries that have achieved dramatic economic growth; and more recently, has been hit severely by economic crisis. Korea belonged at the forefront of a group of countries labelled 'miraculous' by Lucas (1993), at least until 1997. From being one of the poorest countries in 1961, it had grown by 2001 to be the thirteenth largest economy in terms of gross domestic product (GDP) in the world, notwithstanding the setbacks experienced as part of its recent economic crisis. It is hard to investigate the successes and failures of this remarkable economy in a single chapter. Consequently, in this chapter, we will briefly summarize the triumphs and difficulties that this country experienced on the path to growth.

1.2 From nothing to something

1.2.1 Overview

Korea was historically one of the poorest countries in the world endowed with a small landmass, scarce natural resources, and a large population. Added to this, by the time the Korean War (1950–53) ended the entire peninsular had been completely devastated. During the period from 1953–61, Korea made a very slow recovery from the war, and per capita income was lower than that of most of its neighbouring countries. With the introduction of the first Five-Year Plan in 1962, initiated and designed by the military government, Korea accelerated its development and changed the trend curve of economic growth dramatically. It continued its rapid economic growth in the 1970s, in spite of the downturn of the world economy caused by two oil crises. Since then, the Korean economy has been among the most rapidly growing nations over the period, even during the 1980s when the country was in the middle of political turmoil, and generally regarded as one of the most successful developing economies often used to illustrate the superiority of the capitalistic market economies over socialist economies, in particular North Korea. Since the 1980s, it had become known as one of the 'four little Asian dragons (or tigers)' together with Hong Kong, Singapore, and Taiwan, although there have been debates in some quarters about the reality of the rapid economic growth of some East Asian countries (see, e.g. Krugman 1994). When Lucas (1993) discussed the main factors of economic growth, he emphasized that the growth achieved by East Asian countries was miraculous for at least three reasons; it was extremely rare throughout the ages that so many economies in the same region recorded such high growth rates continuously for such a long period. A host of studies attempted to identify the main factors that contributed to these economies' growth. A general consensus was reached that most of these economies had the following common features, in addition to the fast accumulation of production factors that is traditionally used in the neoclassical framework to explain economic growth (e.g. Hughes 1995, Kruger 1997):

1 They actively pursued export-oriented policies.
2 Usually, government intervention in the economy was not excessive.
3 The importance of education was emphasized.
4 And, these economies were able to maintain stable macroeconomic policies.

In addition to these aforementioned common characteristics, the Korean economy had a few more unique characteristics. For example, it was oriented towards conglomerate-oriented growth. Also, its economic growth was more impressive as it achieved such high growth rates even though a significant portion of GDP (or the government's budget) was reserved for defence. As well as being such a direct cost, the opportunity cost of defence was immense, considering that all the young males had to complete two years or more of military service. Another unique characteristic of the Korean economy, which was one of the most important explanatory factors of the crisis, is excessive government intervention in the financial sector up until the early 1990s, which subsequently caused structural weaknesses in this sector. A more detailed review of the history of economic growth in Korea follows in the next section.

1.2.2 The road to growth

The economic growth of the Korean economy prior to the crisis in 1997 can be categorized into four stages, taking into account the leadership and growth strategies. Table 1.1 summarizes the leadership overall and the development plans, and economic growth for the last forty years. When Mr Chung-hee Park seized power in a military coup and then retained it after holding an election, Korea possessed all the bad characteristics of a typically poor country; a small land mass with an extremely high population density, small domestic markets, no natural resources, and low levels of physical capital. The Five-Year Economic Development Plans

Table 1.1 State leadership and economic performance (1961–98)

Economic development plan	*Period*	*President*	*Planned growth rate (%)*	*Actual growth rate (%)*	*State leadership and economic, management*
1	1962–66	Park, C.H. (1961.5–1979.10)	7.1	7.8	Authoritarian and strong leadership. State-guided economy.
2	1967–71	Park, C.H.	7.0	9.6	↓
3	1972–76	Park, C.H.	8.6	9.7	
4	1977–81	Park, C.H. Chun, D.H. (1979.11–1988.2)	9.2	5.8	Authoritarian and strong leadership. Large corporation centred economy.
5	1982–86	Chun, D.H.	7.5	8.6	↓
6	1987–91	Chun, D.H. Roh, T.W. (1988.2–1993.2)	7.3	10	Authoritarian but weak leadership. Large corporation centred economy.
7	1992–96	Roh, T.W. Kim, Y.S. (1993.2–1998.2)	7.5	7	↓ Democratic but weak leadership. Reform oriented economy.

Source: Rearranged from Kim (2001), p. 14.

initiated by the Park government thus emphasized the role of exports to overcome the limitations imposed by small domestic markets. His government believed that, as Korea was not endowed with abundant natural resources, growth should be achieved by a systematic programme of importing raw materials and intermediate goods for processing, and then exporting commodities with added value. Government policy was in general based on market principles; nonetheless, it used a variety of policy tools, and intensively controlled the banking and financial sectors (World Bank 1993). While the government frequently intervened in the market, it could minimize price distortions and the misallocation of resources caused by intervention, through a system of intensive subsidies. Specializing in labour intensive goods such as clothes and shoes, the economy enjoyed annual economic growth rates of between 8 and 10 per cent throughout the duration of the first two Development Plans until 1971.

As a former General, President Park's ambition was to build the country to the point where at the very least it would be superior to North Korea in both economic and military power. To this end, the growth achieved in the last decade largely as the product of selling clothes, toys, and wigs was in his eyes not very satisfactory. Moreover, he recognized the importance of economic growth, generated as a result of high value added commodities in the heavy and chemical industries. As a result, the third Economic Development Plan concentrated on developing 'heavy and chemical industries' (1973–79) and selected six strategic heavy and chemical industries – steel, petrochemicals, non-ferrous metals, shipbuilding, electronics, and machinery – to receive support such as tax incentives, subsidized public services and preferential financing. In return, the government demanded producers in these areas to strive to achieve international competitiveness. Furthermore, as a means of transferring advanced technology from foreign developed countries to the domestic industries, Park's government encouraged invitations to many foreign-trained scientists and engineers. Combined with a strong export-driven growth policy, this policy of strategically supporting heavy and chemical industries seemed to be successful, at least in terms of growth. Despite the First Oil Shock, annual growth rates for the first five years reached almost 10 per cent. However, this policy was criticized as well in some quarters, on the basis that this patronage produced, as an inevitable by-product, a distortion of local industry, particularly in regards to a severe distortion in the structure of domestic industry. Labour intensive firms and small- and medium-sized firms were starved of credit; large firms started to entertain flawed ideas as to 'the survival of the fattest rather than the fittest' and accrued excessively high levels of debt. The links between business and government got stronger and rent-seeking behaviour became more common. Moreover, after the two oil shocks, high oil prices pushed the capacity utilization ratio very low, which caused inefficiencies in the heavy and chemical industries where a large amount of capital was initially invested. As a result, during the period of the fourth Economic Development Plan, the annual growth rate sharply declined to about 6 per cent, which was generally viewed by members of the country as indicative of the economy being in recession.[1]

In 1979, the bureaucrats recognized that the complexity of the economy was in excess of the government's management capacities, and consequently introduced more market-oriented policies and deregulations. Government intervention continued, however, it focused on restructuring distressed industries, supporting the development of technology, and promoting competition (Kim 2001). While the economy experienced a period of political turmoil following Mr Park's assassination (in 1979), and the ascension to power of Mr Doo-hwan Chun, bureaucrats liberalized the country even further and used a variety of incentives to encourage production and exports. Favourable international economic environments such as low energy costs, low interest rates and a strong Japanese yen, helped the economy to recover from the relatively poor rates of growth that emerged in the late 1970s, and the economy was able to record growth rates of 9–10 per cent until the early 1990s. However, the non-competitiveness of the financial sector (resulting from excessive government intervention) as well as large-scale levels of private sector debt continued, which later became major sources of economic crises.

Kim (2001) points out that while the macroeconomic indicators looked fine, the backbone of the economy began to fall apart when President Tae-woo Roh was in office. One of the important reasons for this was, he argued, that Mr Roh compromised unnecessarily over the demands of the workers, which led to frequent labour strikes and an increase in wages that was higher than increases in productivity.

It was unfortunate for Korea also that the next President, Mr Young-sam Kim, did not notice how quickly the economy had become incompetent. Influenced more by his concern over popularity ratings than prudent economic considerations, Mr Kim attempted some large-scale economic reforms, which proved to be failures and only created confusion in an economy that was already weakening. As shown in Table 1.2, Kwack (2001) cited figures to demonstrate the extent to which the economy had lost its competitiveness in the run up to the outbreak of the crisis. While the unit value of exporting goods had been decreasing since 1995, all costs such as material costs, labour costs, and borrowing costs had been consistently increasing.

1.2.3 The Achilles tendon of the Korean economy

Throughout the history of rapid economic growth in Korea, the expansion of industrial capacity has been achieved through the expansion of existing firms rather than through the creation of new firms. This pattern has resulted in the growth of a small number of very large firms, *chaebols*, leading to a tendency towards high industry concentration. The *chaebols* in Korea have made a significant contribution to industrialization during the period of rapid economic growth, and they have constituted an important part of the Korean economy. Nevertheless, as well as enjoying a kind of monopolist position afforded by government protection and subsidies, they also sought unrelated diversification, which has resulted in an unnecessary concentration of industries. By the end of 1996, the top five *chaebols* in Korea accounted for more than 8 per cent of the economy's GDP.

The government utilized financial instruments to support the *chaebols*' activities. The financial intermediary system in Korea has been nationalized or heavily regulated by the government since the 1960s, and most foreign loans have been directed and allocated by the government. The government decided who should receive the policy loans (loans distributed by strategic purposes of government), and most of them were distributed to big conglomerates in the industries targeted by the government. The government loans were subsidized by lower interest rates than the prevailing market rates, and the government implicitly guaranteed to bail out government approved firms through debt cancellation or through granting additional government loans, if these firms ran into financial problems. The government's policy of rewarding *chaebols* through granting them preferential access to credit and implicit guarantees surrounding potential bailouts led to an underdeveloped banking system and raised ethical or 'moral hazard' problems surrounding the behaviour of the *chaebols* and financial intermediaries. Financial intermediaries frequently failed to carry out due diligence and analysis, as they felt obliged to follow the government's guidelines for distributing loans.

The *chaebols* too often ignored whether or not they were capable of paying back the loan or paid insufficient attention to whether they could get a higher return from their investments than the interest they had to pay on the debts incurred to fund these investments, as they felt that they could rely on another round of government support if necessary. Consequently, the large conglomerates financed through subsidized policy loans, too frequently expanded and made acquisitions

Table 1.2 Unit values of export prices, production cost, and make-up, 1990–95 (1995 = 100)

	Export prices		*Cost of production*		*Domestic material cost*	*Imported material cost*	*Unit labour cost*	*Borrowing cost*	*Make-up*	
	(A)	*% change*	*(B)*	*% change*					*(A/B)*	*% change*
Weights			100		60.4	18	15.8	5.8		
1990	86.4		88.3		85.6	92.5	87	86.3	98.2	
1991	90	4.17	91.5	3.62	89.5	95.1	89.3	86.1	98.5	0.31
1992	94.4	4.89	93.8	2.51	91.6	96.5	93.1	91.3	101	2.03
1993	97.4	3.18	93.9	0.11	92.9	93.7	95.8	99.6	103	2.89
1994	99.2	1.85	96.1	2.34	95.5	93.5	101	97.2	103	−0.29
1995	100	0.81	100	4.06	100	100	100	100	100	−3.01
1996	90.3	−9.70	103	3.00	102.7	104.7	99.9	109.3	87.3	−12.70
1997	89.7	−0.66	108.7	5.53	106.7	118.9	101.6	117.7	81	−7.22

Source: Rearranged from Kwack (2001), p. 55.

Notes
Domestic material cost = producer; Import material cost = import prices of materials and energy; Borrowing cost = weighted average of commercial banks' lending rates. Weights used are based on information from the Bank of Korea, input–output table; financial statement analysis. Weight used from 1990 to 1992 are: 57.8 for domestic material cost, 22.3 for imported material cost, 15.1 for unit labour cost, and 4.8 for the cost of borrowing.

Table 1.3 Debt–equity–asset ratio of manufacturing corporations in Korea, Taiwan, Japan, and United States (%)

	1990	*1991*	*1992*	*1993*	*1994*	*1995*	*1996*
Korea	285	306	318	294	302	286	317
Taiwan	113.64	83.4	97.9	92.9	88	87.2	85.7
Japan	226	221	216.4	212.8	209.3	206.3	153
United States	148.7	147.3	168.2	174.5	166	159	153.5

Source: Bank of Korea (various years), financial statement analysis.

by investing in high-risk projects or even marginally profitable projects as has been pointed out by Krugman (1998a).

Given the provision of guaranteed subsidized loans from the government, Korean firms preferred debt financing to equity financing for investment. Consequently, the corporate sector in Korea had a relatively higher debt to equity ratio than many Asian countries, well in excess of 300 per cent, until it faced economic collapse and a fully blown economic crisis (The World Bank 1998, 1999). Table 1.3 indicates that the debt to equity ratio of Korean manufacturing firms was higher than that of Taiwan, Japan, and the United States. Excessive lending to inefficiently operated firms and the mismatching of short-term loans and long-term investments were inevitable as the economy's financial markets, which had been subject to tight government controls, were liberalized without proper precautionary measures being taken.

The 1990s witnessed the liberalization of financial markets in Korea. Over the period 1993–97, capital flows and foreign exchange controls were liberalized in accordance with the Blueprint for Financial Reform in 1993 and the Program for Capital Account Liberalization in 1995. The volume of international capital flows increased, as shown in Table 1.4, where, in particular, liquid short-term portfolio investments comprised the major portion. Large conglomerates and many other small firms in Korea could get easy access to international capital in this period for their long-term investment projects through the operations of financial institutions that made available short-term loans at lower interest rates than the domestic rates. Many firms in Korea were not concerned about the possibility of a run on the banks and their exposure to foreign exchange rate fluctuations, and they invested the short-term loans in long-term projects. *Time* (9 March 1998) describes how Asian companies and financial institutions borrowed heavily from abroad and, moreover, how they displayed an excessive appetite for short-term debt.

1.3 Five minutes to midnight

1.3.1 Economic fundamentals prior to the crisis

Korea celebrated two monumental achievements in 1996: the first was to join the Organization for Economic Cooperation and Development (OECD) and the other was to break through per capita GDP of $10,000. However, contrary to

Table 1.4 Macroeconomic fundamentals (Units: US million/%)

Year	*GDP*	*Exchange rate*		*Current account*		*Investment*		*Exports*		*Imports*		*Export price index*	*Import price index*	*Trade balance*	*Terms of trade*
		Nominal	*Real*		*As % GDP*	*FDI*	*Portfolio*	*Return*	*Growth rate*	*Return*	*Growth rate*				
1988	182,688	684.1	822.8	14,505.4	7.94	1,014.1	−607.4	60,696	28.37	51,811	26.31	86.91	91.08	8,885	95.42
1989	222,440	679.6	810.5	5,360.8	2.41	1,117.8	−2.1	62,377	2.77	61,465	18.63	85.51	87.78	912	97.41
1990	250,350	716.4	829.4	−2,002.8	−0.80	788.0	661.5	65,016	4.23	69,844	13.63	87.94	86.89	−4,828	101.21
1991	294,940	760.8	840.0	−8,317.3	−2.82	1,179.8	2,905.8	71,870	10.54	81,525	16.72	91.25	86.6	−9,655	105.37
1992	315,480	788.4	844.2	−3,943.5	−1.25	728.3	5,874.5	76,632	6.63	81,775	0.31	93.68	87.88	−5,143	106.60
1993	341,207	808.1	850.3	989.5	0.29	588.8	11,087.8	82,236	7.31	83,800	2.48	96	90.99	−1,564	105.51
1994	402,813	788.7	801.7	−3,867.0	−0.96	810.3	8,713.1	96,013	16.75	102,348	22.13	98.7	94.59	−6,335	104.35
1995	488,879	774.7	774.7	−8,506.5	−1.74	1,775.8	14,619.3	125,058	30.25	135,119	32.02	100	100	−10,061	100.00
1996	511,238	844.2	828.1	−23,005.7	−4.50	2,326.0	21,514.4	129,715	3.72	150,339	11.26	95.8	100.65	−20,624	95.18
1997	530,338	1,695.0	1,629.4	−8,167.2	−1.54	2,844.2	13,308.1	136,164	4.97	144,616	−3.81	102.1	110.25	−8,452	92.61
1998	314,859	1,204.0	1,093.1	40,364.9	12.82	5,412.3	774.8	132,313	−2.83	93,282	−35.50	134.08	141.38	39,031	94.84
1999	406,590	1,138.0	1,047.4	24,476.7	6.02	9,333.4	7,907.9	143,686	8.60	119,752	28.38	108.81	124.24	23,934	87.58
2000	471,273	1,264.5	1,176.4	11,404.8	2.42	9,283.4	12,697.0	172,268	19.89	160,481	34.01	107.7	133.75	11,787	80.52

Source: International Financial Statistics, International Monetary Fund, March 2002.

forecasts by the OECD concerning the future economic prosperity in Korea, the Korean economy experienced severe turmoil in late 1997. Many Koreans felt that as one of the miracle economies, it was unacceptable that Korea could have fallen victim to such a catastrophic financial crisis. This section will review how the economy accumulated its major problems during the several years before the crisis.

Various economic models and hypotheses have been advanced to explain the Asian financial crisis in 1997. Corsetti *et al.* (1998a,b) stressed that deteriorating macroeconomic fundamentals and poor economic policies were the main causes of the crisis. They identified several contributing fundamental factors such as exchange rate misalignments, current account imbalances, excessive domestic investment in risky and low-profitable projects, and excessive borrowing and lending with moral hazard problems and lack of regulation and supervision. As an alternative view, Radelet and Sachs (1998a,b) emphasized the role of financial panic to explain the Asian crisis. They argued that weak economic fundamentals and significant structural problems in the region were not sufficiently severe to cause a financial crisis. The crisis underscored the shortcomings of the international capital markets and their vulnerability to sharp and abrupt shifts in market confidence.

In the period immediately preceding the crises, the Korean economy appeared to possess strong macroeconomic fundamentals as reported in Table 1.4. Growth rates ranged from 7 to 10 per cent, which was the norm in Korea since 1962. Furthermore, throughout the 1990s Korea enjoyed a single digit inflation rate, the government's fiscal deficit was less than 1 per cent of GDP, and the rate of saving was high, amounting to over 35 per cent of GDP. In this regard, it was not pure nonsense when the deputy prime minister of Korea announced just before the crisis that the Korean economic fundamentals were still solid and strong.

However, despite the prevalence of these strong market fundamentals, some of the other economic fundamentals were, in fact, very weak before the onset of the crisis. In 1995, the trade deficit in Korea was only 2.2 per cent of GDP, but this increased to as much as 4.3 per cent of GDP in 1996. The current account deficit was even higher; in 1996 it reached the unsustainable level of 4.5 per cent of GDP. These high trade and current account deficits can be attributed to a surge in imports, stagnating exports, and the real appreciation of exchange rates. If only the economy continued to grow rapidly, or 'pongi' game style financing was available, this level of deficit might not have been critical to Korea. On the other hand, high deficit levels could easily become fatal if the economy entered a period of crises or encountered unusual economic circumstances. Since 1992, the Korean economy has also experienced a deterioration in the terms of trade.[2] The slowdown in exports in 1996, along with a deterioration in the terms of trade, severely affected the profitability of the firms in Korea. While the Korean economy recorded a chronic trade deficit, it was due to a deterioration in the terms of trade and a rapid surge in imports, rather than exports stagnating (except for 1996). In particular, the growth of imports had been phenomenal; 32 and 11.3 per cent in 1995 and 1996, respectively. Imports of domestic consumer goods expanded by more than 20 per cent over the period from 1994–96. However, the growth of exports, which had reached 30.3 per cent in 1995, decreased to a mere

3.7 per cent in 1996. This in part was caused by the extended recession in Japan that decreased the demand for exports from Korea and other Asian countries as well. An unexpected and severe decline in the demand for semiconductors, increased competition in manufacturing and textiles exports from China, and tight monetary policy from the United States and Japan in the middle of 1995 had further retarded the growth of Korea's exports.

During the period 1990–96, the Korean won depreciated in nominal terms by more than 17.8 per cent; however, the real exchange rate had a distinct tendency to appreciate over the period from 1993–95 as shown in Table 1.4. Real appreciation of the Korean won eroded the competitiveness of Korean firms and resulted in trade and current account deficits. This real appreciation of the Korean currency could have been the result of the particular exchange rate regime selected. Korea had a Market Average Exchange Rate System (MARS), under which the value of Korean won to the US dollar changed within a daily trading margin whose bandwidth was 2.5 per cent.[3] The effects of MARS could lead to large capital inflows attracted by favourable interest rate differentials and the expectation of low exchange rate fluctuations, given the policy of stable currency values that prevailed at the time.

1.3.2 The private sectors prior to the crisis

The deterioration in economic conditions resulting from the mismanagement of the Korean economy continued in the private sector. The private sector in Korea resorted to excessive and reckless borrowing. The banks in Korea, the main borrowers, were in a position to exploit and arbitrage the gap between the domestic and foreign interest rates. For example, the domestic market interest rate in Korea ranged from 10 to 15 per cent while in the United States it was as low as 6–8 per cent. The Korean banks borrowed short-term debts from America, Japan, and other countries in Europe at low rates of interest without putting adequate hedging in place, converted the loans to the Korean won, and then lent them at higher interest rates to the very highly leveraged Korean firms engaged in risky investment activities. By pursuing this practice, the banks made large windfall profits; however, for the entire economy, the results were disastrous. As a consequence of this profitable but ultimately non-productive pattern of behaviour, net foreign liabilities amounted to $108.8 billion in 1995 and then rose to $138 billion in 1996. To make things even worse, by the middle of 1997, approximately 67 per cent of the total debt ($170.5 billion) in Korea was comprised of short-term debt.[4] The critical mistake made by incompetent financial intermediaries was that they invested a large portion of this short-term debt in long-term projects, which created the possibility of a subsequent run on the banks if the lenders became nervous as conditions worsened. By June 1997, the ratio of short-term debt to foreign reserves exceeded 400 per cent, signalling that the country would face national insolvency if it had to repay about 25 per cent of its short-term debt all at once.

A fragile financial system and poorly developed corporate governance practices contributed to the kinds of visible problems in the banks that were discussed in the previous section. A lack of appropriate financial analysis techniques, and asymmetric information prevailing in the markets resulted in adverse selection, where 'good' lenders were crowded out of the market, and only 'bad' lenders remained as the financial institutions' customers. The fragile financial system and weak banking governance structures that had prevailed before the crisis, and the perceptions of implicit government guarantees, allowed banks to become involved in excessively risky projects; a type of behaviour which has been dubbed 'moral hazard problems' (Diamond 1984, Fama 1985, Boyd and Prescott 1986). Krugman (1998a) also argued that moral hazard problems, resulting from government protection and intervention in the financial market mechanisms, as well as adverse selection due to asymmetric information and the incompetence of financial institutions should be counted amongst the most important reasons for the emergence of the crisis.

The illusory or transient nature of the brief spurts of spectacular economic growth – 'economic bubbles' – that characterized the economy before the crisis was created by just this type of reckless expansion of lending and borrowing. The stock market in Korea had grown in the early 1990s accompanied by a boom of international investment demand in emerging markets. Large portions of capital inflows, however, have been made in the form of short-term portfolio investments in the absence of any adequate hedging mechanisms rather than long-term foreign direct investment (FDI). In the presence of a large number of borrowers and lenders, the problems created by companies seeking a free ride will confound attempts by the regulatory authorities to monitor them. As a consequence, the possibility of excessive *ex-ante* risk-taking by borrowers, including excessive short-term borrowing without adequate hedging mechanisms becomes much more likely. Excessive high-risk lending by these institutions led to inflated asset prices and gave a false impression of the sound financial condition of these financial intermediaries. Inevitably, asset values and stock prices rose to unsustainable levels.

Controversy still exists as to whether it may have been possible to predict the crisis using certain indexes and thus have helped to minimize its impact. Instead of delving into this matter in detail, we present here a summary of selected economic figures for Korea before the crisis. Some of these variables have already been considered in the studies that attempted to develop 'warning indexes' to predict economic crises. Table 1.4 indicates that the economic environment in Korea, represented by selected figures, was deteriorating towards the onset of the crisis, although no empirical evidence or normative hypotheses exist, which one could use as a yardstick to assert that conditions were sufficiently 'bad' to make the subsequent crisis inevitable. In contrast, some of the fundamentals such as GDP growth rates, budget balance, and the volume of capital investment seemed sound until 1997. Even the current account deficit was not disastrously high, except in 1996. This is why some people argue that the Korean economy would not have endured such a difficult time if other South East Asian countries had not fallen victim to the crisis first. It is impossible to pin down the exact causes of the crisis to just a few factors and, indeed, a multitude of reasons must be taken into consideration to understand the phenomenon. While most studies to date have concentrated on how weak the Korean economy was, and how it was destined to collapse, in the following section we will introduce arguments that place principal emphasis on the contagious effect of the crisis throughout the region.

1.4 The day of crisis, the herd effect, and the contagion effect

1.4.1 The day of the crisis

In late 1996, foreign investors speculated on the ability of Thailand to repay its foreign debt and started withdrawing investments from Thailand. The credibility of the Thai government and its ability to maintain its exchange rates at stable levels was called into question. Subsequently, with the bankruptcy of Thailand's largest finance company, Finance One, foreign investors and Thai companies rushed for the exit doors and tried to convert Thai baht to US currencies. In a doomed attempt to halt this stampede, the Central Bank of Thailand raised interest rates; however, foreign reserves dried up rapidly as currency conversion continued unabated. As a consequence, the Bank was unable to defend the value of the baht; the baht collapsed and depreciated dramatically.

Lucas (1993) had singled out for praise the miraculous economic growth in Asia, as the growth happened in so many countries in one region, to such a high degree, and over such a long period. Yet, several Asian countries in the one region were simultaneously engulfed by crisis, and collapsed so severely in such a short period of time. Just as a large number of economists were interested in explaining the growth in this region, a host of other economists started to analyse the 'crisis'. Table 1.5 portrays how the number of publications devoted to this crisis exploded since 1997 and peaked in the following years. In fact, the total number of publications about this economic crisis was at times almost comparable to other very popular topics such as FDI.

1.4.2 Explaining the domino effect

Unstable and deteriorating economic fundamentals can, to some extent, explain the plunge of one nation's currency. In order to examine the almost simultaneous outbreak of economic crisis across many countries, however, we need to refer to a

Table 1.5 Econlit key word search summary

Key word	*1996*	*1997*	*1998*	*1999*	*2000*	*2001*
Economic crisis	29	19	47	111	79	41
Financial crisis	26	19	119	221	152	101
Currency crisis	11	11	43	52	48	31
Asian economic crisis	0	0	8	30	21	9
Korea and economic crisis	0	0	4	19	16	11
Crisis(total)	66	49	221	433	316	193
Interest rate	749	740	803	771	655	555
FDI	53	55	100	117	124	118
PPP	39	34	28	39	46	24

Source: Econlit.

self-fulfilling crisis theory (Azariadis and Guesnerie 1986, Obstfeld 1986, 1994) and the 'bubble effects' theory (Meese 1986), which were published before the Asian crisis.

When agents in currency markets perceive that the present actual value of a currency is substantially higher than its fundamental value, they usually decide to sell the currency. This engenders similar sentiments among other agents, which only further reinforces pessimistic attitudes that in turn may often be sufficient to finally trigger sales of the currency. Continuing with this train of thought, fuelled by the negative sentiments of the speculators, a massive shift in the supply of the currency suddenly occurred, which in turn caused the exchange rate to plummet. Similarly, the bubble effects in the economy in fact formed over a long period before the onset of the crisis, and, it is important to remember that currency prices do not necessarily reflect the values of the underlying market fundamentals (Meese 1986). Once the bubble in a particular country burst, the negative sentiments of investors in the country began to spread to other investors in related countries. Thus, once the Thai bubble burst, the contagion effects spread to the surrounding Asian countries including Korea. The consequent fall in asset prices made the insolvency of the intermediaries become visible, forcing them to cease operations, leading to further asset and currency deflation. The circularity of the pattern of events outlined above, can explain both the remarkable severity of the crisis and the apparent vulnerability of the Asian economies to self-fulfilling crisis. This, in turn, has the potential to increase our understanding of, and affords new insights into the phenomenon of contagion between economies with few visible links.

As the countries geographically close to Thailand were attacked by the crisis one after the other, foreign investors and companies in Korea also started pulling their money out of the Korean economy and began converting local currencies into US dollars. In November 1997, the Central Bank of Korea depleted much of its foreign exchange reserves, which were reduced to just $8.7 billion in order to support the Korean won. News of this event accelerated investors' conversion of local currency into US dollars and made the situation even more serious. On 21 November 1997, the Finance Minister of Korea, in desperation, announced that the government was officially seeking an International Monetary Fund (IMF) rescue package. In December 1997, Korea received an emergency rescue package of $58 billion from the IMF and other multilateral institutions. Nevertheless, the Korean won collapsed and depreciated by more than 50 per cent in 1997, accompanied by a severe credit squeeze and many bankruptcies. The depreciation reduced the per capita GDP of Korea in dollar terms by roughly half; at the same time, it meant a doubling of the foreign debt in Korean won. The foreign lenders concerned about the possibility of a request for a moratorium on debt repayments, refused to roll the debt over, which resulted in a severe credit squeeze.

The overall effect of the financial crisis on the Korean economy was dramatic and desperate conditions prevailed. Hundreds of small and large firms in Korea went bankrupt and many factories closed. Domestic asset markets collapsed and widespread bank failures followed. Due to the tendency of the local business culture to frequently use a firm's promissory notes, the bankruptcy of a small number of firms was capable of inducing the widespread failure of many firms including those in sound financial positions.

Financial panic, widespread speculation, and the withdrawal of short-term capital can adequately explain the dramatic downward spiral of the currencies that occurred. It is a classic case of self-fulfilling prophecies on the part of investors and speculators becoming realized as a result of their belief that the government would not be able to defend the value of domestic currencies leading to an actual devaluation of the currencies. Speculators realized that the cost of maintaining the strength of the currency might prove to be too high for the government to bear. Currencies and financial markets in general are subject to the phenomenon of multiple sunspot equilibria (Azariadis and Guesnerie 1986). Under normal circumstances, the pre-existing adverse macroeconomic conditions disappear and the country regains normalcy. On the other hand, these weak macroeconomic fundamentals can be the source of self-fulfilling expectations and precipitate crises. Thus, depending on the prevailing mindset, some countries placed in a similar macroeconomic situation might escape the descent into a state of disequilibrium or economic chaos while others may not.

Each self-fulfilling crisis is associated with herd and contagion effects. Shiller (1989) argued that financial markets are inefficient and exhibit strong anomalies. The only reason sellers consistently sell their stocks is that the price of the stocks drops and other people are selling. Also, the bandwagon effect can exert a strong influence in foreign exchange markets where agents have asymmetric private information. If one agent leaves the market, other agents, who may possess optimistic perceptions about the economy, leave the market suddenly as well. As a result, private money is highly liquid money (Cole and Kehoe 1996a,b).

This kind of self-fulfilling crisis spreads from one country to another very rapidly. When one country's currency is depreciating, the other countries have to devalue to remain competitive. This string of competitive devaluation aggravates what is already a precarious situation. The sophistication of international markets today enables investors to withdraw huge amounts of capital instantaneously. The results of intense speculation, capital flight, and a loss of credibility undoubtedly exacerbate the crisis and bring about a tailspin in a matter of months. In fact, within a matter of days, capital mobility in Korea dramatically changed from a net inflow of US$95 billion, to a net outflow of US$21 billion.

1.5 The morning after – lucky Korea

1.5.1 The morning after

Most developed countries have established their technological expertise and acquired improvements in productivity in accordance with the transparent market principle: that governments need to establish fair and impartial rules to enhance competition among domestic and foreign firms. After the crisis, partly due to strong advice from the IMF, the Korean government launched a total reform programme. The financial markets were to be restructured fully to restore their tarnished reputation. The government also implemented a substantial package of measures to reform corporate governance structures and to restructure the *chaebols*. Even though a comprehensive reform programme will take time and resources to implement successfully, it will certainly reduce Korea's susceptibility to financial difficulties in the future.

The Korean people were not frustrated by the crisis. While the crisis was caused by financial weakness and an unhealthy business sector, most Koreans faced the difficulties stemming from the crises and co-operated with one another to help efforts by the government to increase the level of foreign reserves. In an extraordinary display of collective enthusiasm, some families even exchanged their family's collection of gold. While some analysts pointed to the possibility of a second wave of crisis emerging around 2001 and 2002, as a percentage of debts rolled over or as a result of fresh borrowings after the crisis maturing in those years, the economy seemed to regain its momentum of rapid economic growth (as shown in Table 1.4). Recently some analysts have even warned about the renewed possibility of inflation.

1.5.2 Lucky Korea

Just as favourable international environments in the early 1980s rescued Korea from the full impact of the Second Oil Shock, the rapid recovery of the economy was again, at least in part, due to very favourable international economic environments, as well as the efforts of the Korean people themselves. First, for a few years after 1997, the Japanese yen did not depreciate significantly and the value of the Chinese yuan was sustained (against the US dollar). The Korean economy lies just in the middle of these two countries in terms of economic development. As a transition country whose specialization was moving from labour-intensive to capital-intensive and skilled labour-intensive industries, Korea had to compete against both countries in the world market. Any serious depreciation or devaluation of the two currencies would have slowed Korea's recovery or even rendered it impossible. Second, while controversy surrounds whether or not the IMF's policy was adequate and whether the rescue loans provided by the IMF and some developed countries were provided in time, with appropriate conditions, it is still true that this support helped to stabilize the economy. As a matter of fact, the loans would not have been possible if there had not been sufficient intervals between the series of economic crisis. Around the time of the Asian crisis, many other non-Asian countries suffered from economic crisis of their own, for example, some Scandinavian countries, Russia, Brazil, Argentina, as well as several Asian countries including Korea. If all these crises had occurred over a short period, or if even some had occurred simultaneously, it would have been difficult for the international institutions or developed countries to provide adequate rescue packages to those affected countries. Third, the US economy, which has been Korea's largest market recorded very high levels of stable growth throughout the 1990s. With the depreciation of the Korean currency, it was therefore, relatively easy for Korean exporters to penetrate the US market and increase their market share. In addition, the health of the US economy made US attitudes towards trade negotiations more flexible, more relaxed, and helped the economy to maintain low barriers to trade between the two countries, even though there have been periodic episodes of conflict over trade imbalances.

A recent article from *Time Asia* (18 March 2002) describes the current Korean economy in the following positive manner:

> Plenty of problems remain, including bankrupt or near-bankrupt corporate giants such as Daewoo Motor and Hynix Semiconductor. But, thanks to restructuring efforts forced by the crisis, the economy is proving to be surprisingly resilient, mature and self-assured ... Unlike China, Korea's engine is increasingly turbocharged by Pocketbook Power. Manufacturing output as a percentage of GDP stood at 32 per cent in Korea in 2000; the services sector was larger at 43 per cent. Domestic spending by the country's 47 million consumers has grown from about 50 per cent of GDP in 1987 to 58 per cent. With more than 1 million service sector jobs added since 2000, it looks like Korea will be the first Asian economy to make the leap from an industrial-led to service-driven domestic economy.
>
> *Time Asia* (18 March 2002)

1.6 Epilogue

The Korean economy seems to be on the path to economic growth again. Some institutions have even cautiously predicted that per capita GDP of Korea will break through the $10,000 threshold again in 2002, six years after it first broke through this barrier. Is it, therefore, now time to open the bottles of champagne?

The rapid recovery of the Korean economy since 1998 surprised many Koreans. The overall consensus as to the reasons for this success can be summarized in the following ways: the economy pursued swift and prudent reforms; the approach was well coordinated; they worked hard to prevent moral hazard problems emerging in various sectors of the economy; they were able to maintain social stability; the market was liberalized consistently, and; the range of the reforms was very wide, including the financial, corporate, labour, and public sectors as well. While the crisis was a disaster for the economy, it also provided a precious opportunity to restructure and reform the whole economy. Unexpectedly, however, the rapid recovery of the economy sapped the country's will to complete the reform process; reform is always painful and usually encounters resistance.

Globalization means that countries today have closer economic links through trade, investment, financial flows, and labour mobility. The Asian crisis demonstrated that international investors could have a significant effect on Korea. Accelerating globalization will lead Korea to be more exposed to the world and, consequently, more vulnerable to international shocks even when the domestic economy is strong and healthy. Those same favourable external environments that helped Korea to recover from the crisis can change at any time, and just as easily precipitate negative effects in Korea. If this happened the impact on Korea would be even more serious, as the reform process is still incomplete.

While economic growth in the United States is relatively stable, the US economy is running an unprecedented current account deficit, which is being financed by capital inflows (ADB 2002). If this imbalance continues, the inflow of capital will bring inflationary pressure to the US economy, and the voices opposed to free trade may become more strident and powerful. Both of these possibilities would affect the Korean economy in a number of ways. Fluctuations in oil prices also pose a constant potential threat to the well-being of the Korean economy. The price of petroleum has risen by more than 300 per cent since December 1998 to late 2000. The possibility always exists that the price of petroleum will soar even further, as occurred previously during the period of the two oil shocks. According to the ADB (2002), Korea has increased its level of commercial energy use per capita more rapidly than any other country in Asia, even though in terms of efficiency (energy consumption per unit of economic output) it has been one of the best performing nations. There is also the ever present threat of the Japanese yen depreciating and of a devaluation of the Chinese yuan, which would significantly erode the competitiveness of Korean commodities on the world market.

As long as it is integrated with the rest of world economies, it is inevitable that Korea will be influenced by foreign factors. Most foreign shocks fall outside the ability of any particular economy to control them. Therefore, the major concern must be how to minimize the impact of external shocks. It is too soon for Koreans to break open the champagne bottles. Rather, now is the time for Korea to remember what it aimed to do on the morning after the crisis.

Notes

1 While it is argued that the intentional encouragement of strategic sectors as an engine of growth produced significant negative by-products, it is also true that these sectors led the country's exports. Most of the top five exporting items in the 1990s are from industries favoured by the Park government.
2 Relatively stagnant exports in the mid-1990s were mainly due to the deterioration in the terms of trade, as well as rising production costs. There was no significant evidence that the volume of Korea's exports declined seriously during this period.
3 Korea switched from MARS to the free floating exchange rate system after the crisis.
4 This ratio is even higher than other Asian countries affected by the crisis. It was 24 per cent for Indonesia, 39 per cent for Malaysia, and 46 per cent for Thailand (World Bank 1998).

Bibliography

Asia Development Bank (2001, 2002) *Asia Recovery Report*, various issues. Available Online, http://aric.adb.org/external/arr2001/arr_mar.htm.

Azariadis, C. and Guesnerie, R. (1986) 'Sunspots and cycles', *Review of Economic Studies*, 53(5): 725–37.

Bank of Korea (various years), *Economic Statistics Yearbook*.

—— *Financial Statement Analysis*.

Boyd, J. and Prescott, E. (1986) 'Financial intermediary-coalitions', *Journal of Economic Theory*, 38(2): 221–32.

Cole, Harold L. and Kehoe, Timothy J. (1996a) 'A self-fulfilling model of Mexico's 1994–5 crisis', Federal Reserve Bank of Minneapolis Staff Report No. 210.

Cole, Harold L. and Kehoe, Timothy J. (1996b) 'Self-fulfilling debt crisis', Federal Reserve Bank of Minneapolis Staff Report No. 211.
Corsetti, G., Pesenti, P., and Roubini, N. (1998a) 'What caused the Asian currency and financial crisis? Part I: A macroeconomic overview', National Bureau of Economic Research Working Paper No. 6833.
——(1998b) 'What caused the Asian currency and financial crisis? Part II: The policy debate', National Bureau of Economic Research Working Paper No. 6834.
Diamond, D. (1984) 'Financial intermediation and delegated monitoring', *Review of Economic Studies*, 51 (July): 393–414.
Fama, E. (1985) 'What's different about banks', *Journal of Monetary Economics*, 15(1): 29–39.
Hughes, H. (1995) 'Why have east Asian countries led economic development?', *Economic Record*, 71(212): 88–104.
Kim, I. (2001) 'Korea's growth potential and crisis management', in I. Kim, S. Kwack, and S. Park (eds), *Growth, Productivity and Vision for the Korean Economy*, Seoul: Pakyoungsa.
Kruger, A. (1997) 'Trade policy and economic development: how we learn', *American Economic Review*, 87(1): 1–22.
Krugman, P. (1998a) 'What happened to Asia?', mimeo, MIT.
——(1998b) 'Bubble, boom, crash: theoretical notes on Asia's crisis', mimeo, MIT.
——(1994) 'The myth of Asia miracle', *Foreign Affairs*, November: 62–78.
Kwack, S. (2001) 'Factors contributing to the financial crisis in Korea', in I. Kim, S. Kwack, and S. Park (eds), *Growth, Productivity and Vision for the Korean Economy*, Seoul: Pakyoungsa.
Lucas, R. (1993) 'Making a miracle', *Econometrica*, 61(2): 251–72.
Meese, R. (1986) 'Testing for bubbles in exchange markets: a case of sparkling rates', *Journal of Political Economy*, 94(21): 345–73.
Obstfeld, M. (1986) 'Rational and self-fulfilling balance-of-payments crises', *American Economic Review*, 76(1):72–81.
——(1994) 'The logic of currency crises', *Cahiers Economiques et Monetaires* (Bank of France), 143: 189–213.
Radelet, S. and Sachs, J. (1998a) 'The onset of the east Asian financial crisis', National Bureau of Economic Research Working Paper No. 6680.
——(1998b) 'The East Asian financial crisis: diagnosis, remedies, and prospects', *Brookings Papers on Economic Activity*, 10(1):1–74.
Shiller, R. (1989) *Market Volatility*, Cambridge: MIT Press.
Time Asia Magazine (18 March 2002) 'Veni, Verdi, Gucci'. Vol. 159, No. 10. Hong Kong, Time Inc.
World Bank (1993) *The East Asian Miracle*, New York: Oxford University Press.
——(1998a) *Global Economic Prospects*, Washington, DC: World Bank.
——(1998b) *Global Development Finance*, Washington, DC: World Bank.
——(1999) *Global Economic Prospects*, Washington, DC: World Bank.

2 The Asian financial crisis[1]

Genesis and exegesis

John Hawkins

2.1 Introduction

The early stages of the 1990s turmoil in Asian financial markets were described as 'a few little glitches in the road'.[2] Now it is recognized as one of a series of major financial crises to have hit the world economy in the past decade. The main features were:

- private capital markets withdrew their support from countries that for several years had been recipients of large capital inflows;
- the defensive package of foreign exchange market intervention, sharp rises in interest rates and selective controls proved inadequate to avert devaluation of some formerly fixed exchange rates;
- large unhedged foreign exchange positions and weak banking and financial systems contributed to vulnerability and sharply constrained the authorities' room for manoeuvre;
- the trauma quickly spread out from its original locus to affect exchange rates and other asset prices in the region (and for a short while, in major industrial countries as well);
- large, multilateral official rescue packages had to be mobilized; and
- the events generated calls (both within the region and beyond) for stronger preventative arrangements to reduce the likelihood and severity of future outbreaks.

While some of these factors were common to earlier (and later) crises, one of the unusual features of the Asian experience is that the affected economies had a record of strong economic growth, generally moderate inflation and disciplined fiscal policy for at least a decade. However, these virtues were eventually overwhelmed by weaknesses in the financial sector, where strong capital inflows, extended periods of rapid economic growth, rising property prices and perceptions of implicit government guarantees led, in some economies, to a degree of complacency by banks in their credit standards, which supervisory systems proved inadequate in disciplining. This was compounded by some loss of confidence by markets in the longer-term export potential of some Asian economies. Once these factors started currency depreciations within the region, contagion effects exacerbated and spread them.

This chapter reviews the origins and aftermath of the Asian financial crisis. Section 2.2 summarizes the key macroeconomic and financial developments and the international rescue packages. Section 2.3 analyses the factors generating the crisis, including the likely transmission channels for contagion. Section 2.4 discusses some of the ramifications of the crisis. Section 2.5 provides some conclusions.

2.2 What happened in the crisis?

Pressure on a country's foreign exchange market is typically reflected in exchange rates, international reserves, interest rates and the temporary imposition of controls on credit or foreign exchange transactions.[3] The combination depends on the circumstances of the particular country affected and on the defensive strategy chosen by the authorities. As background to the subsequent discussion on origins, this section reviews the main developments.

2.2.1 Exchange rates

The Thai baht had been subject to episodic pressures during the previous eighteen months, which intensified in May 1997. The subsequent forced floating of the baht on 2 July ushered in the market turbulence. Figure 2.1 shows the sharp declines in the dollar exchange rates of the ASEAN-4 economies during the second half of 1997 and early 1998.[4] The worst affected was the Indonesian rupiah, which at one stage was worth only a fifth of its June 1997 value against the US dollar. January 1998 marked the worst of the depreciations, with all the affected currencies regaining some strength during the course of 1998.

The combination of the close (explicit or implicit) tracking of the US dollar by many Asian currencies and large swings in the yen–dollar exchange rate meant that the ASEAN-4 currencies had marked medium-term fluctuations against

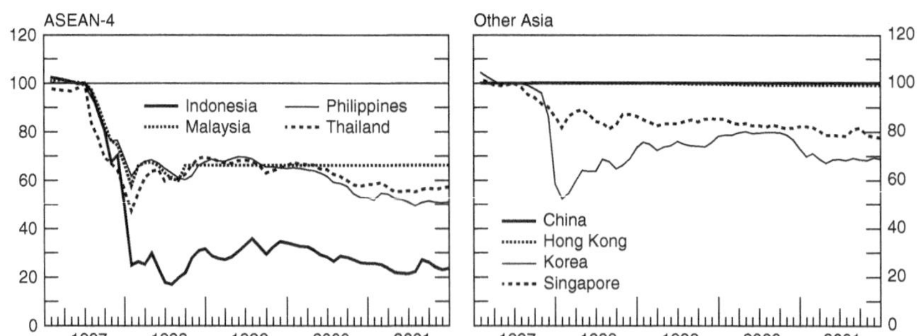

Figure 2.1 Bilateral exchange rates. US dollar per local currency; June 1997 = 100.

Source: Datastream.

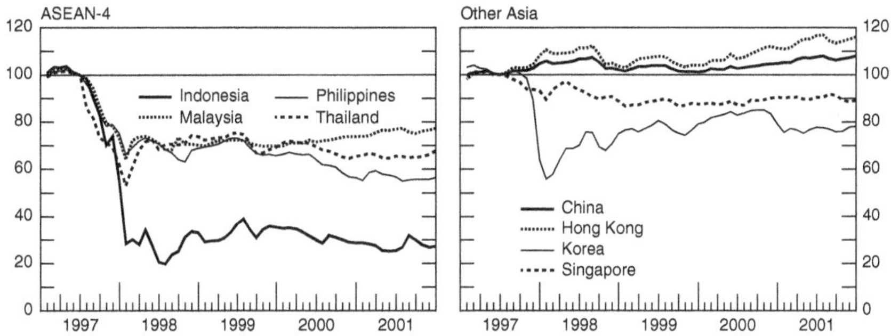

Figure 2.2 Nominal effective exchange rates. An increase indicates an appreciation; June 1997 = 100.

Source: BIS.

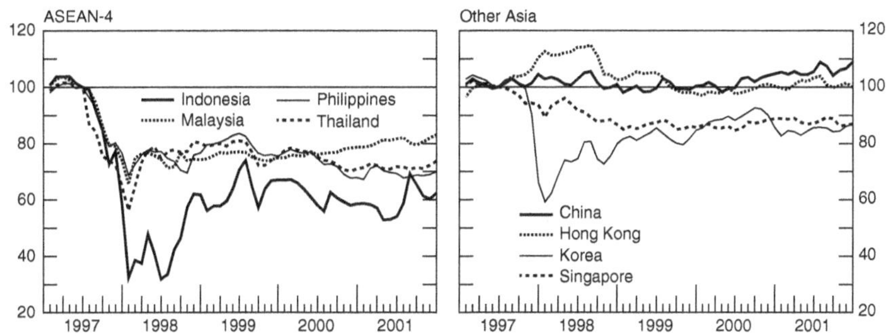

Figure 2.3 Real effective exchange rates – in terms of relative consumer prices; an increase indicates an appreciation; June 1997 = 100.

Source: BIS.

a wider trade-weighted basket of exchange rates (Figure 2.2). Notwithstanding some rise in inflation, the real effective exchange rates of the ASEAN-4 currencies also fell heavily (Figure 2.3).

The ASEAN-4 currencies entered the crisis with differing levels of real effective exchange rates, relative to their historical averages but, notwithstanding uncertainty about equilibrium real exchange rates, any exchange rate misalignments were quite modest compared to the subsequent depreciations.

The large size of the Asian depreciations is placed into perspective in Table 2.1, which shows some of the largest real effective depreciations over six-month periods since 1970. By comparison, the largest six-monthly change in the G-3 currencies over this period was the 1995 real depreciation in the yen of around 20 per cent; some European currencies recorded similar real depreciations in the Exchange Rate Mechanism (ERM) crisis and the Australian dollar had a similar real depreciation in the mid-1980s.

Table 2.1 Real effective exchange rates: twenty large depreciations from 1970 to mid-2002 (% change over six months)

Kuwait	1990	−74
Nigeria	1986	−74
Indonesia	**1998**	**−68**
Argentina	2002	−63
Pakistan	1972	−55
Turkey	2001	−49
Nigeria	1999	−47
Russia	1998	−46
Brazil	1999	−44
Israel	1993	−42
Turkey	1970	−42
Venezuela	1984	−41
Mexico	1995	−40
South Korea	**1998**	**−36**
Malaysia	**1998**	**−34**
Nigeria	1992	−34
Venezuela	1986	−34
Indonesia	1978	−33
Thailand	**1998**	**−33**
Mexico	1976	−32

Source: Derived from IMF, International Financial Statistics, JPMorgan.

2.2.2 Exchange market intervention

It is hard to describe the role played by exchange market intervention. Published data (Figure 2.4) generally referred only to gross reserves. They therefore miss intervention by the authorities in the forward market, which reportedly peaked at US$24 billion in Thailand. The data may also miss co-ordinated intervention undertaken in support of currencies by (third party) monetary authorities or intervention funded through a country's fiscal accounts rather than its international reserves. Furthermore, some of the Korean international reserves were not useable as they had been lent to banks. But at face value, Thailand and South Korea initially relied much more on their reserves in defending the exchange rate than did Indonesia or the Philippines. Figure 2.4 also illustrates the large reserve holdings of China, Hong Kong and Singapore relative to the ASEAN-4 countries.

2.2.3 Interest rates and credit controls

An important element in most currency defences is played by short-term interest rates, shown in Figure 2.5. Real rates, simply measured by subtracting the most recent twelve-month-ended inflation rate, are shown in Figure 2.6. There were three notable developments around the crisis period. First, the ASEAN-4 countries and South Korea entered 1997 with already high short-term real interest rates, as during 1996 they had been endeavouring to rein back excessive credit growth or support the exchange rate. These high interest rates may have left them more vulnerable to attack because efforts by speculators to push up the cost of 'holding on' to exchange rate commitments had begun from a relatively high base.

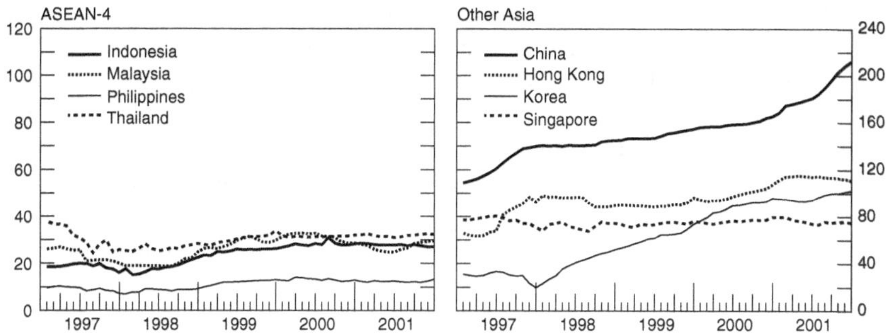

Figure 2.4 Foreign exchange reserves – in billions of US dollars.

Source: IMF.

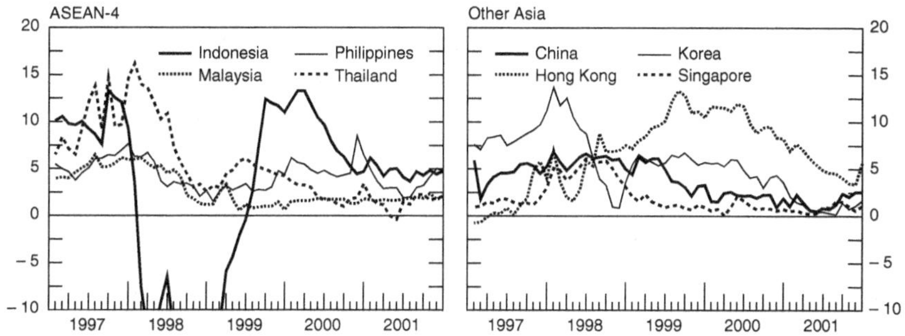

Figure 2.5 Real interest rates. Short-term interest rate deflated by the annual percentage change in consumer price index; in per cent.

Sources: Datastream, IMF.

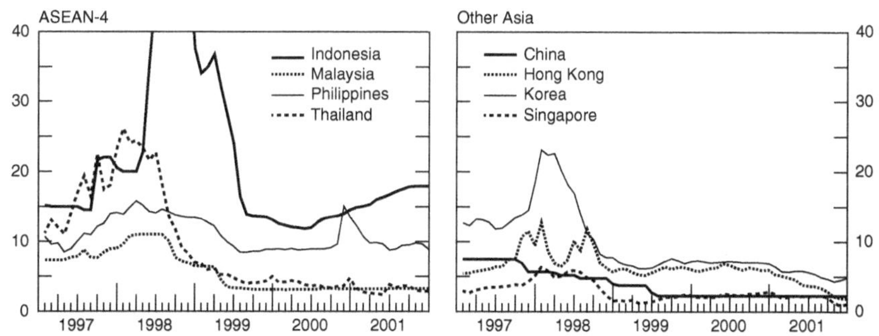

Figure 2.6 Interest rates. Short-term interest rates; in per cent.

Source: Datastream.

Second, exchange market pressures led each of the ASEAN-4 countries to increase short-term interest rates further in 1997.

Third, reminiscent of the tactics employed by several European countries during the 1992–93 ERM crisis, each of the ASEAN-4 countries resorted to a mixture of administrative controls, taxes and moral suasion, aimed at discouraging capital outflows and short sales of both the domestic currency and domestic equities, and at reducing the need for even larger increases in domestic interest rates. But as in the ERM crisis, this did not prevent exchange rates declining sharply, nor did they obviate the need for domestic interest rates to increase significantly.

2.2.4 *Equity prices*

Unsurprisingly, the ASEAN-4 countries suffered steep falls in their equity markets in the second half of 1997. As with their exchange rates, the equity markets turned around in early 1998. In domestic currency terms, most regained pre-crisis levels in 1999–2000, but have since fallen back. In US dollar terms, many remain well below pre-crisis levels.

The behaviour of equity markets is important because they serve as an alternative to bank financing for some companies, they can generate important wealth effects, equities are used as collateral for bank loans and because they are an important channel for foreign capital inflows. Moreover, they are often regarded as an early warning signal; see the references cited in end note 3.

2.2.5 *Real impact of the financial problems*

One immediate effect of the financial crisis was sharp, and unexpected, falls in real output; see Table 2.2 and Figure 2.7. Real GDP contracted severely in 1998, despite the stimulus to net exports from the depreciations, reflecting, *inter alia*, high interest rates, vastly increased foreign currency debt obligations, more widespread corporate and banking failures, higher layoffs, and the generalized uncertainty and loss of confidence associated with such crises.

Table 2.2 Real GDP: annual average % change

	1990–96	*1997*	*1998*	*1998*	*1999–2002*	*2003–10*
			(June 97 forecast)	*(Actual)*	*(Partly forecast)*	*(Forecast)*
Indonesia	7.8	4.5	(7.6)	−13.0	3.1	5.0
Thailand	8.5	−1.4	(5.9)	−10.8	3.5	4.0
South Korea	7.6	5.0	(6.1)	−6.7	7.2	5.1
Malaysia	9.6	7.3	(8.0)	−7.4	4.6	5.9
Singapore	8.8	8.4	(7.3)	−0.1	4.8	5.4
China	10.4	8.8	(10.4)	7.8	7.4	7.3
Philippines	2.7	5.2	(6.3)	−0.6	3.6	n.a.
Hong Kong	5.0	5.0	(5.5)	−5.3	3.8	3.9

Sources: IMF, Asia-Pacific Consensus Forecasts, June 1997, April 2002.

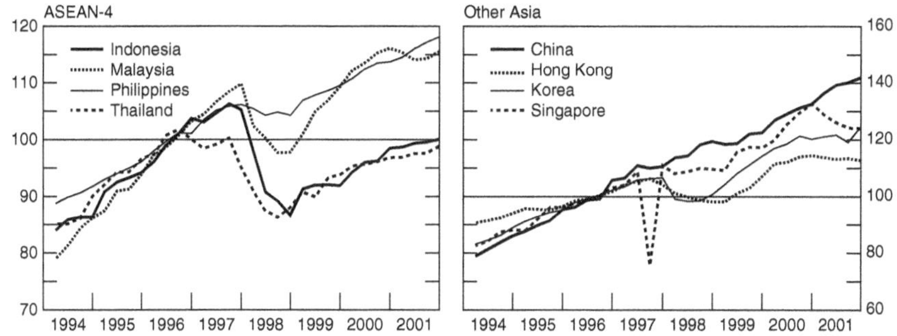

Figure 2.7 Real gross domestic product. 1996 = 100.

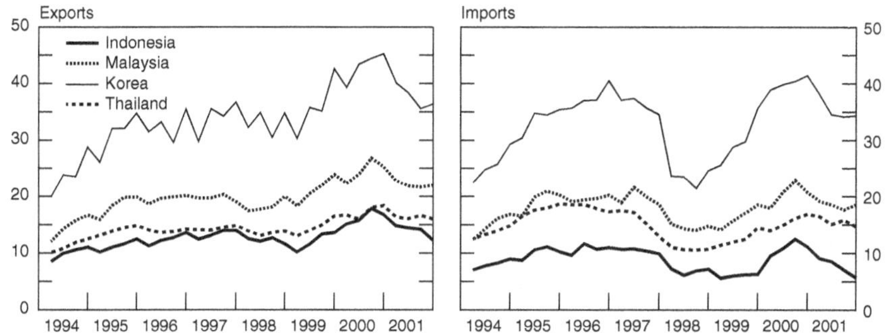

Figure 2.8 Merchandise trade – in billions of US dollars.

Source: IMF.

There were large movements in the current accounts of the affected economies. In 1997–98 the change in trade balances came mainly from a sharp reduction in imports. Initially, the competitiveness benefits for exporters were outweighed by other factors such as difficulties in exporters attracting finance or collapse of neighbouring markets.

Figure 2.8 refers to the US dollar value of merchandise exports and imports. Stability in US dollar value of exports is consistent with increased export volumes (and so greater real GDP) if prices are being cut in US dollar terms, but still mean that exports are not helping to rebuild reserves or increase national income.

2.2.6 International rescue packages

Large IMF-led rescue packages were assembled following requests by Thailand, Indonesia and South Korea (but not by Malaysia) and an existing programme in the Philippines was augmented. Table 2.3 compares them with the rescue packages for Mexico in 1995 (the previous largest). The United States was the largest

Table 2.3 International rescue packages

	Thailand	*Indonesia*	*South Korea*	*Mexico*
Date agreed	20 Aug 97	5 Nov 97	4 Dec 97	1 Feb 95
Total (US$bn) of which:	17	35	58	52
IMF	3.9	9.9	20.9	17.8
World Bank	1.5	4.5	10	2.8[a]
ADB	1.2	3.5	4	—
BIS/G10	—	—	—	10
USA	—	3	5	20
Europe	—	—	6.3	—
Canada	—	—	1	—
Australia	1	1	1	—
Brunei	0.5	—	—	—
China	1	1	—	—
Hong Kong	1	1	—	—
Indonesia	0.5	—	—	—
Japan	4	5	10	—
Malaysia	1	1	—	—
New Zealand	—	—	0.1	—
Singapore	1	5	—	—
South Korea	0.5	—	—	—
Disbursements as of March 1999	13.1	14.3	28.4	—
Time period	34 months	36 months	36 months	—
% of IMF quota	505	490	1,939	688
Targets (1998)	*Original*	*(Revised as of early 1998)*		*(1995)*
Real GDP[b]	3.5 (−3)	3 (−5)	2.5 (−1)	1.5
Inflation[b]	5 (11)	9 (45)	5 (<10)	9 by end 95
Current account[c]	−3 (+4)	−2 (+3)	−2 (+5)	−4
Budget balance[c]	1 ($-1\frac{1}{2}$)	1 (−4)	0 (−2)	0.5

Notes

a World Bank and Inter-American Development Bank.

b Annual % change.

c % to GDP.

contributor to the Mexican package and Japan was the largest contributor to the three Asian packages. This may be related to the fact that US banks are the largest lenders to Latin America and Japanese banks are the largest lenders to Asia; see Hawkins (2002).

The IMF's assistance is subject to policy conditionality. These were subject to substantial revision, notably making the budgetary demands less onerous, as the economic outlook for the economies deteriorated. The original growth targets in these programmes had to be revised downward, as evidence accumulated that the breadth and depth of the crisis would be greater than anticipated.

A distinguishing feature of these rescue packages is that they went much further into reform of the financial sector and corporate governance than most IMF programmes.[5] Common elements of the required conditions included improved prudential supervision of the financial system, privatization and removal of anti-competitive practices. The rationale for including corporate governance and transparency elements in these programmes reflects the view that weaknesses in this structural area (non-consolidated accounting statements, over-leveraged conglomerates, cross-company shareholding arrangements and guarantees, inefficient government monopolies and cartels, absence of official subsidies from published government budget accounts, etc.) were one of the underlying elements of vulnerability.

2.3 Why did it happen?

Like most other financial crises, the Asian financial turmoil was not due to one or two isolated factors. Its multiple origins can be conveniently grouped under three interrelated headings: (i) *financial-sector vulnerabilities* such as poor credit assessment in some Asian emerging economies concurrent with relatively easy global liquidity conditions; (ii) *external sector problems* which generated some concern about these economies; and (iii) *contagion* from Thailand – first to its near neighbours (Indonesia, Malaysia, and the Philippines), thence to some other Asian economies to the north (South Korea, Taiwan, Hong Kong and Japan), and finally much further afield (ranging south to Australia, east to Brazil and west to Russia). For a time, there was even an impact on equity markets in the major industrial countries.

2.3.1 Financial sector vulnerability

Indonesia, Thailand and the Philippines experienced a *credit boom* in the early 1990s. Table 2.4 shows that while nominal GDP growth was rapid, bank and non-bank credit to the private sector grew even faster. This left the ASEAN-4 economies vulnerable to a shift in credit conditions. When concerns about overheating and the defence of exchange rates led to higher interest rates, it caused

Table 2.4 Bank lending: growth of bank lending to the private sector less growth in nominal GDP, annual rates

	1990–96	*1997–99*	*2000*
Indonesia	10	−26	4
Thailand	10	3	−22
South Korea	2	7	12
Malaysia	6	5	2
Philippines	19	−3	−3
Singapore	3	0	−6
Hong Kong	3	2	−2

Source: IMF.

Table 2.5 Capital flows to emerging Asian economies[a] (billions of US dollars)

	1996	*1997*	*1998*	*1999*	*2000*	*2001e*	*2002f*
Direct equity investment	46	52	57	56	53	56	57
Portfolio equity investment	17	6	4	24	21	13	16
Bank lending	86	−6	−64	−45	−19	−10	−6
Non-bank private lenders	38	22	2	2	15	1	1
Official flows	5	42	30	5	3	−5	−2
Total external financing	191	116	29	42	73	56	66

Source: Institute of International Finance (2002).

Note
e is estimates, f is forecast.
a China, India, Indonesia, Korea, Malaysia, Philippines, Thailand.

slackening economic activity, falls in property prices and a rising share of non-performing bank loans.

Large net private capital inflows (Table 2.5) contributed to the credit boom. While Asian banks were only modest lenders to homebuyers, exposures to property developers accounted for between 25 and 40 per cent of bank loans in Thailand, Indonesia, Malaysia and Singapore, and even more than that in Hong Kong.[6] Also, in Thailand, Malaysia and Indonesia this exposure was compounded by high loan-to-collateral ratios. Data is scarce on banks' exposure to the equity market but it likely contributed further to the strains in some Asian economies.

In several of the Asian economies, financial vulnerability was exacerbated by banks and/or their customers trying to reduce their funding costs by borrowing in foreign currencies and at short maturities. In Thailand this was inadvertently encouraged by the government's effort to promote Bangkok as a regional financial centre. The Bangkok International Banking Facility had been established in 1993, with a mandate (and special incentives) to borrow abroad in foreign currency and to lend to other borrowers in the region (so-called 'out-out' operations). In the event, most of the proceeds appear to have been lent to Thai entities ('out-in' operations).

Currency mismatching by companies was the greater problem in Indonesia. Once the rupiah was floated, belated efforts by Indonesian firms to hedge their large short foreign-currency position in the market helped accelerate its decline. This established a vicious circle, whereby the currency weakened further, prompting more defensive selling.

In South Korea, the vulnerability arose from the short-term foreign currency borrowings by banks and the *chaebol*. In Malaysia and the Philippines, the scale of foreign borrowing over the 1990s was also considerable, but on the whole, maturity and currency mismatches were apparently kept under better control.

Table 2.6 provides several measures of liquidity and currency mismatches for the Asian emerging economies (as well as some other developing countries). In short it supports the view that South Korea, Thailand and Indonesia had been particularly vulnerable to liquidity and currency mismatches. Thailand and South

Table 2.6 Liquidity and currency mismatch variables (end-June 1997)

	Broad money/ international reserves	*Short-term external debt to international reserves*	*External debt: short-term/ total*	*Borrowings from overseas banks: short-term/ total*
Indonesia	6.2	1.6	0.2	0.6
Thailand	4.9	1.1	0.5	0.7
South Korea	6.2	3.0	0.7	0.7
Malaysia	n.a.	0.6	0.4	0.6
Philippines	4.9	0.7	0.2	0.6
China	8.2	n.a.	n.a.	0.5
Argentina	3.6	1.1	0.2	0.5
Brazil	3.5	0.7	0.2	0.6
Chile	1.8	0.4	0.3	0.4
Mexico	4.2	1.3	0.2	0.5

Sources: BIS, IMF, World Bank.

Table 2.7 External debt burden

	Total external debt as per cent to 1996 GDP	*Total external debt as per cent to 1996 exports*	*1997 repayments due as per cent to 1996 exports*
Indonesia	49	189	67
Thailand	59	154	90
South Korea	23	72	37
Malaysia	38	42	19
Philippines	59	140	61
Singapore	11	n.a.	n.a.
Hong Kong	21	15	7
China	16	n.a.	n.a.
Argentina	30	320	133
Brazil	15	n.a.	n.a.
Chile	31	117	14
Mexico	44	139	46

Sources: IMF, OECD.

Korea would look even more vulnerable in these comparisons if commitments in forward markets or loans to commercial banks were netted off the gross reserves used in such ratios.

The importance of the composition of foreign borrowing in the vulnerability of the crisis countries is underlined by Table 2.7. In terms of external debt to GDP, Thailand and the Philippines had higher burdens than their neighbours but were not far outside the range experienced by many emerging economies. Similarly, only Indonesia among the five most adversely affected economies has a high debt burden relative to exports (and still below that of both Argentina and Brazil). Table 2.8 likewise reinforces the point that the vulnerability of the crisis countries was not tied to the foreign-currency denomination of external debt *per se*, but

Table 2.8 Currency denomination of long-term foreign debt (1996)

	US$	*Yen*	*Major European*	*Other*
Indonesia	24	35	11	30
Thailand	32	45	4	19
Malaysia	56	28	4	12
Philippines	34	35	3	28
China	65	16	2	17
Argentina	58	9	18	15
Brazil	69	6	8	17
Chile	46	9	5	40
Mexico	68	8	7	17

Source: World Bank, Global Development Finance 1998.

rather to the imbalance between short-term foreign-currency denominated liabilities and liquid foreign-currency denominated assets (international reserves).

These developments were unlikely to have gone so far were it not for the accompanying long-standing deficiencies in financial-sector supervision. Common problems in emerging economies include lax loan classification and provisioning practices; see Goldstein (1997). 'Connected lending' (making loans to major shareholders, bank directors, managers and their related businesses) was allowed to flourish, with the concomitant dangers of concentrated credit risks and lack of impartial credit decisions. Too many banks were owned by governments and became the 'quasi-fiscal' agents of governments, providing an oblique mechanism for channelling government assistance (off-budget) to ailing industries. In some cases this directed lending was also undertaken by privately owned banks. With the exceptions of Hong Kong and Singapore, the riskiness of banks' operating environment was not matched by an appropriate level of capital. History led to the strong expectation that depositors and creditors would get bailed out should banks get into trouble. In the face of strong political pressures for regulatory forbearance, bank supervisors lacked the mandate to resist. Adding to these problems, the quality of public disclosure and transparency was questionable.

Of course, every borrower of foreign funds in these economies had a corresponding lender overseas. These lenders' enthusiasm for emerging markets recovered surprisingly quickly after the Mexican crisis, in part driven by a desire to diversify investments. Indeed 1996 was a record year for private net flows to emerging economies. Spreads on emerging economy bonds narrowed markedly between 1995 and mid-1997; according to Cline and Barnes (1997) by more than can be explained either by upgradings by ratings agencies or by fundamentals. Moreover, maturities were extended and loan covenants were watered down. East Asian economies were major recipients of private capital flows.

The proximity of Tokyo, a large financial centre offering extremely low interest rates, also proved a temptation. The combination of weak economic activity, a huge stock of bad loans in the banking system, and a public antipathy to bailing-out banks, seemed to point to the continuation of low interest rates there.

Table 2.9 Saving and investment, % to GDP; 1996 (2001)

	Current account balance	*Government budget balance*	*Saving*	*Investment*
Indonesia	−4 (4)	1 (0)	31 (26)	30 (26)
Thailand	−8 (6)	2 (−2)	35 (31)	40 (23)
South Korea	−4 (2)	1 (1)	34 (29)	37 (27)
Malaysia	−6 (6)	1 (−6)	43 (44)	43 (26)
Philippines	−5 (12)	0 (−4)	14 (16)	23 (18)
Hong Kong	−1 (3)	2 (0)	30 (30)	30 (26)
Singapore	14 (21)	9 (6)	51 (52)	35 (31)

Sources: IMF, Consensus Forecasts February 2002.

Furthermore, the ASEAN-4 economies were generally regarded by lenders as in the first tier of sovereign borrowers among emerging markets. There were certainly some good reasons for this; over the previous decade they had been the star performers in terms of economic growth, plugged themselves into global markets, and had high saving and investment rates, and enviable fiscal positions; see Table 2.9 and Grenville (1998). The modest levels of public debt may have (falsely) assured lenders that if local financial institutions encountered troubles, the public sector had the capacity to mount a prompt and comprehensive rescue. All these positive attributes led bankers to overlook their weaknesses almost until (or in some cases after) the crisis hit.

2.3.2 External sector problems

As Table 2.9 shows, Thailand's current account deficit reached 8 per cent of GDP in 1996, with the other ASEAN-4 countries also having significant deficits.

However, these current account imbalances were widely viewed as benign (at the time) in two respects. First, there was a belief (known variously as the 'Lawson doctrine', 'Pitchford critique' or 'consenting adults view') that current accounts were only a concern if they reflected public sector deficits. This was not the case in the ASEAN-4 economies. Second, the funds borrowed offshore were being employed to increase investment (rather than consumption), thereby building the potential capacity to service the debts. In both these dimensions, Asian current account deficits were said to be more sustainable than those in Latin America.

Gradually, however, this sanguine interpretation was challenged on at least five counts:

- The quality rather than just the quantity of investment assumed greater importance. Investment ratios of over 30 per cent began to look less attractive when much of it was directed toward speculative activities such as golf resorts and expensive condominiums, industries with incipient overcapacity or overambitious infrastructure projects.
- Real effective exchange rates suggested some possible, albeit small, overvaluation increased vulnerability. In particular, with Japan one of their largest

trading partners, seeking stability of their exchange rates against the dollar made their competitiveness vulnerable when the dollar strengthened against the yen.

- Merchandise export receipts slowed in 1996 (Figure 2.8). While it was acknowledged at the time that some of the slowdown was attributable to temporary factors, such as a deceleration in global trade and an inventory glut in the worldwide electronics industry (which was especially important as electronics account for a large share of Asian exports) it did raise questions about longer-term projections.
- Some analysts perceived (rightly or wrongly) that China was gaining regional comparative advantage at the expense of the ASEAN-4 economies.
- Overproduction and intense export competition in certain industries (automobiles, memory chips, petrochemicals, steel, cement, wood products, frozen chickens) was seen as a looming threat to the sustainability of Asian external deficits.

The large current accounts deficits were the counterpart to strong capital inflows. It would have been hard for the economies to deal effectively with the overheating this involved. A monetary tightening could have encouraged even greater capital inflows. Capital controls may not have been effective for long, and would have raised questions about the authorities' commitment to openness and market-based policies more generally. Fiscal tightening was difficult to justify given the healthy state of public finances and demands for public spending. Even floating the exchange rates may not have helped, as if the currencies appreciated, foreign investors may have extrapolated this and been even keener to invest.

2.3.3 Contagion

The factors discussed above explain why some Asian emerging economies were vulnerable. But these factors did not appear overnight in July 1997. For so many Asian currencies to come under attack in so short a space of time suggests contagion must have played a role. The Asian currency crisis is unusual, in that it originated in a relatively small country (Thailand) and spread to a wide set of economies, both large (Korea, Japan, Brazil, Russia) and small.

There are three ways contagion might spread. The first is via direct linkages, the second is through competitive devaluations and the third is through signalling. The first of these does not seem to provide a good explanation for the recent Asian experience. Table 2.10 shows some indicators of the importance of the bilateral relationship with Thailand. In terms of their bilateral links, Malaysia, Singapore and Hong Kong would have been more vulnerable than Indonesia and South Korea; but this is not consistent with the observed impact of the crisis across economies (e.g. the size of currency and equity declines, the downward revision of 1998 growth forecasts).

The second means by which contagion could arise is through the competitiveness dynamics of devaluation. As one country after another in a region succumbs,

Table 2.10 Bilateral relationships with Thailand

	Distance	*Flying time*	*Export market*	*Telephone calls*	*Export similarity*
Malaysia	1,180	125	4.6	2.5	0.40
Singapore	1,430	135	3.0	3.7	0.43
Taiwan	2,530	330	3.1	4.2	0.50
Hong Kong	1,730	160	0.4	<2	0.50
Philippines	2,210	195	1.8	<2	0.39
Indonesia	2,310	295	2.2	1.3	<0.4
South Korea	3,720	440	1.8	1.3	0.44

Sources and definitions: See table 14 of Goldstein and Hawkins (1998).

those countries surviving find themselves less competitive which in turn makes their currencies more vulnerable to speculative attack, a sort of 'domino theory' of devaluations.[7]

A third possible cause of contagion is signalling; international investors were startled by events in Thailand, leading them to reassess the creditworthiness of all Asian borrowers.[8] They found a number with similar weaknesses, in kind if not in degree, and thus wrote the other economies down as well.

There are at least two reasons for favouring this third characterization. One is that markets appeared to be 'asleep at the wheel' in terms of monitoring latent risks in emerging Asian markets prior to the Thai crisis. Radelet and Sachs (1998) provide a comprehensive discussion of how unexpected was the Asian crisis. One simple indication is the GDP forecasts that were being made in June 1997 – see Table 2.2. Hawkins (1999) shows how publicly available data from the Bank for International Settlements (BIS) showed the large and rapidly increasing international borrowing by these countries, but it was mostly ignored. Eschweiler (1997) documents how interest rate spreads gave no warning of impending difficulties for Indonesia, Malaysia and the Philippines, and produced only intermittent signals for Thailand. The leading credit rating services failed to downgrade long-term debt ratings of Indonesia, Malaysia or Thailand in the year and a half to June 1997. Instead, downgradings followed the crisis – and exacerbated it (Figure 2.9).

A second reason for favouring the third characterization is based on a simple empirical exercise, which examines whether the observed impact on economies during the second half of 1997 was more consistent with some notions of contagion than with others (see Appendix A). Contagion appeared to operate by prompting a belated reassessment of all Asian economies; with the economies most affected being those with the weakest fundamentals (particularly if the weakness was in those fundamentals in which Thailand itself was weak).

2.4 What has happened since the crisis?

The Asian crisis has greatly affected the countries concerned. It has also, along with subsequent crises, affected the global financial system.

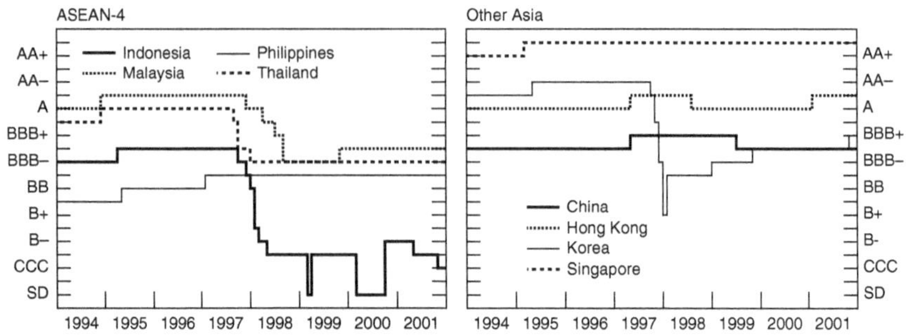

Figure 2.9 Sovereign credit ratings. Standard & Poors long-term sovereign credit ratings for long-term foreign currency debt.

Source: Standard & Poors.

2.4.1 Effects in Asia

As mentioned earlier, other than in Indonesia, the large nominal depreciations of 1997 were partly reversed in early 1998. Against the US dollar, most Asian exchange rates were fairly stable in 1999 and depreciated slightly in 2000 and 2001 (Figure 2.1). The latter movement is perhaps better interpreted as a strengthening of the US dollar. The HK dollar and the Chinese renminbi remained fixed to the US dollar and, from September 1998 so did the Malaysian ringgit. In effective terms, this meant that those currencies fixed to the dollar appreciated in recent years, while the others were relatively stable (Figure 2.2). With inflation rates fairly well contained, other than in Indonesia, the Asian economies have held on to much of the competitiveness gains from the 1997 devaluations (Figure 2.3). As a result, after initial weakness, exports grew quite strongly, before succumbing to the global slowdown, and in particular the fall in demand for electronic products and components, in 2001 (Figure 2.8).

As pressure on the exchange rate eased, and the magnitude of the recessions became apparent, the monetary authorities lowered nominal and real interest rates through 1998 (Figures 2.5 and 2.6). This aided the recovery process by stimulating domestic demand. In some economies there was also fiscal stimulus. Combined with the resurgence of exports, this led to strong recoveries in real GDP (Figure 2.7). In Indonesia and Thailand, real GDP regained its pre-crisis level in 2001. In the other economies, it is now well above pre-crisis *levels* but still below the arguably unsustainable pre-crisis *trends*.

The Asian crisis was followed by steep falls in investment as capacity utilization dropped, perceptions of longer-term growth prospects deteriorated, firms husbanded resources for survival rather than expansion and bank credit became harder to obtain. Investment/GDP ratios have dropped sharply (Table 2.9). It seems likely they will rise again, but it is hard to say by how much. It is generally agreed that the ratios had been too high prior to the crisis; there had been wasteful, speculative investment, particularly in property development.

With exports stronger and import demand generally remaining subdued, in part due to the collapse in investment, the current account moved into substantial surplus (Table 2.9). Even with reduced capital inflows (Table 2.5), this translated into an accumulation of foreign reserves (Figure 2.4), which was probably welcomed by policy-makers. The sharp recessions contributed to changes of government in Indonesia, Korea, the Philippines and Thailand. It was a catalyst for reform in a number of areas. Corporate governance was one particularly important area.

The banking sector remains weak in much of Asia. In many economies analysts believe the extent of the problem is still being understated in data released by the banks and the authorities. Asset management corporations have taken bad loans off the books of banks in China, Indonesia, Malaysia and Thailand. However, only in Malaysia do these agencies appear to have made much progress in selling off the acquired loans or underlying assets.

Credit growth has been weak across much of Asia (Table 2.4); it is still contracting in Hong Kong, the Philippines and Thailand. It is hard to know the extent to which this just reflects low demand for credit and the extent it is resulting from domestic banks adopting an (excessively?) cautious approach to new lending as they focus on cleaning up their existing loan books. The extent to which borrowing from international banks is contracting across the region suggests it may be more a matter of weak demand than weak domestic banks. Many corporations deliberately reduced gearing ratios in the aftermath of the crisis and much of the recovery in the past two years has been financed out of retained export earnings. Surveys of companies do not suggest that large firms are being constrained by access to finance, but it may be a problem for some small companies. In cases where there is some element of 'credit crunch', it could be exacerbating deflationary tendencies. In a number of economies, notably Hong Kong and Korea, banks have shifted the emphasis of their lending from the corporate sector towards the household sector.

2.4.2 *Effects on the global financial system*

The Asian crisis led not only to calls for reforms in the countries afflicted, but also gave further impetus to reforms in what came to be called the 'architecture' of the international financial system. Many of the most ambitious suggestions, such as an international bankruptcy court or global super-regulator, never looked like happening, but there has been some solid, often incremental, progress; see Kenen (2001) and White (2000). Some reforms had started following the Mexican crisis; the 'Rey Report' in 1996 on sovereign liquidity crises had discussed the moral hazard risks of 'bailouts'. But the Asian crisis was more a problem of excessive private sector debt and so raised new issues. New international fora, with broader representation than groups such as the G-7 and OECD, were established which issued a number of influential reports. These included ad-hoc groups such as the 'Willard' group, and ongoing groups such as the G-20, the International Monetary and Financial Committee and the Financial Stability Forum.

It was noted earlier that the IMF attached many more, wide-ranging conditions to its lending to the Asian countries. This was criticized in many circles as diffusing attention away from the core problems (the required abolition of Indonesia's cloves monopoly being a much-cited example). In 2002, the IMF's managing director issued new guidelines to restrict these 'conditionalities'.

The IMF institutionalized large scale lending by establishing the Supplemental Reserve Facility allowing it to make larger amounts of credit available. It also introduced a scheme of Contingent Credit Lines to assist otherwise sound countries at risk from contagion. However, no countries have applied for such lines, apparently for fear that being an early applicant would be interpreted as a sign that a crisis was imminent.

The Asian crisis demonstrated the need for greater transparency and disclosure – both in recipient countries and by international investors – and improved prudential oversight of capital flows; see Yam (1999). Many codes and standards have been established. Examples include the Special and General Data Dissemination Standards and the Core Principles for Effective Banking Supervision.

The Asian crisis also shifted the debate about exchange rate regimes. Fixed-but-adjustable pegs came to be increasingly seen as vulnerable to speculative attacks and no longer credible. Any exchange rate link must be in a stronger form or the exchange rate would need to be floating, according to this view.[9]

2.5 Conclusions

The Asian financial crisis arose primarily from three interrelated sets of factors. The first factor was shortcomings in the financial sector, including deficiencies in the supervision of banks that allowed a degree of exuberance to translate into an excessively rapid expansion of credit. This was compounded by a second factor, a reassessment by markets of the longer-term export potential of some Asian economies. These concerns were initially manifest in Thailand but then quickly spread across the other economies in the region. The third factor, the contagion, appears to have mainly resulted from the sudden realization by the market that a number of other Asian economies had vulnerabilities similar to those in Thailand.

While the origins of the Asian financial crisis are now better understood, this has not prevented further crises erupting in Russia, Brazil, Turkey and Argentina. But perhaps they have at least been better handled. Certainly, there has not been the same degree of contagion, probably because international investors are now more discerning and better informed about the differences between various emerging economies.

Appendix A

To capture the relative impact of the crisis on individual economies in the region, four variables are employed; the bilateral and real effective depreciations in the second half of 1997, the fall in equity prices and the change in the consensus forecast for 1998 real GDP growth.

These four dimensions of the impact of the crisis are complemented by four measures of interdependence with Thailand and fourteen fundamentals in Table 2.11. Given the acknowledged data deficiencies, ordinal rankings are used rather than the cardinal data themselves. The ordinal ranking of economies on each fundamental, as well as on each measure of interdependence with Thailand, is portrayed from left to right, with the most vulnerable country on the extreme left.

The fundamentals used mostly attempt to capture dimensions of financial sector or external sector vulnerability. The choice among the myriad of possible indicators to include draws on some recent studies of variables that leave an economy exposed to the risk of a financial crisis. The results of the exercise are summarized

Table 2.11 Ordinal ranking of country vulnerabilities

Impact							
Depreciation (bilateral)	Indo	Thai	SKor	Mal	Phil	Sing	HK
Real effective depreciation	Indo	SKor	Thai	Mal	Phil	Sing	HK
Equity price fall from peak	Thai	SKor	Mal	Indo	Phil	Sing	HK
GDP downgrading	Indo	Thai	SKor	Mal	Sing	Phil	HK
Capital flow reversal							
Interdependence with Thailand							
Distance	Thai	Mal	Sing	HK	Phil	Indo	SKor
Trade linkage	Thai	Mal	Sing	Indo	Phil	SKor	HK
Telephone calls	Thai	Sing	Mal	Indo	SKor	HK	Phil
Export similarity	Thai	HK	SKor	Sing	Mal	Phil	Indo
Fundamentals							
Liquidity mismatches							
Excess credit growth	Phil	Mal	Thai	Indo	Sing	SKor	HK
s.t. external debt/reserves	SKor	Indo	Thai	Phil	Mal	HK	Sing
Broad money/reserves	Indo	SKor	Thai	Phil	HK	Mal	Sing
Debt/GDP	Thai	Phil	Indo	Mal	SKor	HK	Sing
Banking strength							
Capital adequacy	SKor	Thai	Indo	Mal	Phil	HK	Sing
Non-performing loans	Mal	Thai	SKor	Indo	Phil	Sing	HK
Bank ratings	Indo	SKor	Thai	Phil	HK	Mal	Sing
State-owned banks	Indo	Phil	SKor	Mal	Thai	Sing	HK
External							
International reserves	Phil	Indo	Mal	Thai	SKor	HK	Sing
Current account/GDP	Thai	SKor	Mal	Phil	Indo	HK	Sing
Export slowdown	Thai	Sing	Mal	SKor	HK	Phil	Indo
Real exchange rate							
Deviation from average	Phil	Sing	Mal	Thai	Indo	SKor	HK
Expected depreciation	Indo	Phil	HK	Thai	Sing	Mal	SKor
Deviation from PPP	Sing	SKor	HK	Mal	Thai	Indo	Phil

Table 2.12 Summary measures of vulnerability

Interdependence with Thailand	*Similarity to Thailand*	*Fundamentals (simple average)*	*Fundamentals (Thai factor weights)*
Thailand	Thailand	Thailand	Thailand
Malaysia	Malaysia	Indonesia	Indonesia
Singapore	South Korea	Philippines	South Korea
Hong Kong	Indonesia	South Korea	Philippines
Indonesia	Philippines	Malaysia	Malaysia
South Korea	Hong Kong	Singapore	Singapore
Philippines	Singapore	Hong Kong	Hong Kong

in Table 2.12. The first column shows the average rankings of the economies on their interdependence with Thailand. The second column shows the similarity of their fundamentals to Thailand and the third their rankings on fundamentals. Implicit in this approach is an equal weight being given to each of the 'sins' and a zero weight to other possible indicators. This is, of course, somewhat arbitrary (but then so would be any alternative selection). The final column gives more weight to those fundamentals on which Thailand was weakest.

While only an informal test, it is interesting to observe some pattern to the economies most affected by the crisis. Specifically, the various fundamental measures do clearly distinguish Hong Kong and Singapore from the rest; there seem to be good reasons for their being less affected.

Contagion appeared to operate by prompting a belated reassessment of all economies in the region, with the economies which had the weakest fundamentals being most affected (particularly if the weakness was in those fundamentals in which Thailand itself was weak).

Notes

1 An earlier version of this chapter appeared as Goldstein and Hawkins (1998). The views expressed should not be attributed to organizations with which either are currently or previously associated. I thank Brett Winton for helpful comments and Marc Klau for preparing the graphs.
2 President Clinton at the meeting of APEC heads of government in Vancouver in November 1997.
3 Indeed, these variables typically serve as components of indices of exchange rate crises in the growing literature on early warning indicators of currency crises; see Goldstein *et al.* (2000), Hawkins and Klau (2000) and references cited therein.
4 Changes in exchange rates are calculated in terms of units of foreign currency (e.g. US dollar) per unit of domestic currency, that is, the 'world' price of the domestic currency. This results in smaller changes than using units of national currency per unit of foreign currency. The latter approach yields changes of over 100 per cent for Indonesia, which might be interpreted as implying that the currency has lost all its value.
5 Tables 5 and 6 in Goldstein and Hawkins (1998) provide some key extracts.
6 Mera and Renaud (2000) contains a collection of papers about the role of real estate in the Asian financial crisis.

7 Some (e.g. Thurow 1998) argue that the initial trigger for the devaluations in the region was the Chinese official devaluation in January 1994. However, because of the large share (perhaps 80 per cent) of transactions conducted at the market rather than the official rate before the two were unified by a devaluation of the official rate, the true devaluation was much less.
8 The impact of the news in Thailand was exacerbated by how much of it was received so quickly – the loss of reserves, the float, the approach to the IMF, the problems in the financial system etc. The fact that the rapid growth in the economies was termed by many 'the Asian miracle' implied that its basis was not that well understood, which perhaps exacerbated the tendency to panic when it seemed to be faltering.
9 Crockett (1993) was one of the earliest to make this point, prior to the Asian crisis. It has not gone unchallenged; see Williamson (2000). In practice, as noted by Calvo and Reinhart (2002), countries have shown a 'fear of floating' and still try to stabilize their exchange rates. See also Goldstein (2002).

Bibliography

Calvo, S. and Reinhart, C. (2002) 'Fear of floating', *Quarterly Journal of Economics*, 2: 379–408.

Cline, W. and Barnes, K. (1997) *Spreads and Risks in Emerging Market Lending*, Washington: Institute of International Finance.

Crockett, A. (1993) 'Monetary policy implications of increased capital flows', *Changing Capital Markets: Implications for Monetary Policy*, Federal Reserve Bank of Kansas City.

Eschweiler, B. (1997) 'Did the market see the Asian crisis coming?', paper presented at World Bank Seminar on the Asian Crisis, 4 October, Washington.

Goldstein, M. (1997) 'The case for an international banking standard', Institute for International Economics Policy Analyses in International Economics No. 47.

——(1998) 'The Asian financial crisis: causes, cures and systemic implications', Institute for International Economics Policy Analyses in International Economics No. 55.

——(2002) 'Managed floating plus and the great currency regime debate', Institute for International Economics Policy Analyses in International Economics No. 66.

——and Hawkins, J. (1998) 'The origin of the Asian financial turmoil', Reserve Bank of Australia Research Discussion Paper 9805.

——, Kaminsky, G. and Reinhart, C. (2000) *Assessing Financial Vulnerability: An Early Warning System for Emerging Markets*, Washington: Institute for International Economics.

Grenville, S. (1998) 'Exchange rates and crises', *Contemporary Economic Policy*, April. Available in abbreviated form in Reserve Bank of Australia *Bulletin*, February, 29–34.

Hawkins, J. (1999) 'Economic and financial monitoring', *Australian Economic Indicators*, Australian Bureau of Statistics, cat no 1350.0, January, 3–11.

——(2002) 'International bank lending: water flowing uphill?', WIDER discussion paper 2002/42.

——and Klau, M. (2000) 'Measuring potential vulnerabilities in emerging market economies', Bank for International Settlements Working Paper No. 91.

Institute of International Finance (2002) 'Capital flows to emerging market economies', 22 April. Available Online, http://www.iif.com/verify/data/report_docs/cf_0402.pdf (accessed 17 June 2002).

Kenen, P. (2001) *The New Financial Architecture: What's New? What's Missing?*, Washington: Institute for International Economics.

Mera, K. and Renaud, B. (2000) (eds) *Asia's Financial Crisis and the Role of Real Estate*, New York: ME Sharpe.

Radelet, S. and Sachs, J. (1998) 'The onset of the east Asian financial crisis', in P. Krugman (ed.), *Currency Crises*, Chicago: University of Chicago Press.

Thurow, L. (1998) 'Asia: the collapse and the cure', *The New York Review of Books*, 5 February.

White, W. (2000) 'What have we learned from recent financial crises and policy responses?', Bank for International Settlements Working Paper No. 84.

Williamson, J. (2000) *Exchange Rate Regimes for Emerging Economies: Reviving the Intermediate Option*, Washington: Institute for International Economics.

Yam, J. (1999) 'Causes of and solutions to the recent financial turmoil in the Asian region', *Hong Kong Monetary Authority Quarterly Bulletin*, 18: 52–60.

3 The origin and evolution of the Korean economic system

Wonhyuk Lim[1]

Developing countries typically face three interrelated policy challenges: investment, conflict management, and engagement with the outside world. They must formulate effective strategies to accumulate both physical and human capital, cope with social conflicts, and maximize the benefits of 'openness' while containing the risks (Rodrik 1999). In the early 1960s, the Republic of Korea (South Korea) addressed these developmental challenges by combining state-led financial resource allocation with export market orientation. The government nationalized banks and assumed a dominant role in financial resource allocation, providing selective guarantees on private-sector foreign borrowing. The government in effect formed a risk partnership with large private firms. Replacing the import substitution bias of the 1950s with outward orientation, the government, for the most part, used the performance of firms in competitive export markets as a selection criterion. As for conflict management, successive authoritarian regimes used both the carrot of improving living standards and the stick of ruthless suppression – before Korea was democratized in the late 1980s.

Since the outbreak of an economic crisis in 1997, this Korean model of economic development has come under heavy criticism. In fact, many critics have argued that the risk partnership between the government and big business had resulted in an inefficient financial sector and a highly leveraged corporate sector fraught with moral hazard. Some, predominantly Western, commentators have even contended that the Korean system was little more than a hotbed of corruption and cronyism. What is conspicuously missing in this barrage of criticism, however, is the recognition that the *same* system served as the backbone of 'rapid, shared growth' which catapulted Korea from one of the poorest countries in the world to the ranks of OECD countries in thirty years (World Bank 1993). As Table 3.1 shows, Korea's economic performance over the period of three decades prior to the 1997 crisis was truly exceptional.

It is the objective of this chaper to shed light on the rise and fall of the Korean model of economic development by using the concept of path dependence. In particular, this chapter will argue that the very success of the system made it difficult for reform-minded policymakers to introduce fundamental changes that would have placed Korea on a more sustainable, less crisis-prone development trajectory.

Table 3.1 Comparative growth experience, 1960–90 (per cent per annum)

Regions and countries	*Output*		*Labour*	*Physical capital*		*Human capital*	
	GDP	*GDP per worker*	*Number of workers*	*Total physical capital*	*Physical capital per worker*	*Labour quality*	*Years of schooling*
East Asia	7.46	4.71	2.75	10.89	8.14	1.33	1.94
Latin America	3.27	0.85	2.42	4.51	2.09	0.98	1.57
Middle East	5.14	2.71	2.43	6.43	4.00	1.36	2.93
South Asia	4.10	2.02	2.08	5.38	3.30	1.51	3.39
Sub-Saharan Africa	3.42	0.81	2.61	3.64	1.03	0.77	1.83
Developed countries	3.56	2.38	1.17	4.62	3.44	0.63	0.90
Malaysia	6.86	3.71	3.14	9.43	6.29	1.52	2.47
Indonesia	5.92	3.74	2.18	7.91	5.73	1.75	3.62
Philippines	4.11	1.59	2.52	6.10	3.58	1.40	1.64
Singapore	8.17	5.27	2.90	12.93	10.03	0.69	1.03
Korea	8.49	5.93	2.56	11.90	9.34	2.18	2.83
Taiwan	8.31	5.66	2.66	11.87	9.22	1.83	2.41
Thailand	6.97	4.26	2.72	9.75	7.03	0.39	0.89
Japan	6.17	5.03	1.14	9.35	8.22	0.10	0.48

Source: Hahn and Kim (2000).

Note
Regional averages are weighted by each country's average GDP between 1960 and 1990. The labour quality index is constructed as the weighted average of educational attainment for workers, where the weights are based on the (diminishing) rate of return from each additional level of schooling (i.e. primary, secondary, and tertiary level).

This chapter is organized as follows. Section 3.1 examines the set of initial conditions that affected the choice of economic systems in Korea in the early stages of development. After Korea was liberated from Japanese colonial rule in 1945, the reassignment of property rights and the realignment of political forces provided the background for subsequent economic decisions, but what later came to be known as 'the Korean model' was not the initial choice. A series of 'historical accidents' that led to its adoption in the early 1960s is highlighted. Section 3.2 looks at the evolution of this model of development. The government's decision to forge a risk partnership with large private firms not only encouraged rapid capital accumulation, but it also created a coalition of economic players interested in preserving this system. In the 1960s, the government tried to contain the potential dangers of this risk partnership by making government support contingent on market performance. When a major economic downturn raised the spectre of massive bankruptcies in the early 1970s, however, the government resorted to an emergency decree to bail out heavily indebted firms *and* their incumbent owner–managers at the expense of creditors. Exacerbating moral hazard, the government extended extremely generous financial support to large private firms during the ensuing heavy and chemical industry (HCI) drive. Section 3.3 examines why efforts to reduce state intervention and moral hazard were delayed, even as the Korean system became increasingly dysfunctional in the era of liberalization and democratization. The capacity of the government to control international capital flows and domestic private firms was significantly weakened after the late 1980s, but the installed base of politicians, bureaucrats, and businessmen blocked fundamental reforms centred on the principle of 'de-control with de-protection'. The economic crisis of 1997 should be understood within this context.

3.1 The adoption of the Korean model of economic development

After Korea was liberated from the Japanese colonial rule (1910–45), it was confronted with the crucial tasks of reassigning property rights and re-establishing the external trade and foreign exchange regime. The 'enemy properties' of the Japanese and their collaborators had to be either nationalized or sold off, and the rules governing trade and foreign exchange had to be modified to deal with the vacuum created by the severing of economic relations with Japan. Furthermore, given the lack of domestic capital and technology, policies designed to attract investment had to be implemented. In this regard, Korea's economic situation after liberation was similar to that of Central and Eastern European countries after the collapse of the Socialist Bloc. Faced with these policy challenges, Syngman Rhee, the first president of the Republic of Korea, took a rather myopic and politically motivated approach. In fact, Rhee's use of policy instruments to finance elections and other party activities through a close alliance with select private firms played a dominant role in a succession of economic decisions during his presidency (1948–60).

After the outbreak of the Korean War in 1950, the United States reassessed Korea's geostrategic importance and provided generous aid and assistance.[2] The Korean government deposited the local currency equivalent of all US aid into a counterpart fund whose use would be jointly determined by the Americans and the Koreans. The exchange rate became a contentious issue, however, as Rhee insisted on repaying the advances at a rate that significantly undervalued the dollar. The market exchange rate (as approximated by the rate applied to UN soldiers stationed in Korea) was at times nearly three times as high as the official rate. Rhee's reasoning was clear: the possession of foreign exchange and aid goods at less than their market value would create arbitrage opportunities, and would allow him to distribute favours to businessmen willing to provide kickbacks to his Liberal Party (Haggard 1990: 57).

In the end, what passed for an economic system in Korea in the 1950s was primarily shaped by crony capitalism. The sale of 'enemy properties' resulted in windfall gains for favoured businessmen and an undue concentration of economic power. The overvaluation of the Korean currency, designed to maximize arbitrage opportunities, had the effect of severely discouraging exports.

When a student protest in April 1960 finally put an end to the Rhee government, Korea was in a dismal state. Korea's per capita GDP in 1960 was lower than such sub-Saharan African countries as Mozambique and Senegal – to say nothing of most countries in Asia and Latin America. In fact, a cross-country study on economic development shows that Korea had a rather unusual economic structure in the early 1960s (Perkins 1997). The share of agriculture and mining in the Korean GNP was close to 50 per cent, nearly 15 percentage points higher than the average of other countries of comparable size and per capita income. The share of manufacturing, slightly over 10 per cent of GNP, was unusually low, nearly 20 percentage points below the average. Even more remarkable was the extremely low share of exports, as it amounted to only 3 per cent of GNP when the average was about 15 per cent. This was a dramatic departure from the 1930s and the early 1940s when Korea's exports amounted to about 30 per cent of GNP. The Rhee government's myopic policy was largely responsible for turning a trading nation into an aid-dependent near-autarky.

Following the Student Revolution of April 1960, the 'Military Revolution' of May 1961 provided the political background for the adoption of the Korean model of economic development. Upon seizing power through a bloodless coup, General Park Chung Hee and his followers declared that they were determined to 'focus all energy into developing capability to confront communism, in order to realize the people's long-standing wish for national unification'.

Although Park and his followers had only a rudimentary knowledge of economics, they believed that the state should take a leading role in economic development. In order to centralize economic policymaking, the military government established the Economic Planning Board (EPB) in July 1961. The EPB was charged with the task of formulating and implementing five-year economic development plans based on an 'indicative planning' approach. The military government also took several measures to strengthen the role of the state in resource allocation. After the Student Revolution of April 1960, prominent businessmen were accused of having grown rich through political connections with the previous Syngman Rhee regime. Taking over the task of dealing with these 'illicit wealth accumulators', the military government accused them of tax evasion and other illegal business practices, and forced them to turn in their equity shares in commercial banks as 'fines'. This drastic measure paved the way for the government to exert direct control over commercial banks, in effect re-nationalizing the banks that had been privatized in the late 1950s. In a little more than a year, the military government thus established various levers of control. The question remained, however, as to what kind of state-led system it would be.

Over the next few years, the Park government implemented three interrelated sets of economic policies that came to define the Korean model of economic development. First, primarily to accommodate US demands, the government instituted a set of macroeconomic reforms designed to 'get the prices right' and stabilize the economy. Second, the government adopted drastic measures to share the investment risks of the private sector, providing, in particular, explicit repayment guarantees to foreign financial institutions that extended loans to Korean private firms. Third, in order to enhance economic independence, Park himself spearheaded the effort to boost exports, offering various incentives based on market performance. The resulting government–business risk partnership, for which the export market performance of private firms was primarily used as a selection criterion, defined the core of what later came to be known as 'the Korean model'.

The macroeconomic reforms ensured that Korea's state-led development model would be a market-based one. Building on the stabilization policies of 1963–64, the government devalued the Korean won from 130 to the dollar to 255 to the dollar in May 1964. Also, in order to protect depositors from inflation and to encourage domestic savings, the government raised the ceiling on the one-year time deposit rate from 15 to 30 per cent on 30 September 1965 (Kim 1995: 114).

These orthodox polices, designed to reduce distortions in macroeconomic variables, were accompanied by dirigist measures that deliberately introduced distortions into the microeconomic incentives. The Park government knew that Korea lacked the domestic resources to carry out its ambitious economic development programme, but unlike Latin American countries at the time (or Southeast Asian countries in the 1980s), it was not willing to depend on foreign direct investment (FDI). Seeking to tap into foreign capital while limiting the influence of foreign multinationals, the fiercely nationalistic Korean government decided to rely heavily on foreign loans. The domestic firms at the time lacked the standing in the international capital market, however, the government decided to take up the problem of asymmetric information and allow state-owned banks to issue a repayment guarantee to foreign financial institutions that provided loans to Korean firms.

In taking this measure, the Park government signalled that it was willing to form a risk partnership with business leaders. Although Park Chung Hee and his followers had initially condemned most of these businessmen as 'illicit wealth accumulators', they apparently concluded that combining state monitoring with private entrepreneurship would be the most effective means of carrying out the economic development plans. The alternative of using state-owned enterprises to accelerate industrialization, as in Taiwan (Tien 1989) or Singapore (Low 1991), was not actively pursued. The government decided to use its credibility to raise capital on the international market and allocate financial resources to private firms, in effect *contracting out* the provision of goods and services to the private sector under a system of government monitoring as well as a guarantee on loans. Through direct monitoring and a market test based on export performance, the government tried to contain the potential costs of moral hazard that state-backed debt financing created. Export performance, in particular, provided the government with a relatively objective selection criterion (see Figure 3.1).

In order to increase economic independence through export promotion, the government also introduced a number of export incentives. The short-term export credit system was streamlined as early as 1961. The essence of the new system was the automatic approval of loans by commercial banks to those with an export letter of credit (L/C). The government also gave exporters various tax deductions, generous wastage allowances, tariff exemptions, and preferential policy loans.[3] In order to monitor export performance according to indicative targets set at the beginning of each year, the president himself chaired monthly export

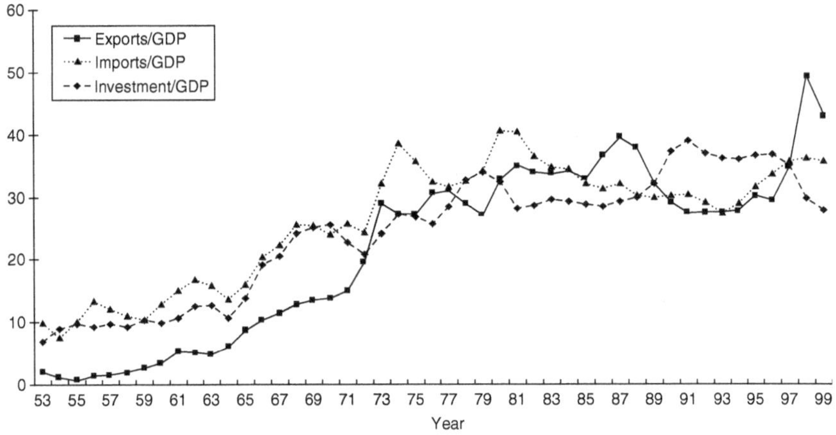

Figure 3.1 Korea's exports, imports, and investment.

promotion meetings. Strong export performers even received medals and national recognition on Export Day, which was established in 1964 to commemorate the day when Korea's annual exports exceeded 100 million dollars for the first time. Aware of Korea's comparative advantage in the 1960s, the government encouraged private firms to concentrate on labour-intensive industries.[4] The rapid increase in export encouraged by the government is illustrated in Figure 3.1.

The Korean model of economic development proved an efficient choice given Korea's resource endowment at the time. In 1965, the primary and secondary enrollments in Korea were similar to the rates in countries with three times its per capita income (World Bank 1993: 45–6). Cheap and high-quality labour could be readily employed to produce a high rate of return on investment in physical capital, if Korea could only tap into foreign capital and technology to compensate for the shortage of domestic resources and exploit its comparative advantage. The government's decision to issue a selective guarantee on the foreign borrowing of private firms and promote exports was a solution to this developmental challenge. The Korean government thus corrected for capital market imperfections and removed the government-imposed constraints that had made it very difficult for firms to exploit profitable investment opportunities in the 1950s.

3.2 The evolution of the Korean model of economic development

Korea's economic development model entered on export-led industrialization and government–business risk partnership encouraged rapid capital accumulation. Reassured by government guarantees and subsequent economic growth, foreign financial institutions expanded loans to Korean firms and provided the lion's share of necessary capital for investment projects.[5] Korean firms, for their part, dramatically increased their leverage while their profitability actually *declined*: the

Table 3.2 Economic trends in Korea before and after the 1972 emergency decree (1964–78) (per cent per annum)

	Growth rate of investment	*Rate of inflation*	*Interest rate on bank loans*	*Interest rate on curb loans*	*Total liabilities/ net worth*	*Net profit/ net worth*
1964	13.3	30.0	16.5	61.80	100.5	15
1965	19.3	5.8	18.5	58.92	92.7	15
1966	84.0	14.6	26.0	58.68	117.7	17
1967	25.2	15.9	26.0	56.52	151.2	17
1968	52.3	16.1	25.8	56.04	201.3	16
1969	45.1	15.5	24.5	51.36	270.0	14
1970	11.3	15.5	24.0	50.16	328.4	11
1971	24.9	12.5	23.0	46.44	394.2	4
1972	3.7	16.7	17.7	39.00	313.4	17
1973	40.7	13.6	15.5	33.24	272.7	30
1974	30.2	30.5	15.5	40.56	316.0	23
1975	24.9	25.2	15.5	47.88	339.5	17
1976	77.1	21.3	16.1	40.47	364.6	22
1977	43.1	16.6	15.0	38.07	350.7	21
1978	45.1	22.8	17.1	41.70	366.8	23

Sources: Bank of Korea, *Economic Statistics Yearbook*, various issues; Bank of Korea, *Financial Statements Analysis*, various issues; Cho and Kim (1997).

debt–equity ratio of manufacturing firms, as measured by their total liabilities divided by net worth, rose from 92.7 per cent in 1965 to 328.4 per cent in 1970 (Table 3.2). While encouraging investment conducive to rapid economic growth, the Korean system thus led to a highly leveraged corporate sector that became extremely vulnerable to shocks.

Although the Korean system was designed to contain idiosyncratic moral hazard by making government support contingent on market performance, it was not prepared to deal with the increased *systemic* risks as manifested in the higher leverage of private firms. Apparently successful firms kept borrowing to expand their business under government guarantees on foreign debt, and neither the government nor the private sector stopped to think seriously about the potential toll that a major economic downturn would take on heavily indebted firms.

When a serious economic slowdown following the investment explosion of the late 1960s threatened to topple the debt-plagued corporate sector in 1972, the Park government decided to bail out heavily indebted firms and issued the Presidential Emergency Decree for Economic Stability and Growth on 3 August 1972. The Emergency Decree placed an immediate moratorium on the payment of all corporate debt to the curb lenders and called for an extensive rescheduling of bank loans at a reduced interest rate. The moratorium was to last three years, after which all curb funds had to be turned into five-year loans at a monthly interest rate of 1.35 per cent, or an annual rate of 16.2 per cent – when the prevailing market rate exceeded 40 per cent.

In retrospect, the 3 August Emergency Decree of 1972 marked a watershed in the evolution of the Korean economy. When the government was forging a risk partnership with private firms in the 1960s by guaranteeing repayment on their foreign borrowing, the government issued a repayment guarantee to foreign financial institutions rather than to Korean firms. Aware of moral hazard created by insurance, the government certainly did not intend to guarantee the governance rights of the incumbent owner–managers. The Emergency Decree of 1972, however, established the precedent that the government would take extraordinary measures to relieve financial distress when necessary – *without* holding the management of firms and banks accountable for their previous investment and lending decisions. Moreover, the Emergency Decree seemed to imply that an excessive dependence on debt would not only go unpunished but might actually be rewarded by the government – as long as other companies also depended heavily on debt. Violating the property rights of the creditors in the informal curb market, the government relieved the debt burden of the private firms it had come to rely on as agents to carry out its ambitious economic development plans. The 3 August Emergency Decree of 1972 thus fundamentally changed the nature of state guarantees and ushered in a new era characterized by the deepening of the government–business risk partnership.

The ensuing HCI drive aggravated moral hazard as the government was increasingly trapped in a vicious cycle of intervention (Stern *et al.* 1995). During the late 1970s, HCIs accounted for almost 80 per cent of all fixed investment in the manufacturing sector when their share in the manufacturing sector's output was around 40 per cent. The banks as well as the newly established National Investment Fund supported the HCI drive by providing policy-oriented loans at a *negative* real interest rate. In order to minimize time and exploit scale economies in establishing the capital-intensive HCI sector, the government relied on a select group of large family-based business groups and provided them with extremely generous financial support. Known as *chaebol*, they drastically increased their share of GDP.

The HCI drive in the 1970s transformed the government–business risk partnership decidedly in favour of these family-based business groups. Unlike in the 1960s, international competitiveness (i.e. 'market test') no longer operated as a selection criterion. The government simply believed in the entrepreneurship of a few *chaebol* founders and directed massive resources to their firms. Although Park Chung Hee might have felt that he could always control the chaebol firms like 'quasi-SOEs', he was in fact creating behemoths that would come to dominate the Korean economy. Having channelled massive resources into the *chaebol* to carry out high-priority investment projects – sometimes over the initial objection of their owner–managers, the government had to take responsibility should these projects turn sour. Moreover, the gigantic size and high leverage of the *chaebol* strengthened the case for a 'too big to fail' argument.

These developments in the 1970s had a profound impact on the Korean economic system. The Emergency Decree of 1972 and the HCI drive consolidated the government–business risk partnership and exacerbated moral hazard.

Subsequently, the industrial targeting approach adopted during the HCI drive trapped the government in a vicious cycle of intervention, and the massive financial support extended to the top *chaebol* consolidated the government–business risk partnership.

3.3 Delayed reform and crisis

By the 1980s, it had become possible for successful Korean firms to raise capital on their own. It had also become increasingly difficult for the government to identify profitable investment opportunities and monitor the performance of individual firms. Moreover, increased domestic and foreign pressure for liberalization and democratization was beginning to force the government to relinquish some important policy instruments that it had used to motivate and discipline private firms. Given the reduced desirability and effectiveness of government intervention in the economy, policymakers should have fundamentally redefined the role of the government.

In fact, as early as the beginning of the 1980s, many technocrats did advocate a transition to a more market-oriented system. They were clearly aware of the dilemma that the government faced. Since the collapse of a large *chaebol* would bury the financial system in nonperforming loans, the government was more or less obliged to guarantee the *chaebol*'s stability. This implicit guarantee, however, encouraged the *chaebol* to undertake excessive investment. Expecting to be bailed out should a crisis strike, they would discount the downside risks and invest wildly – unless restrained by the government. In order to maintain economic stability, the government thus found itself having to intervene in the investment decisions of private firms.

The technocrats believed that the solution to this apparent dilemma required the government to let market forces operate and allow a nonviable *chaebol* to go bankrupt while containing the fallout from its collapse. The technocrats also thought that the government would have to hold the incumbent owner–managers accountable for their previous decisions and refrain from intervening in the investment decisions of private firms in the future. Moreover, autonomous financial institutions, free from the control of the government *and* industrial capitalists, would have to be allowed to make decisions on their own and bear the full consequences of their actions. The government would have to redefine its role and focus on competition policy and prudential regulation rather than allocate financial resources according to its industrial policy objectives. In other words, the government would have to stop providing direction and insurance to private firms, but limit its role to setting and enforcing 'the rules of the game' and providing a social safety net. This series of decisive measures would serve as a credible signal that the regime had indeed changed.

By this time, however, the Korean economic system had produced a coalition of economic players who were interested in consolidating and maintaining the government–business risk partnership. Although domestic and foreign pressure for liberalization and democratization did lead to the adoption of some market-oriented reforms, the government–business risk partnership continued to dominate and blocked fundamental reforms. The state control of the banks continued, and the government took a decidedly bureaucratic approach to competition policy. The *chaebol* tried to expand their influence in the financial sector through the ownership of non-bank financial institutions, and limit the presence of foreign multinationals in the domestic market.

The lack of fundamental reform proved fatal for the Korean economy. In 1995, the average debt–equity ratio of the top thirty *chaebol* was 347.5 per cent. The lower-ranking groups (No. 11–30) were earning a negative average return on assets since 1993. Halla, Jinro, and Sammi, in particular, had a debt–equity ratio of over 2,000 per cent as they piled up losses. Financial institutions, however, continued to provide credit to these companies. In 1996, the average debt–equity ratio of the top thirty *chaebol* climbed to 386.5 per cent, but the financial institutions still propped up the debt-plagued conglomerates. In April 1996, Korea's terms of trade began to decline sharply as the prices of semiconductors collapsed. The decline in the terms of trade reached 20 per cent by the end of the year, and it turned out to be Korea's biggest terms-of-trade shock since the oil shock. In 1997, the average debt–equity ratio of the top thirty *chaebol* reached 519.0 per cent. Korea was on the brink of yet another debt crisis.

Figure 3.2 illustrates the basic nature of the problem with the Korean corporate sector. Korean firms have relied excessively on debt financing, even when carrying out massive investment projects with a long gestation period. It would have been all right if Korean firms had a sufficiently high profit rate to cover interest expenses, but their rate of return on net worth has been below the opportunity cost of capital for much of the past two decades.

From a political economy perspective, the Korean experience illustrates that once an economic system is well established, it is very difficult to introduce fundamental

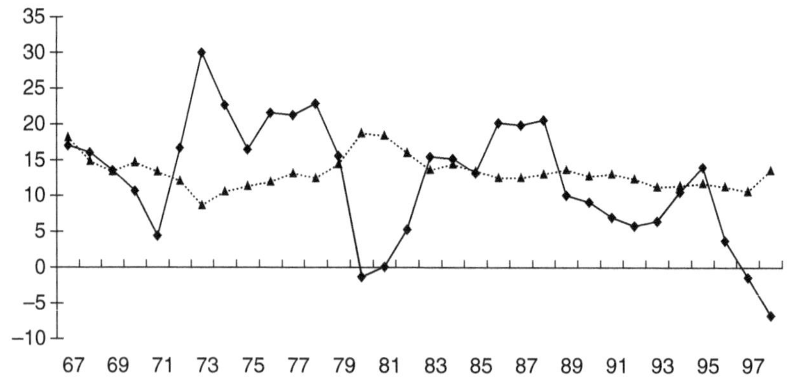

Figure 3.2 Profitability and opportunity cost of capital.

Source: Bank of Korea, *Financial Statements Analysis*, various issues.

Note
Total borrowing does not include non-interest-bearing IOUs.

changes because the economic players interested in preserving the existing system tend to be the ones who wield a great deal of influence in the policymaking process. The Korean model of economic development itself was adopted only when the entrenched interests associated with the old corruption-prone system were wiped out in the wake of a student revolution and a military coup. As for the new economic system based on the government–business risk partnership, the chances for fundamental change were smaller than in the case of the old system. It was not just because the new system was far more successful than the old one. In the case of the old system, which was based on crony capitalism, a political upheaval throwing out the entrenched interests would do the trick – if it is followed by an institutional reform designed to reduce rent-seeking in the economy. In the new system, however, a political upheaval replacing one set of policymakers with another would not result in a fundamental change – unless the new politicians and bureaucrats were willing or forced to relinquish their control over the economy. Even in the wake of the economic crisis, Korea is struggling to make progress in this regard.

Notes

1 The author gratefully acknowledges financial support provided by the National Institute for Research Advancement (NIRA), Tokyo, Japan. The author would also like to thank Paul David, Euysung Kim, Jacob Metzer, and Nobuki Sugita for helpful comments on earlier versions of this paper, as well as Jina Yu for her excellent research assistance.

2 Foreign aid financed nearly 70 per cent of total imports from 1953 through 1962. It was equal to nearly 80 per cent of total fixed capital formation and 8 per cent of GNP. Net foreign savings, as measured by the current account deficit of the balance of payments, averaged 9 per cent of GNP for this decade (Mason *et al.* 1980: 185).

3 The interest rate on export loans was subsidized heavily from the mid-1960s to the beginning of the 1980s. When the 1965 interest rate reform was implemented, the interest rate on export credit was left untouched. Consequently, the rate differential between export loans and general ordinary loans widened sharply, approaching nearly 20 percentage points (Cho and Kim 1997: 36–7).

4 In 1962, labour-intensive manufactures accounted for less than 15 per cent of Korea's total exports of $54.8 million. In 1963, exports increased by $32 million (58.4 per cent jump!) to reach $86.8 million, and labour-intensive manufactures such as textiles and footwear accounted for more than 80 per cent of this increase. Overall, exports increased at an average annual rate of 35 per cent in real terms from 1963 to 1969 (Yoo 1996: 8–9).

5 In the First and Second Five-Year Economic Development Plan periods (1962–71), foreign savings accounted for 52.8 and 39.4 per cent of total investment, respectively. The share of foreign savings in investment remained significant through the 1970s, hovering around 20 per cent.

Bibliography

Cho, Yoon Je and Kim, Joon Kyung (1997) *Credit Policies and the Industrialization of Korea*, Seoul: Korea Development Institute.

David, Paul A. (2000) 'Path dependence, its critics and the quest for "historical economics,"' mimeo, Stanford University.

Haggard, Stephan (1990) *Pathways from the Periphery: The Politics of Growth in the Newly Industrializing Countries*, Ithaca: Cornell University Press.

Hahn, Chin Hee and Jong-Il Kim (2000) 'Sources of East Asian growth: some evidence from cross-country studies', paper prepared for the Global Research Project *Explaining Growth* initiated by the World Bank.

Jones, Leroy P. and Il SaKong (1980) *Government, Business, and Entrepreneurship in Economic Development: The Korean Case*, Cambridge, Mass.: Harvard University Press.

Kim, Chung-yum (1994) *Policymaking on the Front Lines: Memoirs of a Korean Practitioner, 1945–79*, Washington, DC: Economic Development Institute of the World Bank.

——(1995) *A 30-Year History of Korean Economic Policy: A Memoir*, Seoul: Joong-Ang Daily News.

Kim, Eun Mee (1997) *Big Business, Strong State: Collusion and Conflict in South Korean Development, 1960–90*, Albany, NY: State University of New York Press.

Kimiya, Tadashi (1991) *The "Failure" of the Inward-Looking Deepening Strategy in South Korea: The Limits of the State's Structural Autonomy in the 5.16 Military Government*, unpublished PhD dissertation, Korea University [in Korean].

Krueger, Anne O. (1979) *The Developmental Role of the Foreign Sector and Aid*, Cambridge, Mass.: Harvard University Press.

Low, Linda (1991) *The Political Economy of Privatization in Singapore*, Singapore: McGraw-Hill Book Co.

Mason, Edward S., Kim, Mahn Je, Perkins, Dwight H., Kim, Kwang Suk, and Cole, David C. (1980) *The Economic and Social Modernization of the Republic of Korea*, Cambridge: Harvard University Press.

Park, Chung Hee (1963) *The Country, the Revolution and I*, Seoul: Hollym Corporation.

Perkins, Dwight H. (1997) 'Structural transformation and the role of the state: Korea, 1945–95', in Dong-Se Cha, Kwang Suk Kim, and Dwight H. Perkins (eds), *The Korean Economy 1945–95: Performance and Vision for the 21st Century*, Seoul: Korea Development Institute, 57–98.

Rodrik, Dani (1999) *The New Global Economy and Developing Countries: Making Openness Work*, Washington, DC: Overseas Development Council.

Shin, Inseok (2000) *The Korean Crisis: Before and After*, Seoul: Korea Development Institute.

Stern, Joseph J., Kim, Ji-hong , Perkins, Dwight H, and Yoo, Jung-ho (1995) *Industrialization and the State: The Korean Heavy and Chemical Industry Drive*, Cambridge: Harvard Institute for International Development.

Tien, Hung-mao (1989) *The Great Transition: Political and Social Change in the Republic of China*, Stanford: Hoover Institution Press.

World Bank (1993) *The East Asian Miracle: Economic Growth and Public Policy*, New York: Oxford University Press.

Yoo, Jungho (1996) 'Challenges to the newly industrialized countries: a reinterpretation of Korea's growth experience', KDI Working Paper No. 9608, Seoul: Korea Development Institute.

4 A 'stroke' hypothesis of Korea's 1997 financial crisis[1]

Hyun-Hoon Lee

4.1 Introduction

Since the Asian financial crisis erupted in 1997, a number of people including economists, journalists and politicians have expounded many explanations and theories of the causes of the crisis. However, there has been no consensus, and each individual analyst tends to explain the causes of the Asian crisis, subscribing exclusively to one of the explanatory categories. These people can be categorized into four groups.

The first group headed by Radelet and Sachs (1998) argues that the Asian crisis erupted because, even though there was no serious intrinsic problem, self-fulfilling investors suddenly panicked and ran away from East Asia in a herd. The second group headed by Krugman (1998) and Corsetti *et al.* (1998) takes the opposite view and claims that the fundamental problems of these countries had accumulated, gathered momentum and finally erupted all at once when they reached the maximum level. The third group blames mostly the failure of the policies implemented by the crisis countries before the crisis occurred. The fourth group argues that the crisis erupted mainly because of external factors like abrupt changes in international market conditions. Unlike the first and second groups, which include mostly economists, the third and fourth groups seemed to include mostly politicians and journalists.[2]

But, singling out only one factor for the crisis does not seem to be justified. For example, attributing exclusively to the irrational (or rational) speculative attacks and contagion as the cause of the crisis does not seem to make sense, because the contagion varied widely across the East Asian countries. Blaming it solely on an economic system once praised as a successful model for development is also inconsistent.

It seems that there is some truth in each of these explanations. Had at least one of these four factors been different from what they actually were, the financial crisis would not have occurred, or it would not have been as destructive as it actually was. In other words, Korea's financial crisis (and maybe most of the other Asian countries' crises as well) occurred not due to one single reason, but due to elements from all of the four explanatory categories.

This chapter, then attempts to piece together the fragmented causes of the Korean financial crisis. We will do this by drawing an analogy between a financial crisis and a human 'stroke', which occurs when there is a sudden blockage of an artery in the brain by a blood clot, or by other debris carried in the bloodstream of the circulatory system. This approach may be considered as a kind of general systems theory. The 'stroke' hypothesis synthesizes most of the appealing explanations and theories of the financial crisis, and shows how the numerous factors such as fundamental weaknesses, policy mistakes, unfriendly international circumstances and exogenous shocks were systematically intertwined in causing the financial crisis.

This chapter is organized as follows. Section 4.2 introduces the 'stroke' hypothesis and explains how the underlying and direct causes of the financial crisis are systematically intertwined. In Sections 4.3–4.6, this chapter discusses each of the four major causes, respectively. Section 4.7 concludes.

4.2 Analogy between a stroke and a financial crisis

The financial system of the economy is analogous to the human circulatory system in terms of its structure and functions. A financial crisis normally starts with a sudden liquidity crunch in the financial system. This is also analogous to the human stroke, which happens with the sudden blockage of an artery in the brain. These two are also very similar in that a financial crisis can result in the real sector's paralysis and a stroke can limit the body's normal functions such as thinking, movement, speech and the senses.

Therefore, it may be very useful to understand the nature of a stroke in understanding the nature of the financial crisis.[3] To most people, a stroke normally seems to occur all of a sudden in a person who has been living his/her life quite normally. As a matter of fact, however, it does not strike a real healthy person. Figure 4.1 illustrates how strokes normally occur. As illustrated in the figure, the chance of having a stroke is dependent upon how the person's physical constitution is, how well the person responds to the warning signs of stroke and how friendly the surroundings are.

Smoking, heavy alcohol intake, lack of exercise and a high-fat diet normally result in the physical weakness of a person, contributing to high blood pressure, high blood cholesterol, diabetes and obesity, which then speed up hardening of the arteries. When a person's physical constitution becomes weak, the risk of having a stroke increases. Therefore, if a person has high blood pressure or other contributing factors, it is very important for him/her to change his/her life style by stopping smoking, limiting the amount of alcohol intake, having regular exercise and eating less fat. If the person fails to react properly to his/her weakening physical constitution, then he/she becomes constitutionally predisposed to stroke. Unfriendly surroundings such as family dispute, competitive personal relationships and a heavy burden of work also contribute to the likelihood of having a stroke.

Strokes normally occur after giving several different kinds of warning signs beforehand. Sudden loss or blurring of vision in one eye is one important warning

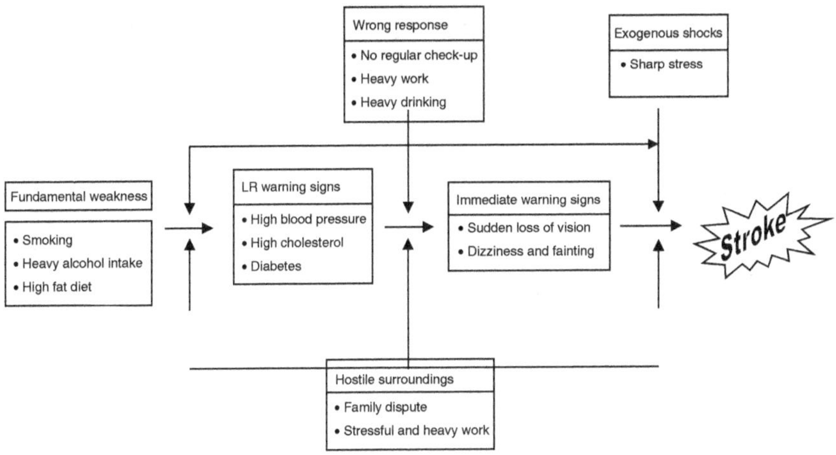

Figure 4.1 Systematic flow of strokes.

sign. Sometimes it may be only a passing weakness, dizziness, fainting or tingling in a limb. If there appears a warning sign and the person fails to take appropriate action, then the stroke risk increases significantly. Finally when there is a sudden sharp stress, worry, heavy exercise or an exposure to the cold weather, which work as a trigger or an exogenous shock, then a stroke may finally occur, with serious damage to the body.

Korea's financial crisis underwent a process very similar to a typical stroke. To most people, it appears to have erupted all of a sudden when the panicked foreign investors turned their backs on Korea. However, like a stroke, it erupted after several early symptoms. Fundamental weaknesses, policy mistakes, unfriendly international circumstances and exogenous shocks all contributed to the crisis. Of course, one may argue that we still need to single out one or two factors, which are considered most critical to the crisis. This is indeed a reasonable argument. But it seems that each of the four factors played a critical role and should be considered equally important causes of the financial crisis.

Using the 'stroke' framework, a systematic and comprehensive process of the Korean financial crisis is illustrated in Figure 4.2. As seen in the figure, each of the four factors played a role and intertwined with each other systematically, resulting in the financial crisis. That is, since the late 1980s the fundamental weaknesses began accumulating, and hence the international competitiveness of Korean corporations weakened. On the other hand, the international environment, which used to be friendly with Korea's export-oriented growth strategy, rapidly become hostile. This also put the downward pressure on Korea's competitiveness, and made the Korean economy even more vulnerable to the sudden changes in the world economy. However, the Korean government overlooked the

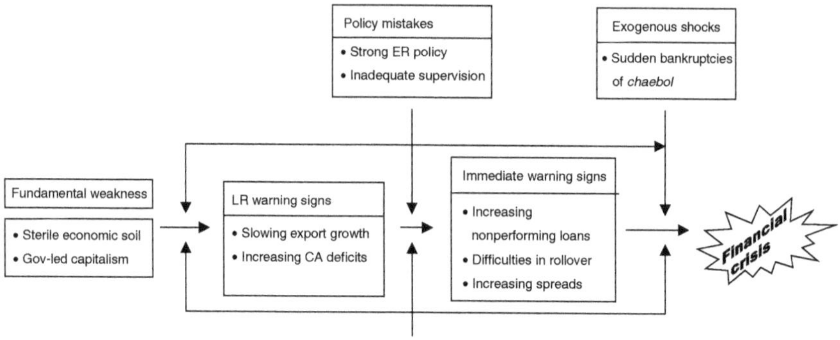

Figure 4.2 Systematic flow of financial crises.

signs of weakening competitiveness and possibility of financial crisis and, instead, aggravated the situation by making consecutive policy mistakes. Finally, a sudden exogenous shock in early 1997 triggered the financial crisis to erupt.

The following sections explain the factors and processes of the financial crisis in more detail. Fundamental weaknesses, unfriendly environment, policy mistakes and triggering factors are considered in that order.

4.3 Fundamental weaknesses

Just like a typical stroke, the financial crisis of Korea had its roots in fundamental weaknesses. The fundamental weaknesses, and consequently the weakening of the international competitiveness of Korea have developed since the late 1980s.

From the early 1960s, Korea has enjoyed extraordinary growth that transformed it from one of the poorest countries in the world to the twenty-ninth member of the OECD.[4] In 1996, Korea was the world's eleventh largest economy in terms of GDP. With regard to the fundamental basis for economic growth, the following two factors contributed to Korea's rapid growth.[5] First, Korean people were diligent as proven by their long working hours and high savings rates. They were also well educated due to the strong Confucian emphasis on education. The second most important cause of the rapid growth was the government's strong leadership in creating and developing strategic manufacturing industries and in moving towards export-oriented growth. This is a somewhat controversial argument, as there is plenty of evidence that Korea's industrial policies did not contribute to the growth of industries' productivity. But at least until the early 1980s, a strong government leadership was somewhat necessary and desirable, because the size of the domestic markets was small, the structure of the domestic industry was rather simple and Korea's exposure to the world market was limited.

Since the late 1980s onwards, however, these two factors have become no longer valid. We discuss the reasons in the following sections.

4.3.1 Sterilizing economic soil

With the advent of democratization in 1987 and the subsequent liberalization of trade unions, nominal wage increased 15 per cent per annum up until 1996, exceeding productivity that rose by 11 per cent. However, tight labour market conditions and strong trade union power ensured that labour market reform went untouched. The labour market was full of rigidities. An excessive degree of job protection prevented lay-offs and encouraged over-manning, inflexible working hours and few limits on strike action (Fitch ICBA 1999).

What was more critical than the rapid rise in the wage rate and labour market rigidities was that the Korean education system no longer provided the economy with a labour force it needed most. Since the late 1980s, as the Korean economy has moved towards the level of developed countries, its products have become more sophisticated and its production processes have become more complex and more deeply integrated into the world economy. All this means that Korea is now in urgent need of a creative and highly skilled labour force – entrepreneurs, workers, bankers and the like. However, the Korean education system has kept its repetitive-memory-oriented education, which once proved to be successful when the Korean economy was in a less developed stage.[6]

On the other hand, Koreans have continued to work longer hours than their competitors, and their savings rates have remained very high.[7] However, the rapid rise in the wage rate, labour market rigidities and the lack of a creative labour force have made the Korean economic soil sterile, and these indigenous factors have weakened the international competitiveness of Korean firms.

4.3.2 Inefficient government-driven capitalism

As indicated earlier, the government-led economic policy was once considered to have led the nation to its remarkable economic success in the 1960s–80s. But it was no longer suited in the 1990s as the Korean economy became larger and more complex, and as the global competition became keen. Excess government involvement in the economy caused inefficiency, overcapacity and imbalances in many sectors (Sohn *et al.* 1998).

The political sector had its ties with some businesses, intervening in the process of extending loans to huge family-controlled conglomerates or *chaebols* and in deciding major state-funded projects for political kickbacks in return. Accordingly, capital, production and exports were heavily skewed towards *chaebols*, with myriad cross-guarantees on borrowing and limited transparency and accountability. And a 'too big to fail' mentality of *chaebols* resulted in their excessive risk-taking, over-investment and insufficient attention to credit and exchange rate risks. Over-indebtedness, overcapacity and poor earning power among *chaebols* were a natural outcome. By the end of 1997, the top thirty *chaebols* had debt–equity ratios of 519 per cent, a sharp contrast with 154 per cent in the United States and 193 per cent in Japan.[8]

On the other hand, the excessive government control of the banking system made banking institutions rely more on government intervention than on profit-first business. This, in turn, resulted in the misguided advancing of bank loans to nonviable or insolvent borrowers.

Thus, the government's active involvement in the market resulted not only in corruption, but also in moral hazard and inefficiency in the general economic sector, and a weakening of the competitiveness of enterprises and banks. These altogether, of course, left Korea vulnerable to shocks in an increasingly globalizing financial market.

4.4 Unfriendly environment

Korea's fast growth was in part due to the international circumstances, which were favourable to Korea until the late 1980s. First of all, the world's free trade movement under the GATT enabled Korea to effectively pursue an export-oriented growth strategy. Following a number of the multilateral trade talks, the developed countries moved towards the opening of their domestic markets, yet Korea, a less developed country, was allowed to keep its domestic market closed effectively until the end of the 1980s. Second, Korea, which became a part of western capitalism after its independence in 1945, received a considerable amount of explicit and implicit economic assistance from the United States during the cold war era. The United States also provided the largest market for Korea's export.

Since the late 1980s, however, Korean companies have faced intense competition with foreign companies in both domestic and international markets. Competition has mainly come from the rapid opening of Korea's domestic market, the rapid catch-up growth of China and the 'new' newly industrializing economies (NNIEs) of Southeast Asia.

4.4.1 Rapid opening of the domestic market

In 1989, Korea announced that it would no longer restrict trade for the sake of its balance of payments (as covered in the GATT Article XVIIIB) and it would follow Article XI, further increasing its pace of import liberalization. With the conclusion of the Uruguay Round and the embarkation of the World Trade Organization (WTO), Korea faced a more rapid opening of its domestic market. Furthermore, former President Kim Young-Sam who came to power in 1993 proclaimed that Korea would join the OECD during his term of office. OECD access required that Korea open its domestic market even wider and faster. As a result, by 1996, the number of restrictions and the average tariff rates for manufacturing goods were comparable to those of most industrial countries.

Compared to the goods market, the financial market, in the name of financial liberalization, underwent an even faster opening. During the early 1990s, restrictions on the inflow and outflow of mobile capital were nearly removed.[9] However, the liberalization happened with little attention to the new kinds of regulation that would be required and with only a thin base of financial skills. The liberalized financial systems enabled inexperienced private domestic banks and firms to take out large, dollar-denominated loans from foreign lenders.

Thus, the rapid opening and liberalization of the financial market in the early 1990s left the economy exposed and vulnerable to the instabilities of the international financial markets.[10]

4.4.2 'A nut in a nutcracker'

Since the early 1980s, China has strongly pursued a so-called 'reform and open-door policy'. This new policy was very successful, and between 1980 and 1996 China's real GDP grew by more than 10 per cent per annum. The rise of China, however, meant intense new competition for Korean firms. China's manufactured exports grew by more than 20 per cent per annum in the US dollar terms between 1990 and 1996, and Chinese firms competed directly with Korean firms in textiles, apparel and electronics. In addition, the rapid catch-up growth of the NNIEs of Southeast Asia, such as Indonesia, Malaysia, Thailand and the Philippines also led to harsher competition for Korea.

Obviously, this new competition put downward pressure on Korea's international competitiveness and hence its exports. Accordingly, to maintain the wage rates higher than the NNIEs, Korea had to change its industrial structure to become more high-tech-oriented. In fact, following the textbook example of Japan, Korea invested a huge amount of capital into the so-called strategic industries such as electronics, automobiles, biochemicals, etc. As a consequence, however, Korean companies found themselves competing directly against Japanese companies in some important industries.

Thus, Korea faced a very difficult economic predicament. It had to compete against China and other NNIEs on the one hand, and against Japan on the other. That is, Korea was being squeezed both from above and from below. In short, Korea was situated like 'a nut in a nutcracker', as stated first in the Booz Allen Hamilton report (1997) on the Korean economy, which was published just before the financial crisis.

Korea, a nut in a nutcracker, faced even more pressure when in January 1994, China devalued the yuan by 50 per cent, and as the Japanese yen progressively depreciated against the US dollar: from Y/$ 85 in June 1995 to Y/$ 127 in April 1997. Semiconductor prices also collapsed by as much as 80 per cent in 1996. This delivered a severe terms-of-trade shock to Korea, for this industry accounted for 20 per cent of Korea's total exports by value.

4.5 Policy mistakes

Just like a typical stroke, there were signs of the weakening of economic fundamentals and warning symptoms of impending crisis. For instance, export growth relative to import growth, measured in US dollars, began to slow in the mid-1990s. For example, exports in the US dollar terms increased by just 12.8 per cent per annum between 1990 and 1996, while imports increased by 14.1 per cent per annum during the same period (Figure 4.3). Specifically, since 1991 Korea has had continuous deficits in trade with the United States, except for 1993 which had

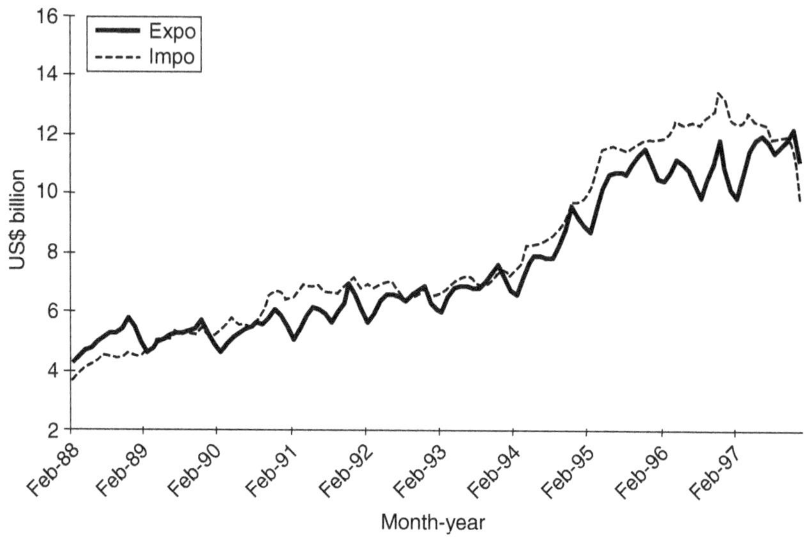

Figure 4.3 Exports and imports (2/88–12/97).

Source: Bank of Korea.

Note
3-month moving average.

US$0.2 billion surplus. This was quite a remarkable sign of the weakening of Korea's competitiveness, because the United States was Korea's largest export market and was the country with which Korea had been enjoying the largest trade surplus.

Accordingly, the current account, which had showed surplus during the period 1986–89, has recorded deficits annually since 1990, except for 1993, which had a minor surplus. Most markedly, the current account deficit widened sharply to US$23 billion in 1996 from US$8.5 billion in 1995. The ratio of the current account deficit to GDP rose to 4.7 per cent in 1996 from 1.7 per cent in 1995. From 1990 to 1996, the cumulative current account deficit amounted to US$48.7 billion, and the current account deficit was financed mainly by the inflow of foreign capital (Figure 4.4). This, in turn, caused a sharp increase in foreign debts. The entire external debts increased from US$29.3 billion in 1989 to US$157.5 billion in 1996. The net external debts increased from US$3.0 billion in 1989 to US$52.9 billion in 1996.

The Korea Stock Price Index (KOSPI), which once reached over 1,100 points in 1994, had dropped to the 600-point level in early 1997 (Figure 4.5). But the Korean government underestimated the early signs and denied the possibility of a financial crisis, repeatedly citing its strong GDP growth rates, high savings rates, budget surplus and moderate inflation rates. Accordingly, even when warnings of the likelihood of a crisis were circulating among foreign investors, it did not react to the signs properly and decisively to prevent the actual crisis.

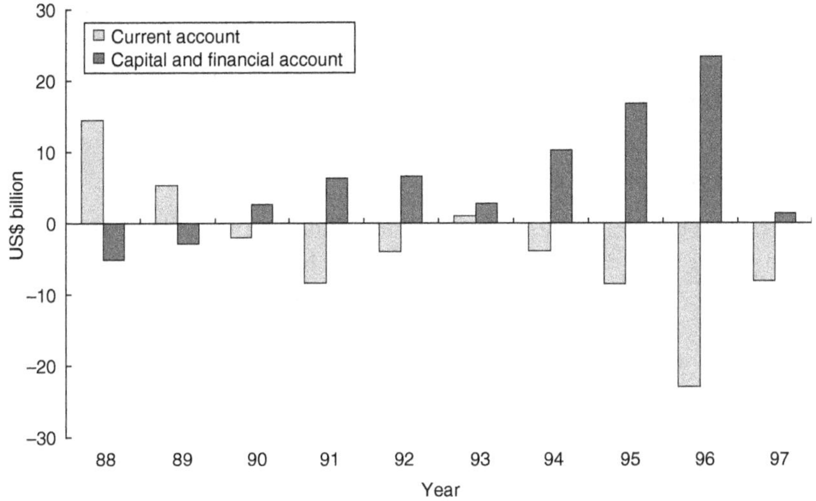

Figure 4.4 Current account and capital account (1988–97).

Source: Bank of Korea.

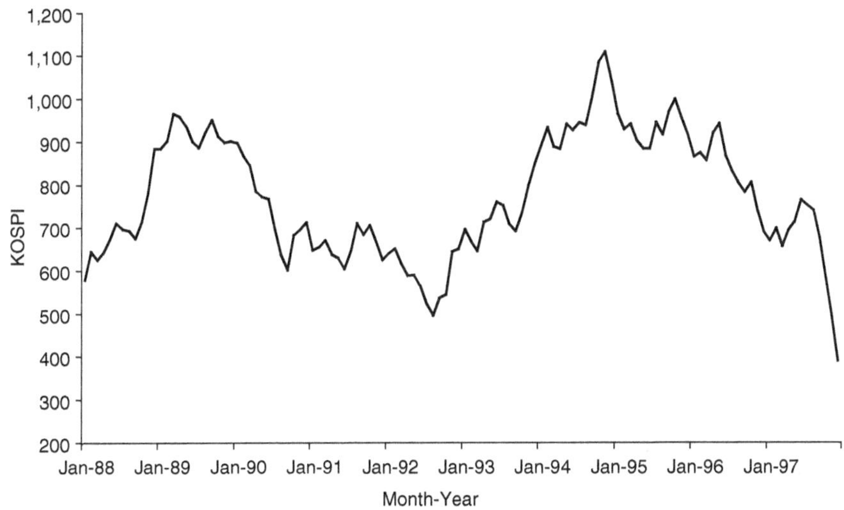

Figure 4.5 Korea stock price index (KOSPI, 1/88–12/97); 1980 = 100.

Source: Bank of Korea.

Among the policy mistakes made by the Korean government before the crisis, three major ones are discussed here. The prime mistake was in its exchange rate policy. Inappropriate financial market supervision also turned out to be a serious mistake. The Korean government also failed to take appropriate action in response to the repeated defaults of *chaebols* and the speculative attacks in early 1997.

4.5.1 Strong won policy

As explained before, since the late 1980s the international competitiveness of Korean industry has continued to falter as the economic fundamentals and international circumstances have deteriorated. Then the Korean won should have depreciated; otherwise the current account deficits would have followed.

However, the Korean government adopted a strong won policy. The strong won policy was maintained with the so-called market average foreign exchange rate system, which was adopted in 1990. The exchange rate was allowed to move within the daily fluctuation band, which was kept narrow[11] (Figure 4.6). Radelet and Sachs (1998) estimate that the Korea won appreciated in real terms about 12 per cent between 1990 and 1997.[12]

Why did the Korean government insist on a strong won policy? First, to achieve the target of one-digit inflation rate per annum, the Korean government insisted on the nominal exchange rate stability. That is, inflation control was the overriding priority of macroeconomic policy and the exchange rate was an 'anchor' for inflation control.[13] Second, the Korean government maintained the position that a strong won would push Korean firms to strive to increase their productivity and hence

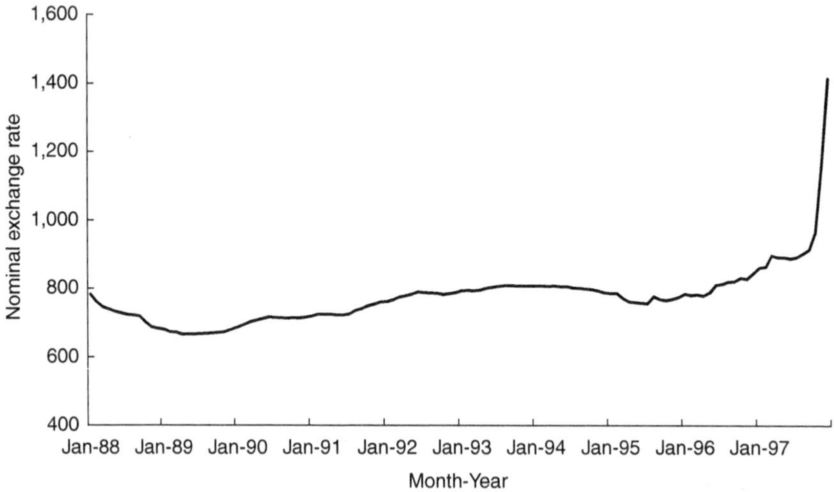

Figure 4.6 Nominal exchange rate (W/US$, 1/88–12/97); 1980 = 100.

Source: Bank of Korea.

international competitiveness. Third, the government wanted to keep the exchange rate stable in order to help domestic corporations and financial institutions by lowering the domestic currency costs of servicing foreign debts denominated in the US dollars. Fourth, a political consideration also made the exchange rate policy less flexible. The then Kim Young-Sam government strongly wished to realize US$10,000 income per capita. Once the per capita income reached US$10,000 in 1995, the government did not want it to slide with the depreciation of the domestic currency.

4.5.2 Inappropriate supervision of financial sector

As noted earlier, during the early 1990s, the financial market underwent a very rapid liberalization and deregulation. This allowed domestic financial institutions to have easy access to foreign capital to finance domestic investment. The problem was that financial liberalization was done without adequate process and provision of the safety net.

First, financial liberalization was carried out mostly on short-term rather than long-term capital inflows. For instance, the net foreign portfolio investment, which was merely US$0.1 billion in 1990, increased drastically to US$3.1 billion in 1991, US$5.8 billion in 1992 and US$10.0 billion in 1993. This upward trend continued until 1996. However, the net direct investment continuously revealed negative values, indicating that the foreigners' direct investment in Korea was smaller than Korea's direct investment overseas (Figure 4.7).

Second, appropriate supervision and prudential regulation did not accompany financial liberalization. Especially, the secondary financial institutions such as merchant banks, which increased sharply from six in 1993 to thirty by 1996, were

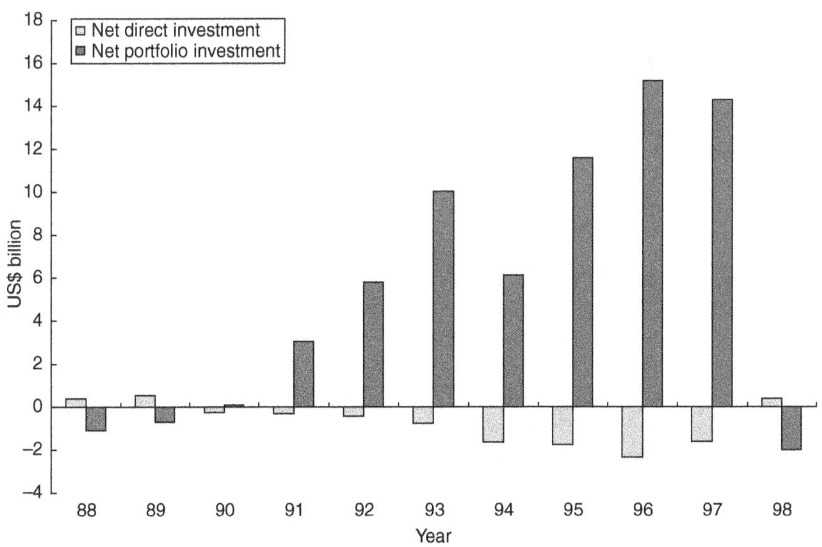

Figure 4.7 Net direct investment and net portfolio investment (1988–98).

not under appropriate supervision. With the belief that the government would not allow financial institutions to fail, Korean banks borrowed unhedged short-run foreign capital at lower rates, denominated in the US dollar, and made long-term loans at higher rates, with the expectation that they could continually renew short-term borrowing. This led to a serious mismatch in maturities between borrowing and lending. Short-term loans accounted for 63 per cent of the total debts on the eve of the financial crisis. With this fragile structure of foreign debt, Korea became very vulnerable to the instabilities of the international financial markets.

4.5.3 Naive policy response to the early warning signs

A series of policy mistakes were also made in response to the early symptoms or warning signs of the impending crisis, which started to appear early in 1997. First, the Korean government did not properly and swiftly cope with the corporate insolvencies, which had a devastating impact on Korea's financial system. The government repeatedly declared that troubled firms would be dealt with on the basis of the market mechanism. However, amid the critical situation in the first half of 1997, the government aggravated the financial turmoil by taking measures counter to market principles such as the Bankruptcy Prevention Accord and state subsidies for the hopelessly ailing *chaebols*. Especially, the Korean government's decision to convert Kia Motors, the insolvent eighth largest *chaebol*, into a public enterprise heightened the confusion and distrust among the foreign investors.

The second mistake made by the government was with the exchange rate policy. With the Thai currency collapse in July 1997, contagion spread to Indonesia, Malaysia, and even to Singapore and Hong Kong. When speculative attacks on the Korean won began in October and accelerated in November, the Korean government maintained a narrow daily fluctuation band and tried to defend the Korean won inexplicably, wasting valuable foreign exchange reserves. As a consequence, Korea's available foreign exchange reserves fell far below the outstanding short-term foreign debts. In fact, the daily band of exchange rate fluctuations was widened from ±2.25 to ±10 per cent on October 16. But the trading band was still narrow so that the Korean won fell to its daily limit against the US dollar as soon as the market opened, and foreign exchange trading had to be suspended. In retrospect, if the band had been widened earlier and the exchange rate had been allowed to float freely, the Korean won would have depreciated gradually and this would have helped limit the extent of the crisis.

Third, the Korean government waited until the country's usable foreign currency reserves plummeted to US$7.3 billion, and the country was on the verge of a debt moratorium, before turning to the IMF on 21 November. As Korean banks faced difficulties in rolling over their short-term foreign liabilities, the Bank of Korea shifted foreign exchange reserves to the banks' offshore branches and announced a guarantee of foreign borrowing by Korean banks. However, this action merely helped many foreign creditors to escape from Korea, and Korea soon found itself on the brink of national insolvency as the country's usable reserves became almost depleted.

Thus, once the financial crisis began to spread from Thailand, the Korean government made a number of mistakes, and these mistakes accelerated the capital withdrawals and caused a serious crisis of its own. Why then did the Korean government, which was once considered shrewd and efficient, make such policy mistakes? Primarily, the then Korean government was in total disarray in its decision-making during the 'lame duck' period of Kim Young-Sam's presidency. Next, the presidential election was scheduled to take place in December 1997.

4.6 Exogenous shocks: the trigger

Normally, a stroke finally occurs when there is a trigger. A great deal of stress or sudden cold weather to which the patient is exposed could be a trigger. The Korean financial crisis also erupted eventually with the exogenous shocks, which acted as a trigger. There were two different shocks in early 1997: one came as a stress from inside, and the other came as cold weather from outside. That is, the drastic increase in corporate insolvencies acted as a stress on the Korean economy and the financial crises of Southeast Asian countries acted as sudden cold weather to which the Korean economy was exposed.

As briefly noted earlier, along with business cycle of downturn, a series of large corporate bankruptcies began with Hanbo Steel, the fourteenth largest *chaebol* in Korea, in January 1997. In fact, before Korea turned to the IMF for assistance in November, seven out of the top thirty *chaebols* including Kia Motors, the eighth largest, faced insolvencies. This resulted in a surge in non-performing loans of commercial banks. At the end of September 1997, non-performing loans of all financial institutions recorded W32 trillion (7 per cent of GDP), about double their level at the end of 1996.[14]

On the other hand, the financial crisis in Southeast Asia acted in two ways as another trigger of the Korean crisis. First, a drastic devaluation of the currencies of the crisis countries impeded Korea's already shredded international competitiveness, and this acted as a great downward pressure on the Korean currency. Second, trouble in Southeast Asia acted as a wake-up call for foreign investors to reevaluate the risk of Korea, and to find out that Korea was already experiencing difficulties in the financial market with the surge in non-performing loans. When the Hang Seng Index of the Hong Kong stock market recorded a big downturn on 23 October 1997, the foreign investors suddenly started together in a panic to withdraw their investment and to cut back their short-term loans to Korea. The won depreciated by about 20 per cent against the US dollar through November 30 and the stock market index fell by about 30 per cent to a ten-year low. Usable foreign currency reserves declined sharply as the Bank of Korea financed the repayment of the short-term debt of Korean commercial banks' offshore branches.

Finally, Korea turned to the IMF on 21 November 1997, as the rollover ratio of short-term external borrowings by domestic financial institutions kept decreasing and the country's usable foreign currency reserves plummeted to US$7.3 billion, down sharply from US$22.3 billion only a month ago.

Thus like a human stroke, the Korean crisis was triggered by the two different shocks: a surge in large corporate bankruptcies inside Korea and the Southeast Asian crisis outside Korea. It should be noted here that the self-reinforcing herding of capital outflows was not a 'cause', but a 'symptom' of the financial crisis, erupting as a combination of the fundamental weaknesses, the unfriendly international surroundings, the policy mistakes and the exogenous shocks.

4.7 Concluding remarks

Drawing the analogy between the economy's financial system and the human circulatory system, this chapter introduced a 'stroke' hypothesis of Korea's financial crisis. With the 'stroke' hypothesis, we were able to synthesize most of the appealing explanations and theories of the financial crisis and show how the numerous factors had been systematically intertwined in causing the financial crisis.

Even though, it appears to have erupted all of a sudden when the panicked foreign investors turned their backs on Korea, it actually erupted after several early symptoms. Each of the four factors (fundamental weaknesses, policy mistakes, unfriendly international circumstances and exogenous shocks) played a significant role and intertwined with each other systematically, resulting in the financial crisis.

To conclude the chapter, we briefly discuss three areas to which the stroke hypothesis can be applied. First of all, the stroke analogy of financial crisis suggests what needs to be done as counter-policy measures after the crisis. That is, an early and appropriate treatment is imperative to help prevent having another stroke and resulting in serious complications, and in the medium and long term, treatment for the fundamental causes of strokes such as high blood pressure and diabetes should follow. Similarly, the first and most immediate way to treat the financial crisis should be to (1) break the self-reinforcing capital outflows and to stabilize the domestic currency (i.e. minimize the likelihood of recurrence) and (2) prevent a collapse in the real sector (i.e. prevent complications). In the medium and long term, structural reforms are needed to address the root causes of the crisis.[15]

Second, the 'stroke' hypothesis could be applied to the financial crises of other countries like Thailand, Indonesia, Brazil, etc. As in the case of Korea, this will allow us to analyse its causes and consequences more systematically and comprehensively. Nonetheless, unlike other approaches such as moral hazard or self-fulfilling models, the stroke framework can allow for significant country differences and explain unique features of each country.

Finally, it may be possible to use the stroke framework in devising an early warning system for the financial crises. Credit rating agencies such as Standard & Poor's, Moody's Investors Service and Fitch IBCA seem to have devices for calculating the creditworthiness of different countries. As proven by the case of the Asian crisis, however, these rating agencies were not able to forecast the financial crisis beforehand. Instead, they have been criticized for aggravating the crisis by, at a later stage, downgrading the ratings of the crisis countries. In academia, there have been few attempts to devise an early warning system. If we use the stroke framework, we could systematically and comprehensively identify the factors of four different causes of the financial crisis, and the long-run and immediate warning signs of the financial crisis. In addition, by marking risk indexes of the responsible factors and warning signs, and summing them up, we could measure each country's likelihood of having a financial crisis.

Notes

1 This work was supported by 2001 Research Grant of Kangwon Naitonal University.

2 For instance, the Korean parliamentary hearing in early 1999 on the causes of the financial crisis was mainly focused on the policy mistakes made by the then president and the government officials. Some advocates of the Asian values claim that the Asian financial crisis was the result of hegemonic conflict between the East and the West.

3 The following discussion on strokes is based on a booklet titled *Preventing Stroke: A Consumer's Reference Guide*, published by National Health and Medical Research Council, Australia, in 1997. Consultations with medical doctors were also carried out. Readers, who are more serious about strokes, are referred to Barnett, Henry, J.P. Mohr, Bennett Stein and Frank Yatsu (eds), *Stroke: Pathophysiology, Diagnosis, and Management*, 2nd edition, Churchill Livingstone, 1992.

4 Up until 1996, Korea enjoyed over 8 per cent annual growth rate of its real GDP for over thirty years. Accordingly, its GDP soared from US$2.1 billion in 1961 to US$484.4 billion in 1996, while its per capita GNP rose from US$82 to US$10,543 over the same period.

5 For more detailed explanation about the sources of Korea's rapid growth, readers are referred to Kim and Hong (1997), and Harvie and Lee (2002).

6 For more discussion, see Kim and Lee (1997), and Harvie and Lee (2002).

7 Korea's gross domestic savings amounted to 36 per cent of GDP in 1995. In contrast, the US gross domestic savings amounted to 15 per cent in the same year.

8 For more discussion on *chaebol*, see Yoo (1995), and Lee and Lee (1996).

9 Park (1996) and Wang (2001) evaluate this liberalization procedure.

10 There have been many authors who point out that financial liberalization is the best predictor of currency crises. Wyplosz (1998), and Radelet and Sachs (1998) noted that Korea became vulnerable to external financial shocks in part because it attempted to reform its financial markets in a market-oriented manner. China and Vietnam were shielded from the crisis because ironically they had not undertaken significant financial sector reforms and accordingly they had much less short-term capital inflow than Korea.

11 Even though the daily fluctuation band had been widened gradually with the progress of financial liberalization, it remained at only ±2.25 per cent just before the crisis.

12 In fact, there have been some arguments that the Korean won was not overvalued before the crisis. For instance, Corsetti *et al.* (1998), and Chinn (1998) among others claim that in Korea, the real exchange rate was roughly in equilibrium on the eve of the crisis. This may reflect the problems with regard to the methods in calculating the real exchange rate. Nonetheless, the fact that until 1997 Korea experienced the consecutive current account deficits and after the onset of the crisis the Korean won depreciated by a large amount, seems to prove that the Korean currency was obviously overvalued.

13 In fact, the nominal W/US$ exchange rate seems to have affected the price level considerably in Korea. Lee and Cheong (1997), for example, show that the exchange rate has been a good predictor of the future movements in prices.

14 At the end of September 1997, non-performing loans of commercial banks stood at W21.9 trillion, which was 6.4 per cent of total credit and was double the W12.2 trillion at the end of 1996. At the same time, merchant banks recorded non-performing loans of W3.9 trillion at the end of October 1997, nearly three times the W1.3 trillion at the end of 1996.

15 In line with the stroke hypothesis, Lee (2001) evaluates the IMF's structural reform programme, which has come under heavy criticism for its macroeconomic stabilization measures of tight monetary policy and fiscal policy, and more fundamental measures of structural reform.

Bibliography

Bank of Korea, Data Base. Available Online, http://www.bok.or.kr/kb/princp-e.

Barnett, Henry, Mohr, J.P., Stein, Bennett and Yatsu, Frank (1992) *Stroke: Pathophysiology, Diagnosis, and Management*, 2nd edn, Churchill Livingstone.

Booz Allen Hamilton (1997) *Revitalizing the Korean Economy Towards the 21st Century*, Seoul: Mael Economic Newspaper Co.

Chinn, Menzie D. (1998) 'Before the fall: were East Asian currencies overvalued?', National Bureau of Economic Research Working Paper No. 6491.

Corsetti, Giancarlo, Pesenti, Paolo and Roubini, Nouriel (1998) 'What caused the Asian currency and financial crisis?' mimeo. Available Online, http://www.stern.nyu.edu/globalmacro.

Fitch ICBA (1999) *Rating Report: Republic of Korea.*

Harvie, Charles and Hyun-Hoon Lee (2002) *The Korean Economic Miracle – Fading or Reviving?*, London: Palgrave.

Kim, Kwang-Suk and Hong, Sung-Duk (1997) *Accounting for Rapid Economic Growth in Korea, 1963–95*, Seoul: Korea Development Institute.

Kim Sookon and Lee, Ju-Ho (1997) 'Industrial relations and human resource development', in Cha, Kim and Perkins (eds), *The Korean Economy 1945–95*, Seoul: Korea Development Institute.

Krugman, Paul (1998) 'What happened to Asia?' mimeo, January 1998. Available Online, http://web.mit.edu/krugman/www/disinter.html.

Lee, Hyun-Hoon (2001) 'The IMF rescue program in Korea: what went wrong?', *Journal of the Korean Economy*, 2(1): 69–86.

—— and Cheong, Yongkyun (1997) 'Real output and inflation in a small open economy: the case of Korea', in D. Kantarelis (ed.), *Business & Economics for the 21st Century*, MA: Business & Economics Society International, vol. I, pp. 273–283.

Lee, Kyu-Uck and Lee, Jae-Hyung (1996) 'Business groups (chaebols) in Korea: characteristics and government policy', Occasional paper No. 23, Seoul: Korea Institute for Industrial Economics and Trade.

National Health and Medical Research Council (1997) *Preventing Stroke: A Consumer's Reference Guide*, Australia.

Park, Won-Am (1996) 'Financial liberalization: the Korean experience', in Takatoshi Ito and Anne O. Krueger (eds), *Financial Deregulation and Integration in East Asia*, Chicago: University of Chicago Press.

Radelet, Steven and Sachs, Jeffrey (1998) 'The East Asian financial crisis: diagnosis, remedies, prospects', *Brookings Papers in Economic Activity*, 1.

Sohn, Chan-Hyun, Yang, Junsok and Yim, Hyo-Sung (1998) 'Korea's trade and industrial policies: 1948–98, why the era of active policy is over', KIEP Working Paper No. 9805, Seoul: Korea Institute for International Economic Policy.

Wang, Yoonjong (2001) 'Does the sequencing really matter? The Korean experience in the capital market liberalization', *Journal of the Korean Economy*, 2(1): 35–67.

Wyplosz, Charles (1998) 'Globalized financial markets and financial crises', the Conference on 'Coping with financial crises in developing and transition countries: regulatory and supervisory challenges in a new era of global financial finance' organized by the Forum on Debt and Development, Amsterdam, March 1998.

Yoo, Seong Min (1995) 'Chaebol in Korea: misconceptions, realities, and policies', KDI Working Paper No. 9507, Seoul: Korea Development Institution.

5 The restructuring of the Korean economy since 1986 and the onset of the financial crisis

The industrial/financial nexus

John McKay

5.1 Introduction

The brutal impacts of the financial crises in Asia in 1997/98 have called into question what had earlier been regarded as an infallible engine of growth, the Asian Development Model. Many of the features which earlier had drawn widespread approval – close cooperation between governments and the private sector, monitoring of investment flows to encourage chosen growth industries, the linking of economic and social plan targets, and even the preference for broader social stability over concern for individual human rights – are now interpreted as major sources of weakness and contributors to the crisis. The triumphalism of some of the more fundamentalist disciples of the free market was to be expected, but what has been more surprising perhaps is the rapid loss of confidence in Asia itself after so many years of unprecedented growth. It seems hardly credible that those Asian strengths that were analysed at such length in all those books on the 'miracle' could have been transformed so quickly into such fatal weaknesses. Hence, there is a need for careful analysis of the causes of the crisis as well as critical evaluation of the new directions being proposed, otherwise there is a real danger of throwing out the baby with the bath water.

In this chapter, I want to take a broad view of the crisis in Korea and its consequences, and present a more comprehensive evaluation of the various reform measures that have been implemented or are being proposed. While the timing and severity of the crisis confounded many critics, for more than ten years questions had been raised about the need for restructuring in a number of Asian economies, including Korea (see, e.g. Garnaut *et al.* 1995, McKay and Missen 1995). These problems are related to: economic structures, the organization of production, the effectiveness of the financial system and its relationship with the organization of production, the development and access to new technology, and a range of labour issues. None was simply a question of economic efficiency, but reflected complex interactions between economic, political, and social factors, and in many cases involved consideration of regional and global forces of various kinds.

In particular, the focus here will be on three key questions. First, while the developmentalist state had been very effective in generating unprecedented growth rates in Korea, it was clear after the mid-1980s that the system could not continue in its old form. To what extent can the onset of the crisis in Korea be traced to the management (or lack of it) of the processes of restructuring that were clearly needed after 1986? Second, if some variant of the original Asian model seems to be the most effective way of generating growth in the early stages of development, what can other nations learn from the recent experience of Korea? Can such a process be managed effectively, or are the risks of longer term instability and crisis too great? Third, how can Korea be brought back on track? I tie these complex questions together within a theoretical framework drawing its inspiration from the concepts of *regime dynamics* and *regime shift*.

5.2 Regime dynamics and regime shift

Interest in the concept of regimes has been stimulated by the simple question of why individual economies continue to differ from one another, and why these differences persist rather than converging on international 'best practice'. Certainly national systems undergo change, even fundamental transformation, but this also raises some questions about the mechanisms of such change and about the relative strengths of local and international factors. Cheng (1990, 1993) has argued that *regime dynamics*, which are the basis of differing national systems, may be thought of as the relational manoeuvres of leading businesses and government that take place in changing political and economic contexts and which are designed to increase political legitimacy and to consolidate political power. Social pressures for restructuring accompany growth, exacerbated by changes in the global economy. Capital and the state adjust their authority patterns and legitimation strategies to these changing environments, but within previously established social contexts. Pempel (1998) argues that a regime is composed of three key elements: socio-economic alliances, political-economic institutions, and a public policy profile. These components are overlapping, and reinforce each other, and each is essential to the stability of the total system. In some situations the elements may be unstable, coalitions may come and go, and new institutions may disappear quickly. But within the post-war industrialized democracies, stability has been the general rule.

Within the industrial sphere, Soskice (1999) has explored the ways in which production systems in different countries have diverged in the 1980s and 1990s, in spite of the multiple influences of globalization. He suggests that there are two major variants of modern industrial economies. The *liberal market economies* operate on short-term time horizons, allow high risk taking, have deregulated labour markets, and strong competition requirements. By contrast, the *business co-ordinated market economies* have financial systems allowing the long-term financing of companies, co-operative industrial relations systems, a strong emphasis on vocational training, and encourage co-operation on technology and standards. This second category includes Germany and Sweden, but he argues that Japan and Korea make up a distinct subgroup of *group co-ordinated economies*. In the case of Korea, the *chaebols* are the key co-ordinating component (Soskice 1999: 106).

These national systems have all evolved, often over long periods, to meet the needs of the local conditions and the heritage of unique institutional configurations.

Boyer and Hollingsworth (1997) emphasize that there is no single optimum institutional configuration for the modern economy, rather a very large array of possible arrangements. The best choice depends upon the external environment and the precise nature of the societal problems that need to be solved. They argue that not even the market should be regarded as the ideal and universal institutional arrangement for co-ordinating economic activity, and numerous problems can arise if efforts are made to organize the world exclusively in terms of markets. All institutional arrangements have their own strengths and weaknesses, and the best choice at any time will depend on the precise context. Hence no new institution can simply be borrowed and implemented in any given social setting. It is not just the nature of the individual institutions that varies between nations, it is the unique configuration of these components in the entire economic system that is important (Gao 2001: 18).

Perhaps the most difficult task in this kind of analysis is to understand how and why regimes change. Pempel (1998) argues that any regime is faced with a variety of pressures for change, but not all changes will destabilize a regime: some will merely cause minor readjustments. He recognizes three levels of disturbance in any system. First order changes are confined to just one of the components of the regime. Adjustments are made, but the essential nature of the regime is unchanged. Second order changes involve shifts in two of the three domains. These pressures are more severe, but again do not bring about a fundamental transformation. It is only the third order changes, involving all three dimensions – institutions, coalitions, and public policies – that bring about a true *regime shift*. Gao (2001) suggests that such a shift may take some time, as the forces for change gather strength and the fundamental contradictions in the existing regime are revealed, and as a new regime emerges, made up of some new elements and some remaining fragments from the old system, but combined in a unique new configuration.

Several authors have highlighted two key dilemmas that must be faced in the development of appropriate institutional structures. The first is the trade-off that seems to be inevitable between co-ordination and control of the entire economy and the monitoring and control of individual companies. Historical evidence suggests that no nation has ever been able to perform both functions effectively at the same time, and has been forced to concentrate on one or the other. Gao (2001) has suggested that Japan has preferred strong co-ordination, resulting in weak control and monitoring mechanisms, and I will argue that the same has been true of Korea. The second dilemma is the choice between the competing demands for economic and social stability and the need to upgrade the economic structure. Japan has opted for stability, but at the cost of an economic system that has become increasingly uncompetitive.

I also want to take a methodological point from this emerging body of literature. Gao has adopted an interesting method of 'reverse thinking'. Rather than simply looking at how the Japanese model became obsolete, Gao analyses the key institutions that sustained the economy during the critical bubble period of the 1980s, and asks whether these structures were also present during the earlier period of high growth. If they did exist, why did they not cause similar serious problems earlier?

The broad concepts of regime dynamics and regime shift also include the more familiar phenomenon of industrial restructuring. In a series of earlier papers with a number of other colleagues, I have argued that restructuring is more than just structural change or technical innovation inserted within the existing relationships of the economy. Rather, restructuring is a deliberate process of re-making of such relationships with respect to an idealized future (Clark *et al.* 1991, 1992, Webber *et al.* 1991). Particularly important here is the realization that restructuring is a highly contested and difficult process, and successful strategies for change may involve considerable amounts of persuasion, exhortation, idealization or even coercion.

5.3 Korea's growth and development regime, 1961–86

The nature of the political and economic system that produced in Korea one of the most dramatic industrial transformations ever achieved has received an enormous amount of attention. Some of these analyses have been economic, others cultural, or political. Some commentators have highlighted local, internal factors, while others have stressed the nature of the particular economic or strategic environments of the period. It is not my intention here to present an extended review of all this literature. Rather, I want to interrogate this large body of earlier work to identify the essential characteristics of this remarkable successful regime.

Cumings (1987) has noted the similarities in the basic structures of Japan, Taiwan, and Korea. All three of them during their initial growth phases were characterized by: relative state autonomy, central co-ordination, bureaucratic short- and long-range planning, high flexibility in moving in and out of industrial sectors, private concentration in big conglomerates, exclusion of labour, exploitation of women, low expenditure on social welfare, and militarization and authoritarian repression. Similar themes have been taken up by Amsden (1989), who has emphasized the role of three key facets of growth: the government as entrepreneur, government economic policies, and the generation of high levels of productivity. In particular, she has praised the government's willingness to rise above the short-term market signals and deliberately get the prices 'wrong'. Woo (1991) has also taken up the dynamics of 'the big push', highlighting the centrality of the links between the state, the *chaebol*, and the financial system. More recently, Kong (2000) has characterized this period as one dominated by the developmentalist alliance of state and *chaebol*, a pervasive objective of economic nationalism and an authoritarian system that excluded labour but achieved a remarkable transformation of living standards.

In my analysis I want to pay particular attention to these generally agreed regime features, but also following the methodological lead of Gao (2001) ask whether the factors identified later as causing problems leading to the financial crisis of 1997 were problematic in this earlier era. I also want to introduce some key features of the industrial production system that appear to have been neglected by other writers. In particular, I want to concentrate on three key questions about the regime and its effectiveness: first, how did the various elements of the regime fit together to produce a unique and coherent whole? Second, in what ways was the regime particularly successful in supporting the dominant development goals of the Korean state at that time? Third, how was this unique regime structure translated into an equally distinctive production system, supported by a set of particular financial institutions?

5.3.1 The coherence of the Korean developmentalist regime

The regime that was progressively implemented in the 1960s was a unique and highly successful developmentalist system, very clear in its goals and remarkably single-minded in their pursuit. In the literature on the Korean 'miracle', great emphasis has been given to certain elements of the Korean system, in particular the role of the government and the *chaebol*. However there have been strong differences of opinion on just how effective this intervention was in creating development beyond what would have occurred through simple market-led processes. Until recently we lacked any detailed evidence on just what the government of Park Chung Hee was aiming to achieve in its approach, and how it thought about and planned its interventions. However, a pioneering study by Kim Hyung-A (1996), who has analysed detailed records from this era, and in particular has gained access to some of the key officials then at the core of the programme and its implementation has provided the answers. Her results make it clear just how detailed the planning was, particularly in the phase of heavy and chemical industrialization after 1972. This was not just a plan for the economy, but involved all parts of the society, and also included in its scope foreign and defence policy. The vision was to create a prosperous, strong, and self-reliant nation, free from outside interference, especially from the United States, and able to defend itself effectively against any threat from North Korea. The creation of new industries was the immediate aim, but in order to achieve the planned targets it was essential to transform the nation through broad economic reconstruction, development of skilled manpower, national land development, and the creation of a strong national defence. The planning approach used was very precise, even scientific. O Wonch'ol, the key official in charge of the programme, argued that his aim was to leave as little as possible to chance, using an engineering approach that left no room for either politics or emotion. He also suggested that an authoritarian approach to government was essential, at least in the short term, to give the technocrats a free hand to implement agreed plans. Thus, to O Wonch'ol the repressive *Yusin* constitution was an integral and necessary part of the drive to industrialization.

Space does not allow any more detailed discussion of this fascinating story, but the basic point I am trying to highlight, one which is entirely consistent with regime theory, is that there was a strong and essential coherence in the Korean system from 1961 into the 1980s, and especially after 1972. The government was quite clear how all the pieces fitted together to create a working whole, and this included areas well beyond the reach of many concepts of economic planning.

5.3.2 Implications for the production system

Given the comprehensive and unique nature of this development regime, it is hardly surprising that the production system that emerged should have some very distinctive features. An obvious feature, and one that has been much discussed in relation to the financial crisis, is the extreme dominance of the *chaebol*, the large, diversified, predominantly family-owned conglomerates. The rates of growth for these conglomerates were truly remarkable, especially in the era of heavy and chemical industrialization. During these decades of economic expansion, the role of the small and medium enterprises (SMEs) was markedly peripheral to that of the *chaebol* (McKay and Missen 1995).

All of these features are in sharp contrast to the structures found in Taiwanese industry. The predominant actors here have been the SMEs, which have become the country's exporters of a large range of industrial products. The rise of the SME as a competitive and flexible exporter depended on three processes: small firm sensitivity to and early entry into niche markets before retreating or diversifying investment into other industries, what has been called 'guerrilla capitalism' or 'industrial nomadism'; a labour force involving complex subcontracting relations amongst small firms, in which flexibility compensated for small scale; and labour-intensive products and technological upgrading (rather than the 'technological leaping' that characterized Korea) that were within the scope of the small firm.

The consolidation of the Korean production system produced in turn a number of more detailed characteristics in the economy, some of which were related to the nature of the *chaebol* themselves, while others were the result of the extensive power over the entire system exerted by the conglomerates. Many of these features have also been indicted by some researchers as contributing to the crisis of 1997. A number of writers (e.g. Kim 1997, Kong 2000) have noted that the *chaebol* were generally highly diversified, much more so than Western companies. Intense competition between the industrial groups meant that each tried to do everything, and was not willing to concentrate on a small number of truly excellent lines. There was a strong emphasis on gaining the benefits of economies of scale through concentration on large-scale production, but this benefit was generally lost through the insistence of the *chaebol* in getting into each new attractive market, resulting in serious overcrowding in key areas. Individual subsidiaries of the conglomerates were sometimes small and technologically backward, and there was frequent cross-subsidization between subsidiaries. If one company was ailing, it was usually taken over by a healthy one within the same group, effectively weakening the entire structure. Virtually all of the *chaebol* had rather fragile financial positions and high levels of debt, partly reflecting the desire of the family to keep control of the group. A strong sense of economic nationalism tended to keep out foreign capital, especially foreign direct investment. There was, however, a heavy dependence on borrowed technology. This facilitated rapid expansion into new areas, and allowed risk to be spread, but resulted in a continued and chronic dependence on Japanese machinery and parts. As the conglomerates grew, there was a widely held belief that the government could not afford to let any fail, given the massive size of potential financial and employment effects. But it was the creation of a uniquely structured financial system, and in particular that part of the financial sector designed to support the production goals of the economy, that needs to be given special attention in terms of future effects and vulnerabilities.

During the 1970s in particular, Korea embarked on a massive and ambitious programme of investment. In part this was financed through the mobilization of local savings. When corporate and government savings are added, total domestic savings rose from 10 per cent in the 1960s to 21 per cent in the 1970s, and a massive peak of 38 per cent in the 1980s (Kim and Leipziger 1997). These local resources were extremely important, generally accounting for the bulk of investment. But this still left a significant gap, which had to be filled through foreign borrowings (Woo 1991). Korea entered the international loan market in a significant way around 1973 and by 1984 owed $43.4 billion on the private money market. The vast majority of this private funding went into new industrial development. Woo (1991: 153–4) has estimated that by 1981, the manufacturing sector absorbed some 60.3 per cent of all private loans, and if one adds in spending on infrastructure to support these new industries, the figure rises to 97.8 per cent. By 1981, total funding through special programmes, the so-called 'policy loans' accounted for 45.7 per cent of all domestic loans. These loans were especially attractive because of their extremely low rates of interest. In 1974, for example, export loans were charged at 9 per cent, compared with the curb loan rate of 40.6 per cent and an inflation rate of 29.5 per cent. The vast majority of these special loans were directed to new export industries, especially those in heavy industry, and all of these industries were dominated by the *chaebol.*

There were several important implications of these clear policy directions. For the conglomerates themselves there was the opportunity for spectacular rates of growth, and for diversification into a range of new industries. However, this expansion of the big business groups was achieved at the cost of extraordinarily high levels of corporate indebtedness, something that was to remain to haunt the Korean economy leading to the 1997 crisis. By the mid-1980s, the top fifty *chaebol* had average debt/equity ratios of more than 500 per cent. The implications for the rest of the economy were also profound. The expansion of large-scale industries generating significant economies of scale was generally predicated on the building of Japanese-style production chains of subcontractors supplying component parts. However, the SMEs expected to fulfil this role were seriously starved of capital, had poor access to new technologies, and were generally not able to attract a well-trained labour force (McKay and Missen 1995).

5.3.3 The development regime in its societal context

How then did this development regime intersect with the wider society that was emerging during this period of very rapid growth? How did the single-minded pursuit of growth sit with the broader aspirations – social and political, as well as economic – of the Korean people? To what extent did the problems that were to become an issue at the time of the 1997 crisis cause any discomfort at this stage?

To some extent, the government itself anticipated some of the problems inherent in the development regime, notably the problem of excessive power wielded by the *chaebol*, and tried to develop some safeguards. In particular, the government attempted to make sure that in return for all of their favourable treatment the conglomerates lived up to their primary task of creative, effective, and viable new export industries (Amsden 1989, Woo 1991). Poor performers were penalized, and only good ones were rewarded.

One defining component of the development regime was that government–business relations were so close that in some ways it was impossible to define clear boundaries between the two entities. The government saw the *chaebol* as essential to its purpose, and subsumed them as part of the state's purpose. This process included the absorption of the risks involved in assigning too much power to the conglomerates, and accepting the distortions created by excessive debt levels inherent in the financial system used to promote industrialization. The regime clearly had its problems, and could not hope to survive into the longer term. It was undemocratic and statist, but as a means of generating a decisive push towards industrial development it was clearly very successful.

5.4 Reforming the developmental regime 1986–97

The developmental regime was faced with a whole series of pressures for change as the country entered the 1980s. Indeed, some commentators have argued that the regime in its purest form did not really survive beyond the end of Park Chung Hee's rule in 1979. Kong (2000), for example, has argued that even before Park's death, neo-classically trained economists were gaining more influence within policy-making circles. These tendencies were intensified by the impact of the 1979–80 economic crisis, itself seen by many as being exacerbated by the distortions flowing from the drive to heavy industry, and resulted in many calls by local commentators and a range of international institutions for less interventionist approaches (Corbo and Suh 1992). The banks were privatized in 1981–82, and interest rate reform was implemented to reduce the level of selectivity between different types of borrowers (Kong 2000). More generally, there were moves to allow business greater choice in its sources of loans: the old reliance on banks was gradually replaced with opportunities for raising funds through equity and corporate bond issues. But, in other ways the system remained substantially unchanged, and throughout the 1980s the government retained very tight controls over the financial system. It was not until later in the decade, especially in the period after 1986 that much more significant pressures for reform began to emerge.

5.4.1 Pressures for restructuring after 1986

Strong pressures for change within both the political and economic systems were manifest around 1986, and were essentially the direct result of the successes of the earlier years. In the economic sphere, rapid growth rates and significant trade surpluses produced upward pressures on the Korean currency. The Won appreciated significantly, rising 16 per cent against the US$ in 1988 alone, with serious implications for the competitiveness of Korean exports. During this period labour unrest also increased as workers demanded a bigger share of the nation's success. Labour shortages appeared in many sectors and for the first time in three decades, wage increases outstripped productivity gains (McKay and Missen 1995).

More fundamentally, Korea began to face the problem of making the difficult transition from a developing to a more mature economy. Central here was a question of technology, as currency revaluations and wage increases necessitated the movement to a more sophisticated industrial base. In the competitive situation of the 1990s, access to new technology from overseas was often restricted (or prohibitively expensive) as advanced nations feared the competition from newcomers such as Korea. The generation of home-grown technology was difficult and slow, given the still poorly developed state of basic science in Korea. Even more fundamental was the question of social change and the movement towards democracy. The Korean population had made significant sacrifices in the national interest, and was now demanding new political freedoms as well as increased living standards. Thus, the successes of earlier years created the conditions and forces to engender significant changes, transformations that could not be accommodated within the parameters of the old regime. The stage was set for a necessary shift to a new regime. I want to argue that the inability to manage that regime shift in an effective way led directly to the crisis of 1997.

5.4.2 Revitalizing the production system

Throughout its drive to development, the modern Korean state had depended more than anything else for its success on its strong production system. However, by the late 1980s it was increasingly clear that while this system still had some fundamental strengths, it was in real need of revitalization. The problems of export competitiveness that derived from wage rises and currency movements have already been noted. At the same time new low-cost competitors, notably China, appeared to challenge Korea's traditional role in several sectors. Even in the areas in which Korea remained very competitive, in electronics in particular, there were wild fluctuations in demand and price. The result was a serious and growing balance of payments problem. In 1988, Korea recorded one of its largest trade surpluses in history, a total of $8.885 billion, but by 1989 this surplus had dwindled to practically nothing, and there followed progressively larger deficits during the 1990s. This was largely made up of two components: a growing deficit with Japan, reaching $15.7 billion in 1996; and a reversal in the former surplus with the United States, a large deficit of $15.7 being recorded in 1996. These deficits were partly offset by a growth in trade with the rest of the world, and in particular with the rest of Asia, but this was not nearly enough. These patterns clearly illustrated the problem of technological dependence on Japan discussed earlier. There was also clear evidence of the failure of several decades of policies designed to increase the strength and capacity of SMEs to provide high-quality component parts at competitive prices, and dependence of the small companies on the *chaebol* remained a problem.

The major strategy adopted by the larger firms (and even some of the medium-sized ones) at this time involved a combination of approaches to gain access to new markets and technology, and to reduce production costs. All of these measures were also designed to generate still further economies of scale and to increase market share, long-term strategies that were given precedence over more immediate issues of corporate profitability. Significantly, these approaches also had the effect of generating still higher levels of company debt. Companies embarked on very bold programmes of asset acquisition. Often these purchases of assets and the construction of new production facilities were in areas of traditional focus for Korean companies, especially in Western Europe, and North America. But there were also moves into countries and regions that even at the time appeared to be very risky, such as Central Asia, Eastern Europe, and parts of Latin America. There were also large-scale relocations of factories into various parts of Asia in sectors that were losing competitiveness. As well as putting even more pressures on corporate financial resources, these initiatives also exposed some severe problems in Korean management systems and even basic knowledge about how to operate in different cultures.

In this frantic attempt to become global and to acquire increased market share, there was a distinct lack of careful analysis and planning. Basic problems, notably access to new technology and the reform of the industrial structure, were not addressed in any systematic and strategic way, and where plans did exist the level of implementation was simply not up to the standards of the past. These, I would argue, were clear signs of an old regime having unravelled, but without any clear new system having yet emerged to take its place.

5.4.3 The growing power of the chaebol

During the 1980s, two trends became clear in relation to the key issue of the role and power of the *chaebol*. The conglomerates continued to be at the core of the Korean system, and indeed were able to extend their power and influence. They were indispensable to the continued export effort, and indeed they were able to point to some impressive successes, especially in the boom years leading up to 1988, when the economy grew at a staggering 12 per cent. But the second trend was particularly important: during the 1980s the conglomerates consolidated their power to such an extent that the old subservience to the state was outgrown and replaced by a new interdependence in which the *chaebol* exercised considerable leverage.

In part, these results were fostered by the very mode of reform that was implemented by successive governments. The emphasis was on gradual rather than abrupt reform, Korean industry was still protected from outside competition in most sectors, and there was still a strong emphasis on encouraging business by severely curtailing the rights of workers and of unions (Cotton 1995, Kong 2000). During this period of change, however gradual, it was essential to keep growth and exports moving, and the big companies were the key to that. The net result of these reforms was that in spite of repeated government statements about the need for *chaebol* reform and for the revitalization of the small business sector, the conglomerates in fact increased their power. One particular loss in this period was the old ability of the government to discipline big business, and there was a perception that the *chaebol* were out of control, and this had important political ramifications in the move towards democracy.

5.4.4 Problems in the transition to democracy

Political commentators have long argued that the Korean system suffers from a number of very serious structural problems: notably regionalism, lack of an effective party system, and over-identification of parties with the personal ambitions of individual leaders (Shin 1999, Kim 2000). But it has also been argued that the way in which a particular form of democratization has emerged has caused particular problems for the whole system, including the economy, and could even be regarded as a contributing factor to the onset of the crisis.

In general terms, it is clear that the transition from authoritarian rule to some form of democracy in Korea has been difficult, largely because it requires a complete shift in political culture. A number of studies have suggested that this process still has a long way to go (Shin 2000). In such a political climate, good policy formulation and implementation becomes difficult. This is doubly so if opposition politicians become obstructionist in their approaches to government proposals. Mo and Moon (1999) argue that this is exactly what happened in the lead up to the economic crisis of 1997. In their view, the Korean economy had suffered from more than a decade of policy gridlock, the direct result of an immature democracy. This is not to suggest that democracy itself is an obstacle to good policy-making, but rather that the particular manifestation of democratization in Korea in 1997 suffered from serious shortcomings. One of the points I made earlier about the success of developmental regime related to the clarity of goals and the precision of implementation. A return to the authoritarian rule of an earlier era is neither possible nor desirable, but in an intensely competitive world policy gridlock can be fatal, as events of 1997 demonstrated.

5.4.5 Kim Young Sam's globalization agenda

During the period of Kim Young Sam's government, especially between 1994 and the onset of the crisis, an ambitious attempt was made to transform the Korean society yet again, but this time in the image of a new globalized future. This *segyehwa* strategy aimed to use the forces of globalization to transform and modernize all aspects of the Korean society (Moon and Mo 1999, Kim 2000). In terms of the reform of the production system, which is my concern here, there were a whole series of targets. These included financial and corporate reform, labour reform, public sector restructuring, educational modernization, knowledge-intensive industrial policy, economic diplomacy, and OECD membership. There were however some fundamental weaknesses in the government's approach.

Whereas in earlier periods there had been detailed strategic planning of both problems and proposed solutions, the *segyehwa* approach was extremely vague, and seemed to be based on the assumption that if the Korean society was simply opened up to outside influences the resultant democratic liberal market system would solve all difficulties that might be encountered on the road to a modern future. There was no analysis of the existing systems and institutions and the ways in which these might be used, transformed, or swept away. Given this staggering level of naivety, it is hardly surprising that so little was really achieved. Membership of the OECD was certainly gained, but even the process of gaining acceptance into this club of the successful nations generated some serious policy and reform blunders that can even be linked to the events of 1997. Some authors have dismissed this programme as somewhat frivolous and now irrelevant bit of Korean history, but I would argue that these years represented a serious loss of opportunity to find solutions to some pressing problems.

5.4.6 Fundamental problems of financial reform

Since the events of 1997 in Korea have generally been labelled a *financial* crisis, it is not surprising that a great deal has been written about the financial system and its weaknesses, and the various programmes of reform both before and since the crisis (see, e.g. Lee and Orr 1999, Choi 2000, Kim and Park 2000, Cho 2001, Cho and Hong 2001). Here, I want to highlight a number of key points around my theme of the production system and the various supporting structures which are essential for its health.

One of the major problems of the 1990s, and one which was not addressed in the largely wasted years of that decade, was that the old system was not adequately replaced. Government withdrew to a large extent from the process hence the old co-ordinating mechanisms ceased to exist. But new mechanisms of monitoring or control were not put in place to regulate the new market driven practices. Thus, in regime terms neither the systems of co-ordination nor monitoring were working effectively. Thus, I would argue that the crisis was not essentially financial in nature, but was more systemic and involved a total regime failure.

Part of the failure of the financial reform programme involved an unsystematic approach to dealing with some of the problems inherited from the old system. The high levels of *chaebol* debt have already been discussed, and there was a failure to deal with this legacy. One approach might have been to underwrite corporate debt while embarking on thorough and speedy reform. Another, would have been to give the conglomerates target dates by which certain levels of debt/equity ratio targets would have been met. But government did none of these things, but succeeded only in confusing the international markets. There had been an expectation of continued government support for the *chaebol*, but the sudden repudiation of any responsibility in the case of the Hanbo crash, caused panic in the markets.

Another fundamental problem concerns the sequencing of financial reforms (Cho 2001). There was no attempt to differentiate between financial instruments of a long-term nature and those of a short-term nature. The result was that there was a rapid expansion of short-term financing before any reforms had been put in place to strengthen the financial structure of corporations. General financial infrastructure, including an adequate regulatory framework, was not built up as a first step. The domestic financial system was deregulated before anything had been done about corporate debt or the development of equity markets. International capital flows were deregulated before the local capacity to deal with them was in place.

5.5 The failure of regime shift and the onset of the crisis

To sum up my argument, the Korean crisis of 1997 was not simply a financial or currency crisis. It was a failure of the system more generally. The old regime which had served Korea so well for so many years was no longer viable, but the process of a shift to a new regime was badly managed by a series of governments, culminating in the idealistic but simplistic globalization campaign of the Kim Young Sam administration. The old regime had a number of key features that were essential to the development of the country. There was careful planning and co-ordination, goals were clearly addressed and articulated, there was an almost fanatical attention to the detail of implementation. The production system, its growth targets and export goals came first, and other systems were designed to support this priority. In particular, a financial system was developed to feed the needs of the production complex.

When internal and external pressures demanded a fundamental transformation of the system, this proved to be very difficult. The serious problems in the areas of financial reform, *chaebol* governance and structure, industrial restructuring, revitalization of the small business sector, and in a number of other areas I have highlighted, were not addressed. Nor was there any real vision of how the new regime might fit together in its totality. The flawed nature of democratic reform produced a political system and a style of leadership that was just not up to the task. The result was a progressive crisis in the system, beginning in the mid-1980s if not earlier, and this led inevitably to the crash of 1997.

This does not mean that the Korean system itself was or is a failure – as I said at the beginning, let us not overreact or throw out the baby with the bath water. Many of the fundamentals of the Korean economy were quite sound at the time of the crisis, and in many ways the country did not deserve to be punished so severely by the international markets. I certainly do not support the argument that what Korea needed to do both before and after the crisis was to implement thoroughgoing market reform, perhaps using a big bang approach. Modern approaches to questions of international competitiveness do not support the idea that market liberalization can by itself produce everything that is necessary. This is especially true for middle-sized powers such as Korea with problems of how to generate new technology to keep their production systems competitive. Nor can reforms ignore the historical and institutional legacies of earlier periods. The aim then is to create a new regime to meet the new circumstances and challenges, and yet be compatible with the society and its heritage. What such a regime will or might look like for Korea is a new challenge that will require some extremely creative thought, but the legacy of the old developmental regime might not be so irrelevant as some commentators might have us believe.

Bibliography

Amsden, A. (1989) *Asia's Next Giant: South Korea and Late Industrialization*, New York: Oxford University Press.

Boyer, R. and Hollingsworth, J.R. (1997) 'The variety of institutional arrangements and their complementarity in modern economies', in J.R. Hollingsworth and R. Boyer (eds), *Contemporary Capitalism: The Embededness of Institutions*, Cambridge: Cambridge University Press, 49–54.

Cheng Tun-Jen (1990) 'Political regimes and development strategies: South Korea and Taiwan', in G. Gereffi and D. Wyman (eds), *Manufacturing Miracles: Paths of Industrialization in Latin America and East Asia*, Princeton NJ: Princeton University Press, 139–78.

—— (1993) 'Distinctions between Taiwanese and Korean approaches to economic development', *Journal of East Asian Affairs*, 7: 116–36.

Cho Dongchul and Hong Kisoek (2001) 'Currency crisis in Korea: internal weakness or external dependence?', in T. Ito and A. Kreuger (eds), *Regional and Global Capital Flows: macroeconomic Causes and Consequences*, Chicago: University of Chicago Press, 337–79.

Cho Yoon Je (2001) 'The role of poorly phased liberalization in Korea's financial crisis', in G. Caprio, H. Honohan, and J. Stiglitz (eds), *Financial Liberalization: How Far, How Fast?* Cambridge: Cambridge University Press, 159–87.

Choi Young Back (2000) 'Financial crisis and perspectives on Korean economic development', in J. Choi (ed.), *Asian Financial Crisis: Financial, Structural and International Dimensions*, Amsterdam: JAI.

Clark, G.L., McKay, J., Missen, G., and Webber, M. (1991) 'Objections to restructuring and the strategies of coercion: a comparison of Australia, the US, and South Korea', Monash-Melbourne Joint Project on Comparative Australian–Asian Development, Development Studies Centre, Monash University Working Paper No. 91.3.

—— (1992) 'Objections to economic restructuring and the strategies of coercion: an analytic evaluation of policies and practices in Australia and the United States', *Economic Geography*, 68: 43–59.

Corbo, V. and Suh Sang-Mok (eds) (1992) *Structural Adjustment in a Newly Industrialized Country: The Korean Experience*, Baltimore: World Bank/Johns Hopkins University Press.

Cotton, J. (ed.) (1995) *Politics and Policy in the New Korean State: From Roh Tae-woo to Kim Young-sam*, New York: St Martin's Press.

Cumings, B. (1987) 'The origins and development of the Northeast Asian political economy: industrial sectors, product cycles, and political consequences' in F.C. Deyo (ed.), *The Political Economy of New Asian Industrialism*, Ithaca: Cornell University Press, 44–83.

Gao Bai (2001) *Japan's Economic Dilemma: The Institutional Origins of Prosperity and Stagnation*, Cambridge: Cambridge University Press.

Garnaut, R., Grilli, E., and Riedel, J. (eds) (1995) *Sustaining Export-Oriented Development: Ideas from East Asia*, Cambridge: Cambridge University Press.

Kim Daesik and Park Jaeha (2000) 'Korean financial crisis and reform: an overview', in J. Choi (ed.), *Asian Financial Crisis: Financial, Structural and International Dimensions*, Amsterdam: JAI.

Kim Eun Mee (1997) *Big Business, Strong State*, Albany: State University of New York Press.

Kim Hyung-A. (1996) *Park Chung Hee's Self-Reliance Ideology, 1961–79: Modernization and National Restoration*, unpublished PhD dissertation, Division of Pacific and Asian History, Research School of Pacific and Asian Studies, Australian National University.

Kim Kihwan and Leipziger, D. (1997) 'Korea: a case of government-led development', in D. Leipziger (ed.), *Lessons from East Asia*, Ann Arbor: University of Michigan Press, 155–212.

Kim Sunhyuk (2000) *The Politics of Democratization in Korea: The Role of Civil Society*, Pittsburgh: University of Pittsburgh Press.

——(ed.) (2000) *Korea's Globalization*, Cambridge: Cambridge University Press.

Kong Tat Yan (2000) *The Politics of Economic Reform in South Korea: The Fragile Miracle*, London: Routledge.

Lee Soo-Won and Orr, A. (1999) 'The financial restructuring and reform programme in the Republic of Korea: progress and constraints', in B. Herman (ed.), *Global Financial Turmoil and Reform*, Tokyo: United Nations University Press, 93–108.

McKay, J. and Missen, G.J. (1995) 'Keeping their miracles going: questioning big firms in Korea and small firms in Taiwan', in R. Le Heron and S. Ock Park (eds), *The Asian Pacific Rim and Gobalization: Enterprise, Governance and Territoriality*, Aldershot: Avebury, 61–86.

Mo Jongryn and Moon Chung-in (1999) 'Epilogue: democracy and the origins of the 1997 Korean economic crisis', in Mo Jongryn and Moon Chung-in (eds), *Democracy and the Korean Economy*, Stanford, California: Hoover Institution Press, 171–98.

Moon Chung-in and Mo Jongryn (eds) (1999) *Democratization and Globalization in Korea*, Seoul: Yonsei University Press.

Pempel, T.J. (1998) *Regime Shift: Comparative Dynamics of the Japanese Political Economy*, Ithaca, NY: Cornell University Press.

Shin Doh Chull (1999) *Mass Politics and Culture in Democratising Korea*, Cambridge: Cambridge University Press.

——(2000) 'The evolution of popular support for democracy during Kim Young Sam's government', in L. Diamond and Shin Doh Chull (eds), *Institutional Reform and Democratic Consolidation in Korea*, Stanford, California: Hoover Institution Press, 233–56.

Soskice, D. (1999) 'Divergent production regimes: coordinated and uncoordinated market economies in the 1980s and 1990s', in H. Kitschelt, P. Lange, G. Marks, and J.D. Stephens (eds), *Continuity and Change in Contemporary Capitalism*, Cambridge: Cambridge University Press, 101–34.

Webber, M., Clark, G.L., McKay, J., and Missen, G. (1991) 'Industrial restructuring: definition', Monash-Melbourne Joint Project on Comparative Australian–Asian Development, Development Studies Centre, Monash University Working Paper No. 91.3.

Woo Jung-en (1991) *Race to the Swift: State and Finance in Korean Industrialization*, New York: Columbia University Press.

6 The impact of ownership and capital structure on the productivity performance of Korean firms in the 1990s

Euysung Kim

6.1 Introduction

There are many competing explanations for the Korean economic crisis of 1997. There are stories that blame weakened domestic fundamentals as well as those that seem to blame external factors for Korea's crisis (such stories as contagion, herding and market manipulation). However, an important point is that even those explanations that emphasize external factors can only be justified when the fundamentals are sufficiently weak. That is, financial crisis does not simply happen just anywhere. Capital outflows in 1997 were responding to real weaknesses in Korea's corporate sector, weaknesses that had been revealed quite clearly by the bankruptcy of a number of large groups with the onset of the crisis.

In the past, when a number of similar crisis threatened the Korean economy (such as the August 1972 Emergency Decree and the 1979–81 bailout), the "restructuring" efforts in these incidences was really little more than debt rescheduling designed to restore the basic terms of the government–business risk partnership. Corporate bankruptcies were avoided because creditors and taxpayers were forced to bear the burden. In contrast, the Korean government that faced the crisis in 1997 could not possibly avoid the bankruptcies in the same way. With the democratization of Korea and the growing specter of global recession, the government faced limited options both internally and externally and could not muddle through the crisis like before. The government this time had to face the crisis straight on and fundamentally reform corporate Korea.

In pursuing corporate restructuring, the policymakers and academics alike agree that reform in corporate governance is central to Korea's recovery effort. Many have pointed out the deficiencies in the "Korean way" of corporate governance that led to weakened fundamentals and the poor economic performance of Korean firms. However, direct evidence on the effects of different governance systems on corporate performance and competitiveness is still sparse. Using firm level data (from 1991 to 1998), this chapter provides empirical evidence on the link between corporate governance (measured in terms of ownership and financial structure) and productivity performance of Korean firms in the 1990s.[1] While a number of other studies on corporate performance focus on profitability, this chapter uses productivity as the performance measure because it best reflects efficient investment by all stakeholders of the firm and their potential for long-term growth.[2] That is, productivity is a more fundamental measure, which is what, in part, *determines* profitability. In an era of global competition where technological superiority determines the competitiveness of firms and industries, it is of critical importance to understand the ways in which different systems of corporate governance affect innovative activities and entrepreneurship of corporations.

In the remainder of this chapter, Section 6.2 discusses the analytical linkages between corporate governance structure and firm performance. Section 6.3 covers the data and sources used. Sections 6.4 and 6.5 identify some stylized facts about Korean firms' corporate governance structure and performance focusing on ownership and capital structure respectively. Section 6.6 analyzes corporate performance during the 1991–98 sample period. Section 6.7 presents the estimation results of the relationship between corporate governance structure and firm performance.

6.2 Corporate governance and firm performance

While "corporate governance" could be defined in a number of different ways, it essentially defines rules, incentives and goals for various stakeholders in a firm (including management, capital suppliers, employees, etc.) and hence determines the mechanism by which the firm's capital and resources are allocated, profits are distributed and performance is monitored. According to this perspective, it is possible to identify a number of different dimensions of corporate governance structure for the purpose of understanding their impact on firm performance. However, in this chapter, we focus our attention on two central aspects of Korea's corporate governance: ownership concentration and capital structure.[3]

There are many well-known hypotheses as to why both ownership and capital structures are important determinants of a firm's corporate governance. Unfortunately, however, there is no analytical clarity as to how these aspects of corporate governance impacts on corporate performance. For example, with regard to a firm's ownership structure, a frequently heard debate is whether owner-controlled (insider) system is better than manager-controlled (outsider) system. Concentrated ownership has an advantage in that it provides better monitoring and is thus able to overcome the agency problem posed by misalignment of interest between shareholders and managers. But, at the same time, the controlling shareholder, with privileged access to the management, might be less concerned with firm performance but be more interested in the extraction of private rents at the expense of minority shareholders.

In addition, a firm's ownership concentration is often argued to have an important impact on investment horizons. In outsider systems, widely dispersed ownership offers enhanced liquidity of stocks and better risk diversification for investors. Hence, diversified investors would be more likely to support a firm's risky venture into innovative activities than those investors in outsider systems. Yet, from the firm's perspective, it is also possible that a governance system that allows high investor turnover may encourage managers to focus excessively on projects with short-term payoffs and provide weak incentives for stakeholders to make firm-specific investments (Mayer 1996). That is, projects with long-term payoffs, such as research and development and firm-specific human capital investments, may be undervalued as a result of stock market myopia. This, in turn, could lower the firm's innovation, technological development and long-term growth. In sum, there is no clear-cut analytical understanding as to how ownership affects corporate performance.

With regard to the debate on capital structure, it is not most often a recognized issue in the corporate governance literature but is nonetheless controversial. Clearly, under certain conditions, a firm's debt–equity structure should have no effect on the firm's value (Modigliani and Miller 1958). But, there are also those who argue that changes in debt–equity mix can have important effects on a firm's behavior (Grossman and Hart 1986, Jensen 1986, Williamson 1988, Stulz 1990). Since a rise in debt increases default risk, debt financing could have a disciplinary effect on managers who fear bankruptcy. Bond covenants specifying the manager's discretionary use of funds can constrain management behavior. In general, a governance system based on debt financing can be characterized as one functioning through strict rules, while a governance system based on equity financing is one that allows greater flexibility and discretion.

These hypotheses about firms' ownership and capital structure offer testable conjectures about the relationship between firms' capital structure and firm performance. Since there are no clear analytical presumptions, the question of how ownership and capital structure affect corporate performance essentially becomes an empirical question. Furthermore, there are a number of reasons to believe that empirical tests of these hypotheses will reveal important aspects about corporate governance specific to Korea. For example, in Korea, one could argue that, at least before the crisis, there was a widely held presumption that the government's implicit guarantee has virtually eliminated the default risk for the *chaebol*. Hence, *chaebols* with preferential bank financing could exhibit more risk-taking behavior than those *non-chaebol* firms with similar levels of debt financing. It would therefore be interesting to see whether capital structure has a different impact on the performance of *chaebol* and *non-chaebol* firms. For instance, if the risk-taking behavior made *chaebols* more innovative and entrepreneurial, their dependence on debt financing could be associated with *better* firm performance. Also, with lower capital costs, they would be better able to purchase technology from abroad. On the other hand, if *chaebols*' risk-taking behavior is better explained by the recklessness associated with moral hazard and crony capital, debt financing would have quite the opposite impact on their performance. In our model, we introduce a separate *chaebol* dummy variable[4] and also interact it with corporate governance variables to see if the *chaebol* status has the impact hypothesized.[5]

To test these hypotheses, we must also control for a variety of other factors that can jointly affect corporate governance structure (measured in terms of ownership concentration and capital structure) and firm performance (measured by productivity). One obvious candidate would be to include exposure to trade (also measured as log of firm-level exports). Firms' exposure to trade, in particular, would be important to include in the analysis because it could not only affect productivity performance but also have non-trivial effects on shaping firms' corporate governance systems. A growing body of literature suggests that the globalization of capital markets and liberalization of trade could force convergence of corporate governance systems (Shinn 1999). If true, the exclusion of trade could lead to classic omitted variable bias.

In addition, there might be other factors, such as industry-specific characteristics (market or product-related) or political, and macroeconomic instability, which are important determinants of firms' productivity. Because they are difficult to measure on a firm-level basis, we employ a dummy-variable approach. An industry-specific dummy is introduced to capture the effects of all omitted attributes that vary across industries but do not change over time.[6] A time-specific dummy captures discrete productivity shocks specific to the period in which they occur but which are common to all firms (such as macroeconomic and political shocks).

6.3 Data

This study employs detailed financial information on publicly traded firms between 1991 and 1998, collected by National Information and Credit Evaluation, Inc. (NICE). Each firm reports its financial statement to the Korea Securities Supervisory Board. Upon receiving the financial data from the board, NICE checks the integrity of the data. All dependent and independent variables used in this chapter (with a few exceptions such as price deflators) are based on the NICE data. After excluding financial institutions and state-controlled firms from the analysis, our data set includes 18,356 observations on manufacturing firms, of which 731 observations belong to *chaebols*.

A few comments about some of the explanatory variables are in order. As for ownership information, the NICE data set includes the names of large individual and institutional shareholders, their family members and their shareholdings. After identifying all institutional owners and their shareholdings, we subtracted them from the sum of large shareholders' ownership. Through this calculation for each firm, we derived the controlling family's direct ownership stake.[7]

The selection of the *chaebols* follows Korea Fair Trade Commission (KFTC) classification based on the size of total assets. These groups are subject to several restrictions on bank lending and a ceiling on the groups' equity investment.

As for dependent variables, total factor productivity (TFP) performance will be estimated using a multilateral index approach originally developed by Caves *et al.* (1982) and later extended by Good *et al.* (1996).[8] The index provides a measure of the proportional differences in TFP for each firm in each year relative to a hypothetical firm in the base year. This multilateral productivity index is particularly useful in panel-data applications because it provides a consistent way of summarizing the cross-sectional distribution of firm productivity, using only information specific to that time period and how the distribution moves over time.[9]

Measurement of firm-level productivity performance requires data on output, intermediate, capital, and labor input and factor shares (see Haggard and Kim 1997). For manufacturing firms listed in Korea's stock exchange, detailed financial information included in the NICE dataset provides most of the data required for the measurement of productivity index. We have constructed estimates of TFP indexes for the period from 1991 to 1998, for which we have matched ownership data.

Firm output is defined as total sales deflated by a wholesale price index at the two-digit industry level. As for labor inputs, we used the total number of both production and non-production workers, adjusted by annual changes in average work hours per day in the manufacturing sector and by two-digit level average monthly workdays. The measure of capital input is the book value of capital stock of the firm. Following Aw *et al.* (1998), we have adjusted the book values for yearly price changes in addition of new capital equipment. The measure of material input includes raw materials and manufacturing costs (such as electricity, water, fuel and subcontracting costs), and it is deflated by an intermediate input price index. All price indices used come from the Bank of Korea's yearly publication of price statistics.

For factor shares, labor income share is measured as total salaries (including retirement benefit payments) to total workers divided by the value of output. The intermediate share is measured as the expenditure share of intermediate input in the value of output. Applying the standard assumption of constant returns, the capital income share is obtained as a residual by subtracting labor share and intermediate input share from one. Kim (2000) actually showed that constant returns is not such a bad assumption in the Korean case.

Using the data on Korean firms, the index of the proportional difference in TFP for plant f in year t relative to the hypothetical plant in the base year can be calculated using the following equation (following Aw *et al.* 1998):

$$\begin{aligned} \ln TFP_{ft} = {} & (\ln Y_{ft} - \overline{\ln Y_t}) + \sum_{s=2}^{t} (\overline{\ln Y_s} - \overline{\ln Y_{s-1}}) \\ & - \left[\sum_{i=1}^{n} \frac{1}{2} (S_{ift} + \overline{S_{it}})(\ln X_{ift} - \overline{\ln X_{it}}) \right. \\ & \left. + \sum_{s=2}^{t} \sum_{i=1}^{n} \frac{1}{2} (\overline{S_{is}} + \overline{S_{is-1}})(\overline{\ln X_{is}} - \overline{\ln X_{is-1}}) \right] \end{aligned} \tag{6.1}$$

where Y_{ft} is the output of firm f in year t; X_i is the input i; and S_i is the factor income share of input i. The overbars denote the average value over all firms in year t.

6.4 The ownership structure of Korean firms

There has been a long held popular misconception about ownership structure of Korean firms, in particular about *chaebols* in Korea. In both popular media and academia, it is still quite common to find a chairman or CEO of *chaebol* groups being referred to as the "owners" (i.e. managers with high ownership concentration).

However, recent studies have shown that these perceptions are not supported by empirical evidence. La Porta *et al.* (1998a,b) and Claessens *et al.* (1998), for example, have shown that Korean firms typically have a widely dispersed ownership structure.[10] Our data also confirms the view that control of Korean corporations can be achieved with significantly less than an absolute majority of the stock. In our sample, controlling family members in firms listed in Korean stock exchanges owned 22.4 percent on an average[11] and 54.9 percent in non-listed firms. There is also a vast difference in the ownership between the *chaebol* firms and *non-chaebol* firms. Among listed firms, the ownership in *chaebol* firms averaged 16.7 percent, compared to 28.4 percent in *non-chaebol* firms (Table 6.1).

According to Joh and Kim (2003), virtually uncontested family control with low ownership concentration is possible for a number of reasons. First, relatively weak laws protecting small shareholders allow controlling shareholders to maintain low ownership stakes. For example, during the 1993–97 period, Korean law required at least 5 percent ownership for a shareholder to exercise rights such as demanding convocation, inspecting account books and filing derivative suits.[12] With such stringent requirements, small shareholders did not have effective means to monitor the controlling family.

Second, the restriction on the voting rights of institutional investors in listed companies is an additional factor allowing effective control with low ownership stakes. For example, with shadow voting regulations, institutional investors always had to take a neutral stance by casting their votes proportionate to other votes. Despite their significant ownership stakes in Korean corporations, institutional investors posed no threat to the controlling shareholder despite their low ownership stake.

Last, controlling families in *chaebol*-affiliated firms are also able to exercise control through interlocking ownership among subsidiaries. The patterns of institutional interlocking ownership found in *chaebol*-affiliated firms are complicated

Table 6.1 Estimated family control in Korean firms

	Average ownership share 1991–98 (weighted by total assets)
Listed firms	
All listed	0.224 (2,853)
Chaebol	0.167 (376)
Non-chaebol	0.284 (2,477)
Non-listed firms	
All non-listed	0.549 (15,502)
Chaebol	0.352 (355)
Non-chaebol	0.625 (15,147)
Total sample	34.5 (18,356)

Source: NICE; the number of observations are in parenthesis.

because of their need to circumvent regulations on ownership which prevent direct circular interlocking ownership (firm A owns firm B, and firm B in turn owns firm A).[13] Nonetheless, according to the KFTC, the average interlocking inter-subsidiary ownership exceeded 33 percent in the 1990s. Interlocking shareholdings imply that in-group ownership friendly to the controlling family could be quite high, making any challenges to management virtually impossible. That is, while the direct ownership in Korean firms is dispersed, the in-group ownership (direct controlling family ownership plus interlocking ownership between affiliates) is quite concentrated in Korean firms.

According to Lim (2003), the ownership structure of Korean firms cannot be understood without a historical perspective. Lim notes that, in fact, prior to the mid-1970s, the ownership of the *chaebol* firms was characterized by a high degree of concentration. The significant decline in ownership concentration started with the government's concerted efforts in the mid-1970s to push Korean firms to go public. In the aftermath of the debt crisis in 1972, the government believed that opening up family-owned enterprises to public sharing would allow firms to reduce excessive dependence on debt and improve the corporate governance by promoting "modern" corporations characterized by dispersed ownership and professional management. Moreover, the government believed that dispersion of ownership will help disperse economic power that had been concentrated among *chaebol* owners.

The *ex post* outcome clearly indicates that the government policies have been obviously successful in dispersing the ownership structure. However, it is not clear that they were successful in producing the intended result. When the firms that greatly benefited from the Emergency Decree of 1972 were reluctant to go public, the government had to coerce and, at the same time, provide incentive for them to do so. The government thus allowed weak protection of the property rights of minority shareholders to provide incentive for those *chaebol* owners who feared losing control of their firm. But, the dispersion of ownership achieved in this manner actually worsened the principal–agent problem of Korean firms. Moreover, the policies that promoted the dispersion of ownership were clearly inappropriate instruments for achieving the equity in wealth distribution because the ownership dispersion only changed the *chaebol* owner's wealth portfolio, not the wealth itself.

6.5 The financing of Korean firms

The financial crisis of 1997 clearly revealed the vulnerability of the Korean economy due to the high leveraging of its corporate sector. By the end of 1997, the average debt–equity ratio of manufacturing firms hit around 400 percent. The ratio exceeded 500 percent for the thirty largest *chaebols* and reached 3000 percent for several large groups (Lee *et al.* 1999).

Figure 6.1 traces debt–equity ratios for the Korean manufacturing sector from 1965 through the onset of the crisis. What we can learn from this historical data is that the excessive leveraging of the Korean corporate sector is not a recent

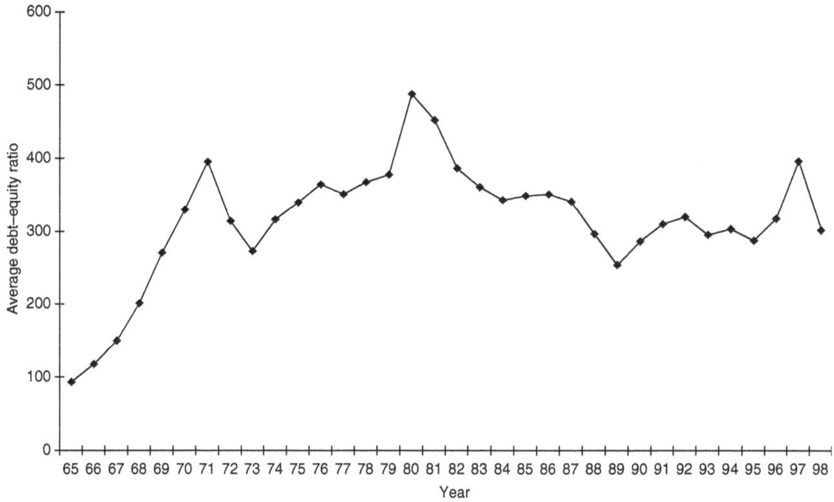

Figure 6.1 Average debt–equity ratio of the Korean manufacturing sector.
Source: Bank of Korea, *Financial Statements Analysis*, various issues.

phenomenon but had been the same throughout the development era. Since the late 1960s, the debt–equity ratio generally hovered above 300 percent, except for two periods: the brief period after 1972 when the corporate sector's debt burden was artificially reduced by the Emergency Decree of 1972 and the period around 1988 when the Korean economy enjoyed the "three-low" boom characterized by low oil prices.

In other words, the financial crisis of 1997 was not the only period in which the Korean corporate sector suffered from excessively high debt–equity ratios. In comparison, the increase in the debt–equity ratio during the period leading up to the Decree of 1972 had been just as dramatic. During the period after the second oil shock, the average debt–equity ratio of Korean manufacturing firms reached nearly 500 percent, much higher than that of the 1997 crisis. In sum, the Korean corporate sector had always been characterized by high leveraging throughout its development history and bouts of debt crisis had not been uncommon. Hence, it is not simply a change in the level of debt financing, a sudden credit expansion and lending boom that caused the 1997 crisis.[14] But, the question posed in this chapter is whether Korea's high reliance on a debt-based corporate governance system, as opposed to equity-based financing, can be linked to fundamental weaknesses in the Korean corporate sector.

While there are many plausible explanations as to why Korean corporations overwhelmingly chose a debt-based corporate governance structure instead of an equity-based one, heavy debt reliance in the Korean corporate sector most critically reflects the extent of the government–business relationship in Korea. After the military coup of 1961, the new government nationalized the banks and assumed a dominant role in financial resource allocation. In effect, the government formed a risk partnership with the firms that are willing to carry out its economic development plans. While it can be debated as to whether this relationship was the reason behind Korea's rapid capital accumulation and economic growth, the Korean corporate sector's heavy reliance on debt clearly indicates the government's intervention in the economy, especially in the early development period.

In this respect, it is quite revealing that the biggest rise in the debt–equity ratio came about during the heavy and chemical industry (HCI) drive (see Figure 6.1). Launched in 1973, the government provided extremely generous support to private firms to carry out specific investment projects in favored industries. The real interest rate on bank loans extended to these firms, for example, was negative! During the 1970s, HCIs accounted for almost 80 percent of all fixed investment in the manufacturing sector when their share in the manufacturing was around 40 percent (Lim 2003). However, the firms that received preferential bank loans were not always profitable and faced periodical financial distress. In these instances, the government rescued troubled companies by extending more loans from government-controlled banks. Lim (forthcoming) points out that the HCI drive aggravated the problem of moral hazard and resulted in an undue concentration of economic power among *chaebol* groups. With the logic of "too-big-to-fail," *chaebol* groups were particularly capable of raising bank financing by taking advantage of interlocking ownership and debt payment guarantees. Table 6.2 shows that the average equity ratio (i.e. equity divided by assets) in our sample for *chaebols* was much lower than that for the *non-chaebol* firms.

Table 6.2 Equity–asset ratio in Korean manufacturing firms

	1991	*1992*	*1993*	*1994*	*1995*	*1996*	*1997*	*1998*
Listed firms								
All listed	0.344	0.349	0.347	0.334	0.345	0.360	0.307	0.273
	(308)	(418)	(432)	(381)	(351)	(332)	(257)	(374)
Chaebol	0.2756	0.27424	0.2436	0.2452	0.2289	0.2323	0.16862	0.18485
	(59)	(80)	(48)	(36)	(32)	(34)	(31)	(56)
Non-chaebol	0.3606	0.36674	0.36013	0.3430	0.35626	0.37402	0.3260	0.28888
	(249)	(338)	(384)	(345)	(319)	(298)	(226)	(318)
Non-listed firms								
All non-listed	0.183	0.195	0.193	0.186	0.178	0.173	0.173	0.269
	(2,039)	(1,931)	(2,013)	(2,082)	(2,066)	(2,129)	(1,749)	(1,494)
Chaebol	0.14118	0.1366	0.09470	0.08025	0.1230	0.0477	0.0943	0.1805
	(63)	(80)	(33)	(40)	(43)	(36)	(34)	(26)
Non-chaebol	0.18442	0.19758	0.1951	0.18797	0.17930	0.17530	0.1744	0.27083
	(1,976)	(1,851)	(1,980)	(2,042)	(2,023)	(2,093)	(1,715)	(1,468)

Source: NICE; the number of observations are in parenthesis.

It is interesting to note (from Figure 6.1 and Table 6.2) that the average debt–equity ratio did not decline in the 1990s, even thought it is long after policy lending had stopped and banks were re-privatized. Despite government efforts to ensure the soundness of the banking system and to control bank credit toward the *chaebol*, Hahm (2003) notes that heavy debt reliance continued into the 1990s with the emergence of non-bank financial institutions (NBFIs) and opening up of more direct and overseas financing opportunities. Moreover, with continued practice of the government's indirect and occasional intervention, there was a widely held belief in the financial market that the government's implicit guarantee was still valid and extended also to NBFIs. As a result, the moral hazard continued and the investment boom of the early 1990s ultimately ended up in the crisis of 1997.

6.6 Performance of the Korean corporate sector in the 1990s

Using the data on Korean manufacturing firms, we have constructed estimates of TFP indexes for the period from 1991 to 1998. Table 6.3 summarizes the movement in the firm productivity distribution by reporting the 25th, 50th and 75th percentiles for each year. For example, the estimate of 0.0984 for the median firm in 1995 means that productivity performance was 9.84 percentage points higher than that of our hypothetical benchmark firm in the 1993 base year. In other words, the output performance of the median firm in 1995 was higher by 9.84 percentage points than that of the benchmark firm, for the given changes in the factor inputs. Likewise, it is important to note that the negative signs in Table 6.3 imply that estimated productivity *differentials* are negative, not *levels* of productivity.

With respect to the changes in the shape of the distribution from year to year, there is no evidence of substantial widening or narrowing until the mid-1990s. In comparison, the dispersion in the interquartile range increased in the latter portion of the 1990s. It is interesting to see that the interquartile range continued to increase in 1998 while the median firm's productivity dropped to a whopping 5 percentage points, reflecting Korea's economic crisis in full bloom. Before the crisis, however, the productivity in general did increase over time, averaging about 3 percentage-point increases per year.

Table 6.4 shows the average productivity differential between *chaebol* and *non-chaebol* firms. Although these figures represent comparisons of simple averages,

Table 6.3 Percentile of the distribution of lnTFP across firms

	1991	*1992*	*1993*	*1994*	*1995*	*1996*	*1997*	*1998*
25th percentile	−0.3687	−0.3511	−0.3398	−0.3007	−0.2727	−0.2306	−0.2046	−0.3125
Median	−0.0170	0.007	0.0091	0.0544	0.0984	0.13234	0.16406	0.1143
75th percentile	0.3275	0.3593	0.3532	0.4042	0.4831	0.50966	0.5719	0.56688

Table 6.4 Average productivity differential between *chaebol* and *non-chaebol* firms

	1991	*1992*	*1993*	*1994*	*1995*	*1996*	*1997*	*1998*
Non-chaebol	−0.018	0.024	0.0217	0.080	0.124	0.159	0.212	0.163
Chaebol	−0.172	−0.219	−0.213	−0.116	−0.187	−0.089	−0.131	−0.244
Productivity differential	0.154	0.243	0.2347	0.196	0.311	0.248	0.343	0.407

Note
Simple averages.

it is interesting to note that *chaebol* firms' productivity performances were consistently lower than that of *non-chaebol* firms throughout our sample period. In the latter half of the 1990s, the difference became quite substantial, leading to about 40 percentage point differential in 1998. The question we would like to address is whether any portion of these differences in productivity performance between different groups of firms and over time can be accounted for by the corporate governance structure of Korean firms.

6.7 Empirical tests and results

The call for corporate governance reform in Korea is rarely based on a solid empirical foundation. Simple cross-country benchmark case comparisons serve as the bases for policy recommendations without any consideration of the context under which different governance systems operate. In this section, we evaluate the relationship between corporate governance structure (as characterized by each firm's ownership concentration and capital structure) and firm performance using a sample of manufacturing firms in Korea.

Table 6.5 presents the estimated impact of corporate governance on relative productivity differences of Korean firms using the full sample of 18,356 for which all the relevant data is available. The benchmark regression (1) shows that productivity is significantly and positively related to ownership concentration. The coefficient of 0.13 implies that a 10 percentage point increase in the ownership will increase productivity by about 1.3 percent. Even with changes in specification, we can see that the impact of controlling shareholder's ownership concentration on corporate performance is quite robust.

As we had expected, the equity ratio also has a significant and positive impact on productivity performance, which is consistent with the presumption that an equity-based governance structure is more conducive to innovative activities than a debt-based governance structure. The result shows that a 10 percentage point increase in the equity ratio would result in about 3 percent increase in the productivity performance. As with ownership concentration, this result is quite robust with respect to various other specifications.

In regressions (2), (3) and (4), we introduce two control variables, *chaebol* dummy and exports.[15] It is important to note that the *chaebol* dummy is highly

Table 6.5 Impact of corporate governance on firm-level productivity difference (full sample)

Dependent variable		*(1)*	*(2)*	*(3)*	*(4)*
Corporate governance variables	Ownership concentration	0.131 (8.95)	0.107 (7.13)	0.101 (6.73)	0.047 (2.85)
	Equity ratio	0.289 (12.62)	0.284 (12.46)	0.294 (12.47)	0.328 (12.55)
Control variables	Chaebol dummy		−0.218 (−9.240)	−0.227 (−5.91)	−0.325 (−6.00)
	Ownership × *chaebol*			0.162 (1.49)	0.277 (2.04)
	Equity-ratio × *chaebol*			−0.270 (−3.61)	−0.358 (−4.27)
	ln Export				0.027 (5.57)
	Dummy controls	Industry/ Time dummies	Industry/ Time dummies	Industry/ Time dummies	Industry/ Time dummies
	Number of observations	18,356	18,356	18,356	16,276
	R^2	0.0889	0.0936	0.0943	0.0963

Note
Numbers in parentheses are *t*-values controlling for White's heteroskedasticity.

significant and negative. The common presumption that *chaebols*' cost advantages and ability to diversify risk make them better innovators and acquirers of technology turns out to be wrong; *chaebol* underperform *non-chaebol* firms with productivity as the performance measure. The interaction variables introduced in regressions (3) and (4) tell us that, for *chaebol* firms, the impact of equity ratio on productivity is less than that for *non-chaebol* firms. With the benefit of the government guarantees and subsidies, debt financing for *chaebols* was not perhaps constraining as it would be for *non-chaebols* in financing risky but innovated projects. When ownership is interacted with *chaebol* dummy, a significant result is only obtained in regression (4). The positive coefficient implies that the ownership concentration is more important for *chaebols*' performance than for *non-chaebol* firms' performance. If diversified, interlocked ownership structure of *chaebol* firms creates greater opportunities for controlling families to expropriate from other shareholders. The greater would be the benefit from the reduction of such incentives.

Finally, the export variable introduced in regression (4) tests the conventional wisdom in the growth and development literature that exposure to trade is one of the most important determinants of productivity performance. The relation is positive and significant, suggesting that a greater exposure to international trade helps productivity enhancement. With the introduction of the export variable, the coefficient on ownership concentration is reduced by almost half, but retains its significance.

Table 6.6 reports the result from a subsample of publicly traded firms. The main purpose here is to see if the result obtained in Table 6.5 is robust across subsamples.

Here, we see that ownership maintains significance in regressions (1), (2) and (3). Equity ratio does not appear significant in this subsample. On the other hand *chaebol* dummy is consistently highly significant and negative. With substantial loss of degrees of freedom, the result is not as clear-cut as that of Table 6.5, but the variables that are significant convey the same message as before.

6.8 Conclusion

This chapter has examined the impact of controlling shareholder's ownership concentration and financial structure on firm-level productivity performance. In a panel data of Korean manufacturing firms from 1991 to 1998, we have identified that higher ownership concentration is associated with stronger firm performance. This finding is consistent with the hypothesis that higher ownership concentration leads not only to greater convergence of interest between the controlling shareholder and other shareholders, but also to greater investment in firm-specific investments that results in a better productivity performance. The significant positive impact of equity ratio on firm performance was also found in the regression analysis, suggesting that equity governance, rather than one that is based on debt, is more conducive to innovative activities.

Table 6.6 Impact of corporate governance on firm-level productivity difference (listed firms)

Dependent variable		*(1)*	*(2)*	*(3)*	*(4)*
Corporate governance variables	Ownership concentration	0.260 (6.22)	0.218 (5.20)	0.206 (4.65)	20.087 (20.91)
	Equity ratio	0.118 (1.68)	0.100 (1.44)	0.108 (1.49)	0.082 (0.75)
Control variables	*Chaebol* dummy		−0.157 (−5.86)	−0.139 (−2.29)	−0.258 (−2.12)
	Ownership × *chaebol*			0.107 (0.74)	−0.050 (−0.13)
	Equity-ratio × *chaebol*			−0.187 (−1.18)	−0.279 (−1.37)
	ln Export				0.002 (0.25)
	Dummy controls	Industry/ Time dummies	Industry/ Time dummies	Industry/ Time dummies	Industry/ Time dummies
	Number of observations	2,853	2,853	2,853	782
	R^2	0.1983	0.2088	0.2095	0.2432

Note
Numbers in parentheses are *t*-values controlling for White's heteroskedasticity.

In addition, we found a significant and negative impact of *chaebol*-affiliation on corporate performance, both directly and also indirectly by affecting the governance variables. Despite many possible *chaebol* advantages, this study shows that *chaebol*-affiliated firms show inferior performance when compared to *non-chaebol* firms in terms of productivity.

The findings of this study must be carefully interpreted within the given Korean context and caution must be exercised in carrying the lesson in other country contexts. The effectiveness of a different corporate governance system is influenced by history, culture and differences in countries' legal and regulatory frameworks, as well as the structure of product and factor markets (Maher and Anderson 1999). That is, the search for good practice should be based on identification of what works within a given country. Unlike many existing studies based on cross-country evidences, this chapter has attempted to draw lessons for Korea's corporate governance reform based on Korean data.

There are, of course, a number of other reasons to be cautious about taking these conclusions too far. For example, our ownership data is limited in that it only accounts for direct ownership by the controlling shareholder. Our results might change if one could get at the "ultimate" ownership data (including indirect ownership via ownership in the affiliates). Also, we have not explored the possibility that the relationship between corporate governance data might be nonlinear or more importantly, endogenous. Corporate performance might determine corporate governance structure.

Notes

1 There are several previous studies of Korea that are related to this issue. For example, Chang and Choi (1988) focus on the impact of transaction costs on firm performance and Chang and Hong (1998) focus on performance consequences of resource sharing among group affiliated firms. Joh (2000) examines the relationship between firm profitability and corporate governance.

2 There is a strong theoretical presumption in both traditional and new growth theories that the main engine of sustained long-run economic growth is productivity growth. The new endogenous growth theories in particular show a number of different ways in which productivity advances can occur: learning by doing, human capital accumulation, R&D. If corporate governance system affects any of these mechanisms, it would be an important factor in determining the rate of technological progress.

3 Other features of governance often emphasized include the market for corporate control and the role of boards of directors.

4 We include a separate *chaebol* dummy variable to test whether the performance of *chaebol* is different from that of independent firms for reasons apart from differences in corporate governance structures. For example, the typical argument is that their ability to diversify risk allows them to be better innovators. On the other hand, there are also strong arguments suggesting that *chaebols*' growth mostly resulted from crony capitalism and had little to do with efficiency. In fact, their excessive diversification into unrelated areas and monopolistic behavior caused *chaebols* to be inefficient and unprofitable.

5 The definition of chaebols can be quite illusive. See Lim (forthcoming). Our definition of *chaebols* simply follows those business groups designated by the Korea Fair Trade

Commission as "Daegumo Guiup Gipdan" (which is literally translated as "big business groups").

6 A study by Zeckhauser and Pound (1990), for example, found that owner-controlled firms outperform manager-controlled firms in industries with relatively low asset specificity (e.g. machinery and paper products) but found no difference in industries with relatively high asset specificity (e.g. computers). Hence there might be some interactive relationships, which also should be explored.

7 Because it is not always possible to identify whether an individual shareholder identified in the NICE data is related to the controlling family, our approach can be considered an upward estimate of the overall controlling family's direct ownership.

8 The approach has been used recently by Aw *et al.* (1998) to estimate the TFP of Taiwanese and Korean plant-level data and this study follows the same methodology to calculate the Korean firm-level TFP estimates.

9 Good *et al.* (1996) provide a detailed discussion on methodology.

10 Among 356 publicly-traded Korean corporations in their sample, Claessens *et al.* (1998) find that less than 4 percent of the firms were controlled by families that own at least 40 percent of the shares, while 20 percent of all firms were controlled by families with less than 30 percent of the shares. Families with at least 10 percent of the total shares controlled more than 67 percent of Korean firms. La Porta *et al.* (1998a) studied a sample of the ten largest nonfinancial corporations from a cross-section of fourty-nine countries and found that the average ownership by the three largest shareholders in Korean corporations was 23 percent, much lower than the ownership concentration of 46 percent found for the whole sample.

11 The estimate is a weighted average by total assets.

12 The minimum ownership requirements for shareholders' rights have been lowered since 1998.

13 Moreover, holding companies were not allowed in Korea until 1998.

14 That is, even though the debt–equity ratio was much higher after the second oil shock, Korea did not face the crisis in the magnitude of the 1997 crisis. Moreover, it is now a well-known fact about the 1997 crisis that the portion of short-term debt in the overall debt portfolio did rise significantly and exposed the Korean corporate sector to term structure risk. But, analytically there is no reason to presume that this change in term structure would lead to fundamental weakness in corporate performance. Our focus, however, is on whether a debt-based corporate governance structure is intrinsically worse than equity-based corporate governance in terms of performance.

15 Joh and Kim (2003), on which much of this chapter is based, also introduced the R&D ratio as control variable. It was found to have a significant and negative impact on productivity in their sample. This puzzling outcome could perhaps be attributed to a specification problem. For example regression (1) in Table 6.5 is in reduced form; we do not specify the precise mechanism through which corporate governance impacts productivity performance. But if ownership and capital structure affect productivity performance by encouraging firm-specific investments such as R&D, then measuring the impact of R&D on firm performance, apart from what is already captured by corporate governance variables, may produce a spurious result. Moreover, a reliable data on the R&D stock is very hard to come by, not alone finding an appropriate price deflator.

Bibliography

Agrawal, A. and Knoeber, C.R. (1996) "Firm performance and mechanisms to control agency problems between managers and shareholders," *Journal of Financial and Quantitative Analysis*, 31(3): 377–98.

Aw, Bee Yan, Chung, Sukkyun and Roberts, M.J. (1998) "Productivity and the decision to export: micro evidence from Taiwan and South Korea," National Bureau of Economic Research Working Paper No. 6558, Cambridge, MA, USA.

Caves, Douglas W., Laurits R. Christensen and Erwin W. Diewert (1982) "Multilateral comparisons of output, input, and productivity using superlative index numbers," *The Economic Journal*, 92: 73–86.

Chang, H.J., Hong-Jae Park and Chu Gyue Yoo (1998) "Interpreting the Korean crisis: financial liberalization, industrial policy, and corporate governance," *Cambridge Journal of Economics*, 22(2): 735–46.

Chang, Sejin and Choi, Unghwan (1988) "Strategy, structure and performance of Korean business groups: a transactions cost approach," *Journal of Industrial Economics*, 37(2): 141–58.

—— and Jaebum Hong (1998) "Economic performance of the Korean business groups: intra-group resource sharing and internal business transaction," mimeo.

Claessens, J., Fan, P.H. and Lang, L. (1998) "Ownership structure and corporate performance in East Asia," mimeo, the World Bank.

Cho, M.H. (1998) "Ownership structure, investment and the corporate value: an empirical analysis," *Journal of Financial Economics*, 47: 103–21.

Demsetz, H. and Ricardo-Campbell, R. (1983) "The structure of ownership and the theory of the firm," *Journal of Law and Economics*, 26: 375–90.

Edwards, S. (1998) "Openness, productivity and growth: what do we really know?," *The Economic Journal*, 108: 383–98.

Gale, Bradley T. (1972) "Market share and rate-of-return," *The Review of Economics and Statistics*, 54(4): 412–23.

Good, D.H., Nadiri, M.I. and Sickles, R.C. (1996) "Index number and factor demand approaches to the estimation of productivity," NBER Working Paper No. 5790.

Grossman, S. and Hart, O. (1986) "The costs and benefits of ownership: a theory of vertical and lateral integration," *Journal of Political Economy*, 94: 169–79.

—— and Maskin, E. (1983) "Implicit contracts under asymmetric information," *The Quarterly Journal of Economics*, 98: 123–96.

Gugler, K. (1999) "Corporate governance and economic performance: a survey," mimeo, University of Vienna, Austria.

Haggard, Stephan and Euysung Kim (1997) "The source of East Asia's economic growth," *Access Asia Review*, 1(1): 31–63.

Hahm, Joon-Ho (2003) "The government, chaebol and financial institutions in pre-crisis Korea" in Haggard *et al.* (eds), *Economic Crisis and Corporate Restructuring in Korea: Reforming the Chaebol*, Cambridge: Cambridge University Press.

Jensen, M. (1986) "Agency costs of free cash flow, corporate finance and takeovers," *American Economic Review*, 76(2): 323–9.

—— (1988) "The takeover controversy: analysis and evidence" in J. Coffee, L. Lowenstein and S. Rose-Ackerman (eds), *Knights, Raiders, and Targets: The Impact of the Hostile Takeover*, New York: Oxford University Press.

Joh, Sung Wook (1999) "The Korean corporate sector: crisis and reform," Working Paper, Seoul: Korea Development Institute.

—— (2000) "Does shareholder conflict reduce profitability? evidence from Korea," in Shin (ed.), *The Korean Crisis: Before and After*, Seoul: Korea Development Institute.

Joh, Sung Wook and Euysung Kim (2003) "Corporate Governance and Performance of Korean Firms in the 1990s" in Haggard *et al.* (eds), *Economic Crisis and Corporate Restructuring in Korea: Reforming the Chaebol*. Cambridge: Cambridge University Press.

Kim, Euysung (2000) "Trade liberalization and productivity growth in Korean manufacturing industries: price protection, market power, and scale efficiency," *Journal of Development Economics*, 62: 55–83.

La Porta, Rafael, Florencio Lopez-de-Silanes, Andrei Shleifer and Robert W. Vishny (1998a). "Law and finance," *The Journal of Political Economy*, 106: 1113–55.

——(1998b) "Agency problems and dividend policies around the world," mimeo, Harvard University.

Lee, Jong-Wha, Young Soo Lee and Byung-Sun Lee (1999) "The determinants of corporate dept in Korea," Harvard Center for International Development working paper.

Lee, Young-Ki (1995) "Corporate governance: the structure and issues in Korea," mimeo, Seoul: Korea Development Institute.

Leech, D. and Leahy, J. (1991) "Ownership structure, control type classifications and the performance of large British companies," *Economic Journal*, 101(6): 1418–37.

Leff, N. (1978) "Industrial organization and entrepreneurship in the developing countries: the economic group," *Economic Development and Cultural Change*, 26: 661–75.

Lim, Wonhyuk (2003) "The emergence of the chaebol and the origins of 'the chaebol problem'" in Haggard *et al.* (eds), *Economic Crisis and Corporate Restructuring in Korea: Reforming the Chaebol*, Cambridge: Cambridge University Press.

Maher, M.E. (1997) "Transaction cost economics and contractual relations," *Cambridge Journal of Economics*, 12: 219–29.

——and Anderson, T. (1999) "Corporate governance: effects on firm performance and economic growth," *OECD.*

Martin, S. (1993) *Advanced Industrial Economics*, Cambridge: Blackwell.

Mayer, C. (1996) "Corporate governance, competition and performance," OECD, *Economic Studies*, 27: 7–34.

Modigliani, F. and Miller, M.H. (1958) "The cost of capital, corporation finance, and the theory of investments," *American Economic Review*, 48: 261–97.

Morck, Randall, Shleifer, A. and Vishny, R.W. (1988) "Management ownership and market valuation: an empirical analysis," *Journal of Financial Economics*, 20: 293–316.

Nam, S.W. (1979) "Hankook Kiupui Chaemoo Koojowa Chabon Cost [Financial structure and capital cost of Korean companies]" Hankook Gaebal Yunkoo (KDI).

Prowse, S.D. (1992) "The structure of corporate ownership in Japan," *Journal of Finance*, 47(3): 1121–40.

——(1994) "Corporate governance in international perspective: a survey of corporate control mechanisms among large firms in the United States, the United Kingdom, Japan and Germany," BIS Economic Paper No. 41.

Rajan, Raghuram G. and Luigi Zingales (1998) "Financial dependence and growth," *The American Economic Review*, 88(3): 559–86.

Randlesome, C. and Myers, A. (1998) "Cultural fluency: the United Kingdom versus Denmark," *European Business Journal*, 4th Quarter, 10(4): 184–95.

Shinn, J. (1999) "Bringing the state back in to the boardroom: corporate governance convergence in Japan and Korea?," mimeo, Princeton University.

Shleifer, A. and Vishny, R. (1986) "Large shareholders and corporate control," *The Journal of Political Economy*, 94: 461–88.

——(1997) "A survey of corporate governance," *Journal of Finance*, 52(2): 737–83.

Stulz, R.M. (1990) "Managerial discretion and optimal financing policies," *Journal of Financial Economics*, 26: 3–27.

Von Thadden, E. (1995) "Long-term contracts, short-term investment and monitoring," *Review of Economic Studies*, 62: 557–75.

Williamson, O.E. (1975) *Markets and Hierarchies*, New York: Macmillan.
——(1985) *The Economic Institutions of Capitalism*, New York: The Free Press.
——(1988) "Corporate finance and corporate governance," *Journal of Finance*, 45: 567–91.
Zeckhauser, R. and Pound, J. (1990) "Are large shareholders effective monitors? An investigation of share ownership and corporate performance," in R. Hubbard (ed.), *Asymmetric Information, Corporate Finance and Investment*, University of Chicago Press.

7 Financial reporting of selected Korean listed companies

Disclosure practices

Youngok Kim[1]

7.1 Introduction

The importance of corporate disclosure practices has been increasing with the internationalization of capital markets and business activities (Saudagaran and Biddle 1992, Wallace and Nasser 1995). Their significance is well reflected in the recent revision of the Korean Financial Accounting Standards (KFAS hereafter) that occurred in South Korea (Korea hereafter), following the country's 1997 economic crisis. The current KFAS particularly stresses the importance of comparable and reliable financial statements produced by Korean companies in raising capital on both domestic and international capital markets (KFAS 1998).

This chapter attempts to provide empirical evidence regarding the state of corporate disclosure practices prior to the country's 1997 crisis. In particular, it examines the relationship between various firm-specific characteristics and the extent of financial disclosure. To achieve this objective, a disclosure checklist is developed based on the KFAS and KFAS Working Rules effective as of December 1994 and a list of company-specific variables is drawn from significant prior research on disclosure practices.

The chapter begins with a review of prior research on disclosure practices, from which a series of hypotheses are developed. It further discusses approaches to sample selection and data sources, measurement of variables, and statistical tests used to test the hypothesized relationships. Then it provides major limitations of the study, followed by conclusion with suggestions for further research.

7.2 Literature review and hypotheses development

This section provides a review of major literature on corporate disclosure practices by focusing on single-country studies that relate the extent of disclosure to company-specific factors within a country. However, this study also incorporates some relevant findings of comparative studies to the Korean context.

7.2.1 Prior research

As indicated in Table 7.1, the explanatory variables tested include: size (assets, sales, or other similar measures), listing status, industry type, profitability, financial

Table 7.1 Studies on corporate disclosure practices using disclosure indices

Author	*Data used*	*Method*	*Factors*	*Results*
Cerf (1961): USA	Annual reports 527 firms Financial analysts	Class means Least squares regression	Size (total assets) No. of share-holders Profitability (net income/net worth) Listing status	Positive Positive Positive Mixed
Singhvi and Desai (1971: USA)	Annual reports 155 firms Financial analysts	Chi-square regression	Size (total assets) No. of share-holders Profitability Return on S.E.^ Earnings margin Listing status Audit firm size	Positive, not sig. Positive, not sig. Positive, not sig. Positive, signif.* Positive, signif.** Positive, not sig.
Buzby (1975: USA)	Annual reports 88 firms Financial analysts	Kendall rank corr. Wilcoxon matched-pairs, signed-ranks test	Size (total assets) Listing status	Positive, signif.** No effect
Stanga (1976: USA)	Annual reports 80 firms Financial analysts	Regression	Size (net sales) Industry	Positive, not sig. Effect, signif.**
Belkaoui and Kahl (1978: Canada)	Annual reports 200 firms Char. accountants Financial analysts	Kendall rank corr.	Size Total assets Net sales Profitability Liquidity Capitalization ratio Industry	 Positive, signif.** Positive, signif.** Negative, signif.** Positive, signif.** Negative, signif.** Effect
Firth (1979: UK)	Annual reports 180 firms Financial analysts	Kendall rank corr.	Size (sales + capital) Listing status Audit firm size	Positive, signif.** Positive, signif.** No effect
Chow/Wong-Boren (1987: Mexico)	Annual reports 52 firms Loan officers of banks	Regression	Size (equity + debt) Leverage Fixed assets ratio	Positive, signif.** Positive, not sig. Positive, not sig.
Ilace (1988: Nigeria)	Annual reports 47 firms No specific focus	Regression	Foreign equity	Positive, signif.**
Cooke (1989: Sweden)	Annual reports 90 firms No specific focus	Regression	Listing status Size Total assets Net sales No. of share-holders Parent company	Positive, signif.** Positive, signif.** Positive, signif.** Positive, signif.** Positive, not sig.

(*continued*)

Table 7.1 (Continued)

Author	*Data used*	*Method*	*Factors*	*Results*
Cooke (1992: Sweden)	Annual reports 35 firms No specific focus	Factor analysis regression	Size (8 variables)	Positive, signif.**
			Listing status	Positive, signif.**
			Industry	Significant
Ahmed/Nicholls (1994: Bangladesh)	Annual reports 63 firms No specific focus	Regression (stepwise)	Size (assets or sales)	Mixed, not sig.
			Total debt	Positive, not sig.
			Multinational owner	Positive, signif.**
			Accounting officer qualification	Positive, signif.*
			Audit firm size	Positive, signif.**
Diga (1995: ASEAN)	Annual reports 145 firms No specific focus	Kruskal–Wallis ANOVA Principal component regression	Size (assets or sales)	Positive, signif.**
			Leverage	Positive, not sig.
			Industry	Signif.**
			Ownership	Signif. for foreign-owned**
			Country of origin	Signif.**

Notes
* Significant at a range of between 0.05 and 0.10.
** Significant at a conventional level (i.e. $p \leq 0.05$).
^ Denotes shareholders' equity.

leverage, financial liquidity, size of auditing firm, foreign ownership, and country of origin. While a disclosure checklist and weighting systems based on the opinions of financial analysts were used in earlier studies, no specific user group was employed in later studies (e.g. Wallace 1988, Cooke 1989, 1992, Ahmed and Nicholls 1994, Diga 1995). This discrepancy in measuring instruments appears to limit a strict comparison of the findings of these studies.

Despite comparison difficulties, the prior studies highlight the importance of some company characteristics in explaining the levels of disclosure, with size and listing status being consistently the most powerful variables in companies of different nationalities. However, mixed evidence on the effects of other variables on disclosure practices pose an obstacle to the development of a contingency framework that would explain the theoretical linkages between company-specific variables and reporting practices within a country. Nonetheless, coupled with comparative studies on disclosure practices, findings from these single-country studies are potentially useful in uncovering the basis for the "contingent" relationships.

7.2.2 Hypotheses development

Among the several variables tested in prior studies, the following variables are viewed most relevant in the context of the Korean business environment. They include: size (measured in terms of total assets, sales turnover, and number of employees), profitability (i.e. net income to net worth; net income to net sales; ordinary income to total assets) and degree of financial leverage (i.e. debt to equity). In addition, two new variables are included in this study: affiliation with *chaebols*[2] given the increasing regulatory and public attention to the power of *chaebols* in Korea and affiliation with any of the multinational "Big-Six"[3] audit firms because of the unavailability of audit firm size. The following is a discussion of the relevance of each independent variable included in this study to Korea's particular business environment.

7.2.2.1 Affiliation with chaebols

As discussed earlier, big business groups called *chaebols* have been increasingly exposed to the attention and scrutiny of the public and regulatory bodies in Korea because of their rapidly growing political and economic power, particularly since the early 1980s. This attention has led to calls for more stringent financial reporting requirements for *chaebols*. To reduce political costs arising from potential adverse regulatory action (Watts and Zimmerman 1978), *chaebols* are most likely to endeavor to improve their disclosure practices. Based on this argument, the following hypothesis is developed.

H1: There is a difference in disclosure level between chaebol *companies and* non-chaebol *companies.* Chaebol *companies are expected to disclose more than* non-chaebol *companies.*

7.2.2.2 Size

Size was found to be positively associated with the extent of disclosure in various studies (Cerf 1961, Buzby 1975, Belkaoui and Kahl 1978, Firth 1979, Chow and Wong-Boren 1987, Cooke 1989, 1992, Diga 1995). This significant positive relationship between size and disclosure level can be explained in numerous ways, which are discussed next.

One plausible reason is that large firms, in general, have resources and expertise to produce and disseminate more sophisticated financial information for their internal management purposes. In addition, management of large corporations is likely to realize the benefits of quality disclosure, especially in raising capital. In contrast, smaller firms generally lack both resources and expertise to produce sophisticated information and, more importantly, feel more than larger firms that their competitive position might be threatened by disclosing quality information. Second, agency costs theory may provide another explanation because managers of larger firms tend to increase their disclosure level in an attempt to reduce agency costs that increase with the size of firms and are ultimately borne by them (Chow and Wong-Boren 1987). Finally, political costs theorists would assert that larger firms tend to disclose more information because they are more subject to adverse government control or regulation (Watts and Zimmerman 1978). On the basis of these arguments, the following hypothesis is proposed:

H2: There is a positive association between the extent of disclosure and firm size.

7.2.2.3 *Profitability*

Profitable companies are expected to have higher disclosure levels because they may want to be differentiated from poorly performing firms through disclosing more. When a company is profitable, managers may disclose more detailed information in order to support the continuance of their positions and compensation arrangements, especially in a competitive labor–market environment. In addition, minimization of political costs may be applicable in a sense that profitable firms, in general, tend to attract more public and regulatory attention than poorly performing firms. The following hypothesis is, therefore, proposed:

H3: There is a positive association between the extent of disclosure and profitability.

7.2.2.4 *Financial leverage*

Studies of the relationship of financial leverage (i.e. debt to equity) with the extent of disclosure have shown mixed results (Belkaoui and Kahl 1978, Chow and Wong-Boren 1987). Despite these conflicting results, a company with a higher leverage ratio is expected to disclose more to provide greater assurance about its ability to pay. However, this expectation needs to be refined in a country's particular business environment. In Korea, for example, firms with higher leverage ratios have been traditionally viewed as safer companies because the Korean government has guaranteed most of their corporate debt. For this reason, high-debt Korean firms may not feel the need for disclosing sophisticated quality information to the public. However, these government guarantees are not as relevant to the current business environment of Korea as they used to be in the 1960s and 1970s. Therefore, it is expected that firms with high financial leverage disclosure are likely to disclose more than firms with low leverage in an attempt to signal their ability to pay. The following hypothesis has been developed:

H4: There is a positive association between leverage and extent of disclosure.

7.2.2.5 *Affiliation with Big-Six accounting firms*

The primary responsibility for preparing annual reports rests with company directors. However, auditors of the companies may significantly affect the quality of information disclosed in those annual reports (Singhvi and Desai 1971, Firth 1979, Ahmed and Nicholls 1994). It may be argued that larger and better-recognized accounting firms (e.g. multinational accounting firms) as auditors may exercise greater influence on companies' disclosure levels. In the early 1980s, with the enactment of the External Audit Law (EAL), the Korean government changed the audit environment from government-directed allocation to market-based competition. Coporatization of audit firms and their affiliation with multinational audit firms has since become a common feature in Korea as an important way of enhancing audit independence and quality and ultimately disclosure practices of Korean firms. Accordingly, whether a firm's Korean audit firm is affiliated with the Big-Six or not has become important in determining the quality of information provided by Korean firms being audited. The following hypothesis has thus been proposed:

H5: There is a positive relationship between affiliation with Big-Six multinational accounting firms and disclosure level.

7.3 Research design

7.3.1 Sample selection and data sources

Out of the total of 699 companies listed on the Korean Stock Exchange as of December 31, 1994, twenty-eight *chaebol*[4] and thirty-three *non-chaebol* companies were selected (Table 7.2). As an important source of financial information (Baker and Haslem 1973, Chang and Most 1981), audited financial statements with notes for the fiscal year ended December 31, 1994 were investigated because of their comprehensiveness in providing financial information.

7.3.2 Operationalization of variables

7.3.2.1 Dependent variable-disclosure level

This study focuses on the financial disclosure level that is measured by constructing a disclosure checklist. The disclosure checklist is based on the KFAS and KFAS Working Rules effective as of December 31, 1994. Disclosure requirements of Korean listed companies are also influenced by various other legislation, namely the Commercial Code (CC), the Securities and Exchange Law (SEL), and the EAL. Among them, however, the KFAS and KFAS Working Rules most comprehensively prescribe financial disclosure requirements that need to be provided in audited reports.

Instead of selecting disclosure items subjectively, the disclosure requirements mandated by the KFAS and KFAS Working Rules were used for construction of a disclosure checklist. The total of 338 disclosure items[5] is classified into thirty-nine groups, as shown in Table 7.3.

Following Wallace (1988), Cooke (1989, 1992), and Diga (1995), each item was scored in a dichotomous way; that is, one if disclosed and zero if not disclosed in the financial statements with notes and supplementary schedules included in the audited reports. The aggregate disclosure level was then computed by adding all individual scores.

Table 7.2 Distribution of firms – *chaebol* vs *non-chaebol*

	Chaebol	Non-chaebol
1	Asia Automobile	Chongkeun Dang
2	Daerim Yo Up	Chosun Naewha
3	Daewoo Chungmil	Chungsan
4	Dongkook Jekang	Daehan Joongsuk
5	Dongyang Cement	Daewoo Keumsok
6	Dongyang Jekwa	Dongsuh Sanup
7	Dongyang Maekjoo	Dongsung Hwahak
8	Dongyang Nylon	Hanchang
9	Doosan Yuri	Handok Pharmaceuticals
10	Goldstar	Hankook Cosmetics
11	Hanhwa Energy	Hankook Koa
12	Hyundai Kangkwan	Heungchang
13	Hyundai Mokjae	Jinwoong
14	Jeil Mojik	Kabul
15	Kia Teuksookang	Keukdong Jehyuk
16	Kohap Sangsa	Kunsul hwahak
17	Kolon	Kwangdong
18	Kookje Junsun	Kyeyang Electric
19	Kumho	Kyemongsa
20	Kumho Petroleum	Kyungnong
21	Lotte Samkang	Maxon
22	Mando Kikye	Namsun Aluminium
23	Miwon	Paekkwang Sanup
24	Sammi	Pyunghwa Sanup
25	Samsung Junkwan	Samrip
26	Samsung Jungmil	Sepoong
27	Ssangyong Yanghoe	Sewon
28	Yukong	Suhkwang
29		Suhtong
30		Taeil Jungmil
31		Woongjin
32		Youngwon
33		Yuhwa

The disclosure items were not weighted because of a number of methodological problems associated with the weighting system, such as scaling problems and scoring bias. More importantly, this study examines general-purpose financial statements which are prepared to provide information to a diversity of user groups. Equal weighting to disclosure items was also supported by prior research (e.g. Firth 1979, Chow and Wong-Boren 1987, Wallace 1988, Cooke 1989, 1992, Ahmed and Nicholls 1994, Diga 1995). The unweighted index permits analysis independent of perceptions of a particular user group (Chow and Wong-Boren 1987: 536) and allows an evaluation of financial statements in a 'general-purpose' context because all disclosure items are treated as equally important to the average user.

Table 7.3 Disclosure requirements checklist* – KFAS and KFAS Working Rules (1994)

1	General disclosures**	21	Appropriations
2	Supplementary schedules**	22	Dispositions
3	Cash	23	Leases
4	Marketable securities	24	Accounting changes
5	Receivable-current	25	Prior period adjustment
6	Inventories	26	Transactions with related parties
7	Other current assets	27	Contingencies
8	Investments (long-term)	28	Post balance sheet events
9	Other investments (long-term)	29	Revenue recognition
10	Tangible fixed assets	30	Extraordinary or unusual items
11	Intangible fixed assets	31	Segment reporting
12	Research and development costs	32	Business combinations
13	Deferred charges	33	Foreign currency translations
14	Current liabilities	34	Earnings per share
15	Long-term liabilities	35	Severance and retirement benefits
16	Capital stock	36	Income taxes
17	Capital surplus	37	Asset revaluation
18	Retained earnings (or deficits)	38	Insurance coverage
19	Capital adjusting accounts	39	Cash flow statement
20	Income statement		

Notes

* The thirty-nine groups contain all the disclosure requirements (i.e. 338 items), excluding items on consolidation.

** Relate to broad disclosure requirements, while the others (3–39) are requirements on specific accounts.

Every mandatory requirement was considered relevant to each company in this study because it was extremely difficult to determine the applicability of each disclosure item to a company based on financial statements and their footnotes only. The assumption that all disclosure items are equally relevant to the sample companies may be justified by the fact that all the companies in the sample are listed manufacturing companies.

The scores were not converted into an index (i.e. ratio of actual score to total possible score) because of the same problems raised by Ahmed (1993) and Ahmed and Nicholls (1994). Constraints on using the ordinary least square (OLS) regression thus do not exist in this study.

7.3.2.2 *Independent variables*

7.3.2.2.1 AFFILIATION WITH CHAEBOLS (H1)

The affiliation with *chaebols* was treated as a dichotomous variable. Companies from *chaebol* groups were assigned one, while companies from *non-chaebol* groups were assigned zero.

7.3.2.2.2 SIZE (H2)

The literature has indicated that various measures were used as proxies for size. They include total assets, sales turnover, shareholders' equity, and number of shareholders. The problem of using these accounting numbers is noted because of the availability of alternative asset valuation methods or revenue recognition methods in different countries (Diga 1995). However, this problem does not appear to be of major concern in this study because the study investigates firms within a country. Among these various measures, total assets, sales turnover, and the number of employees are thus used as three important measures of size in the current study.

7.3.2.2.3 PROFITABILITY (H3)

Profitability can be measured in a number of different ways. Rate of return (i.e. net profit to net worth) and earnings margin (i.e. net profit to net sales) were used in several studies (e.g. Cerf 1961, Singhvi 1968, Singhvi and Desai 1971, Belkaoui and Kahl 1978). In addition to these two variables, another profitability variable, ordinary income to total assets, was included in this study. Because of potential multicollinearity among these three profitability variables, stepwise regression was employed to include the most powerful explanatory profitability variable in the final model. Profitability in the final regression model was measured by a company's net income-to-net sales ratio.

7.3.2.2.4 LEVERAGE (H4)

The degree of leverage was measured by a company's debt-to-equity ratio (DE ratio). It is the proportion of total book liabilities to total shareholders' equity.

7.3.2.2.5 AFFILIATION WITH THE BIG-SIX (H5)

Companies whose audit firms were affiliated with the Big-Six multinational accounting firms were assigned one, while the companies not affiliated with the Big-Six were assigned zero.

7.3.3 Statistical methods

7.3.3.1 Univariate tests for group differences

Both non-parametric and parametric tests were used to test whether statistically significant differences in *chaebol* and *non-chaebol* companies exist in terms of their disclosure scores and continuous independent variables, namely total assets, sales, number of employees, profitability, and leverage.

Table 7.4 Pairwise Pearson correlation coefficients among dependent and continuous explanatory variables

	Scores (ln)	*Assets* (ln)	*Sales* (ln)	*Employees* (ln)	*Leverage* (ln)	*Profit2* (ln)
Scores (ln)	1.0000					
Assets (ln)	0.6313**	1.0000				
Sales (ln)	0.5756**	0.9297**	1.0000			
Employees (ln)	0.5800**	0.8379**	0.8101**	1.0000		
Leverage (ln)	0.2775*	0.3338**	0.3609**	0.2934*	1.000	
Profit2 (ln)***	0.2728*	0.0640	−0.0202	0.0637	−0.2780*	1.0000
VIF^		10.0370	8.1420	3.8580	1.7830	1.2600
Tol.^^		0.0996	0.1228	0.2592	0.5610	0.7936

Notes
* Significant at or below 0.05 (two-tailed).
** Significant at or below 0.01 (two-tailed).
*** Profit2 denotes net income to net sales.
^ Variance inflation factor.
^^ Tolerance level.

7.3.3.2 *Multivariate tests*

In order to determine the impact of multiple company characteristics on the disclosure level of individual companies, multiple regression analysis was used because the relationship between the dependent variable and a number of independent variables is of a multiplicative nature. OLS regression was then applied to a new model that was generated by taking natural logs of the initial multiplicative model. Before applying statistical tests on the multiple regression model, diagnostic tests were conducted to determine if all the assumptions underlying the regression model held. The tests were multicollinearity, non-constant variance of residuals (i.e. heteroscedasticity), non-normal distribution of residuals, outliers, or influential observations.

Multicollinearity among continuous explanatory variables was detected by correlations, variance inflation factors (VIF), and tolerance (Weisberg 1985: 196–200, Maddala 1992: 274–6). Table 7.4 presents the correlation matrix among the log-transformed dependent and continuous explanatory variables, including VIFs and tolerance level of each explanatory variable.

Statistically significant correlation between the dependent and individual explanatory variables provides an overall evidence of relationship among them. In particular, as anticipated, potential size variables (assets, sales, and number of employees) were found to be highly correlated (r = more than 80 percent).

Even though multicollinearity may not be a problem as discussed in Maddala (1992: 269–70), various methods have been applied in prior studies to address the problems that multicollinearity poses. They include factor analysis, principal components analysis, stepwise regression, and ridge regression. Cooke (1989, 1991) and Ahmed and Nicholls (1994) used stepwise regression by including each of the highly correlated variables separately in the proposed model until they found the model providing the greatest explanatory power. However, with this method, the explanatory power of variables dropped from the final model may be lost, especially when the correlation is not perfect (Diga 1995). To minimize the loss of explanatory power of original variables, Cooke (1992) and Diga (1995) employed factor analysis and principal components analysis, respectively.

There is "no overwhelming theoretical reason to prefer one size variable to another because each variable may contain an interesting and possibly unique aspect of size" (Cooke 1992: 532). Instead of dropping variables used in the stepwise regression, therefore, this study used the principal components analysis (PCA) which decomposes the information content inherent in the original size variables into information about an inherent set of meaningful factors (Aczel 1993: 804). PCA maintains the information content in the original variables while removing the multicollinearity problem.

Prior to performing the analysis, other diagnostics of multicollinearity were also employed to determine whether the leverage ratio (i.e. debt to equity) should be included in the size variable. The VIF for leverage was very low (VIF = 1.783), which means that the correlation between leverage and any of the remaining explanatory variables is very low (*n.b.* VIF = 1 means that the variable is not collinear with any of the remaining explanatory variables). In addition, the tolerance level for leverage was comparatively high (Tol. = 0.561006) showing that the variable is not correlated significantly with any of the remaining explanatory variables (*n.b.* tolerance = 1 means that the variable has no correlation with any of the remaining variables at all).

Principal component analysis was applied to the above size variables (i.e. total assets, sales, and number of employees) by following three steps. Initially, the Bartlett's test of sphericity was undertaken to test the hypothesis that the correlation matrix of the five variables is an identity matrix. The test statistic of 180.9 is significant at less than 0.01, which provides statistical justification for the use of PCA.

Second, preliminary (initial) components were extracted by principal components analysis, which also computes both eigenvalues and percentage of variance explained by each component. Any components with an eigenvalue less than 0.7, as discussed in Jolliffe (1972) and Diga (1995), were not used in this study. Only the first component satisfies this condition, as shown in Table 7.5.

Table 7.5 shows that the three size variables load highly on the first component which accounts for approximately 90.6 percent of the variance of the original variables. All the three new variables (components) account for all the variance of the original variables; however, the application of all the three variables may not guarantee better coefficient estimates in the original regression model and may also lack parsimony (Aczel 1993: 806).

Third, factor loadings between the first component and the original variables were computed by varimax rotation which is designed to find the best distribution of the factor loadings in terms of the meaning of the factors (Aczel 1993: 808).

Table 7.5 Principal components analysis

Factors	*Eigenvalue*	*% Variation explained*	*Cumulative % variation*
First p.c.	2.71882	90.6	90.6
Second p.c.	0.21179	7.1	97.7
Third p.c.	0.06939	2.3	100

Table 7.6 Factor loadings of original variables

Variable	*First p.c.*
Assets (ln)	0.96988
Sales (ln)	0.96015
Employ (ln)	0.92535

Only one component was found to be meaningful in explaining the original variables. They are shown in Table 7.6.

The factor loadings represent correlations between the principal component and the original variables. The new size variable was computed by a regression method (Norusis 1993). Thus, the first principal component could be interpreted as the latent variable that incorporates the effects of the original three collinear size variables.

The multiple regression model incorporating this new size variable is as follows:

$$D = c + a_1 S + b_1 P + c_1 L + \sum_{i=1}^{1} x_i A_i + \sum_{i=1}^{1} y_i B_i + \varepsilon \tag{7.1}$$

where D = disclosure level (ln); S = new size measures derived using PCA (ln); P = profitability measured by net income-to-net sales ratio (ln); L = leverage measured by the debt-to-equity ratio (ln). A_i = affiliation with *chaebols*; 0 = *non-chaebol* companies (default level); and 1 = *chaebol* companies. B_i = affiliation with Big-Six accounting firms; 0 = not affiliated with Big-Six; and 1 = affiliated with Big-Six. c, a_1, b_1, c_1, x_i, y_i = coefficients to be estimated; ε = stochastic error term which is part of disclosure level not explained by the explanatory variables in the model.

7.4 Results and discussion

7.4.1 Descriptive statistics

Descriptive statistics for the untransformed dependent and explanatory variables are provided in Table 7.7. Results show that skewness and kurtosis are significant for all variables, except for disclosure scores and profitability (i.e. profit1). Frequency histograms also support high skewness and kurtosis. Data transformation using natural logs was made because the range of values is dispersed widely.

The descriptive statistics for the log-transformed variables are presented in Table 7.8. Table 7.8 indicates that both kurtosis and skewness of the log-transformed

Table 7.7 Descriptive statistics of dependent and explanatory variables (untransformed variables)

Parameter	*Minimum*	*Maximum*	*Mean*	*Standard deviation*	*Skewness*	*Kurtosis*
Disclosure scores						
All groups	159	220	185.557	12.820	0.299	0.502
Chaebol	170	220	191.821	12.614	0.488	0.030
Non-chaebol	159	200	180.242	10.509	−0.409	−0.498
Assets*						
All groups	21,431,812	6,453,272,480	614,981,269	1,053,727,433	3.834	17.589
Chaebol	98,688,506	6,453,272,480	1,164,951,629	1,369,808,144	2.728	8.532
Non-chaebol	21,431,812	391,720,334	148,339,752	97,372,271	0.923	0.241
Sales*						
All groups	24,619,506	5,865,699,176	508,912,940	1,007,273,317	4.294	19.948
Chaebol	35,499,530	5,865,699,176	974,107,588	1,354,483,686	2.968	8.740
Non-chaebol	24,619,506	284,916,172	114,202,329	66,241,861	0.686	−0.238
No. of employees						
All groups	131	30,621	2,495	4,352	5.021	30.648
Chaebol	411	30,621	4,24.2	5,849	3.662	15.94
Non-chaebol	131	2,714	918	638	0.835	0.453
Leverage (%)						
All groups	53.1	1,067.2	288.810	205.554	2.079	5.351
Chaebol	53.1	1,054.0	343.826	217.917	1.641	3.254
Non-chaebol	63.7	1,067.2	242.131	185.096	2.952	11.963

(*continued*)

Table 7.7 (Continued)

Parameter	*Minimum*	*Maximum*	*Mean*	*Standard deviation*	*Skewness*	*Kurtosis*
Profit1 (%)**						
All groups	−5.8	11.5	2.393	3.665	0.150	0.408
Chaebol	−5.8	7.0	1.668	3.421	−0.310	0.118
Non-chaebol	−5.1	11.5	3.007	3.804	0.348	0.342
Profit2 (%)***						
All groups	−13.1	11.5	2.310	3.703	−0.895	5.498
Chaebol	−13.1	11.2	1.910	4.169	−1.466	6.339
Non-chaebol	−7.2	11.5	2.648	3.284	0.222	3.085
Profit (%)****						
All groups	−28.4	42.9	6.799	11.397	0.494	3.442
Chaebol	−28.4	42.9	7.495	14.386	0.286	2.197
Non-chaebol	−13.7	32.9	6.208	8.255	0.784	3.563

Notes

* In Korean currency, *won* (000s).

** Profit1 denotes ordinary profit to total assets.

*** Profit2 denotes net profit to net sales.

**** Profit denotes net profit to net worth.

Table 7.8 Descriptive statistics of dependent and explanatory variables (log-transformed variables)

Parameter	*Minimum*	*Maximum*	*Mean*	*Standard deviation*	*Skewness*	*Kurtosis*
Disclosure scores						
All groups	5.07	5.39	5.221	0.069	0.065	0.326
Chaebol	5.14	5.39	5.255	0.065	0.323	−0.073
Non-chaebol	5.07	5.30	5.193	0.059	−0.427	−0.521
Assets*						
All groups	16.88	22.59	19.406	1.253	0.400	−0.284
Chaebol	18.41	22.59	20.372	1.040	0.004	−0.384
Non-chaebol	16.88	19.79	18.587	0.724	−0.145	−0.419
Sales*						
All groups	17.02	22.49	19.175	1.230	0.577	0.076
Chaebol	17.39	22.49	20.121	1.078	0.017	0.915
Non-chaebol	17.02	19.47	18.373	0.638	−0.749	−0.322
No. of employees						
All groups	4.88	10.33	7.135	1.135	0.238	0.168
Chaebol	6.02	10.33	7.802	1.048	0.229	−0.244
Non-chaebol	4.88	7.91	6.533	0.845	−0.686	−0.541
Leverage (%)						
All groups	3.97	6.97	5.462	0.643	0.015	0.071
Chaebol	3.97	6.96	5.661	0.630	−0.450	1.234
Non-chaebol	4.15	6.97	5.293	0.612	0.386	0.331
Profit1 (%)**						
All groups	−2.30	2.44	0.654	1.217	−0.657	−0.380
Chaebol	−2.04	1.95	0.441	1.188	−0.448	−0.607
Non-chaebol	−2.30	2.44	0.830	1.233	−0.923	0.220
Profit2 (%)***						
All groups	−1.90	2.44	0.666	0.995	−0.443	−0.160
Chaebol	−1.51	2.41	0.604	0.981	−0.220	−0.500
Non-chaebol	−1.90	2.44	0.717	1.020	−0.645	0.337
Profit (%)****						
All groups	−0.80	3.76	1.675	0.999	−0.071	0.014
Chaebol	−0.80	3.76	1.723	1.142	−0.170	0.100
Non-chaebol	−0.12	3.49	1.635	0.879	0.006	−0.393

Notes

* In Korean currency, won (000s).

** Profit1 denotes ordinary profit to total assets.

*** Profit2 denotes net profit to net sales.

**** Profit denotes net profit to net worth.

variables are much smaller than those of the untransformed variables. Histograms of log-transformed variables also approximate normal distribution. The normality distribution of the variables implies that parametric tests can also be used to analyze those variables.

Table 7.9 Results of Mann–Whitney U test for group differences (untransformed)

Variable	*Mean ranks*		*Z-statistic*	*p-value*
	Chaebol ($n = 28$)	Non-chaebol ($n = 33$)		
Disclosure scores	39.41	23.86	−3.4132	0.0006**
Assets	44.89	19.21	−5.6300	0.0000**
Sales	45.29	18.88	−5.7892	0.0000**
Employees	39.88	21.08	−4.1972	0.0000**
Leverage	37.04	25.88	−2.4459	0.0144*
Profit1^	28.30	33.29	−1.0927	0.2745
Profit2^^	29.61	32.18	−0.5645	0.5724
Profit^^^	31.36	30.70	−0.1447	0.8849

Notes

* Significant at $p \leq 0.05$ (two-tailed).
** Significant at $p \leq 0.01$ (two-tailed).
^ Denotes ordinary profit to total assets.
^^ Denotes net profit to net sales.
^^^ Denotes net profit to net worth.

7.4.2 *Univariate tests*

The untransformed variables were used for the non-parametric Mann–Whitney U test. Results of this test are provided in Table 7.9.

The results support the existence of highly statistically significant (at $p \leq 0.01$) differences between *chaebol* and *non-chaebol* companies in Korea in terms of all the variables except profitability variables. *Chaebol* companies tend to rank much higher than *non-chaebol* companies, in particular, in assets, sales, and number of employees. Z-scores are used because of larger sample size ($n \geq 30$) with *p*-value denoting the percentage. We can observe the difference of this magnitude in rankings when the two-population mean ranks are equal.

Second, for the parametric two-sample *t*-test, the log-transformed variables were used because the normality assumption holds for those transformed variables. Results of this parametric test are given in Table 7.10.

The results are consistent with the Mann–Whitney U test results reported earlier. Both parametric and non-parametric tests thus appear to indicate that the *chaebol* and *non-chaebol* groups have different firm characteristics (i.e. financial) which may, in turn, affect their disclosure practices.

7.4.3 *Multivariate tests*

Before discussing the results of multiple regression analysis, selection of the most powerful profitability variable and results of various diagnostic tests are addressed. In respect of the profitability variable, stepwise regression[6] was employed on the three profitability variables. It was found that profit2 (i.e. net profit/net sales) was the most powerful explanatory variable. Adjusted R^2 (i.e. 0.43357) approximates the results obtained from similar studies dealing with disclosure

Table 7.10 Results of two-sample *t*-test for group differences (log-transformed)

Variables	Chaebol ($n = 28$)		Non-chaebol ($n = 33$)		*Df*#	*T-score*	*p-value*
	Mean	*Standard deviation*	*Mean*	*Standard deviation*			
Disclosure scores	5.2545	0.065	5.1926	0.059	59	−3.89	0.000**
Assets	20.3722	1.040	18.5868	0.724	59	−7.87	0.000**
Sales	20.1213	1.078	18.3727	0.638	42.30	−7.54	0.000**
Employees	7.8016	1.048	6.5331	0.845	57	−5.14	0.000**
Leverage	5.6610	0.630	5.2934	0.612	59	−2.31	0.025*
Profit1^	0.4411	1.188	0.8296	1.233	51	1.16	0.251
Profit2^^	0.6044	0.981	0.7170	1.020	55	0.42	0.674
Profit^^^	1.7227	1.142	1.6353	0.879	55	−0.33	0.745

Notes

* Significant at $p \leq 0.05$ (two-tailed).

** Significant at $p \leq 0.01$ (two-tailed).

# Denotes degree of freedom.

^ Denotes ordinary profit to total assets.

^^ Denotes net profit to net sales.

^^^ Denotes net profit to net worth.

indices such as Singhvi (1968) (i.e. 0.42) and Singhvi and Desai (1971) (i.e. 0.43). The adjusted R^2 of 0.43357 is lower than that of Cooke (1989) and Ahmed and Nicholls (1994), which were 0.60 and 0.52, respectively. Lower adjusted R^2 may be due to the fact that two important explanatory variables, industry effect and listing status, are already controlled for in this study.

Various diagnostic tests were undertaken to examine if the assumptions underlying the multiple regression model held. All of them support the assumptions underlying the model. First, a histogram and normal probability plot of the standardized residuals shows that the distribution of the residuals appears to be fairly normal. Second, a plot of the standardized residuals against the predicted values shows the constant variance of residuals (i.e. homoscedasticity). Finally, a casewise plot of standardized residuals shows no significant outliers. Results of the multiple regression analysis are provided in Table 7.11.

7.4.3.1 H1: Affiliation with chaebols

Affiliation with *chaebols* appears to exert a positive impact on financial disclosure level. This positive relationship may be attributable to higher political costs of companies affiliated with *chaebols*, mainly arising from the public and regulatory attention to their enormous economic concentration and power. This argument appears to be convincing, given the huge combined sales of the top thirty *chaebol* groups that comprise approximately 75 percent of Korea's GNP in 1995 (Haskins *et al.* 1996). However, the non-significant results seem to suggest that other factors are more important in explaining levels of disclosure in Korea.

Table 7.11 Results of Korean disclosure model

Variable	*Estimated coefficient*	*Standard error*	*t-statistic*	*p-value*
Constant (c)	5.132354	0.070245	73.064	0.0000**
Chaebol	0.011972	0.019353	0.619	0.5390
Size (S)	0.035804	0.009891	3.620	0.0007**
Profitability (Profit2)	0.018776	0.007532	2.493	0.0161*
Leverage	0.013083	0.012472	1.049	0.2993
Audit firm	−0.002655	0.015219	−0.174	0.8622
F-value: ($p \leq 0.01$) 9.267				
Adjusted $R^2 = 0.43357$				

Notes
* Significant at $p \leq 0.05$ (two-tailed).
** Significant at $p \leq 0.01$ (two-tailed).

7.4.3.2 *H2: Size*

A statistically significant positive relationship between company size and disclosure level was found for the sample at the level of $p \leq 0.01$. This result strongly supports the findings of prior disclosure studies in the USA, the UK, India, Sweden, and Japan. As previously addressed, the positive relationship can be explained in various ways. Two widely accepted explanations are operational complexity and political costs associated with large companies. Large Korean companies tend to engage in complex operations which may necessitate high disclosure levels. Similarly, large Korean companies have been constantly exposed to more public attention and regulatory scrutiny than smaller firms because of their enormous economic and political leverage.

7.4.3.3 *H3: Profitability*

Profitability was found to be positively associated with disclosure level at the level of $p = 0.0161$. The statistically significant positive relationship between profitability and disclosure level can be explained by the incentives of profitable companies to disclose more to differentiate themselves from poorly performing companies, and to minimize political costs arising from their higher profitability.

7.4.3.4 *H4: Degree of financial leverage*

The sign of the coefficient for the degree of leverage is positive as expected in the model. However, the relationship is statistically significant approximately at the 30 percent level ($p = 0.2993$), which implies that the disclosure level of companies in the country is explained better by other important variables, rather than the degree of financial leverage. The nonsignificant result may be explained by the unique relationship between major debt providers (i.e. financial institutions) and *chaebol* firms. The main-bank system launched in 1976 has actually allowed each

Table 7.12 Distribution of sample firms across auditing companies

Korean Big-9 audit firms	*International affiliation*	*No. of sample companies audited*
Samil	Coopers & Lybrand	12
Ahnkun-Sewha	Deloitte Tohmatsu Touche International	9
Sandong	Klynveld Peat Marwick Goerdeler	8
Anjin	Arthur Andersen	1
Youngwha	Ernst & Young	7
Sedong	Price Waterhouse	3
Samduck	NEXIA International**	8
Chungwoon	Howarth International**	7
Shinhan	RSM International**	5
Samkyung Hapdong*		1
Total		61

Notes

* Not a member of the Korean Big-Nine.

** Not a member of the International Big-Six.

group's main bank (i.e. debt providers) to participate in management decision making of its borrowing firms. More importantly, the monitoring role allows the main bank to obtain access to significant financial and business information (Park and Kim 1994). Therefore, financial information provided for external purposes may not be as significant as expected.

7.4.3.5 H5: Affiliation with the Big-Six

Contrary to our initial expectation, affiliation with a Big-Six multinational accounting firm is negatively related to the level of disclosure. However, the statistically nonsignificant result ($p = 0.8622$) suggests that the affiliation with the Big-Six may not be an important explanatory variable in determining the disclosure level of Korean companies. The nonsignificant result may also be attributable to the fact that all the firms in the sample (except for one company) were audited at least by one of the nine largest audit firms in Korea, although some of them are not affiliated with the Big-Six, as shown in Table 7.12.

7.5 Limitations

This study is not without its limitations. First, it is limited to profit-seeking listed companies in Korea. So, findings may not be generalizable to unlisted companies, government or "not-for-profit" organizations in the country. As discussed in Singhvi and Desai (1971) and Cooke (1989, 1992), listing status was associated with level of disclosure in the USA, Sweden, and Japan. Even though the advantages of including unlisted companies in the study are recognized, there are some advantages of limiting the study to listed companies only. Both domestic and international attention has been paid mostly to listed companies because of their economic importance in Korea. This importance is reflected in growing regulation and control over listed companies, particularly *chaebol* companies. In addition, access to the financial reports of unlisted companies is extremely difficult because unlisted companies are not required to file their reports with the country's regulatory bodies, unless they are subject to the EAL.

Second, unlike most prior disclosure studies that used annual reports, only financial statements with notes and supplementary schedules are examined. The study of financial information only is limited under current circumstances in which nonfinancial information such as social responsibility accounting has been steadily growing in its significance. However, the regulation of nonfinancial information in the country had not been systematic until 1996, when disclosure requirements relating to the impact of economic transactions on environment and employees were adopted. A separate study of *Operating Report* including nonfinancial as well as financial information will generate more comprehensive findings of disclosure practices of listed companies and also enhance comparability with other disclosure studies, which examined not only financial information but also nonfinancial information disclosed in annual reports.

Third, the study of unconsolidated statements rather than consolidated statements limits the findings. Consolidation is an important area that has been continuously strengthened in financial reporting regulation in Korea. Without an examination of consolidated statements of Korean firms, it seems difficult to appropriately measure the compliance level of Korean companies with mandatory reporting requirements.

Last, this study, which is cross-sectional in nature, fails to identify general trends and problem areas because it examines disclosure practices of Korean firms only at a specific point in time. Future longitudinal studies will be more useful in providing policy implications for accounting standard setters and regulatory organizations in the country.

7.6 Conclusion

This chapter has identified company-specific characteristics that influence the disclosure level of Korean listed companies. The findings support prior disclosure studies in the size variable. A composite of three different size variables (i.e. total assets, net sales, and number of employees) show a statistically significant positive relationship to disclosure level. This may be related to higher political costs associated with corporate size in Korea where government has continuously taken measures to control rapidly increasing economic power of the private business sector, especially large business conglomerates. Interestingly enough, however, rather than a mere affiliation with *chaebols*, size appears to be the most powerful explanatory variable in determining the corporate disclosure level in Korea. The terseness of financial information disclosure by *chaebols* is also noted in the literature (Haskins *et al.* 1996). This prevailing belief and perception of *chaebols*' poor disclosure practices led to changes in financial reporting requirements of *chaebols*, especially the top thirty *chaebols*, in 1996. The changes include appointment of outside auditors to board of directors and introduction of minority shareholders' right to scrutinize financial statements of the top thirty *chaebols*.

With respect to the degree of profitability, the result is consistent with the initial expectation. The degree of profitability (i.e. net income-to-net sales) is found to be positively associated with disclosure level at the level of $p \leq 0.05$. Similar to the size variable, this finding can be supported by the political costs hypothesis as well as by the firms' initiative to disclose more to differentiate themselves from poorly performing firms.

Unlike the two variables discussed above, results regarding the remaining three variables are not statistically significant at conventional levels: affiliation with *chaebols*, financial leverage, and affiliation with Big-Six. These nonsignificant results may suggest that there are other more important variables in explaining the disclosure level of companies in the country. However, the sign of the coefficients for the affiliation with *chaebols* and the degree of financial leverage is as expected (i.e. positive), although the negative association between the affiliation with the Big-Six accounting firms and the extent of disclosure is contrary to our initial expectation.

Overall, the findings suggest the importance of national business environments as well as company-specific variables in influencing disclosure practices of individual companies within a country. Findings concerning the effects of financial leverage and profitability on the extent of disclosure by Korean companies add to the mixed results of prior disclosure studies. Thus it can be drawn that company-specific characteristics appear to play differential roles in influencing disclosure practices of individual companies depending on national environments where companies operate.

7.6.1 Suggestions for further research

A logical and promising area for future research would be a longitudinal study of financial reporting of *chaebols*. Despite the significant concentration of wealth and economic power in a small number of *chaebols*, very little attention has been paid to their financial reporting practices. An historical study of financial reporting of the *chaebols* will provide useful insight into future policymaking regarding Korea's financial reporting regulation. As part of such a study, the historical emergence and development of the *chaebols* and their unique management system may also be examined.

Another area would be a study of financial reporting (i.e. disclosure) practices of Korean companies in the post-IMF (International Monetary Fund) period by building upon the findings of the current study. Since the IMF's massive financial aid to Korea in late 1997, the Korean government has been under increasing pressure to further liberalize its financial markets and to urge Korean companies, especially *chaebols*, to become more transparent in their disclosure of business and financial information. This future study will help identify changes in company disclosure practices that may have occurred during the post-IMF period.

Finally, a comparative study of Northeast Asian economic powers (Japan, Korea, and Taiwan) could be undertaken to identify any differences and similarities in financial reporting regulations and practices. The initial economic, cultural, and geographical proximity between these countries will provide both interesting and informative theories to the existing literature of international accounting. A similar approach could also be applied to a comparative study of financial reporting of four Newly Industrialized Economies (NIEs: Korea, Taiwan, Hong Kong, and Singapore).

Notes

1 The author gratefully acknowledges insightful comments provided by Professor Russell Craig and Dr Joselito Diga at the Australian National University, two anonymous reviewers of her master's thesis, and participants of the inaugural KSAA conference held in Sydney, Australia, 1999.

2 Among the various definitions of *chaebols*, this study adopts a definition used by Yoo and Lee (1987: 97) in which a *chaebol* is defined as "a business group consisting of large companies which are owned and managed by family members or relatives in many diversified business areas."

3 Big-Six accounting firms as of December 1994 were: Coopers & Lybrand, Deloitte Tohmatsu Touche International, Klynveld Peat Marwick Goerdeler (KPMG), Arthur Andersen, Ernst & Young, and Price Waterhouse. The Big-Six became the Big-Five since the merger of Price Waterhouse and Coopers & Lybrand in July 1998.

4 These companies were selected from the top thirty *chaebol* groups whose borrowings from financial institutions were strictly controlled and monitored by relevant government regulatory agencies in order to minimize economic concentration in *chaebols* and resulting monopolistic competition and to improve the financial structure of the *chaebols*. However, there was an announcement in 1996 that the number of *chaebols* whose borrowings were controlled would be reduced from thirty to ten.

5 The complete list can be obtained from the author upon request.

6 Three profitability variables were initially selected in this study. However, because of the high collinearity among these variables, stepwise regression was used to select the most powerful profitability variable. Among them, profit2 (i.e. net income to net sales) has been found to be the most powerful, with adjusted R^2 of 0.43357. The multiple regression model including profit1 (i.e. ordinary income to total assets) has adjusted R^2 of 0.35008, while the model including profit (i.e. net income to net worth) has 0.40210 for adjusted R^2.

Bibliography

Aczel, A.D. (1993) *Complete Business Statistics*, 2nd edn, Homewood, Illinois: Irwin.

Ahmed, K. (1993) "An empirical study of the quality of disclosure in corporate annual reports in developing countries: the case of Bangladesh," unpublished PhD thesis, The Australian National University.

—— and Nicholls, D. (1994) "The impact of non-financial company characteristics on mandatory disclosure compliance in developing countries: the case of Bangladesh," *International Journal of Accounting Education and Research*, 29: 62–77.

Baker, H.K. and Haslem, J.A. (1973) "Information needs of individual investors," *Journal of Accountancy*, November: 64–9.

Ball, R. and Foster, G. (1982) "Corporate financial reporting: a methodological review of empirical research," *Journal of Accounting Research*, 20, Supplement: 161–234.

Belkaoui, A.R. and Kahl, A. (1978) "Corporate financial disclosure in Canada," *CGA Research Monograph No. 1*. Vancouver: Canadian Certified General Accountants Association.

Buzby, S.L. (1975) "Company size, listed versus unlisted stocks, and the extent of disclosure," *Journal of Accounting Research*, 13(1): 16–37.

CC (Commercial Code) (1994) in *Daehan Minkuk Hyunhaeng Popryungjip* (*Korean Current Statutes Book*) (1995), Seoul, Korea: Statutes Compilation Committee.

Cerf, A.R. (1961) *Corporate Reporting and Investment Decisions*, Berkeley, CA: University of California.

Chang, L.S. and Most, K.S. (1981) "An international comparison of investor uses of financial statements," *International Journal of Accounting Education and Research*, 17(1): 43–60.

Chow, C.W. and Wong-Boren, A. (1987) "Voluntary financial disclosure by Mexican corporations," *Accounting Review*, 62(3): 533–41.

Cooke, T.E. (1989) "Disclosure in the corporate annual reports of Swedish companies," *Accounting and Business Research*, 19(74): 113–24.

——(1991) "An assessment of voluntary disclosure in the annual reports of Japanese corporations," *International Journal of Accounting Education and Research*, 26(3): 174–89.

——(1992) "The impact of size, stock market listing and industry type on disclosure in the annual reports of Japanese listed corporations," *Accounting and Business Research*, 22(87): 229–37.

Diga, J.G. (1995) "The effects of company and national characteristics on financial disclosure," unpublished working paper, The Australian National University.

EAL (External Audit of Joint-Stock Companies Law) (1993) *Daehan Minkuk Hyunhaeng Popryungjip* (*Korean Current Statutes Book*) (1995), Seoul, Korea: Statutes Compilation Committee.

EAL Implementation Ordinance (1994) *Daehan Minkuk Hyunhaeng Popryungjip* (*Korean Current Statutes Book*) (1995), Seoul, Korea: Statutes Compilation Committee.

Firth, M.A. (1979) "The impact of size, stock market listing, and auditors on voluntary disclosure in corporate annual reports," *Accounting and Business Research*, 9(36): 273–80.

Haskins, M.E., Ferris, K.R., and Selling, T.A. (1996) "Republic of South Korea" *International Financial Reporting and Analysis: A Contextual Emphasis*, Chicago: Irwin.

Jolliffe, I.T. (1972) "Discarding variables in a principal component analysis 1: artificial data," *Applied Statistics*, 21(2): 160–73.

KFAS (Korean Financial Accounting Standards) (1981, 1984, 1985, 1990, 1992, 1994, 1996, 1998) Seoul, Korea: Korean Institute of Certified Public Accountants (KICPA).

KFAS for Construction Industry (1992) Seoul, Korea: KICPA.

KFAS for Leasing Industry (1993) Seoul, Korea: KICPA.

KFAS and KFAS Working Rules on Consolidation (1994) Seoul, Korea: KICPA.

KFAS Working Rules on Business Combinations (1986) Seoul, Korea: KICPA.

KFAS Working Rules on Research and Development Costs (1987) Seoul, Korea: KICPA.

Kim, S.Y. and Paik, S.H. (1996) "OECD Hoewonkuk Shidae" (OECD Membership: Significance, Background, and Prospects), *Dong-A Daily*, July 10.

Maddala, G.S. (1992) *Introduction to Econometrics*, 2nd edn, New York: MacMillan.

Norusis, M.J. (1993) *SPSS for Windows Professional Statistics 6.0*. Chicago, IL: SPSS Inc.

Park, Y.C. and Kim, D.W. (1994) "Korea: development and structural change of the banking system," in H.T. Patrick and Y.C. Park (eds), *The Financial Development of Japan, Korea, and Taiwan: Growth, Repression, and Liberalization*, New York: Oxford University Press.

Saudagaran, S.M. and Biddle, G.C. (1992) "Financial disclosure levels and foreign stock exchange listing decisions," *Journal of International Financial Management and Accounting*, 4(2): 106–47.

SEL (Securities and Exchange Law) (1994) *Daehan Minkuk Hyunhaeng Popryungjip* (*Korean Current Statutes Book*) (1995), Seoul, Korea: Statutes Compilation Committee.

SEL Implementation Ordinance (1994) *Daehan Minkuk Hyunhaeng Popryungjip* (*Korean Current Statutes Book*) (1995), Seoul, Korea: Statutes Compilation Committee.

Singhvi, S.S. (1968) "Characteristics and implications of inadequate disclosure: a case study of India," *International Journal of Accounting Education and Research*, 3(2): 29–43.

——and Desai, H.B. (1971) "An empirical analysis of the quality of corporate financial disclosure," *Accounting Review*, 46(1): 129–38.

Stanga, K. (1976) "Disclosure in published annual reports," *Financial Management*, Winter: 42–52.

Wallace, R.S.O. (1988) "Corporate financial reporting in Nigeria," *Accounting and Business Research*, 18(72): 352–62.

——and Nasser, K. (1995) "Firm-specific determinants of the comprehensiveness of mandatory disclosure of corporate annual reports of firms listed on the stock exchange of Hong Kong," *Journal of Accounting and Public Policy*, 14(14): 311–68.

Watts, R.L. and Zimmerman, J. (1978) "Towards a positive theory of the determination of accounting standards," *Accounting Review*, 53(1): 112–34.

Weisberg, S. (1985) *Applied Linear Regression*, 2nd edn, New York: John Wiley.

Yang, D.C. and Lee, C.M. (1994) "An empirical analysis of pan-pacific accounting practices in the 1970s," *Advances in International Accounting*, 6: 133–45.

Yoo, S.J. and Lee, S.M. (1987) "Management style and practice of Korean chaebols," *California Management Review*, Summer: 95–110.

8 The *chaebol* and Korean capitalism

The Hyundai business group

Seung-Ho Kwon and Chung-Sok Suh[1]

8.1 Introduction

The historical development of large-scale capitalist business entities is a frequently canvassed topic of research across the economics, business history and organizational structure disciplines. Most of these studies have focused on large-scale capitalist enterprises in advanced countries such as the United States, England, Europe and Japan.[2] In contrast, scant attention has been paid to these enterprises in the newly emergent capitalist economies of the East Asian regions, especially those in South Korea (hereafter Korea). This is surprising, given the dominant role of family-controlled conglomerates, the *chaebol*, in the course of Korea's rapid industrialization and the position of Korean economy in the world. Hence, this chapter addresses the evident gap in the literature through a detailed, in-depth case study of a leading industrial conglomerate, the Hyundai Business Group, in Korea from its origins in the 1940s to the 1990s.

One of the prevalent themes in the study of large-scale industrial enterprises is the evolutionary nature of capitalism, including the logic of economic transformation. One of the pioneering works in the area came from Chandler's two theses, *Strategy and Structure* (1962) and *The Visible Hand* (1977), which analysed the historical transformation of industrial capitalism in the United States. Based on his strategy and structure framework, Chandler charts the transformation of American capitalism from that of single entrepreneur-owned and controlled enterprise to stock exchange listed companies governed by professional managers. He contends that the transformation was imperative. At the time of the transformation, single family-owned and controlled firms confronted increasingly complicated and expanding business systems and highly competitive market forces. In response, the traditional nature of business activities regulated solely by free market forces is replaced by the development of monopolistic enterprises which had grown to economies of scale and scope being able to take advantage of reduced transaction costs, resulting in increased productivity and a stable supply of resources for production. In the course of developing such monopolistic enterprises, the levels of strategic activities and structural units become more diversified. Chandler (1990a) defines that these various diversification strategies deployed are horizontally combined and vertically integrated to achieve economies of scale and scope.

Given such a context, it was imperative for the single entrepreneurs in the United States to develop professional management, which then functioned as a critical strategic agent to initiate the development of large-scale and multi-divisional industrial capitalism in the early twentieth century. In so doing, there was separation between the ownership and managerial control. While the ownership of entrepreneurs was listed in the stock exchange, their managerial control was taken over by the professional managers. Because of this change, Chandler applies the term, 'managerial capitalism', to later American capitalism (Chandler and Daems 1980, Chandler 1990a, 1992).

Chandler's studies have been a major force behind the rise of studying large-scale industrial enterprises in other advanced countries. Some studies focusing on European capitalism have provoked controversy by asserting that variations in the timing, degree and forms of growth as between European and American firms, gave rise to somewhat disparate enterprise and country-specific paths of capitalist transformation (Schmitz 1993: 28–48). However, many studies have thrown up somewhat similar patterns of capital transformation, for example, those of large-scale industrial enterprises in Europe, with those in the United States.[3]

In contrast, the historical transformation of industrial capitalism in Japan has been seen differently with those in the United States and Europe due mainly to the different pattern of Japanese industrialization in different politico-economic contexts. Lazonick (1991) identifies a different pattern in Japanese capitalist transformation whereby 'collective capitalism' superseded the family-controlled *zaibatsu*. Large-scale Japanese conglomerates, the family-controlled *zaibatsu*, emerged in the early twentieth century with strong support from the imperial state. Over time, the ultimate control by family members of the business and managerial activities of *zaibatsu* was lost to the top management of core companies in the *zaibatsu*, who implemented vertically integrated business systems across core and satellite companies to obtain competitive advantages for all conglomerate activities (Lazonick 1991: 36–43).

The dominant theme running through most literature on Korean capitalism is the role of the state because of its 'developmentalist' (Amsden 1989) and 'interventionist' (Wade 1990) approach to the rapid industrialization of Korea's economy. It is argued that the *chaebol*, Korean family-controlled conglomerates, emerged as a consequence of the Korean state's rapid industrialization programmes. The state-guided economic policies directed the growth strategy and structure of the *chaebol* to be monopolistic for their competitive edges in the international market. Therefore, the role of the state is a critical factor in the transformation of Korean capitalism from originally small, family capitalist enterprises in the late 1940s to large-scale industrial conglomerates in the 1990s. In addition, it is the dominant feature of Korean capitalism that the *chaebol*'s business operations and governance have been under the direct control of family owners since their inception. Hence, the process of Korean capitalist transformation is generally characterized as *state initiated family capitalism*. Because of the evident similarities such as family ownership and managerial control and the monopolistic nature of business practices, the Korean *chaebol* is often compared with the *zaibatsu* in pre-Second World War in Japan (Kuk 1988, Kang 1990, Yang Yoo-jin 1991[4], Rhee 1994, Eun-Mee Kim 1997).[5]

These arguments can be summarized into three key propositions, as a basis for the study of the historical transformation of the Hyundai Business Group and also for the analysis of the cause and ramifications of the current economic crisis. The first theoretical proposition is simply related to the nature of external environments shaping the pattern of historical transformation. As discussed above, the influences of different external forces produce different characteristics of capitalism. Examples can be found in the differences in the speed and patterns of growth between European and American firms and in the role of the state in western and Asian economies.

The second proposition comes from the strategy and structure argument, which was put forward by Chandler as a main theoretical tool in understanding the transformation process of the American firms. This became the essential proposition in many subsequent studies. Chandler (1962) defines the strategy of a firm concerns various long-term business and managerial decisions and explained that changes in such strategy inevitably leads to structural changes in the firm's managerial organization and businesses.

The final proposition is that professional management plays the role of a strategic agent in initiating historical transformation of business, from small, family businesses to large-scale industrial enterprises. This role of professional management results in separation between the ownership and managerial control over the large industrial enterprises. As mentioned before in the case of American firms, their initiative role stands out as one of the distinctive features in modern capitalism and thus the term 'managerial capitalism is used to distinguish it from family capitalism in the past. Based on these propositions, diversified interactions that occurred during the process of historical transformation of the Korean capitalism will be analysed in this chapter with particular emphasis on the Hyundai Business Group.

This chapter examines the historical transformation of the Hyundai Business Group from its humble origins in the 1940s, to a large-scale industrial conglomerate in the 1990s through a detailed in-depth and historical case study of its three major leading subsidiaries, the Hyundai Construction and Civil Engineering (HECC), Hyundai Motor Company (HMC) and Hyundai Heavy Industries (HHI). The analysis is divided into three chronological parts, following the distinctive stages of growth patterns and structure of Hyundai, which also reflect socio-political and economic changes in Korea. Then, the historical transformation of Hyundai is compared with that of other Korean large companies, to identify the distinguishing characteristics of Korean capitalism. The concluding section discusses some implications of the findings in this chapter in the context of the current economic crisis in Korea and for future directions.

8.2 Family business and expansion: 1946–60s

The HECC was founded in 1947. Until the mid-1950s, the growth of the HECC's construction business was negligible. It operated as a small civil engineering subcontractor, undertaking mostly simple maintenance and repair work. After being awarded the First Han River Bridge Reconstruction Project in 1957, one of the largest national projects, at 32 million won, the HECC became Korea's sixth largest construction company (Lee Jong-nam 1985: 102–7, Kong Jae-wuk 1994: 221–2, 236, Lee Jung-jae 1994: 107–9, 127–38).

The HECC was selected as a representative construction company by the incoming Park Chunghee military government (1961–79) under its policy of rapid industrialization of the Korean economy. During the First (1962–66) and Second (1967–71) Five Year Economic Development Plans (FYEDPs), the HECC was successful in obtaining a series of large national infrastructure construction projects, such as highways and dams, power plants and factories, enabling it to grow rapidly. The contribution of the government projects to HECC earnings grew from 41 per cent (732 million won) between 1953 and 1961 to 88 per cent (44,555 million won) between 1963 and 1971 under the Park government (HECC 1982: 579, 638–9, 1096–143).

Once it was well established at home, the HECC entered the overseas construction market with the Pattani–Narathiwat Highway project (1966–68) in Thailand, followed by the projects in Vietnam, Guam, Papua New Guinea and Australia. This diverse international experience provided the basis for its rapid expansion into the Middle East construction market in the 1970s, and resulted in the HECC becoming the leading Korean construction exporter.

During the 1950s and 1960s, Hyundai's growth strategy was premised on the 'one-set' approach. This 'one-set' strategy constituted a typical diversification strategy of the *chaebol* in the 1960s, the objective of which was to vertically integrate related business areas in order to obtain a combined competitive advantage and capability. The core company, the HECC, generated a sizeable demand for building materials in connection with the large-scale construction projects it obtained, mostly from the government projects. Hyundai met this demand internally, by establishing seven subsidiaries during the 1960s, six of which were dedicated to the production, for internal use, of various construction materials such as slate, cement and concrete. These subsidiaries supplied construction materials to the HECC at a lower cost than that obtainable from external suppliers.[6] The HMC, established in 1968, was also incorporated into the 'one-set' system to augment the heavy construction equipment capacity of the HECC, when its large-scale projects required a greater use of complicated heavy construction equipment. The 'one-set' approach to construction was vital to sustaining the leading position of the HECC in the construction market, which needed to pursue a low cost and high volume business strategy.

8.2.1 Expansion and family control

Until the mid-1950s, the management of Hyundai was typical of a small-scale single-family business employing less than 100 workers. Its managerial structure was informal, and organized based on Chung's kinship, his friendship with business associates, and engineering experts. Chung was intimately involved in daily management decisions, and managers were assigned tasks by him directly. However, this protean, idiosyncratic managerial structure and style yielded to the development of a formal managerial structure, largely based on kinship. The formalization of management was undertaken in parallel with the growth in scope and size of the business. By the mid-1960s, the sectional organization of the HECC had largely been converted to a department oriented one.[7] The continued expansion of the business was the factor which contributed most to the evolution of the HECC's organizational structure (HECC 1982: 144–628, Cheon Beomseong 1984: 62–85, *Monthly Chungkyeong Munhwa*, December 1984: 150–1, Kim Beoyong-ha 1991: 259).

The number of top executives increased from a single person, President Chung, in 1950 to eleven in 1964 and seventeen in 1968. The expansion of hierarchical positions at the top management board level included adoption of the chairman system. Expansion at the top management level was necessary for Chung Juyung to maintain effective and efficient control over the increasing number of subsidiaries in the various areas of the business. Each of Hyundai's essential subsidiaries was managed by a member of his family.

The emergence of a cadre of professional managers within a structure dominated by the family hierarchy was a significant, albeit inevitable, development. Of the twenty-two managerial executives hired in 1970, eleven were the product of the open recruitment system (ORS) for four-year university graduates, a system which Hyundai had first implemented in 1958. These recruits were internally promoted from their entry point at the bottom rung of the white-collar employees' ladder where they were supervised by the founder's kin and personal associates. The professionalization of management effected a significant gain in the scope and quality of decision-making.

The formalization of management was constrained however by the overall scarcity of managerial resources relative to demand. For example, informal and *ad hoc* practices emerged as one of the critical issues in the resistance of workers (including middle managers) employed on the Pattani–Narathiwat Highway Project (1966–68) in Thailand. Despite their shortcomings, the management structure and practices employed by Hyundai in this period functioned sufficiently well to allow development of monopolistic capitalism in the 1970s.

8.3 Diversity and concentraion: 1970s to early 1980s

During the 1970s, the Park Government, as part of its policy to rapidly industrialize the Korean economy, promoted the establishment of large-scale chemical and heavy industries. This policy prompted some of the *chaebol* to aggressively diversify into these industries. Hyundai was able to diversify into the automobile and shipbuilding industries by establishing the HMC in 1968 and the HHI in 1974. This diversification was based on the construction business of the HECC, which took on projects requiring heavy and industrial machinery, thereby creating an internal market for such equipment. To this end, the existing 'one-set' approach for low-cost market competition, was revised to suit the various heavy and machinery industries in which Hyundai was now engaged. Heavy and machinery industries became the dominant business of three major companies of Hyundai: the heavy construction works of the HECC, the automobile production of the HMC and the shipbuilding of HHI. This enabled Hyundai to develop a monopolistic production and market position in the Korean economy.

Though the HECC faced financial insolvency when the economic boom generated by the Vietnam war ended, the decline in overseas contracts was compensated for by a series of large-scale government construction projects as part of the Third and Fourth FYEDPs in the 1970s.[8] However, the HECC's most important business development was its entry into the Middle East construction market, starting with the Arab Shipbuilding and Repair Yard project (US$114 million, 1975–78, Bahrain). The aggressive entry into the Middle East market had important implications for the growth of the HECC and Hyundai. With the resultant sharp increase of its total sales, this market expansion enabled the HECC to become an international construction company no longer dependent on its domestic market, which decreased from over 80 per cent of total projects up until 1975 to less than 30 per cent between 1976 and 1981.

In 1968, Hyundai set up the HMC with support from the Park government. Like the existing Korean automobile companies, the HMC began as a completely knocked down (CKD) assembler, under Assembly and Technological Cooperation Agreements with the Ford Motor Company of the United States. In early 1973, the partnership between the HMC and Ford ended due to disagreements over managerial control of the HMC. Consequently, in 1976 the HMC developed and produced its own model, the *Pony*, using a low-cost concept (around US$2,000) of a small sized passenger car (under 1,500 cc) with the technological support and 10 per cent capital participation of Mitsubishi Motors of Japan. Based on the success of the first model, the initial stage of a mass production system was established in 1979 to annually produce 100,000 passenger cars, with the development of the models, *Pony II* and *Excel* (HMC 1987: 34–8, HMC 1992: 362–547).

However, Hyundai's expansion was hit by the second oil price hike, a crisis from which it then recovered with the assistance of the industrial restructuring policies of the new Chun Doohwan military government (1981–88), which granted a monopoly for the production of small-sized passenger cars to the HMC. Internally, the HMC changed its production strategy from being content with the small domestic market to an export focus, entering the export market in 1983 with the shipment of automobiles to Canada. As a result of the establishment of the initial stage of its mass production system in the late 1970s, its sales sharply increased from 528 million won in 1968 to 26,092 million won in 1976 and 430,149 million won in 1982 (HMC 1992: 418, 548–628, 1084, 1099, Lee Ho 1993: 121).

The establishment of HHI in 1974 was a significant milestone in the history of the Korean economy and the turning point for its entry into large-scale shipbuilding industry. This industry, along with the automobile industry, was central to the government's economic policies. Thereafter, whenever the shipbuilding industry hit a crisis, the government intervened to protect it. For example, in the aftermath of the first oil shock of 1974, HHI received the most assistance of all

Korean shipbuilding companies, gaining 67.2 per cent of all government-backed orders from 1975 to 1980. The expansion of HHI was also associated with the expansion of the HECC into the Middle East construction market. The HECC functioned as a supportive base through its requirements for various heavy industrial products, such as offshore steel structures and barges. Sales rapidly increased from 58,840 million won in 1974 to 992,876 million won in 1983 and HHI became the leading international shipbuilder in 1983 (HHI 1992: 391–2, 459, 461–3, 547, 1487).

Overall, the total sales of Hyundai increased more than a hundredfold over the period from 1973 to 1984, from 5,200 million won to 69,792 hundred million won. Its contribution to the national economy increased from 8.56 to 9.5 per cent of GNP between 1978 and 1980 (Park Dong-sun 1979: 364). Table 8.1 shows the rapid growth of Hyundai with the significant role of the HECC, HMC and HHI in Hyundai clearly apparent from the late 1960s. However, owing to the intensive diversification practices of Hyundai away from a construction dominated business base into large-scale heavy industrial businesses, as seen in Table 8.2, the role of the three main companies (HECC, HMC and HHI) in the growth of

Table 8.1 Total annual sales of Hyundai business group, selective years, 1968–80 (hundred million won)

Year	*1968*	*1973*	*1977*	*1978*	*1979*	*1980*
Group Total (A)	129	520	14,799	19,049	22,428	32,620
HECC	124	315	5,360	6,353	6,173	10,517
HMC	5.	179	930	2,158	2,690	2,249
HHI	na	na	4,309	4,013	2,051	3,751
Total (B)	129	484	10,500	12,424	10,914	15,751
Ratio (%: B/A)	100.00	93.07	70.95	65.22	48.66	51.35

Source: Kwon and Suh 1998: 9.

Note
Total sales amount in 1968 is calculated by only those of HECC and HMC due to absence of other data.

Table 8.2 Changes in the number of industrial plant projects of HECC by type of source, 1961–81 (million won, %)

Period	*1961–70*	*1971–75*	*1976–81*	*Total*
Number of project				
Total number	15	15	27	57
Internal source	1	6	21	28
Contract amount				
Total (A)	4,042	633,635	84,233	151,910
Internal source (B)	1,780	2,132	56,438	60,342
B/A (%)	44.0	33.0	66.9	47.9

Source: Kwon and O'Donnell 2001: 61.

Hyundai's total sales declined from the mid-1970s. This does not imply that the role of the three companies had been replaced by others. Rather, it shows the increased role of Hyundai's other supporting subsidiaries, which occurred as a result of the systematic organization of monopolistic production and market strategies in the heavy and machinery industries from the late 1970s.

The previous 'one-set' approach, involving vertical integration of various construction businesses of the HECC in the 1960s, was revised in relation to Hyundai's large-scale heavy and machinery industries in order to gain the benefit of economies of scale and scope in the 1970s. By 1985, a total of eleven support companies had been set up to supply common materials and parts, such as steel and paint materials for the three companies or Hyundai as a whole. For example, Inchon Steel supplied steel materials for the production of heavy industrial structures by the HECC, shipbuilding by HHI and automobiles by the HMC, at low internal prices. Integration, however, extended beyond support companies and the core companies, HECC, HMC and HHI. Table 8.2 shows the extent of internal business cooperation between the HECC and other Hyundai companies with respect to the construction projects undertaken by the HECC in the 1970s.

By utilizing the 'one set' approach to the large-scale heavy and machinery industries of Hyundai, the three major companies were able to secure a sizeable, often dominant, share of domestic and international product markets. For example, in 1977, Hyundai produced sixteen products which had monopoly or semi-monopoly status, including automobiles, slate, steel, pipe and ships in the domestic market (Cho Dong-seong 1991: 193). From 1977 to 1981, the HECC obtained over 20 per cent of the total value of projects undertaken by Korean construction companies in overseas markets (HECC 1982: 659, 836). The share of the domestic motor vehicle market held by the HMC increased from 19.4 per cent in 1970 to 62 per cent over the second half of the 1970s (HMC 1992: 116).[9] While HHI held 77.4 per cent of the domestic ship construction market between 1976 and 1978, its share of the international shipbuilding industry increased from 1.7 per cent in 1973 to 3 per cent in 1974. In 1983, HHI became the world's largest shipbuilder (HHI 1992: 370, 449, 547).

Due to its rapid growth, by the late 1970s, Hyundai became the leading *chaebol* in Korea. Its annual average growth rate, as measured by total sales, was over 11 per cent between 1980 and 1984, whereas other top *chaebol*, such as Samsung and Daewoo, grew at less than 9 per cent (Kim Hyo-gun 1986: 175). The rapid expansion of Hyundai's heavy and machinery industry businesses in the 1970s, utilizing the 'one-set' approach gave rise to large-scale workforce. Regional concentration of its production businesses also occurred, particularly in the Ulsan Industrial Estate of Southeast Korea where by 1982, 50,695 workers were employed in eighteen Hyundai companies (Lee Jong-seon 1989: 15, 35).

8.3.1 Combined family and managerial hierarchy

In response to sustained growth occurring in the large-scale heavy and machinery industries of Hyundai, formalization of both managerial structure and activities was undertaken to consolidate the central authority of Chung Juyung, his kin and associates. Professional management groups, especially those in the HECC, were relocated to form a second tier position in the revised hierarchical structure to underpin the central control of top management.

The first major structural change involved the replacement of the existing department system by the division system in the 1970s. The size of departments rapidly increased from the mid-1970s in line with rapid growth of their businesses. This was paralleled in the increased size of the managerial structure from department-oriented to division-oriented structure, especially in the number of executives (Kwon 1997: 91). All in all, the changes constituted a bureaucratization of the large-scale division system from the mid-1970s. Figure 8.1 simplifies the formal managerial structure of Hyundai which developed from the late 1970s.

With the development of a formal Hyundai managerial structure, important changes occurred at the top decision-making level, with the broad application of the chairman system and the introduction of a Group Planning Office in 1979. In 1982, except for the chairman of HHI, all chairman positions were held by the founder, Chung Juyung, to enable him to be formally involved in every aspect of the business and management of subsidiary companies, especially the three major companies. The Group Planning Office was introduced in association with the Group Chairman system. The Group Planning Office grew out of the planning

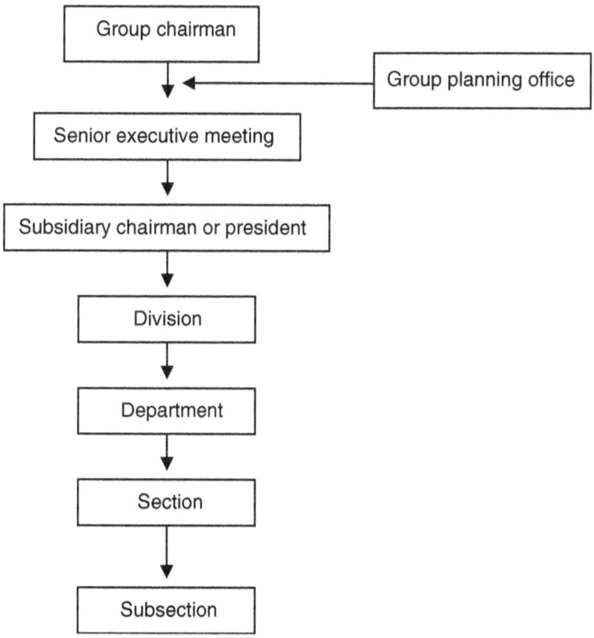

Figure 8.1 Formal managerial structure of Hyundai since 1979.

Source: Developed by authors.

office which had been set up in the HECC in the 1960s to develop a management science capability in general, and in particular to support top management in the creation, implementation and monitoring of long-term business plans (HECC 1982: 627, 776, 786, HHI 1992: 533). The role of the Group Planning Office was critical to Hyundai's ability to derive benefits from economies of scale and scope and the systematic integration of its businesses, or what Ansoff describes as the 'synergy effect' (Ansoff 1969).[10] From the Group Planning Office, Chung Juyung was able to maintain oversight and control of Hyundai's businesses.

With the operation of a centrally controlled managerial structure, two additional supporting mechanisms were necessary: the development of a kinship structure in the Hyundai top management class and the diffusion of HECC-backed professional managers into the second tier of top decision makers. In the 1970s, Chung Juyung's brothers were placed in the top management positions of the most important subsidiaries under Chung's central authority (Park Dong-sun 1979: 360, Kim Young-ho 1985: 269–70).

The kinship structure was expanded further with the emergence of a second generation of the founder's family in the early 1980s. While the major companies presided over by Chung's four brothers were legally separate from Hyundai, they nevertheless functioned as satellite *chaebol* through an interconnected business structure and the exchange of senior executives. From the 1980s, members of the second generation of Chung Juyung's family, who had been employed as middle or senior managers in the 1970s, gradually took over central positions in the managerial structure under the direct guidance of Chung Juyung. A strong patriarchal kinship system was particularly effective in securing the central authority of Chung Juyung in the context of a well entrenched Confucian socio-cultural tradition in which the father and the eldest son are given authority in decision-making. Therefore, cultural values favoured the central authority of Chung Juyung as the eldest brother and father, in managerial decision-making (*Monthly Chosun* September 1980: 281–3, HECC 1982: 1081, Cheon Beom-seong 1984: 436–44, Kim Young-ho 1985: 269–70, 290–1, Chang 1988: 51–7, Chung Ku-hyeon 1989: 291, Kim and Kim 1989: 27–46).

With the extension of the middle layer in the managerial structure through kinship in the 1970s and 1980s, professional managers, especially HECC-backed managers, were placed in the second tier of top management in Hyundai. An initial diffusion of professional managers into top management positions in the subsidiaries during the 1960s was accelerated in the 1970s with the rapid expansion of Hyundai as a whole. In the organizational chart in 1981, of 61 top managerial executives in 16 Hyundai subsidiaries, 28 executives came from those who had been hired in the late 1960s under the formal recruitment system and had served over 10 years in the HECC. With such service, they had in effect supported the kinship structure and central authority of the top management (HECC 1982: 1081–2).

Several factors contributed to the emergence of the HECC-backed professional executives in Hyundai. First, the HECC historically functioned as the parent company in executing Hyundai's growth strategy. With the growth in interrelated business operations between HECC and other companies, the diffusion of

HECC-backed managers to other companies was necessary. Second, these executives were mostly those middle managers who had worked a long time under the direct supervision of the founder in the 1960s and thus had proven their capabilities and loyalty to him. Most importantly, their long working relationship with the founder was crucial for the implementation of the founder's managerial decisions. Last, the experience of the founder in construction work led him to prefer HECC-backed managers. The HECC was also the place where his sons were initially trained to be senior executives for other Hyundai companies. However, these executives were also an agency for extending the patriarchal aspects of managerial control with the formalization of work and employment relations in these years. As the professional management class was regarded as a means of enforcing the central authority of Hyundai top management, so employment conditions were extended to effectively control the mass of production workers. In this way, the central control of the founder in the formal organization was reinforced – it was combined with the kinship structure in the family hierarchy and the diffusion of HECC-backed executives. As a result, during this period, the founder of Hyundai was able to maintain managerial control of a large, rapidly expanding conglomerate.

8.4 Crisis and transition: early 1980s–1990s

The excessive dependence of Hyundai on large-scale heavy and machinery industries in the 1970s had made it vulnerable to changes in the international supply and price levels of natural resources, for example, the second oil price hike in 1979. Further, the business crises which periodically beset Hyundai were exacerbated by the emergence, from the mid-1980s, of a mass, independent trade union movement.[11] These developments undermined its low-cost market approach and thus its competitiveness. Furthermore, politically and economically, the state became less well disposed to the monopolistic capitalism of the *chaebol*. Therefore, from the mid-1980s, Hyundai redirected its investment from heavy and machinery industries to technologically intensive, high value added industries such as microelectronics and services. The three major companies, HECC, HMC and HHI, reorganized their business strategies to accommodate these changes.

In the early 1980s, the HECC suffered a sharp decline in its Middle East construction contracts due to adverse political and economic developments in that region. Meanwhile, the increasing cost of Korean labour weakened its competitiveness, and outdated construction technologies limited its potential expansion into more advanced construction projects, such as nuclear power plants. To overcome its regional concentration in the Middle East, especially in Saudi Arabia, the HECC diversified to other countries in the Middle East, and in Asia, Africa, and Central and South America (HECC 1982: 882–3, 913–6). At the same time, to maintain its low labour costs, the HECC's Korean construction labourers were replaced by those from Third World countries on overseas projects, who increased from 30 per cent of overseas project workforce in the early 1980s to 70 to 80 per cent from the late 1980s (*Korea Economy Newspaper* 24 March 1992, *Chungang Economic Newspaper* 7 June, 10 July 1990, 6 July, 18 May, 24 October 1993,

28 February 1994, *Monthly Chungkyeong Munhwa* April 1983: 346, *Monthly Chungang* October 1988: 378–81).

The timing of the HMC's entry into the mass production market for automobiles in 1979 was unfortunate. The Korean automobile industry experienced an economic recession in the aftermath of the assassination of President Park Chunghee and the second OPEC oil price shock. To facilitate its recovery, the HMC was granted a monopoly over small-sized passenger cars under the *Rationalization Policy for Heavy and Chemical Industries* by the Chun military government (1981–88). The HMC was compelled to reduce employment levels and implement a wage freeze to lower production costs. These policies ensured that the company succeeded in turning a 19,300 million won loss into a 25,700 million won profit (32 million US dollars) between 1980 and 1983. This turnaround in its financial affairs enabled the HMC to increase its mass production for the international market from 110,000 cars in 1979 to 300,000 in 1985 and to 890,000 automobiles in 1990 (Chung Kuhyeon 1989: 299–301, HMC 1992: 491–8, 500).

With the rapid expansion of its production output for the international car market, HMC also developed a range of models, such as the *Excel* (1,400 cc, 1985), *Stellar* (1,439 cc and 1,597 cc, 1982), *Sonata* (1,800 cc and 2,000 cc, 1985) and *Elantra* (1,500 cc and 1,800 cc, 1990) through technological cooperation with Mitsubishi. Canada was its first overseas market and the HMC opened its first branch there in 1983. The HMC sold some 79,072 models of the *Pony* in 1985, representing 7 per cent of the Canadian small passenger-car market. This success gave the HMC the confidence to enter the US car market in 1986 with its competitively priced *Excel*. This model sold 168,882 cars, the third largest number of sales in the small sized and imported passenger category in the United States in 1986. Nevertheless, from the mid-1980s the pace of the HMC's overseas expansion slowed because of a combination of increased market protection in countries to which it exported and rising labour costs at home. The HMC's dependence on the US export market in late 1988 was overcome by diversifying its car exports to other national markets. The HMC exported to sixty-five countries in 1986 and this increased to 141 by 1994.[2] HMC has also diversified its production and in 1999 produced some 800,000 cars per annum in Korea and 320,000 in plants in China, Turkey and India (*Chosun Ilbo* 21 July 1993, 4 January, 7 December 1994, *Donga Ilbo* 24 November 1995, interview with HMC engineer 13 March 2000).

The economic crisis of the late 1990s brought a substantial change in the Korean automobile industry. First, other competitors' entry into the industry failed because of the excess production capacity that the economic crisis created. Second, Kia and Daewoo went into bankruptcy when their debt-driven growth strategy backfired and they were unable to meet their debt repayments. Kia was eventually taken over by the HMC. Daewoo was left technically bankrupt as a result of the financial crisis and remains under the control of its major debtors, the state controlled banks and the government. In 2000, government attempts to find a new foreign owner for Daewoo, to increase the level of competition in the domestic automobile market, gave rise to widespread strike action by workers in Daewoo and other automobile companies over concerns regarding potential job losses. The economic crisis therefore created opportunities and imposed constraints on the HMC's growth. By taking over Kia, the HMC was able to bring its annual production capacity up to two million cars in domestic plants. At the same time, it secured a monopoly market position in the domestic passenger-car market, with over 70 per cent of sales. The economic crisis, however, greatly affected the domestic car market, with sales decreasing from 116,619 hundred million won in 1997 to 86,980 hundred million won in 1998 (US$7.2 billion). Furthermore, the Korean domestic car market was opened to international competition from foreign multinationals who were seeking to enter the South Korean domestic market by taking over bankrupted automobile companies such as Daewoo. Large multinational automobile producers have also begun exporting to Korea in line with the free trade policies of the World Trade Organization. These developments will inevitably intensify competition in the domestic automobile market in future years (HMC 1997, *Chosun Ilbo* 6 June 1998 – 20 July 1999, Samsung Securities 1999: 822–3).

Among the three companies, HHI suffered most seriously from the 1979 worldwide depression which resulted in a decline in the movement of natural resources and thus marine transportation. Consequently, the Chun government provided HHI with a monopoly over the production of marine engines in excess of 6,000 horsepower, as well as financial support. HHI also adopted a very aggressive low-cost market approach to gain orders. As a result, HHI contracted nine Very Large Crude Carriers (VLCCs) of a total of fifteen new VLCCs offered in the international market and twenty other tanker projects in 1986, so that its international market share increased from 3 per cent in 1974 to 18 per cent in 1986 (Korean Shipbuilding Industries Association 1991, HHI 1992: 514–35, 686–90).

However, HHI's shipbuilding business had inherent structural deficiencies due largely to its low-cost market practice and labour-intensive mode of production. These features of its business were contrary to industry trends. Since the late 1970s, its competitors had gradually moved from large-scale, bulk carrier ship construction to micro and technologically intensive product carriers. Moreover, the development of a mass trade union movement in HHI from the mid-1980s directly undermined its low-cost market advantage, which was further aggravated by the emergence of shipbuilding in other developing countries such as China and Brazil with low labour costs. As a result, its market position continuously declined over the 1986 and 1989 period from 74.4 per cent to 31.4 per cent of the domestic market, and from 18 per cent to 10 per cent of the international market (*Monthly Economic Review* September 1987: 73–86, HHI 1992: 532–5, 544–7, 617–24, 730–5).

Therefore, it was imperative for the HHI to abandon its outmoded production methods and adopt a growth strategy based on the production of high value added ships that required a high level of marine engineering. With assistance from government policies, labour-intensive production was intensively automated with shipbuilding technology through various R&D institutes. These efforts helped boost the average value of ships constructed from US$30 million in 1981 to US$60.5 million in 1990, and production of the most technologically advanced ships, liquefied natural gas carriers (LNG), in 1993. In addition, HHI diversified into other heavy industrial products such as marine developments, industrial plant and industrial robots in order to reduce its dependency on the fragile shipbuilding industry. In the process of diversification, Hyundai Steel Tower (1987), Hyundai Industrial Robots (1987) and Hyundai Heavy Machinery and Equipment (1988) became independent subsidiaries of HHI (HHI 1992: 594, 659–65, 786, 961, 984–5, *Chungang Ilbo* 21 July 1995).

In response to the structural problems resulting from its over dependence on heavy and machinery industries, Hyundai diversified into higher value added industries, such as microelectronics and services. Of fifty-four total subsidiaries of Hyundai, twenty-five subsidiaries were founded after the mid-1980s as part of its diversification strategy (Hyundai Public Relations Office 1994: 80–1). Among the new companies of Hyundai founded in the 1980s, a typical example is Hyundai Electronic Industries (HEI), founded in 1983 to produce semiconductor and various microelectronic products such as computers, automotive electronic products and telecommunications systems. The semiconductor was the key product of HEI under the government's new economic policies that favoured technologically intensive industries. Based on an internal market demand, for example automotive electronics for the HMC, HEI began a strategy of becoming a leading international electronics company. To that end, HEI succeeded in developing the 4M Dynamic Random Access Memory (DRAM), 16M DRAM and 64M DRAM in 1989, 1991, and 1993 respectively, under collective research and development projects with other semiconductor companies, such as Samsung and LG, with government support. These significant developments increased HEI sales from three million to 4,419 billion won over the 1984–99 period (*Shin Dong-Ah* February 1987: 340–8, *Chosun Ilbo* 24 July 1994, HEI 1994; Samsung Securities 1999: 824). The increased role of subsidiaries was evident in the diminishing contribution of the HECC, HMC and HHI, to the growth of Hyundai in the 1980s. The dependence of Hyundai's growth on the sales of these three core companies decreased from over 70 per cent in 1977 to 31 per cent in 1993, while total sales of Hyundai have steadily grown from 106 hundred billion won in 1977 to 1,252 hundred billion won in 1993 (Kwon 1997: 108).

Figure 8.2 also shows the burgeoning structure of Hyundai in 1994. It outlines the expansion of a wide range of business areas, from the production of resources to manufacturing, the retail sector, mass media, banking and the knowledge-based service industries. This broad based expansion occurred as the result of its wholesale revision of the 'one-set' system which was undertaken in order to reduce the dominance of heavy and machinery industries. This large-scale 'one-set' approach of Hyundai was a pervasive feature of national economic growth in the 1980s and the early 1990s, with the consequence that Hyundai became increasingly dominant in the Korean economy.

Another significant change in the 1990s was that Hyundai's globalization strategy involved locating or transplanting production systems overseas, for example, Southeast Asia, Europe, and North and Central America. There were various reasons for this strategy. First, to overcome market protection in advanced countries.

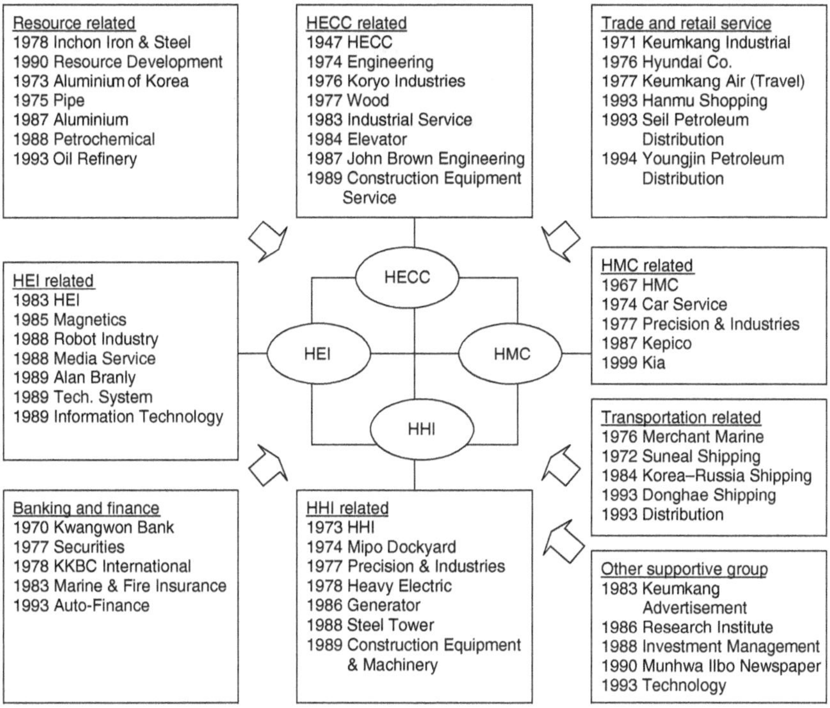

Figure 8.2 Growth structure of Hyundai in 1994 by type of business, with foundation year.
Source: Kwon and O'Donnell 2001: 109.

This led HEI, in 1996, to establish a US$1,300 million electronics plant in the United States. Second, to maintain low-cost production. To this end in 1996, HHI set up heavy construction machinery factories in China. Labour-intensive industries were the prime targets for relocation to developing countries such as Vietnam, China and India (*Maeil Economic Newspaper* 29 July, 19 August 1991, 19 January 1993, *Chungang Economic Newspaper* 25 May 1994, Kong Jae-wuk 1994: 46–7, *Chosun Ilbo* 29 September 1995).

8.4.1 Combined patrimonial and managerial hierarchy

Despite extensive reorganization of the business structure of Hyundai, the centralized authority of Hyundai's top management, especially the family hierarchy of the founder, remained a key institution of control. As at 1994, ten of seventeen chairmen in Hyundai have kinship ties. In contrast with the phase of rapid expansion in the 1970s, the managerial structure of Hyundai in the 1980s reflected a more stable period of growth for the three core companies (Table 8.3).

Since the early 1980s, however, there have been significant changes in the role of the Group Planning Office in providing support to top management at Hyundai.

Table 8.3 Annual changes in the total number of executives in HECC, HMC and HHI, 1983–93

Year	*1983*	*1984*	*1985*	*1986*	*1987*	*1988*	*1989*	*1990*	*1991*	*1992*	*1993*
HECC	84	86	99	102	90	102	89	85	na	86	101
HMC	21	29	33	38	44	46	52	54	51	35	73
HHI	52	67	69	84	91	92	93	108	76	79	81

Source: Derived from Maeil Economic Newspaper Co., selective years, 1983–93.

Note

The executives selected for the data were based on employment conditions and only those who were appointed by the shareholders' meeting.

Its operations have been extended to encompass long-term managerial policies of the diversified, conglomerate business at the Group level. The Group Planning Office was expanded from twenty-five employees and a vice-presidentship to forty employees and a presidentship between 1982 and 1990.[12] These upgraded service functions served to support the central authority of Hyundai's top management. For example, the Group Planning Office has been involved in a revision and consolidation of collective personnel and labour management policies and practices at the Group level in close liaison with the personnel and labour sections of the subsidiaries (HECC 1982: 627, 766, 786, *Monthly Observer* July 1990: 175–6, *Shin Dong-A* September 1991: 257, HHI 1992: 533).

However, a significant change occurred in the character of general management and of the kinship and HECC-backed structure of Hyundai top management in the late 1980s. Its kinship structure had been formed by the enhancement of the managerial positions of the sons of the founder, while his brothers had separated from Hyundai in the late 1970s and early 1980s. The founder's sons took over key decision-making positions in the main subsidiaries of Hyundai from the early 1980s. Their positions were strengthened with the official retirement by the founder, Chung Juyung, from the Group chairmanship in 1987. However, Hyundai remained subject to his indirect control through his kinship hierarchy and links to professional executives originating from HECC though a number of non-HECC-backed professional managers gradually increased.[13] By 1994, kinship relations to Chung and managerial experience originating in HECC were still the dominant backgrounds of top managers in Hyundai.

8.5 Family and managerial capitalism in the Korean *chaebol*

So far, this chapter has sought to identify and explain three developmental stages of Hyundai from its inception in the 1940s to that of a large-scale conglomerate in the 1990s, based on the three propositions selected.

Three distinctive features in the transformation of the three developmental stages of Hyundai have been explored. First, government support for the *chaebol*, as part of rapid industrialization strategies, underpinned and facilitated the expansion and diversification of Hyundai businesses. Second, through the 'one-set' growth strategy and structure, Hyundai achieved vertical and horizontal integration of its diversified businesses in the construction industry (1950–60), heavy and machinery industries (1970s to the early 1980s), and the electronics and service industries (the mid-1980s onwards). The most critical goal behind deployment of this 'one-set' strategy was to reinforce market competitive advantages obtained from economies of scale and scope.

Third, in spite of the transformation from small to large industrial economies of Hyundai, there has been no separation between the managerial control and ownership and was still under the leadership of the owner founder, Chung Juyoung and his family members. To maintain the central authority of the family top management, the governing structure of its businesses was modified over time from informal patriarchal control by the founder, to a combined hierarchy of patriarchal and managerial control, and to a transitional character which combined, on succession of the second generation, the patrimonial and its subordinated managerial hierarchy. This does not deny the significant role of the professional management which has been the main sustainer for such capitalism through its strategic functions. These three aspects of Hyundai's transformation are summarized in Table 8.4, which highlights the main characteristics distinguishing each developmental stage of Hyundai.

Given that Hyundai has emerged as Korea's leading business group or *chaebol*, it is not unreasonable to make the assumption given the paucity of detailed case studies, that Hyundai constitutes the quintessential *chaebol*, whose historical development provides a more or less general model of Korean capitalist transformation. Such evidence, as is available, suggests that other *chaebol* have indeed followed a somewhat similar path of capital transformation. As mentioned earlier, most of such research argues that development of large-scale monopoly capitalism in Korea through the

Table 8.4 Developmental patterns of Hyundai since its inception in 1946

Period	*1946–1960s*	*1970s–early 1980s*	*1980s–1990s*
Political economy	Liberation and war economy Initial industrialization	State-guided economy Rapid industrialization	Transition to less regulated market economy
Growth pattern	Family to industrial economy 'One-set' system in construction industry	Monopoly capitalism 'One-set' system in heavy and machinery industries	Transition 'One-set' system in diverse industries
Growth structure	Single company Section/department system	Conglomerate structure Division system	Transitional character Small business groups
Managerial pattern	Formalization of patriarchal control	Development of patriarchal and managerial hierarchy	Development of patrimonial and managerial hierarchy

Source: Drawn from the analysis by the authors.

chaebol is largely attributable to the rapid industrialization policies of the state, especially since the 1960s.[14] The main characteristics of the diversification strategy of the *chaebol* were, to a greater or lesser degree, similar to the 'one-set' systems of Hyundai in various businesses. For example, the diversified businesses of Samsung or Daewoo range from textiles, to electronics and to the automobile and shipbuilding industries. Furthermore, the central governing system of Hyundai through the Group Planning Office, which implements the strategic decisions of the family top management, is typically seen in the other *chaebol*.[15] In relation to changes in the dimensions of family ownership, in 1990 among the fourty-nine top *chaebol* in Korea, the second generation of twenty-one *chaebol* succeeded the managerial control of the founder, while twenty-eight *chaebol* were still controlled by the founder's family members (*Monthly Chosun* February 1990).

The historical developments of Korean capitalism or, at least, those of Hyundai constitute a similar but unique and distinctive process *vis-à-vis* western capitalism in which the family business was transformed into managerial enterprise, and Japanese capitalism, where the family-controlled *zaibatsu* gave way to collective capitalism. Overall the growth strategy that Hyundai employed to diversify and expand is somewhat similar to those in many American, European and Japanese industrial enterprises, as it aimed to achieve economies of scale and scope for competitive market advantages. In association with development of its large-scale and conglomerate businesses, Hyundai devised the central governing system, Group Planning Office, which enabled top management to centrally control various businesses to obtain the potential synergy effects. This is in a manner similar to that of comparable American firms, which functioned as a central administration unity to achieve horizontal and vertical integration of diversified businesses for the economies of scale and scope (Chandler 1982).

Despite these similarities, three distinctive features of the Hyundai case study mentioned before can be extended to all the *chaebol*. These differences require the pre-stated propositions to be revised.

First, in relation to external environments, as discussed, different environment forces exerted influence resulting in different patterns of capitalist transformation with their international variations. Hence, a contingent approach is required rather than the unilateral application of one dominant external force. The role of the state was a significant contributor to the transformation of Korean capitalism. This is in sharp contrast with the *laissez-faire* role of the state in western countries in the early twentieth century. In these countries, the market economy formed dominant external forces. In such contexts, continued growth of enterprises depended on how they utilized various resources such as advanced technology, capital, distribution channel, natural resources and production capacity through merger or acquisition of other firms. Given limited such resources in Korea, the state played a leading role in controlling these resources for the rapid industrialization of Korean economy. Hence, the cosy state–business relationship has been the most critical external source for the growth of the large industrial conglomerates, rather than market forces.

In relation to the strategy and structure framework of Chandler, the second proposition also needs to be revised. Chandler (1962) sees the function of the structure as subordinated to the strategy adopted. However, as Gospel (1983: 169) argues, there exists a two-way causal relationship between them. On the one hand, strategy calls for structural reforms. On the other hand, structure either facilitates or confirms further strategic activities. For example, as identified throughout the case study in this chapter, Hyundai used an intensive diversification strategy – first in construction in the 1950s and 1960s, then the automobiles and shipbuilding in the 1970s, and later in the electronics and service industries. In the process of this diversification, the previous business structure facilitated the new strategic decisions, for example, by the creation of internal market demand for the new business. Therefore, the theoretical relationship between these two variables needs to be understood as an interactive and dynamic relationship.

This growth strategy and structure of the Korean *chaebol* is quite distinctive from those in the West and Japan. In contrast with diversification practices of the West being exercised within similar industrial or business boundaries, the *chaebol*'s strategy has often been cynically described as an 'Octopus Arm' style which operates across industrial boundaries (Kim Beoyong-ha 1991: 16–25). For example, Hyundai's businesses range from shipbuilding to mass media, finance and chemical industry. LG Business Group also produces from toothpaste, to clothes, semiconductor and heavy machinery. In 1997, on average, the top thirty *chaebol* owned 27.3 subsidiaries in 19.8 unrelated industries (*Chosun Ilbo* 23 January 1998).

Furthermore, although, in the light of a functional aspect, the central governing system of the *chaebol*, Group Planning Office, is similar to the central administrative unit of those in western Countries or a holding company of Japanese conglomerates, its organizational character is substantially different from them. As mentioned earlier, the Group Planning Office is neither an organizational unit in the managerial structure of a company nor an independent holding company. The Group Planning Office system has been developed based on *de facto* existence as a consequence of the kin ownership control over various subsidiaries of the *chaebol* without a legal status. As each subsidiary of Hyundai has been operating with an independent legal status, the *ad-hoc* unit, Group Planning Office, has been devised by kin ownership of each *chaebol* to centrally control every aspect of the management of subsidiaries.

In relation to the third proposition as to the nature of capitalism, transformation from the family to managerial capitalism has not yet taken place in Korea. As discussed earlier, family capitalism still is and will be a dominant character of Korean capitalism through its patrimonial transfer to next generations. The founders' family members are still able to maintain a close control of conglomerate business activities, whereas by comparison, managerial capitalism is well entrenched in large industrial enterprises in the United States and Europe.

However, the role of professional managers in the historical transformation of the *chaebol* should not be underestimated. These managers underpinned the hierarchical managerial structure, which enabled family dominated top management to retain central control of increasingly extensive, complex conglomerate businesses (Kwon 1997: 25–6). However, they functioned as strategic but subordinated agents for the kin ownership of the *chaebol*.

These three propositions need to be understood in conjunction with one another, as they are interrelated and interdependent. External conditions do influence the dynamics between the strategy and the structure. Policies adopted by the Korean government undoubtedly changed the strategy and structure of the Korean *chaebol*. In the Korean case, the fact that the separation between owners and managers has not taken place may reflect a relatively short history of the Korean capitalism. However, but it was also due to the policies adopted by the government as well.

8.6 A new era for the Korean capitalism?

As to the future development path of Korean capitalism, it is still uncertain whether and how much Korean capitalism will continue to be dominated by the *chaebol*, owned and controlled by the founder's family members, and also whether there will be a degree of convergence with the model of managerial capitalism predominant in western countries. To understand future directions of Korean capitalism, however, this concluding section discusses structural changes in the Korean capitalism in the context of the economic crisis since late 1997 by using three theoretical propositions revised in the previous section.

The Korean economy has been severely affected since the end of 1997 by what has been termed as the 'IMF Crisis', during which the banking system was unable to repay its large external debt nor to maintain the stability of the currency. The causes and the implications of this crisis can also be understood within the context of the three distinctive features of the Korean capitalism summarized in this chapter.

First, the origin of this crisis lies in the close relationship between the *chaebol* and the state, which controlled the banking sector. This resulted in widespread corruption and provided the *chaebol* with ready access to state supports at times of difficulties. To rescue strategic industries of Korean economy from difficulties, the state created market demands or provided generous financial options for the state-favoured *chaebol* which took over other financially insolvent firms.

Second, the relationship between the government and the *chaebol* influenced the dynamics between the strategy and structure of firms. Examples can be found in their financial management strategy. The non-performing debts held by Korean banks and the *chaebol* increased considerably. The average debt ratio of the top thirty *chaebol* (excluding finance and banking sector) reached to 4.5 times (247.6 trillion won) of their capital size (55.1 trillion won) as at December 1997 (*Hankyorae Shinmun* 24 March 1998). The four largest *chaebol*, Hyundai, LG, Samsung and Daewoo, account for more than half of Korea's debt. In addition, while they were pursuing the 'one-set' growth strategy, firms within each *chaebol* have cross-guaranteed the debts of other firms, which totalled about 33 trillion won among the top thirty *chaebol* (*Korea Herald* 13 February 1998). This debt-driven growth strategy was workable during the rapid expansion period.[16] Yet, when the economy turns to crisis and thus decrease of sales and increase of interests, this growth approach is confronted with serious financial problems (*Business Review Weekly* 6 April 1998). The adoption of this expansionist strategy by all *chaebol* across the board was possible due to the tight control of the owner managers over the entire group through their group planning offices.

The inability of the *chaebol* to handle their debts caused the currency crisis in the Korean banks and Korean economy. In this context, the former President Kim Youngsam requested urgent financial support from the IMF. In return for financial assistance, the IMF demanded that the Korean economy be opened up to increased foreign competition, that the *chaebol* be pressured to restructure and that the Korean labour market be deregulated to increase flexibility (*Chosun Ilbo* 13–18 November, 1–9 December 1997).

Due to this crisis, the growth rate of Korean economy is predicted to decrease from 7 per cent in 1997 to −5 per cent in 1998. This economic downturn is expected to last, at least, over the next three or four years, although the length of this recovery period will depend on the success of the crisis management of the whole economy (*Hankyorae Shinmun* 9 April 1998). However, what is more important than its short-term effect on the performance of the economy is the restructuring process. The economic crisis called for radical changes both in the government and in the Korean corporate sector. The ramifications of these structural changes can also be summarized into three categories, adopted in this chapter.

First, there has been a critical change in the role of the state after the 1997 presidential election. The long repressed opposition leader, Kim Daejung was elected. Subsequently, the new government aimed to achieve 'harmony of democracy and market economy' (*Korea Economic Weekly* 2 March 1998). The emergence of the new Kim government implies the end of authoritarian practices of the state and development of various democratic apparatus. Hence, the authoritarian state-guided economy is to change and the removal of other corrupt business has become one of the focal areas for the changed policy.

The new government pressured the *chaebol* to restructure their 'Octopus Arm' style of business practices. These diversified businesses of the *chaebol* are being forced to focus on a small number of key subsidiaries which possess their own competitive advantages. Other subsidiaries are required to be sold off, in order to meet the government's control programme reducing their total debt size from 450 to 200 percent by the end of 2002. In addition, a consolidated financial statement is now required, with accounting practices to secure transparent managerial operations of the *chaebol*. To minimize the economic and ownership concentration, the government banned the cross-guaranteeing system and capital investments among their subsidiaries by revision of the *Fair Trade Act* in February 1998 and intended to strongly implement high tax rates on the inheritance income, especially for the owners of the *chaebol*.

Second, in response to these unfavourable politico-economic environments, the *chaebol* strive to modify such unfavourable external forces, including the state's new economic policies, through their collective organization, the Federation of Korean Industries (FKI). This effort resulted in the moderation of the aggressive government approach to the *chaebol*, accompanied by the public criticism on the *chaebol*'s responsibility for the current economic crisis. In spite of such collective efforts, they are still being forced to accommodate into the 'IMF Crisis' without state protection. Therefore, the *chaebol* began to slim down their excessively diversified and vast business size to a few strategic businesses in order to rebuild or enhance their competitiveness. For example, the Hyosung Business Group, the seventeenth largest *chaebol* ranked by sales in 1997, massively reorganized its twenty-four businesses into six sectors with five major subsidiaries. In the case of Hyundai, its newspaper corporation, Munhwa Ilbo, was the first target to separate from its business conglomerate because of its financial debt and unrelated business nature. In the case of Ssangyong, the sixth largest *chaebol* in 1997, its automobile company, Ssangyong Motor, was sold out to Daewoo Motor in 1998 (*Hankyorae Shinmun* 10–19 January 1998).

Globalization of business was one of the new characteristics of the *chaebol*'s growth strategy in the 1990s. Among others, Daewoo's internationalization strategy is noticeable. Daewoo's international operations include thirty-two domestic subsidiaries, 590 overseas business sites. They have 320,000 employees in 110 countries and the revenue reached US$80 billion in 1997 (*Hankyorae Shinmun* 28 December 1997, *Business Review Weekly* 6 April 1998). The globalization drive of the Korean *chaebol* has slowed down somewhat due to the economic crisis in 1997. However, globalization remains to be an indispensable option for the Korean *chaebol*, in order to overcome increasing domestic production costs, intensifying global competition and the market protection of OECD and Asian economies.

Third, following state pressure, an immediate change has occurred in the managerial structure of the *chaebol*. Restructuring has also begun in the central governing unit, Group Planning Office system. The government requested the *chaebol* to remove their informal but central administration unit, the Group Planning Office, and instead the *chaebol* owners are being asked to be legal representatives of each subsidiary rather than legally hidden controllers using the Group Planning Office system (*Chosun Ilbo* 24 January 1998, 16 February 1998, *Hankyorae Shinmun* 26 February 1998, *Korea Economy Weekly* 23 February 1998, *Sisa Journal* 19 February 1998).

In response to the demand from the new government, the top ten *chaebol* are reorganizing this informal central control unit. Its functions are divided and taken over by the key or mother company of the *chaebol*. For example, the major functions of the Group Planning Office in Hyundai have been transferred to HECC and those in Samsung to Samsung Co and Samsung Electronics. In line with such change, the family owners and their immediate family members are appointed as multiple representatives of key subsidiaries of the *chaebol*. Examples include Kim Woochoong, the founder of Daewoo, as the representative of Daewoo Motor and Daewoo Co and Chung Mongku, the eldest son of Chung Juyoung, as representatives of its six subsidiaries on the basis of their share proportion (*Chosun Ilbo* 8, 27, 16 February 1998, *Hankyorae 21* 19 February 1998).

In doing so, the vast conglomerate businesses of the *chaebol* is expected to be decentralized into a number of smaller business groups being managed by the founder's sons. However, these smaller business groups are likely to function as *satellite* groups cooperatively, as a looser version of the 'one-set' system to promote their co-joint growth in response to unstable politico-economic environments. An example of this type of cooperation in the history of Hyundai can be drawn from the companies of Chung's brothers and sons which formally separated from the Hyundai *chaebol* in the late 1970s and late 1990s. In this context, professional managers will play an expanding role in governance of the *chaebol*, in an increasingly competitive, globalized business environment, though still subject to contingent managerial oversight and the dominance of family ownership. All these imply that the large-scale conglomerate structure of the *chaebol* is likely to be decentralized and reconfigured to some indeterminate extent to the patrimonial mode of managerial capitalism.

In sum, the fast growth period of the Korean economy has ended, and a road to maturity requires a substantial realignment of strategies by both government and the business sector. The relationship between the state and the business sector has begun to change. Accordingly, the business sector needs to redefine its strategies and establish a new dimension of internal structure befitting the new goals and external constraints. As the role of owner managers is bound to decrease, the role of professional managers will become increasingly important in the new century.

The Korean business sector is at its important cross roads. As the past development of the Korean *chaebol* can be characterized by three factors identified in this chapter, the future development of the Korean *chaebol* will also depend on successful restructuring of the business sector and the whole economy. In all three areas identified in this chapter, more researches and debates are warranted urgently in order to contribute positively to the restructuring of the government and the business and also to the establishment of policies, strategies and structures.

Notes

1 This research was sponsored by a research grant (2001–2) from the *Korea–Australasia Research Centre.*
2 See, for example, Chandler 1962, 1990a, Prais 1976, Fligstein 1990, Lazonick 1991, Schmitz 1993.
3 For arguments of variations in the historical transformation, see British case studies in Elbaum and Lazonick 1986 and of similarities, Chandler *et al.* 1980, Lazonick 1986, Chandler, 1990b, Schmitz 1993.
4 In this chapter, Korean names are given in their proper order, with the surname proceeding the given name. However, in the case of Korean authors writing in English, the order natural to English is preserved.
5 See, for example, Tamio 1986.
6 Here, Chandler (1977)'s term, the 'visible hand' can be applied in this context, that is, the supply and processing of every major resource occurs within the extended business enterprise.
7 The 'section' stands for an organizational unit hierarchically located between a department (*Bu*) and subsection (*Gae*). It is usually organized by five to eight members including a manager.
8 In the 1970s, typical construction projects from government bodies were an iron and steel mill for Pohang Steel Corporation (1970–80), a series of Kori Nuclear Power Plants (1971–78), a series of subway projects (1972–80) and chemical industrial plants in Ulsan Industrial Park (1972–74).
9 The market share of the HMC is calculated by the total amount of domestic sales of passenger cars of four major Korean passenger-car companies, Hyundai, Daewoo, Kia and Ssangyoung.

10 This kind of internal structure was defined as an M-form industrial group by Chandler (1982: 3–23).
11 For the details of an independent trade union movement at Hyundai workplaces and its impact on Hyundai businesses, see Kwon, 1997.
12 In the course of implementing the new growth strategy, its previous public relations and research functions were transferred to the Keumkang Advertising Agency and Hyundai Research Institute which had been established in 1983 and 1984, respectively to enhance the provision of such professional services to the subsidiaries.
13 Of the total fourty-four presidents in Hyundai, twenty-five presidents were non-HECC backed in 1994 (Hyundai Group Public Relations Office 1994: 80–1). This implies a gradual evolution in the second level of top management away from dominance by Chung Juyoung and his subordinates to those in each of the subsidiaries being promoted to top management positions.
14 For the supportive arguments, see Jones *et al.* 1980, Kuk 1988, Amsden 1989, Kang 1990.
15 For further details of the Group Planning Office systems in the Korean *chaebol*, see Park Hee 1992.
16 In 1996, the top fifty *chaebol* had profits of only US$32 million on sales of US$274 billion (Business Review Weekly 6 April 1998).

Bibliography

Ansoff, H. (1969) *Business Strategy*, Penguin: London:

Amsden, A. (1989) *Asia's Next Giant: South Korea and Late Industrialization*, New York: Oxford University Press.

Bank of Korea (1990) *Annual Reports on Economic Statistics*, Seoul: BOA.

Chandler, A. (1962) *Strategy and Structure*, Cambridge: MIT.

——(1977) *The Visible Hand: The Managerial Revolution in American Business*, London: Belknap Press.

——(1982) 'The M-form: industrial groups, American style', *European Economic Review*, 19: 3–23.

——(1990a) *Scale and Scope: The Dynamics of Industrial Capitalism*, Cambridge: Belknap Press.

——(1990b) 'The enduring logic of industrial success', *Harvard Business Review*, 68(2), March–April: 130–40.

——(1992) 'Managerial enterprises and competitive capabilities', *Business History*, 34(1), January: 11–41.

——and Daems, H. (eds) (1980) *Managerial Hierarchies: Comparative Perspective on the Rise of the Modern Industrial Enterprise*, Cambridge: Harvard University Press.

Chang, C. S. (1988) '*Chaebol*: the South Korean conglomerates', *Business Horizons*, 31, March and April: 51–7.

Cheon Beom-seong (1984) *Chung Juyung*, Seoul: Seomundang.

Cho Dong-seong (1991) *Hankukchaebol Yeonku (A Study of Korean Chaebol)*, Seoul: Maeil Economic Newspaper.

Chung Ku-hyeon (1989) *Hankukkiyeobeui Seongjang Jeonrakkwa Kyungyoungkujo (Growth Strategy and Managerial Structure of Korean Companies)*, Seoul: Korean Commercial Industry.

Church, R. (1993) 'The family firm in industrial capitalism: international perspective on hypotheses and history', *Business History*, 35(4): 17–43.

Elbaum, B. and Lazonic, W. (eds)(1986) *The Decline of the British Economy*, Oxford: Clarendon Press.

Fligstein, N. (1990) *The Transformation of Corporate Control*, Cambridge: Harvard University Press.

Gospel, H. (1983) 'New approaches to industrial relations: major paradigms and historical perspective', *The Journal of Industrial Relations*, June, 162–76.

Jones, L. and SaKong, Il (1980) *Government, Business and Entrepreneurship in Economic Development: The Korean Case*, Cambridge: Council on East Asian Studies, Harvard University Press.

Hofstede, G. and Bond, M. (1988) 'The confucius connection: from cultural roots to economic growth', *Organizational Dynamics*, 16 (4): 5–1.

Hong Deok-rul (1985) Hankukchaeboleui Hwankyungtongjae Kijaeea Kwanhan Yeonku (Environment Control Systems of the *Chaebol*), Master's Thesis, Seoul: Seoul National University.

Hyundai Electronics Industries (HEI: 1994) *Hyundai Jeonja 10nyeonsa (A Ten Year History of Hyundai Electronics Industries)*, Seoul: HEI.

Hyundai Engineering and Construction Corporation (HECC: 1982) *Hyundai Geonseol 35nyeonsa (A Thirty-five Year History of Hyundai Engineering and Construction)*, Seoul: HECC.

Hyundai Group Public Relations Office (1994) *'94 Hyundai*, Seoul: Hyundai Group Public Relations Office.

Hyundai Group Trade Union Association (1994) *Hyunchongryeon Danhyeobjaryojib (Collective Bargaining of the Hyundai Trade Union Association)*, Seoul: HGTUA.

Hyundai Heavy Industries (HHI: 1992) *Hyundai Junggongeobsa (History of Hyundai Heavy Industries)*, Seoul: HHI.

Hyundai Motor Company (HMC: 1987) *Hyundai Jadongcha 20nyeonsa(A Twenty Year History of Hyundai Motor Company)*, Seoul: HMC.

——(HMC: 1992) *Hyundai Jadongchasa (The History of Hyundai Motor Company)*, Seoul: HMC.

——(HMC: 1997) *Hyundai Jadongchasa 35sa (The 35 years History of Hyundai Motor Company)*, Seoul: HMC.

Kang, Y. G. (1990) The Rise of Korean Chaebols from the Perspective of Organization Theory, PhD Thesis, Arizona: University of Arizona.

Kim, K. C. and Kim, S. (1989) 'Kinship group and patrimonial executives in a developing nation: a case study of Korea', *The Journal of Developing Area*, 24, October, 27–46.

Kim Beoyong-ha (1991) *Chaebolheyoungkwa Kiyeobka Hwaldong (Formation of Chaebol and their Entrepreneurs)*, Seoul: Hankuk Neungyeulhyeobhoe.

Kim Eun-Mee (1997) *Big Business, Strong State: Collusion and Conflict in South Korean Development, 1960–80*, New York: State University of New York Press.

Kim Hyo-gun (1986) Hankukcaeboleui Seongjang Baljeoneoinae Kwanhan Yeonku (The Developmental Factors for the Growth of the *Chaebol*), Master's Thesis, Seoul: Seoul National University.

Kim Young-ho (1985) *Kyungjaeeui Hyeonjang (Reality of Economy in Korea)*, Seoul: Dongcheonsa.

Kong Byeong-ho (1992) *Chaebol, Binanbadaya Hanneunka? (Why Should The Chaebol Be Criticized?)*, Seoul: Yeyeumsa.

Kong Jae-wuk (1994) *1950nyeondaeui Hankukeui Jabonga Yeonku (Korean Capitalists in the 1950s)*, Seoul: Baeksan.

Korean Shipbuilding Industries Association (1991) *Annual Reports on Shipbuilding Industries*, Seoul: KSIA.

Kwon, S.H. (1997) Control and Conflict: The Historical Development of Labour Management within the Hyundai Business Group, 1946–95, unpublished PhD Thesis, Sydney: University of New South Wales.

Kwon, S.H. and Leggett, C. (1994) *Industrial Relations and the South Korean Chaebol*, A Proceeding of the 8th AIRAANZ Conference, February 1994, Sydney.

Kwon, S.H. and Suh, C. (1998) *Growth Strategy and Structure of the Korean Chaebol*, A paper for the 4th Pacific and Asia Conference on Korean Studies, 10–14 May, Vancouver.

Kwon, S.H. and O'Donnell, M. (2001) *The Chaebol and Labour in Korea*, New York: Routledge.

Kuk, M.H.(1988) The Relationship between Government and Private Companies in the Industrial Development of South Korea, PhD thesis, Urbana: University of Illinios.

Lazonick, W. (1986) 'Strategy, structure and management development in the United States and Britain', in K. Kobayashi and H. Morikawa (eds), *Development of Managerial Enterprise*, Tokyo: University of Tokyo, 101–46.

——(1991) *Business Organization and the Myth of the Market Economy*, Cambridge: Cambridge University Press.

Lee Ho (1993) *Jeongsangeun Yuyeonhi Ojianneunda: Chung Seyungkwa Hyundai Motor Company (Chung Seyung and Hyundai Motor Company)*, Seoul: Wukseok.

Lee Jong-nam (1985) *Chaebol*, Seoul: Heyonjae.

Lee Jong-seon (1989) Jungkongeob Geodaedogjeomkieobeaseoeui Nodongwundongea Kwanhan Yeonku (The Labour Movements in Large Scale and Monopolistic Heavy Industries), Master's thesis, Seoul: Korea University.

Lee Jung-jae (1994) *Chaebol Iryeokseo (The Chaebol and its Status)*, Seoul: Hankuk Newspaper.

Lee Sung-tae (1990) *Gamchueojin Dokjeomchaeboleui Yeoksa (Hidden History of Monopolistic Chaebol)*, Seoul: Nokdu.

Maeil Economic Newspaper (1975–94) *Annual Corporation Reports*, MEN: Seoul. K. Nikagawa (ed.) *Strategy and Structure of Big Business*, Proceedings of the First Fuji Conference, Tokyo: University of Tokyo.

Park Byung-yun (1982) *Chaebolkwa Jeongchi (The Chaebol and Politics)*, Seoul: Hankuk Yangseo.

Park Dong-sun (1979) *Chaeboleui Bburi (Roots of the Chaebol)*, Seoul: Taechang.

Park Hee (1992) *Hankuk Daekieubeui Jojik Kwanriwa Nosakwangaeei Kwanhan Yeongu (Organizational Operation and Labour Relations in Big Corporations*, PhD thesis, Seoul: Yonsei University.

Park, Moon-Kyu (1987) 'Interest representation in South Korea', *Asian Survey*, 27(8): 904–19.

Prais, S. (1976) *The Evolution of Giant Firms in Britain*, Cambridge: Cambridge, University Press.

Rhee, J. C. (1994) *The State and Industry in South Korea: the Limits of the Authoritarian State*, London: Routledge.

Sakong, I. (1993) *Korea in the World Economy*, Washington: Institute for International Economics.

Samsung Securities (1999) Sangjang Kieob Bunseok (Analysis of Stock Listed Companies), Seoul: Samsung Securities.

Schmitz, C. (1993) *The Growth of Big Business in the United States and Western Europe*, London: Macmillan.

Steers, R., Shin, Y. K. and Ungson, G. (1989) *The Chaebol: Korea's New Industrial Might*, New York: Harper Collins.

Tamio, H.(1986) *Hankukkieubeui Kujowa Jeonrak (Strategy and Structure of Korean Firms)*, Seoul: Beobmun.

Yang Yoo-jin (1991) *Hankuk Jabonjuei Bunseok (Analysis of the Korean Capitalism)*, Seoul: Ilbit.

Wade, R. (1990) *Governing the Market: Economic Theory and the Role of Government in East Asian Industrialization*, New York: Princeton University Press.

9 Real exchange rate and inward FDI in crisis-ridden Korea

Jung-Soo Seo

9.1 Introduction

Since mid-1997, a highly contagious financial crisis swept through the economies in East Asia, resulting initially in a free fall of their respective currency values. The crisis subsequently led to bulging unemployment rates and a general economic downturn in these economies. Among others, Thailand, Indonesia and Korea were the hardest hit by the crisis. Such currency crises were not new and had occurred a few times previously in other economies. However, the depth and consequences of the Asian crisis alarmed many people, in the business sector and in the academia, who had touted the remarkable success of the Asian economies as the 'Asian miracle'.[1] However, there were some economists, such as Paul Krugman (1998a), who had predicted a crisis in Asia.

The Asian crises were also followed by a vast flood of literature explaining the causes and the effects of the crises in the region. This literature produced several models and efforts which attempted to explain the Asian crisis. Not only were they diverse in their approach to accounting for the causes of the crisis, but also the origins of the crises were apparently more complex than allowed for in these models. Some models considered the moral hazard of financial intermediaries causing an over-borrowing syndrome (Krugman 1998b). Others like Radelet and Sachs (1998) considered, in their model, the financial fragility to the self-fulfilling panic such as a bank run. In particular, Krugman's model (1999) highlighted the role of the balance sheet and international transfer (Krugman 1999). On the other extreme, some like for example, Cho (1999), took the stance of a political economic approach for the cause of the Asian crisis pointing out US policy towards the Asian region.[2]

While these models and efforts shed light on the causes of the Asian crisis, the countries that have been affected by the crisis have undergone significant reforms and industrial restructuring by implementing various measures to rectify and improve the situation. The reforms and restructuring were a mandatory part of the International Monetary Fund's (IMF) rescue package. In this context, Korea undertook a series of economic and social reforms.[3] The reforms included industrial restructuring and rationalization of the Korean economy mainly through 'big deals' among *chaebols* which were notorious for their high gearing ratios and excessively diversified business and management systems. While reforms ensued in the labour market financial sector reforms included primarily selling off some underperforming banks to foreign investors. The liberalization of the Korean economy was accelerated.

In the turmoil of the financial crisis, the Korean government considered inward foreign direct investment (FDI) as a way out for the crisis-ridden Korean economy. For example, President Kim Dae Jung (1998) during his visit to the United States addressed the role of foreign investment as a critical element for the improvement of the Korean economy. Subsequently, significant changes took place in FDI policies, especially towards foreign ownership. With accelerated liberalization efforts by the Korean government, inward FDI flows in Korea have significantly increased, amounting to US$8.85 billion in 1998 alone. The great increase of inward FDI flows into Korea was surprising since capitals, foreign and domestic, had been fleeing the country when the crisis struck. What are the factors responsible for the increased inward FDI flows to Korea? Is it merely a reflection of policy changes? Or are other factors involved?

The increased FDI inflows into Korea also saw a significant increase in the number of mergers and acquisitions (M&As) of Korean firms and businesses by foreign multinational enterprises (MNEs). As a result, M&As became an increasingly important market entry modality of FDI into Korea. The increased number of M&As of Korean business enterprises by the foreign MNEs created public concern and doubts over the increased foreign ownership in Korea. Some argued that the Asian currency crisis opened up opportunities for MNEs, especially for the US MNEs, to acquire assets in a way to pursue their global long-term growth strategy. However, the skepticism and public concern at the same time focused primarily on the issue of 'selling Korea'.[4]

The principal aim of this chapter is twofold. First, it is to survey recent trends and the development of inward FDI policy changes in crisis-ridden Korea. Particular attention will be paid to policy changes towards foreign ownership in Korea. Second, this chapter intends to deal with the role of exchange rate movements in the inward FDI. The previously mentioned models of the Asian crisis noted, to some extent, the potential acquisition of cheap domestic assets by foreign investors, that is, the 'fire-sale' of domestic assets. Previous efforts at explaining 'fire-sale' FDI were made primarily for the developed countries' experience, especially the Japanese acquisition of the US assets in the 1980s.[5] So far, no systematic efforts have yet been made to examine the issue in the crisis-ridden Asian context. Korea provided a good opportunity for the study in this direction due to accelerated liberalization efforts of inward FDI policies and the more rapid increase of the inward FDI than the other crisis-ridden Asian economies.

This chapter is structured as follows. The next section introduces a brief review of the FDI policies, highlighting recent policy changes by the Korean government towards inward FDI and foreign ownership in a historical context. Also presented in this section are trends and patterns of inward FDI in Korea. Subsequently, an effort will be made to examine if the recent development pattern of inward FDI differs from that of the pre-crisis period in its industrial distribution or in its main characteristics. In Section 9.3, theoretical considerations will be discussed for the role of exchange rate movements in the inward FDI. Particularly focused are the wealth effect and the competitiveness effect on the inward FDI arising from the exchange rate movements. In Section 9.4, we develop a simple econometric model in an effort to disentangle the respective effects of exchange rate movements on the recent inward FDI flows into Korea. The results are discussed in this section. Section 9.5 concludes this chapter with a brief summary of major findings and implications.

9.2 Evolution of policy measures and trends of inward FDI in Korea

Since the enactment of the Foreign Capital Inducement Act in 1960, the Korean government has taken various efforts to promote inward FDI. However, the nature of the FDI policies during the early stages (1960–83) remained fundamentally restrictive and the Korean government considered inward FDI merely as an aid to carrying out policies to achieve its industrialization goal. Thus, the Korean government maintained control over the direction, size and operational schemes of foreign capital in Korea (Kim 1997). During the early period of industrialization FDI was encouraged primarily in export-oriented light manufacturing in an effort to ease the balance of payment problem and exploit export markets. The amount of the inward FDI remained minuscule until the early 1980s with the total approved amount being US$1,179 million in only 375 cases during the period 1962–83.[6]

However, in the early 1980s, structural imbalances appeared in the Korean economy, which followed excessive investments in the heavy and chemical industries in the 1970s.[7] These structural imbalances were coupled with growing current account deficits and snowballing external debts. The Korean government needed to improve the structure of the Korean economy more towards technology- and skill-intensive industries such as optical instruments, industrial robots and electronic switching systems. Thus, the Korean government took a more active approach in the 1980s towards inward FDI and laid particular emphasis on the technology transfer effect of FDI. The adoption of the new approach to the inward FDI was also assisted by changes in the world economy. A heavy reliance, as in the 1970s, on foreign borrowing became extremely costly at the prevailing interest rate arising from the US government's strong dollar policy. The new approaches to FDI were also in line with the general shift of the industrialization policy by the Korean government from the growth first strategy to macroeconomic stability and equity concerns.

For inward FDI approvals, a negative list system was adopted in 1984 by the Korean government. Under this system, any industry not on the list was open to foreign investment. Since then, the Korean government has continued to reduce restrictions and regulations previously imposed on inward FDI, such as performance requirements, while improving market access for the inward FDI. By the time the notification system for FDI was introduced in 1991, the overall liberalization ratio of FDI had reached 79.4 per cent of the total industry. The manufacturing industry was more rapidly opened to foreign investment with a liberalization of 97.7 per cent in 1991 (Kim 1997). Easier market access and an improved business environment due to the liberalization efforts, as well as improved macroeconomic conditions in Korea in the mid-1980s augured well for the level of FDI inflows. The amount of FDI inflows rapidly increased to US$193 million in 1984 and in 1988 reached a peak of US$895 million, as measured on an arrival basis. However, the amount of the inward FDI has since declined due to serious labour disputes and subsequent wage hikes in the late 1980s, soaring real estate prices, and the emergence of the Association of Southeast Asia Nations (ASEAN) as an alternative destination for export oriented, labour-seeking FDI in East Asia.

At the conclusion of the Uruguay Round, the world trading environment in the 1990s created serious challenges for developing countries, including Korea. Globalization of the world economy has become an irreversible trend while regional economic integration has unprecedentedly deepened as manifested by, for example, in the 'Fortress Europe' or in the North America Free Trade Association (NAFTA). At the same time, industrialized countries such as the United States and Japan became increasingly reluctant to transfer advanced technologies to developing countries through licensing. Under such a changed international economic climate, it was necessary for the Korean government to upgrade economic structure and enhance international competitiveness.[8] Thus, the Korean government increased further its efforts in FDI liberalization. For example, a one-stop service system for FDI was established in 1995 and its services were improved in subsequent years.[9] The Korean government also allowed friendly M&As in 1997 although there was a limit of 15 per cent ownership if the firm under M&A consideration had assets of more than 2 trillion won. As a result of such liberalization efforts and expansion of industries open for foreign investment, the amount of FDI increased rapidly to US$1.3 billion in 1994, US$3.2 billion in 1996 and further to US$6.9 billion in 1997.

While pursuing this liberalization effort for FDI in accordance with OECD principles of capital movement, the Asian crisis inflicted a severe blow to the Korean economy in late 1997. The Korean government actively sought foreign investment by accelerating liberalization efforts as a way out of the crisis for the Korean economy. Although new FDI policies may be considered as an extension of the previous liberalization effort for FDI, there occurred subtle but more fundamental changes within the inward FDI policies. The nature of post-crisis FDI policies changed fundamentally from the previous regulation and administration of FDI to supporting and promoting FDI. The Foreign Investment Promotion Act was enacted in November 1998 in an effort to create an investor-oriented policy environment. This new legislation emphasized the streamlining of FDI procedures and strengthening of incentives for FDI, especially in high technology areas. Tax reduction or exemption incentives were extended to foreign investors while restructuring and improving institutional support for FDI through the Korea Investment Service Centre at Korea Trade Association (KOTRA). Under the new system, even fully fledged hostile M&As were allowed, together with foreign land ownership. Categories of business open to foreign investment were expanded, so that the liberalization of FDI in total industry reached 98.9 per cent in May 1999. Thus, only thirteen categories are completely restricted and eighteen categories are partially open for foreign investment. Those restricted categories were scheduled to gradually open for foreign investment from 2000. As a result of such rapid and fundamental changes in FDI policies, the inward FDI flows in 1998 increased by 27 per cent compared with 1997, amounting to US$8.85 billion.[10] Notable during this period was an increase of cross border M&As through acquisition of outstanding shares, that is, friendly M&As. Cross-border M&As increased from around 10 per cent in 1997 to 14 per cent of the total inward FDI of US$1.24 billion in 232 cases. The increasing trend for M&As continued in 1999 such that M&As accounted for 14.5 per cent of the total FDI by July 1999. If we include factory acquisitions or acquisition of ongoing projects in M&As, then M&As' proportion further increased to 53.1 per cent of total FDI in 1998.[11] In 1998, the total cumulative amount of inward FDI in Korea stood at almost US$33.5 billion in 11,686 cases since the first inward FDI in 1962. However, as seen in Table 9.1, about two-third of total inward FDI is a recent phenomenon, particularly after 1994, reflecting the evolution of FDI policies towards liberalization and the changes in the overall economic situation and institutions in Korea.

In terms of industry distribution, the manufacturing sector has been traditionally strong for inward FDI until the early 1990s. Since then its relative importance has declined and the service sector's importance increased. The manufacturing sector accounted for 66 per cent of the total amount of FDI during 1962–93 while the services sector absorbed approximately 34 per cent. Recently, the relative importance of the manufacturing sector fluctuated significantly from around 34 per cent in 1996 to 65 per cent in 1998, with an average of about 51 per cent of the total amount during the 1994–98 period. Within the manufacturing sector, more inward FDI has been directed towards capital- and technology-intensive industries such as chemicals (14 per cent), electrical and electronics (12 per cent) and transport equipment (7 per cent). Light manufacturing industries such as textiles and clothing (2 per cent) attracted only minuscule amounts of the total inward FDI, reflecting changes in Korea's comparative advantage. Among the services sector, hotel, finance and insurance and trading accounted for around 15, 11 and 4 per cent, respectively.[12]

Table 9.1 FDI inflows into Korea 1962–98* (US$ million)

	Manufacturing	*Non-manufacturing*	*Services*	*Total*
1962–86	2,321	1,313	1,285	3,634
1987–90	2,829	1,411	1,400	4,240
1991–93	2,244	1,090	1,087	3,335
1994	402	915	915	1,317
1995	883	1,058	1,057	1,941
1996	1,930	1,273	1,254	3,203
1997	2,348	4,623	—	6,971
1998	5,735	4,781	—	8,852
Total	18,693	14,798	—	33,491

Source: Ministry of Finance and Economy.

Note
* Approved.

9.3 Exchange rate and inward FDI

While being actively pursued by the Korean government as a way out of the crisis, rapid increases of inward FDI into Korea in the recent period have also created public concerns over 'selling Korea'.[13] These concerns were amplified by an increased number of cross-border M&As of Korean firms and assets which were also coupled by the substantial currency depreciation of the Korean won during and after the Asian crisis. What is the source of this concern? Is the depreciation of the Korean currency the source of concern?

Real exchange rate (REXR) movements can affect inward FDI through various channels, and the importance of exchange rate movements has been emphasized in a variety of economics and international business literature (Caves 1982, Cushman 1985, 1988, Froot and Stein 1991, Barrell and Pain 1996). First, it creates a cost of production effect and thus affects FDI. In this argument, it is presumed that FDI is a kind of capital, seeking cheap labour (Goldsbrough 1979, Klein and Rosengren 1994). Depreciation of the REXR reduces the cost of production, particularly that of labour. The reduction in labour cost subsequently leads to an increased quantity of labour demand and thus employment. With a given production technology, the increased quantity of labour demand raises the return to capital which may induce inward FDI into the country whose currency depreciated. Therefore, we expect that real depreciation of the Korean won will lead to an increase of FDI flows into Korea. This line of argument is pertinent especially to a developing country with abundant cheap labour. The developing country specializes and usually exports labour-intensive manufacturing products either by using local resources or by assembling imported materials, parts and intermediate products, rather than exporting high-value added niche products to the world market, due to its apparent disadvantages in these products.[14] Under this situation, changes in exchange rates might have a significant effect on the country's international competitiveness. Maintaining a competitive edge in the labour-intensive products attracts inward FDI because the production process or assembly process may require labour services more than capital services. Therefore, depreciation of the REXR can lead to boosting the host country's competitiveness. This has been a common explanation of the Japanese FDI in the 1970s and 1980s and more recently for the FDI from Asian Newly Industrialized Economies (NIEs) in East Asia (Seo and Suh 1999).[15]

Another source of influence on the FDI due to exchange rate movements follows the idea that there is a link between wealth positions and investment. That is, exchange rate movements create the wealth effect when there is an information asymmetry in a capital market (Froot and Stein 1991). In this model, a firm's wealth position determines the amount that it bids for foreign assets. Currency movements alter the firm's relative wealth position and thus affect FDI. For example, the depreciation of domestic currency raises the wealth of foreign investors relative to domestic investors. Because this lowers the relative costs of capital, foreign investors outbid domestic investors. Thus, the depreciation of domestic currency leads to an increase of inward FDI which may cause a 'fire-sale' FDI issue, and conversely for the real appreciation of domestic currency. The wealth effect of REXR movements may be more relevant to M&A bids by foreign investors than for greenfield investments (Froot and Stein 1991, Goldberg and Klein 1998: 83). Note also that if wealth matters, a surge in the foreign currency value of a foreign stock market should raise inward FDI, even if the exchange rate is fixed (Froot and Stein 1991).

Exchange rate movements can also have an impact on the inward FDI in anticipation of future movements by the host government which may try to mitigate the effects arising from REXR movements. In this case, the exchange rate movements can generate the opposite effect on the inward FDI to the above discussed wealth effect. Real appreciation of the domestic currency makes imports relatively cheaper, thus raising the level of imports. The increased imports, in turn, create pressures on the host government to opt for a protectionist stance, thus foreign investors make FDI in anticipation of potential tariff barriers. As a result, the real appreciation of the host country's currency can lead to the increased inward FDI.[16] In the case of real depreciation, we may observe a reversed impact on the inward FDI.

9.4 An econometric model and a discussion of the results

In this section an empirical econometric model is developed to investigate the effect on the inward FDI of REXR movements in the Korean economy. Of course, there are other factors involved as determinants in the inward FDI (see, e.g. Seo and Suh 1999). However, the aim of this chapter is more specific and narrowly focused based on the effect of REXR movements, through a wealth effect and a production cost effect, on the inward FDI into Korea. In particular, we try to investigate the effect of the level of the real exchange rather than the volatility of the REXR.

Following Froot and Stein (1991) and Klein and Rosengren (1994), the model is specified:

$$(\mathrm{FDI})_t = a_0 + a_1(\mathrm{REXR})_t + a_2(\mathrm{RLC})_t + a_3(\mathrm{VSM})_t + \varepsilon_t$$

where FDI indicates the inward FDI flows to Korea, measured in million US dollars; REXR is real exchange rate index of the Korean won, relative to the US dollar; RLC means real labour costs and VSM presents the value of stock market.

Seasonally adjusted quarterly data for the variables specified in the model were collected for the time span from the first quarter of 1994 to the first quarter of 1999. The selection of the base period was chosen on the following two grounds. First, the inward FDI in Korea was a relatively recent phenomenon. As seen in the previous sections, the 1994–98 period accounted for almost two-thirds of the total cumulative flows into Korea since 1962. Second, during this period the Korean government adopted a relatively more free FDI policy stance. As discussed earlier, the inward FDI policy in Korea changed its nature from regulation and administration to promotion and support of the inward FDI in 1998. However, it may be more appropriate to interpret the changes of the FDI policy as the continued liberalization efforts by the Korean government started in 1994 in order to follow the OECD principles of capital movements.

The FDI flow data were obtained from the balance of payment accounts prepared by the Bank of Korea. Although the total realized FDI in Korea may be appropriate, total FDI usually includes the retained profits by MNEs. However, it is believed that FDI inflows in the balance of payment account may be more sensitive to REXR movements. So, FDI inflows in the balance of payment accounts were used in this study. Then, inward FDI data were adjusted by using the US capital equipment price index (Sung *et al.*, 1998). REXR is the bilateral nominal exchange rate of the Korean won per US dollar, adjusted by the ratio of wholesale price in Korea and in the United States. A price adjusted monthly earnings index was used as a proxy for the RLC, and the value of stock market was captured by the industrial share price index, available at the Korea Stock Exchange. A couple of further modifications were made in the subsequent estimation process. First, as discussed in the previous section, the relative position of the variables matters. Thus, exogenous variables in the model, except REXR, were normalized as ratios by using the corresponding US variables, the choice of the US counterparts being purely an expedient purpose. Second, lagged exogenous variables were used in the estimation so as to avoid potential simultaneous bias and the lag order was determined within the model by using a prediction efficiency criterion. All the variables in the model were measured in logarithmic value so that the estimates of coefficients will represent the elasticity of respective variables. The model was estimated by using an ordinary least squares (OLS) method, and the results are presented in Table 9.2.[17]

Table 9.2 Regression of REXR, RLC, value of stock market on the inward FDI flows in Korea, 1994Q1–99Q1

Dependent variable: LFDI	*Coefficients*
LVSM(−1)	−2.44 (0.63)*
LVSM(−2)	1.42 (0.82)
LREXR(−1)	−1.87 (0.63)*
LREXR(−2)	2.74 (1.32)**
LRLC(−1)	0.71 (2.41)
Constant	−9.19 (7.46)*
Adj R^2	0.72
Standard error of regression	0.41
F	10.21
D.W.	2.70
RESET(1)	0.06
RESET(2)	0.11
LM(1)	3.39
LM(2)	2.27
ARCH(1)	2.27
ARCH(2)	0.87
Heteroscedasticity	0.58

Notes

1 Figures in parentheses are standard errors.

2 * and ** represent 1% and 5% level of significance.

3 Dependent variable was the ratio of FDI inflows to total trade.

A few remarks on the results are in order. First of all, a large proportion of variations in the recent inward FDI flows into Korea are explained by the lagged values of REXR, value of stock markets and relative real wage costs, as indicated by the adjusted R^2 value of 0.72. Second, REXR movements are important for the inward FDI into Korea although the precise direction of the influence differs between the lag orders. One per cent real depreciation of the currency that occurred two periods ago encourages inward FDI by 2.7 per cent, whereas in the immediate past it discourages the FDI inflows by 1.9 per cent. Nevertheless, for the longer period of over six months, the positive effect dominates over the negative one, that is (2.74 − 1.87). This interpretation is plausible considering that there is usually implementation lags associated with FDI, thus having a positive sign, whereas, in the immediate period, the currency depreciation may indicate a possibility of further depreciation or increase an associated macroeconomic instability.

Although an accurate behavioural interpretation of the impact of the REXR movements on the inward FDI may not be warranted from this result, such a positive long-run effect may indicate a relatively improved wealth position of foreign investors arising from real depreciation of domestic currency. This interpretation of a positive wealth position of foreign investors as compared with domestic investors is further supported by two more observations. The first is that inward FDI flows into Korea are not seriously influenced by the relative labour cost advantage, that is, competitive production costs. The sign of the variable is contrary to our expectation, and it lacks statistical significance. However, this may not be surprising if we consider that the FDI inflows into Korea during the period considered in this chapter were directed towards more technology-intensive and heavy industries, as well as service industries such as banking and insurance. They are relatively high wage industries, compared with other manufacturing sectors. The relative labour costs are likely to be more important for export oriented, cheap labour seeking FDIs, in which MNEs and mobile exporters tend to use the host country as an export platform, than for FDI in high-value adding industries. As discussed earlier, Korea in the mid-1990s is no longer a cheap labour country, although labour costs are cheaper than in the United States. Korea has lost its comparative advantage in many labour-intensive industries to neighbouring ASEAN countries and China.

The other factor influencing FDI inflows into Korea during the period is the movements of the value of the stock market, which, as argued earlier, is another source of a wealth effect even if the exchange rate is fixed. A one per cent slide of the Korean stock market value relative to that of the United States leads to about 2.4 per cent increase of FDI inflows, which is persistent even for a relatively longer period, that is (−2.44 + 1.42), thus holding up the wealth effect of REXR movements.

9.5 Concluding remark

The Korean government's continued liberalization efforts towards inward FDI in the 1990s was designed to facilitate FDI flows by improving institutional foundations and extending incentives and support to foreign investors. The rapidly increased FDI flows during the 1997 financial crisis, coupled with the fallen currency values raised public concerns and doubts over 'selling Korea', although it was believed to be the only way out from the crisis. The econometric results in the previous section indicated that, foreign investors during the period took full advantage of the relatively improved wealth positions arising from the currency depreciation and the fall in the value of Korean stock markets. Another interesting result was that foreign investors seemed not much concerned with production cost competitiveness based on labour costs in Korea.

Nevertheless, these findings cannot be sufficient enough for a source of public concern. If the MNEs with superiority in technology and management know-how help to improve efficiency and productivity through various mechanisms and also enhance competition in Korea, then the selling of the troubled Korean firms to foreign MNEs with the relatively improved wealth position via acquisitions and mergers may be desirable. This can eventually be welfare improving in the long run. However, if foreign investment in Korea was based merely on the relatively improved wealth positions and adopted a profiteering strategy, then the increased FDI inflows would have serious negative implications, thus being welfare decreasing in the long run. At this stage it is still too early to make a judgement on this aspect. As this is an important concern to the Korean people, however, more research is warranted.

Notes

1 See World Bank (1993), for example. However, Paul Krugman was one of those who predicted such a crisis in Asia. Refer to Krugman (1998a).
2 There is also a group of people who attribute the Asian crisis to the poor development of institutions in the region. For such an aspect, refer to Kasper (1998).
3 Adelman and Song (1998) chronologically explore the causes of the Korean financial crisis.
4 This is a so-called 'fire-sale' of assets. The issue has been considered first by Mundell (1988) and also more recently by Graham and Krugman (1991) for inward FDI for the United States. Krugman (1998b) constructed a model for fire sale of assets based on moral hazard and over-borrowing for Asia.
5 For example, see Graham and Krugman (1991) and Klein and Rosengren (1994).
6 There was a boom in the 1970s as a result of Japanese FDI in Korea following the Korean government's promotional efforts and Japan's confidence in the potential of Korean investment (Seo 1997).
7 For the details of the Korean heavy and chemical industries' drive and their impact on the economy in the 1970s, refer to Stern *et al.* (1995).
8 Ungson *et al.* (1997) discuss the new challenges lying ahead for the Korean government and also for the Korean enterprises, especially for Korean *chaebols* (see Chapter 1).
9 The one-stop service system was reorganized into 'Investing in Korea Service Centre' in 1997.
10 Such an increase may also be attributed to restoration of confidence of foreign investors in the Korean economy as the reform and restructuring efforts proceed.
11 If we include factory acquisitions or acquisition of ongoing projects in M&As, then M&As' proportion further increased to 53.1 per cent of total FDI in 1998 (Ministry of Finance and Economy).
12 Industry shares are out of the cumulative total up to 1996.
13 For example, *Hangaeraye21* (vol. 276, 23 September 1999) allocated a special section to this issue (in Korean).
14 Trade theories and product life cycle theory of FDI are silent on this aspect of a developing country's exports.

15 Empirical support of this hypothesis for industrialized countries can be found in Cushman (1985, 1988) for the US outward FDI.
16 This may be more strictly classified as 'tariff-jumping' FDI.
17 An alternative specification of the dependent variable, FDI inflows in level form, produced almost the same result.

Bibliography

Adelman, I. and Song, B.N. (1998) 'The Korean financial crisis of 1997–8', mimeo.

Barrel, Ray and Nigel Pain (1996) 'An econometric analysis of US foreign direct investment', *Review of Economics and Statistics*, 200–7.

Caves, R. (1982) *Multinational Enterprise and Economic Analysis*, Cambridge: Cambridge University Press.

Cho, Y.J. (1999) 'Asian financial crisis and the future of Korean economy', *Korea Focus*, 7(1): 1–14.

Cushman, D. (1985) 'Real exchange rate risk, expectations and the level of direct investment', *Review of Economics and Statistics*, 67: 297–308.

Cushman, D. (1988) 'Real exchange rate risk, expectations and foreign direct investment in the US', *Weltwirtschaftliches Archiv*, 124: 322–36.

Froot, Kenneth A. and Stein, Jeremy C. (1991) 'Exchange rates and foreign direct investment: an imperfect capital markets approach', *Quarterly Journal of Economics*, 106: 1191–217.

Glick, R. (ed.) (1998) *Managing Capital Flows and Exchange Rates: Perspectives from the Pacific Basin*, Cambridge: Cambridge University Press.

Goldberg, Linda S. and Klein, M. (1998) 'Foreign direct investment, trade, and real exchange rate linkages in developing countries', in R. Glick (ed.), *Managing Capital Flows and Exchange Rates: Perspectives from the Pacific Basin*, Cambridge: Cambridge University Press (chapter 3).

Goldsbrough, D.J. (1979) 'The role of foreign direct investment in the external adjustment process', *IMF Staff Papers*, 26: 725–54.

Graham, E. and Krugman, P. (1991) *Foreign Direct Investment in United States*, Washington, DC: Institute for International Economics.

Kasper, W. (1998) 'Rapid development in East Asia: institutional evolution and backlog'. A paper presented at ASEAN Regional Conference/Malaysian Economic Convention, Kuala Lumpur, October 15–17.

Kim, Dae Jung (1998) *A Way Out for the Korean Economy: Foreign Investment.* Available Online, http://www.mofe.go.kr/ENGLISH/DATA/E_POLICY_ISSUE/9806eb_16

Kim, J.D. (1997) 'Impact of foreign direct investment liberalisation: the case of Korea', KIEP Working Papers No. 97-01, Seoul, Korea.

Klein, Michael W. and Rosengren, E. (1994) 'The real exchange rate and foreign direct investment in the United States', *Journal of International Economics*, 36: 373–89.

Krugman, P. (1998a) 'Asia: What went wrong', *Fortune*, 2 March 1998.

——(1998b) 'Fire-sale FDI', mimeo. Available Online, http://web.mit.edu/krugman/www

——(1999) 'Balance sheets, the transfer problem, and financial crises', in P. Isard, A. Razin and A.K. Rose (eds), *International Finance and Financial Crises – Essays in Honor of Robert P. Flood*, Kluwer Academic Publishers and International Monetary Fund.

Lee, C.H. and Ramstetter, E. (1991) 'Direct investment and structural change in Korean manufacturing', in E. Ramstetter (ed.), *Direct Foreign Investment in Asia's Developing Economies and Structural Change in the Asia-Pacific Region*, Boulder, Colorado: Westview Press.

Mundell, R. (1988) 'New deal on exchange rates', *Research Institute of International Trade and Industry*, Tokyo: MITI.

Radelet, S. and Sachs, J. (1998) 'Onset of the financial crisis', mimeo. Available Online, http://www.hiid.harvard.edu/

Seo, J.S. (1997) *Dynamics of Comparative Advantage and Foreign Direct Investment in Korea and Taiwan: An Analysis of the Relationship Between FDI and Trade*, School of Economics, the University of New South Wales, unpublished PhD thesis.

Seo, J.S. and Suh, C.S. (1999) 'Location advantage of foreign direct investment in east Asia'. A paper to be presented at the Academy of International Business, 1999 Annual Meeting, November 20–3, Charleston Place, Charleston, South Carolina, USA.

Stern, J., Kim, J., Perkins, D. and Yoo, J. (1995) *Industrialization and the State: The Korean Heavy and Chemical Industry Drive*, Cambridge: Harvard Institute for International Development and Korea Development Institute, Harvard University Press.

Sung, Y.W., Seo, J.S. and Suh, C.S. (1998) 'Inward foreign direct investment in transitional economy: an analysis of regional differences in China', in S.J. Gray and S. Nicholas (eds), *The Challenges of Globalization*, Proceedings of the Inaugural Conference on the Australia–New Zealand International Business Academy. November 13–14, Melbourne, Australia.

Ungson, G.R., Steers, R.M. and Park, S.H. (1997) *Korean Enterprise: The Quest for Globalisation*, Boston: Harvard Business School Press.

World Bank (1993) *The East Asian Miracle: Economic Growth and Public Policy*, Oxford: Oxford University Press.

10 The financial system in Korea after the 1997 financial crisis

A legal perspective

Sunseop Jung

10.1 Introduction

Since the late 1997, when the Korean government requested a bailout loan from the International Monetary Fund (IMF), there have been considerable changes in Korea.[1] The crisis began as a balance-of-payments problem flowing from a shortage in foreign currency reserves in the late 1997. The immediate causes of this crisis were the trade deterioration in 1995 and 1996, a series of insolvencies of major *chaebols*,[2] and the subsequent erosion of market confidence in international financial markets. International market sentiment, already shocked by events in Southeast Asia, was aggravated by inappropriate policy responses, by the Korean government, to the evolving problems. However, the long-term source can be traced back to the structural weaknesses of the Korean economy. In legal terms, these structural weaknesses can be explained as the failure of the legal system to adjust itself to rapidly changing economic circumstances.[3] These challenges required Korea to initiate major reforms in all areas of the economy. This chapter explores the legal dimensions of the crisis and the legal changes implemented to deal with it. There are four sections. Section 10.2 considers the sources of the crisis, which are directly related to the financial sector. In Section 10.3, the setup of the financial institutions and financial regulatory system is reviewed. In Section 10.4, the major features of the legal changes to deal with the crisis are examined. The main areas include market integration, financial sector restructuring, and financial regulation. In Section 10.5 some conclusions are given.

10.2 Sources and tasks of the financial crisis

10.2.1 Sources of the financial crisis

10.2.1.1 Overview

There are two approaches to the sources of the financial crisis (Arner 1998: 391–2). One is to emphasize external conditions including the contagion effect of the overall Asian financial crisis and the movement of international "hot money." The other approach explains the crisis through internal factors such as structural weakness in the Korean economy. This chapter uses this second approach by considering deficiencies in the Korean legal system.[4]

To find the legal dimension of the crisis, the role of law in Asian economic development needs to be explored. This role has not been fully appreciated in studies, as Asian legal systems have developed their own style.[5] However, the function of the law was strongly influenced by the economic policy of each state. According to Pristor, the shift in government economic policy followed broadly similar patterns of movement across the Asian economies from state-led to market-led policies. Changes in economic policy affected both economic development and the legal systems, which then further affected economic development (Asia Development Bank 1998: 5–6). In different periods, state-led or market-led law combined with rule-based or discretionary procedures to create a legal system that generally supported the prevailing economic strategy during that policy period.

In Korea, we can see a similar tendency in the relationship between law and economic policy. There was a turning point in Korea around the early 1980s after about thirty years of strong performance, when domestic and foreign economic circumstances called for a change in economic paradigms (see Borensztein and Lee 1999: 4–7, Samsung Economic Research Institute 1998: 82–5). This was influenced by such structural changes as globalization in the world economy and the radical deterioration of Korea's competitiveness, which required new legal or regulatory approaches to economic issues. However, Korea resisted this by pursuing higher investment policy, rather than accepting it by restructuring its economy and legal system. The government continued market intervention to facilitate financial support for such higher investment and intervened in the credit decisions of financial institutions and corporations. Thus, the stability of the financial system itself was sustained by government guarantees, rather than through prudential regulation and management principles.

In the financial sector, the government liberalized and deregulated financial markets by gradually eliminating credit and interest rate ceilings and other restrictions affecting lending and borrowing activities (Park 1996: 247–60, Baliño and Ubide 1999: 1–16, Bisignano 1999: 5, Borensztein and Lee 1999: 16–19). However, these changes were not supplemented or safeguarded by adequate legal institutions. This situation can be seen as a failure of the legal sector to incorporate the economic factors into a finely tuned legal regime. The factors shown in the following sections are examples of such legal failure.

10.2.1.2 Structural weakness

These problems have their roots in Korea's history of government-led industrialization strategy, which was based on promoting the growth of large conglomerates, the *chaebols*. The government played a significant role in selecting specific industries for development and allocating credit to them.[6] The financial system, in particular the banking sector, played a central role in this strategy by intermediating funds to finance investment and expansion of export-oriented corporations. This pattern of "selective investment and credit allocation" has delayed the need for a well-developed financial market. As a result, the government intervention in the financial sector from the 1960s reduced the market's flexibility to respond to change. Thus, continuing government involvement in the financial sector stymied the development of a commercially sound financial system (Bank of Korea (BOK) 1998a: 7).

Chaebols pursued highly leveraged expansion, which resulted in high debt/equity ratios and low profitability. In turn, the financial sector largely depended on the viability of the *chaebols*. Where external factors such as administrative guidance or government intervention other than the economic interest of shareholders, managers, and creditors determine the sources of financing and business strategies of a corporation, the general legal framework for a corporation is less important. The existence of corporate law does not necessarily imply that the governance of corporations is determined primarily by norms set forth in the law (Asia Development Bank 1998). Moreover, Korean *chaebols* were for the most part owned and managed by a handful of family members with no strict responsibility for business performance. Consequently, the corporate sector was considerably damaged by excessive debt burdens and investment losses. At the same time, the financial sector was weakened by bad loans and the subsequent erosion of its capital base.

10.2.1.3 Insufficient regulatory regime

The insufficient regulatory regime allowed financial institutions to incur excessive risks without building an adequate capital base to withstand unexpected shocks. Factors such as an industry-specific multiple regulatory system, lack of accounting transparency, and other prudential regulations precipitated the crisis.

First, there was no unified regulatory system covering all financial institutions (Baliño and Ubide 1999: 16).[7] Industry-specific regulatory regimes, each with its own approach and enforcement principles, created difficulties in efficient regulatory cooperation and consistent supervisory policies across the industry. For example, commercial banks were subject to the jurisdiction of the Office of Banking Supervision (OBS) under the authority of the Monetary Board, whereas, specialized banks (including development banks) and nonbank financial institutions (NBFs) were subject to the direct supervision of the Ministry of Finance and Economy (MOFE). This lack of consistent and coordinated arrangements for regulation made many prudential rules ineffective as shown in the case of trust accounts of the commercial banks, merchant banks, and other financial institutions (Baliño and Ubide 1999: 16). Trust accounts were subject to less stringent controls than normal banking business, which encouraged the deviation of business towards less regulated areas.[8] Moreover, as the supervisory authority had the power to waive certain requirements, supervisors sometimes waived the full application of regulations, such as provisioning rates, to avoid weakening the earning reports of banks.[9]

Second, there was a lack of accounting transparency that made it difficult to estimate the financial status of a financial institution (BOK 1998a: 6, Baliño and Ubide 1999: 17, Bisignano 1999: 6–38) For example, loan classification and provisioning standards were significantly relaxed in Korea.

Nonperforming loans (NPLs) were defined as loans that had been in arrears for six months or more, compared to the usual standard of three months or more. In addition, they were underestimated by excluding substandard loans, which are loans covered by collateral that have been in arrears for six months or more. In addition, the classification system was based on the loan's servicing record and the availability of collateral (the "look-back approach") without regard to the borrower's future capacity to repay. Accordingly, a bank's apparent soundness was based on unreliable figures. There was also no strict examination carried out on the scale of NPLs of NBFs (BOK 1998a: 6).

Banks were required to set up provisions for loan losses enough to cover 100 percent of expected losses at the end of each fiscal year. This was based on a five-grade credit classification of normal, precautionary, substandard, doubtful, and estimated loss credits. The required provision rate was 0.5 percent of normal credits, 1 percent of precautionary credits, 20 percent of substandard credits, and 100 percent of doubtful and estimated loss credits. But losses were not expected to be over 2 percent of total loans. In fact, loan loss reserves over 2 percent were not eligible for tax deduction, which discouraged banks from providing in excess of that figure (Baliño and Ubide 1999: 17).

Third, standards regarding risk concentration and large exposure to a single borrower were also very soft, which facilitated the highly leveraged corporate finance structure of Korean *chaebols* (Baliño and Ubide 1999: 19). In the case of the banking sector, the exposure limit for a single borrower was fixed in 1991 by Article 35 of the Banking Act, at 20 percent of the bank's equity capital for loans and 40 percent for guarantees. But this standard was not strictly enforced on account of a generous grandfathering clause and a phase-in period of three years. The exposure limits on the *chaebols* were set on a case-by-case basis by each bank under which the shares of loans to the top five and thirty business groups over total loans of the bank should not exceed the designated ratios set by the supervisory authority (the "basket control system"). These limits were tightened in August 1997 and limited the lending to a single borrower (including guarantees) at 45 percent of the bank's equity capital for commercial banks and 150 percent for merchant banks (Baliño and Ubide 1999: 19).

Finally, banks lacked good internal liquidity management controls, and regulations were not sufficiently stringent, particularly regarding foreign exchange (Baliño and Ubide 1999: 17). In order to ensure the liquidity of banks, the OBS required that long-term loans should be financed by funds with a maturity of at least one year (Baliño and Ubide 1999: 17).[10] However, all of these controls included only domestic liquidity positions. The positions of overseas branches and offshore funds were not considered (Samsung Economic Research Institute 1998: 81). Further, despite the growing maturity mismatches in banks' balance sheets that resulted from the capital account liberalization process, no special consideration was given to the prudential regulation and liquidity management in foreign exchange as shown in the following section. This is an example of legal failure to incorporate market change.

10.2.1.4 Foreign-exchange liquidity and market integration

The increased demands for funds made Korean financial institutions rely further on external borrowings. Those external debts often had short-term maturity. By September 1997, total Korean external liabilities amounted to US$170.6 billion, of which 55 percent constituted short-term debts.[11] Their overexposure to short-term external debt made them particularly susceptible to various changes in market expectations. This excessive reliance on short-term funding may be explained by the following noneconomic factors such as interest differentials between the domestic and international market (Baliño and Ubide 1999: 22–8).

First, while the capital account had been partially liberalized, there remained a strong policy preference of intermediation through domestic foreign-exchange banks to foreign direct investment and direct corporate borrowing (Baliño and Ubide 1999: 22). For example, regulations limited international issuance of securities to corporations with an international credit rating of BBB or higher. Second, restrictions against short-term external debts taken by financial institutions were relaxed without full consideration of the side effects (Baliño and Ubide 1999: 22). Therefore, limits on long-term borrowing and foreign investment in domestic capital markets were retained causing the development of large maturity mismatches in bank balance sheets. For example, merchant banks borrowed short-term and lent or invested in long-term deals, especially to Southeast Asian and other emerging markets.[12] Third, the lack of expertise in Korean financial institutions in risk management and international banking led them to take greater risks than prudent management would have advised (Baliño and Ubide 1999: 22).

10.2.2 Policy tasks

As a condition precedent to the bailout package, the IMF required the government to commit to full-scale economic reform focusing on structural measures. The Korean government signed the Memorandum on the Economic Program prepared by the IMF on December 3, 1997.[13] The gist of this program is a series of structural reforms to restore confidence through strengthening financial systems, increasing transparency, and opening markets (see Arner 1998: 394–5, Lane *et al.* 1999: 31–3, 101–12). This program includes the following three measures: first, the closure of non-viable financial institutions; second, the restructuring and recapitalization of viable institutions to meet internationally accepted best practices, including BIS capital adequacy standards and internationally accepted accounting practices and disclosure rules; and third, institutional reforms to strengthen financial sector supervision and regulation, increase transparency in the corporate and government sectors, create a more level-playing field for private-sector activity, and increase competition.

Considering the above-mentioned sources of the crisis and contents of the IMF economic program, the policy tasks to be carried out in respect of the financial system may be classified into:

1 *Market integration.* Full integration of domestic financial markets with global markets should be an essential part of the reform program. This task may be achieved through the liberalization of capital markets and foreign-exchange trade.
2 *Financial sector restructuring.* Restructuring and recapitalization of the financial sector to resolve NPLs and to build up the weak capital base is one of the most urgent measures to enhance the confidence of investors in the Korean market. Various measures to increase the commercial orientation of the financial system are to be considered.
3 *Strengthening of financial regulation.* For preventing the recurrence of similar problems in the future, a coordinated and consistent regulatory regime is to be established. This includes coordination of the regulatory system and introduction of international best practice to enhance accounting transparency.
4 *Corporate sector restructuring.* The problems of the *chaebols* are to be addressed. This issue is beyond the scope of this chapter, but is closely linked to financial sector restructuring.[14]

The rest of this chapter considers what laws need to be implemented to complete the listed tasks.

10.3 The basis of Korea's financial system

10.3.1 Financial institutions

10.3.1.1 Overview

The main activities of the financial system are to transfer funds between lenders and borrowers, enable individuals to switch from one type of financial asset to another, and provide payment systems (Blay and Clark 1993: 4). Each of these functions is generally performed through financial institutions and in Korea there are three main types: the central bank, banking institutions including commercial, specialized, and development banks, and NBFs including investment, savings, and insurance institutions (see generally, Financial Supervisory Service (FSS) 2000: 1–18).

The institutional bases of the modern financial system in Korea were laid down during the early 1950s when the central and commercial banking systems were realigned under the new system provided by the Bank of Korea Act 1950 (BOKA) and the Banking Act 1950 (BA). Specialized and development banks, wholly or partially owned by the government, were established during the 1950s and 1960s to facilitate financial support for underdeveloped or major industrial sectors. Most of the NBFs were established during the 1970s for the purpose of diversifying financing sources, promoting the development of the money market, and attracting funds into the organized market from the kerb market.[15] Several commercial banks and NBFs were newly added as part of liberalization and internationalization measures carried out from the early 1980s. Nowadays, the financial system in Korea has been undergoing unprecedented changes in the course of economic reform agreed upon between the Korean government and the IMF.

10.3.1.2 Bank of Korea

The Bank of Korea (BOK) was established for the purpose of contribut[ing] to the sound development of the national economy by pursuing price stability through the formulation and implementation of efficient monetary and credit policies (BOKA 1). To achieve this purpose, the BOK performs the typical functions of a central bank, such as an issuer of bank notes and coins, a banker for banking institutions, a banker to the government, and a controller of money supply.[16] The BOKA also provides for the central bank's independence and neutrality in formulating and implementing monetary policy. The BOK has to set a goal for achieving price stability in consultation with the government, and to materialize the operational program of the monetary policy for the stabilization of prices.

Until the amendment of the BOKA in December 1997, the BOK had been empowered to supervise banking institutions through the OBS. The BOK also had the power to authorize the opening and closing of banking institutions (including foreign bank branches), mergers among banking institutions, and the liquidation of banking institutions. However, in accordance with the 1997 amendments to the BOKA, the bank supervision power was divested from the BOK and instead the Financial Supervisory Commission (FSC), the newly established financial supervisory authority under the Act Concerning Establishment of Financial Supervisory Organizations 1997, was vested with that power.

Now, the BOK has only a limited bank examination power. The BOK may, when the Monetary Board (the governing body of the BOK) deems necessary for implementing its monetary and credit policies, request banking institutions to submit relevant materials (BOKA 37). In addition, the BOK may, when the Monetary Board deems necessary for implementing its monetary and credit policies, request the FSS, executive arm of the FSC, to examine banking institutions within a specific scope.

10.3.1.3 Banking institutions

Article 2 of the BA defines "banking institutions" as "all juridical persons which, regularly and in an orderly manner, engage in the business of lending funds acquired through the assumption of obligations to the public in the form of deposits received, securities or other evidences of debt issued." Banking institutions consist of two groups: commercial banks and specialized banks. This definition also includes the development banks. While "commercial banks" are incorporated under the BA, "specialized and development banks" have their own organization laws.

Specialized banks consist of the Industrial Bank of Korea for the financing of small and medium enterprises and three banks centered on agricultural, fishery, and livestock cooperatives.[17] Specialized banks were established to provide funds to particular sectors to which commercial banks could not supply sufficient funds on account of limited availability or low profitability. With subsequent changes in the financial environment, however, they have expanded their business into commercial bank areas, although their share of funds allocation to their relevant sectors is still relatively high.

There are two development banks – the Korea Development Bank and the Export-Import Bank of Korea. They were established to facilitate financial support for specific sectors such as major industries, trade, and overseas investment, which needed medium- and long-term credits. Their main sources of funding are the issue of financial debentures (such as the Industrial Finance Bonds of the Korea Development Bank), inducement of foreign capital, and borrowing from the government. These banks have not been subject to the same prudential standards and supervision as commercial banks and were overseen by the MOFE until April 1998.

10.3.1.4 Nonbank financial institutions

Nonbank financial institutions broadly comprise investment, savings, and insurance-related institutions (FSS 2000: 7–18). As generally known, most NBFs have been directly or indirectly owned by the *chaebols* and other large shareholders, although some were partly owned by foreign banks. Accordingly, they have been mainly used as financing vehicles to fund business activities within the *chaebols*.

10.3.1.5 Foreigners' ownership of domestic financial institution

Korea had until recently strictly restricted foreign entry into the banking industry.[18] After the crisis, ownership of financial institutions was liberalized by amendments to relevant laws and regulations on February 1998. In the case of commercial banks, the stake holding ceiling of a single shareholder is 4 percent of the total issued stocks with voting rights of each bank (BA 15(1)). However, foreign investors may hold 4–10 percent stakes after filing with the FSC and 10 percent or more stake holdings subject to the approval of the FSC (BA 15(2)). Foreigners may establish commercial banks in the form of a joint venture or subsidiary subject to the approval of the FSC (BA 15(3)). In case of NBFs, there is no special regulation on the foreigners' stake.

Accordingly, foreign investors contributed to the recapitalization of the banking system. In June 1998, the International Finance Corporation invested US$152 million in Hana Bank, and US$25 million in the Korea Long Term Credit Bank. Germany's Commerzbank invested US$249 million in the Korea Exchange Bank, acquiring a stake of 30 percent chiefly by converting existing credits to this bank into equity (through a debt–equity swap). In December 1998, a US consortium agreed to purchase a 51 percent stake in the previously nationalized Korea First Bank (FSC December 31, 1998: 1).

10.3.2 Financial regulatory system

10.3.2.1 Unified system

On April 1, 1998, the FSC was established as an integrated financial supervisor in Korea (see generally, FSS 2000: 32–42). In addition, the Securities and Futures Commission (SFC) was established under the FSC to oversee securities and futures markets. It is in charge of deliberating matters related to securities and futures markets prior to the FSC's deliberation and investigating market abuses such as insider trading and market manipulation.[19] As an executive body of the FSC and the SFC, the FSS was established on January 1, 1999.[20] The FSS inspects the assets and business conditions of financial institutions and imposes penalties for the perpetrators. It also set up a Standing Mediation Committee to settle a variety of financial disputes between financial institutions and their customers.

In Korea, the FSC is responsible for deciding and ensuring the level and performance of prudential oversight. It exercises extensive powers such as the promulgation and amendment of relevant rules and regulations, the approval and permission for the business of financial institutions, and the deliberation and resolution of agenda with respect to any inspections, examinations of, and sanctions on financial institutions. As a single regulator, the FSC is expected to enhance the efficiency and appropriateness of financial supervision in a rapidly changing financial environment. Moreover, the FSC holds the initiative to implement all restructuring processes for financial and corporate sector reform.

10.3.2.2 Legal basis

The legal basis for this change is the Act for the Establishment of Financial Supervisory Organizations (AEFSO), which was enacted on December 31, 1997. This act was submitted to the National Assembly for legislation on August 23, 1997, prior to the crisis, together with other financial reform acts to execute the recommendations of the Presidential Committee on Financial Reform. However, the acts were not passed in the National Assembly due to some disputes on the independence of the BOK and the jurisdiction of financial regulation. The National Assembly passed these reform acts on December 29, 1997 under the guidance of the IMF.

The concept of an integrated financial supervisory agency was not new in Korea. Since the late 1980s, there were calls for a single supervisory body of the entire financial industry. These opinions were supported by the growing convergence of financial services and blurring distinctions between financial sectors, which have demonstrated the need for a single supervisor for the full range of financial businesses. In fact, the previous industry-specific supervisory regime, each with its own approach and administration, created difficulties in efficient regulatory cooperation and consistent supervisory policies across the industry. This lack of a unified regulatory and supervision system created conditions for regulatory arbitrage and the development of risky practices.[2]

10.4 Legal changes

10.4.1 Overview

In December 1997, the National Assembly passed a number of financial reform acts to transform Korea's financial industry. These reform acts were, in part, the result of financial sector reform efforts staged by the government throughout the year just before the financial crisis hit Korea. In January 1997, the then President of Korea, Mr Young Sam Kim, announced plans for the establishment of the Presidential Committee on Financial Reform and the sweeping reforms of financial system through this committee. However, the bills to execute the recommendations of this committee were not passed in the National Assembly due to some controversies. In the end, the National Assembly passed these reform acts on December 29, 1997, eleven days after the election of the new President Dae Jung Kim, under the guidance of the IMF.

10.4.2 Market unintegration

10.4.2.1 Capital market

Given the huge requirements for new capital in implementing the economic reform program, market integration is an essential element of the economic restructuring program. Korea also recognizes that it must fully integrate its domestic market with the global market. The focus of capital market development in Korea is on two interrelated initiatives: market liberalization and augmentation. Market liberalization will directly increase Korea's access to foreign capital and technology, while market augmentation will improve the operational efficiency of the capital market.

To achieve this, Korea has rapidly liberalized its capital markets. First, foreign investment ceiling on listed bonds was abolished completely on December 1997. Second, foreign equity ownership ceilings were eliminated in May 1998. Third, foreigners are allowed to invest in short-term money market instruments such as certificates of deposit (CDs) or repurchase agreements (RPs) without restriction from May 1998. Fourth, hostile Mergers & Acquisitions (M&As) by foreigners were fully liberalized in May 1998. Finally, Korea enacted the Foreign Investment Promotion Act on November 17, 1998 to completely reshape the legal basis of foreign direct investment in Korea from a "regulatory and administrative nature" into a "promotion and support oriented" system.

10.4.2.2 Foreign-exchange market

As pointed out frequently, one of the major obstacles to increasing foreign investment in Korea was the cumbersome legal and regulatory environment. In particular, laws and regulations governing foreign-exchange transactions were especially complex. On the other hand, Korea's overexposure to short-term external debt, partially due to its poorly managed transition towards full economic integration, was one of the crucial factors in precipitating the crisis. Because of these problems, the previous Foreign Exchange Management Act[22] was replaced by the Foreign Exchange Transaction Act (FETA) in September 1998. The objects of this new act are to liberalize the capital account and to develop the foreign-exchange market. The MOFE planned to implement the liberalization in two stages: the first stage from April 1, 1999 and the second stage from January 1, 2001 (see Ministry of Finance and Economy March 27, 1999: 1–7, Choi 2001). The reason for this gradual approach was to have time to establish safeguards such as prudential regulation and a monitoring system to minimize potential side effects of the liberalization.

10.4.2.2.1 FIRST-STAGE LIBERALIZATION MEASURES

First-stage liberalization measures include the liberalization of capital account transactions, the streamlining of procedures for current account transactions, the introduction of a less-onerous licensing system, and other measures to further develop and deepen the foreign-exchange market. However, restrictions on nonresident local currency funding will remain effective.[23]

10.4.2.2.2 CAPITAL ACCOUNT LIBERALIZATION

The main focus of foreign-exchange liberalization is the change to the legal framework for capital account transactions from a "positive list system" to a "negative list system." A negative list system means that all capital account transactions other than those identified in the negative list (which are stipulated in the FETA and relevant presidential decree) will be liberalized other than less stringent notification requirements. In Korea, "notification" operated like *de facto* approval by requiring an official document issued by the government certifying the completion of the notification procedure. In this case, notification can be made by a simple report of the transaction without the further requirement of an official certificate.

First, foreign-exchange transactions between residents entailing no capital flows will be liberalized, together with offshore transactions in Korean won between nonresidents.

Second, nonresidents will be permitted to open domestic Korean won deposit accounts (including trust accounts) with maturity of more than one year and permitted to freely withdraw funds from those accounts. However, those with maturity of one year or less will be subject to obtaining permission by the governor of the BOK. Third, offshore and domestic issuance of securities denominated in Korean won with maturity of more than one year will be liberalized. However, those with maturity of one year or less will require permission by the Minister of the MOFE. Fourth, domestic corporation short-term external borrowings with maturity of one year or less will be liberalized. Borrowings with maturity of more than one year were already liberalized in 1998. However, short-term borrowings of financially unsound corporations are subject to permission by the minister of the MOFE. Corporations will be prohibited from providing guarantees or collateral for affiliates' short-term overseas borrowing. Head offices or affiliates' guarantees or collateral for offshore branches will be limited to the amount of guarantees by the end of 1998. Capital transactions of residents other than private corporations will remain subject to permission. Fifth, overseas issuance of securities in excess of US$30 million by domestic corporations and financial institutions other than foreign exchange and merchant banks will no longer require notification certificates from the MOFE. The same rule will be applied to the overseas issuance of securities in excess of US$50 million by commercial and merchant banks. Sixth, all derivatives transactions concluded through foreign-exchange banks by residents and nonresidents will be liberalized. In addition, the "real demand principle" applicable to the forward transactions involving foreign or domestic currency, and derivatives transactions will be abolished. Finally, restrictions placed on the usage of the proceeds of offshore borrowings will be removed.

However, financial institution foreign direct investment, including the establishment of offshore branches and representative offices will require notification acceptance from the MOFE. As mentioned previously, the restrictions on holding by nonresidents of Korean won denominated funding will be maintained. Therefore, the current ceiling of 100 million won on the amount of borrowing for each nonresident will be maintained. Nonresidents will be restricted from issuing Korean won denominated bonds with maturity of less than one year. Also, residents will be prohibited from acquiring Korean won denominated securities with maturity of less than one year issued by nonresidents.

10.4.2.2.3 EXPANSION OF FOREIGN-EXCHANGE BANKS

In order to reduce inefficiencies flowing from the selective licensing of foreign-exchange banks, financial institutions, which meet previously set conditions such as the maintenance of an effective management system, will be permitted to engage in foreign-exchange businesses. In other words, the current approval system for foreign-exchange banks will be replaced by a simple registration system.

10.4.2.2.4 SECOND STAGE LIBERALIZATION MEASURES

Initially, the MOFE announced that almost all foreign-exchange controls would be abolished at the end of 2000. However, the final version of the second-stage liberalization was mainly concerned with the external payment of resident individuals, along with many reservations for other transactions. This was to minimize side effects of rapid liberalization (see Choi 2001: 17–23).

10.4.3 Financial sector restructuring

10.4.3.1 Legal basis

The legal basis of financial sector restructuring is the Act Concerning the Structural Improvement of the Financial Industry 1997. This act originally was called the Act Concerning Merger and Conversion of Financial Institutions when adopted on March 8, 1991. It was fully amended on January 13, 1997 and renamed. The act was amended again on January 8, 1998 in compliance with the provisions of the Act Concerning Establishment of Financial Supervisory

Organizations. The purpose of the Act Concerning the Structural Improvement of the Financial Industry 1997 is to contribute to the balanced development of the financial industry by encouraging financial restructuring (§1). The structure of this act may be classified into three parts.

10.4.3.1.1 MERGER AND CONVERSION OF FINANCIAL INSTITUTIONS

Any financial institution may merge with another regardless of the type of counterpart and/or convert to any other type of financial institution subject to the prior authorization of the Minister of the MOFE (§4(1)). The merger and conversion procedures stipulated in the Commercial Code and Securities and Exchange Act have also been simplified by this act (§§ 5 and 9). Other governmental assistance such as tax exemptions and fiscal support may be granted if necessary to encourage restructuring of financial institutions (§5(9), §8).

10.4.3.1.2 MANAGEMENT REFORM FOR TROUBLED FINANCIAL INSTITUTIONS

In order to prevent the failure of financial institutions, prompt corrective actions are provided (§10). The FSC may request debt-ridden financial institutions to increase capital, retire shares, seek merger and acquisition by a third party, and suspend duties of the directors and appoint an administrator to such institutions. In addition, special procedures for investment by the government or the Korea Deposit Insurance Corporation (KDIC) in under-capitalized financial institutions have been introduced (§12). The FSC may request the government or the KDIC to invest in any under-capitalized financial institutions in order to accelerate and facilitate the normalization of the management of such financial institutions. In this case, the FSC may ask those financial institutions to decrease the capital of such financial institutions through the retirement of shares or through any other methods, procedures for which are also streamlined by this act.

10.4.3.1.3 SPECIAL PROVISIONS REGARDING BANKRUPTCY PROCEEDINGS FOR FINANCIAL INSTITUTIONS

In Korea, as there is no special bankruptcy regime exclusively applicable to financial institutions, general bankruptcy laws apply to financial institutions. Korea's bankruptcy laws consist of three acts: the Bankruptcy Act, the Composition Act, and the Corporate Reorganisation Act.[24] However, in consideration of the specialties of financial institutions, this act has special provisions for certain procedural matters. The act also enables the FSC to file a petition of bankruptcy and recommend a receiver or liquidator for eligible financial institutions (§§15–16).

10.4.3.2 Closures, mergers, and recapitalization

Korean banks and other financial companies have undergone an unprecedented restructuring process over the last few years (Table 10.1). Prior to the full-scale restructuring, the government guaranteed all deposits in financial institutions

Table 10.1 Financial institutions suspended or closed

	Dec. 1997	*Mar. 2001*	*License revoked*	*Merger*	*Newly created*
Banks	33	22	5	6	—
Securities companies	36	43	6	1	14
Merchant banks	30	5	23	3	1
Insurance companies	50	40	7	6	3
Leasing companies	25	19	8	1	3
Investment trust companies	31	29	9	1	8
Mutual savings and finance companies	231	146	72	25	12
Credit unions	1,666	1,311	258	101	4
Total	2,102	1,615	388	144	45

Source: FSC.

until the year 2000[25] and provided temporary liquidity support to banks when needed as an interim measure to maintain public confidence in the financial system during the restructuring period. According to the FSC, Korea completed the first round of financial sector restructuring in September 1998.[26] The FSC applied basically the same principles and methods to NBFs.

10.4.3.3 Fiscal support for financial restructuring

Financial restructuring in Korea has involved a considerable amount of public funds. These funds have been provided through the issuance of bonds by the Korea Asset Management Corporation (KAMCO) and the KDIC, budgetary allocations, and the exchange of assets. KAMCO is a government-funded entity similar to the Resolution Trust Corporation in the United States and was established pursuant to a special law, the Act Concerning Efficient Management of Non-performing Assets of Financial Institutions and Establishment of Korea Asset Management Corporation 1997. These public funds have been injected into financial institutions through (1) purchases of shares, (2) purchases of subordinated debt, (3) purchases of NPLs, and (4) repayment of depositors.[27]

10.4.3.4 NPLs and asset-backed securitization

Asset securitization is broadly defined as "the process by which loans, consumer installment contracts, leases, receivables, and other relatively illiquid assets with common features are packaged into interest bearing securities with marketable investment characteristics" (Bhattacharya and Fabozzi 1996: 2). Asset securitization may be used for various purposes, such as liquefying the balance sheet, improving leverage ratios, and creating alternative sources of capital, especially if the process leads to favorable gain on sale accounting treatment and lower costs of funding.

After the crisis, the Korean government felt the urgency to dispose of a huge amount of NPLs, foreclosed real estate, and other assets. Asset-backed securities were considered to be a good means for this purpose and were introduced as a method of resolving NPLs by the Act Concerning Asset-Backed Securitization 1998 (ABSA). As Korean financial institutions strive to improve their soundness by cleaning up NPLs under toughened financial supervision and enhancing the efficiency of asset–liability management, the ABSA is designed to expand the sources of their funds and improve their competitiveness.

In early 1997, certain Korean financial institutions tried to obtain financing through securitization in the international capital market. However, the process was delayed for various reasons such as the lack of experience of the parties concerned, certain legal issues, and delays in the due diligence of procedures of rating agencies and financial guarantors and was put on hold after the crisis.[28] The ABSA attempted to give solutions for these problems. Following the introduction of this act, there were many ABS deals reported in Korea.[29]

10.4.4 Financial regulation

10.4.4.1 Overview

To prevent a reoccurrence of problems, the financial sector needs consistent supervision and coordinated management. International organizations such as the IMF and the IBRD have strongly recommended that the Korean supervisory authority improve its supervision level according to the Core Principles for Effective Banking Supervision 1995 issued by the Basle Committee on Banking Supervision. Above all, the previous industry-specific, multiple regimes were integrated into a single supervisory system under the authority of the FSC. Accordingly, the FSC took on the responsibility of improving Korea's financial supervision levels to meet international standards.

According to the FSC, the goals of financial supervision are the maintenance of a sound credit system, the establishment of fair financial transaction practices, and consumer protection. The FSC expressed the paradigms underlying these reforms as "from direct regulatory methods to indirect regulatory methods," "from the positive system to that of a negative system," "from the application of abstract and subjective principles to that of transparent and objective principles," "from organizational supervision to functional supervision," and "from the regulatory posture to the service offering one."[30]

10.4.4.2 Changes after the crisis

10.4.4.2.1 LOAN CLASSIFICATION AND PROVISIONING

The loan classification system has been strengthened to classify all loans three months in arrears as substandard and to increase the loan loss provisioning rate for precautionary assets from 1 to 2 percent. Loan loss provisions will also be required for payment guarantees of commercial banks. Commercial papers, guaranteed bills, and privately placed bonds in trust accounts, which are virtually equivalent to credit extensions, have been included in the asset category subject to loan loss provisions. The requirement of 100 percent of loan loss provisions for trust accounts with guarantees of principal has been added to those with guarantees of yields. The criteria for the calculation of BIS capital adequacy ratio have been revised to deduct the provisions for those classified as substandard or lower from Tier 2 Capital (FSC 1998e: 6). In addition, the definition of loan classifications was further revised in January 1999 so as to reflect borrowers' repayment capacity as well as past performance ("forward looking approach").

10.4.4.2.2 ENHANCING ACCOUNTING TRANSPARENCY

First, to improve the accounting transparency of financial institutions, the mark-to-market system of accounting has been introduced. Mark-to-market accounting is an accounting method that values the assets at current market value on the valuation date, amends the book value, and recognizes the gains or losses from the difference (FSC 1998e: 6). Second, the accounting standards for public disclosure and the accounting standards for supervision has been separated and is to be administered separately. Third, accounting standards relating to consolidated statements encompassing the parent bank and its subsidiaries have been introduced (FSC 1998e: 6).

10.4.4.2.3 STRENGTHENING SUPERVISION ON FOREIGN-EXCHANGE LIQUIDITY

Supervision of foreign liquidity and exposure has been strengthened. Off-balance sheet items are also included. For example, the FSC changed the frequency of monitoring from a quarterly to a monthly basis and enlarged the scope of monitoring to overseas subsidiaries and offshore accounts. Financial institutions are permitted to hold short-term foreign assets amounting to over 70 percent of foreign liabilities with a maturity of less than three months and to fund over 50 percent of long-term foreign assets with a maturity of more than one year in the form of long-term foreign liabilities (FSC 1998e: 5).

10.4.4.2.4 PUBLIC DISCLOSURE SYSTEM OF MANAGEMENT PERFORMANCE

The public disclosure system of management performance is regarded as a supervision measure that aims to foster sound management of individual financial institutions and the stability of the financial system as a whole. It offers accurate and timely information about the management and financial status of individual financial institutions to depositors, stock holders, creditors, and other users. Though individual supervisory bodies have administered the public disclosure system on the management of financial institutions, disclosure contents have been limited to the status of financial statements and have not been up to the minimum level of public disclosure requested by the International Accounting Standards (IAS). Regular disclosure items have been increased, as requested by the IAS, to include risk management, off-balance sheet transactions (including derivatives) and asset classification. Special disclosure items such as those related to financial mishaps and losing a lawsuit involving a large sum have been included. The frequency of regular disclosure has been increased from once a year to twice a year.

10.4.4.2.5 ADOPTION OF PROMPT CORRECTIVE ACTION

A Prompt Corrective Action (PCA) is generally defined as a step involving gradual imposition of obligatory corrective measures by supervisory authorities on unsound financial institutions that fall below a certain level of the capital adequacy ratio. Since a legal basis for the enforcement of PCA was established by the Act Concerning the Structural Improvement of the Financial Industry 1997, the FSC has continuously made specific regulations concerning banks, securities companies, insurance companies, and merchant banks. The criteria for deciding the soundness of a certain financial institution has been simplified through the use of capital adequacy standards.[31]

A three-step corrective measure composed of management improvement recommendations, management improvement measures, and management improvement orders, will be imposed on unsound financial institutions in accordance with the degree of their unsoundness.

Management improvement recommendations include the improvement of human resources and organization management, the increase or decrease of capital, restriction of profit dividends, special provisioning, and a warning against the institution and senior management. Management improvement measures include the merger or closure of establishments, restriction of additional establishments, sale of risky assets and subsidiaries, change of senior management, and the partial suspension of operations. In the worst case, the FSC can order a management improvement that includes the merger of shares, the firing of senior management or the suspension of senior management activity, appointment of an acting manager, transference of operations and merger or purchase and assumption (P&A), among other measures (FSC 1998).

10.4.4.2.6 CONTROL ON LARGE EXPOSURE AND CONCENTRATION OF RISKS

The controls on large exposures and the concentration of risks were also strengthened after the crisis. Article 35 of the BA stipulates that a banking institution shall not extend loans to a single person in excess of 15 percent of its equity capital. Further, a banking institution must not guarantee the obligations of a single person in excess of 30 percent of its equity capital.

10.4.4.2.7 SUPERVISION FOCUSED ON RISK MANAGEMENT

In the past, financial supervision used only quantified standards based on balance sheet items such as capital regulation for the maintenance of solvency and liquidity regulation for temporary liquidity. However, since the exchange rate system was floated and the liberalization and internationalization of financial industries intensified from the 1980s, financial institutions became greatly susceptible to many risks such as interest rate, exchange rate, and price fluctuation. To cope with this situation, the FSC has already made and carried out "A Working Plan on the Financial Supervision Policy Focused on Risk Control" in order to monitor consistently and control all risks arising in operations (FSC 1998e: 2–3).

10.4.4.2.8 IMPROVEMENT OF THE MANAGEMENT APPRAISAL SYSTEM AND SANCTION SYSTEMS ON THE MANAGEMENT OF FINANCIAL INSTITUTIONS

The management appraisal system makes possible step-by-step supervision measures based on the appraisal results. It can enhance management efficiency by assessing the performance of financial institutions and providing corresponding incentives or penalties.[32] In the past, each supervisory authority including the OBS has carried out management appraisal on financial institutions under its jurisdiction with respective methods and goals. However, maintaining these methods after the creation of the FSS may hamper the efficiency and consistency of the appraisal. Therefore, the FSS is planning to revise the management appraisal system placing focus on risk assessment. The revised management appraisal is applied to all financial institutions that are supervised by the FSS and the appraisal, which will take into account the reports from the financial institutions themselves, will be undertaken during normal on-site examinations. In the final stage, the results will be combined into a composite management appraisal.

Under the previous law, no sanctions could be imposed on the majority shareholder or *de facto* directors who have exerted a direct or indirect influence on the management of failed financial institutions. In response, the FSC has established and executed an efficient sanction system on *de facto* directors by investigating the responsibility for insolvency of the majority shareholder when the ruling on a failed financial institution imposed civil and criminal liabilities on the majority shareholder or *de facto* directors (FSC 1998e: 7–8).

10.5 Conclusion

The Korean crisis erupted suddenly and shocked Korean society, however, the fundamental sources of the problem remained dormant in the backdrop of rapid growth. Korea's failure to correct structural imbalances in a timely manner and its poorly managed transition towards full economic integration, were fundamental problems that developed into a crisis when foreign investors decided to lower their exposure to Korea, because of losses in other Asian economies.

The legal dimension of the crisis was a series of legal failures to address economic factors. Market interests had requested a more market-oriented legal regime with regard to the financial system and the government had taken various legal measures to liberalize and deregulate the financial sector. However, these measures were not fully coordinated to respond to or control the misconduct or abuse by market participants. In short, the legal system did not completely incorporate explicit market demands and rapidly changing economic circumstances within its structure. Many examples of such legal failures have been presented.

Korea has now carried out a variety of legal reforms in response to these challenges. With regard to market integration, Korea adopted a range of liberalization measures as discussed in Section 10.4. Korea also established the legal basis for future financial restructuring under which it is pushing ahead with ongoing restructuring tasks. These reform measures also comprise efforts to establish a coordinated and consistent financial regulatory system. The notable and promising feature of these reforms may be the fact that they were mainly achieved by legal reform based on pre-established rules and regulations. The crisis will hopefully provide an opportunity to reconsider the role of law in the economic and financial development of Korea.

Notes

1 An official request for a bailout loan was made on November 21, 1997. The Korean government signed the memorandum concerning the economic reform program prepared by the IMF on December 3, 1997.

2 *Chaebol* is a Korean word meaning "large business conglomerate(s) with diversified business area owned or controlled by a family group."

3 In this chapter, the term "legal system" refers to all laws, decrees, regulations, and any other rules and guides that have effects to bind or inflict any influence on the operations of the financial institutions.

4 For the sources of the crisis, this section mainly draws on the following materials: Baliño and Ubide (1999: 20–30); Bank of Korea (BOK) (1998: 6–9); Bisignano (1999: 2–42); Borensztein and Lee (1999: 4–16); Ministry of Finance and Economy (1998: section 1).

5 Asia Development Bank (1998), this study covers the People's Republic of China, India, Japan, Malaysia, the Republic of Korea, and Taipei, China.

6 Given the absence of well-developed financial markets and the size of required investments, government intervention in investment decision-making and credit extension may be desirable and welfare-improving in the early stages of economic development. Such "directed credit programmes" were commonly used by many East Asian countries including Japan in the past. For government intervention in credit allocation and its results, see Baliño and Ubide (1999: 11–12), Bisignano (1999: 2–14), Borensztein and Lee (1999: 11–16), Euh and Baker (1990: 15–18).

7 See also below III.B. *Financial Regulatory System.*

8 For example, banks could pay and charge higher interest rates on operations from trust accounts than on operations from normal banking accounts. There were no specific exposure limits or provisioning rules on loans from trust accounts and they were not subject to reserve requirements. In principle, trust accounts are not counted when computing a bank's capital adequacy ratio. In practice, however, a large segment of trust accounts in Korea have an economically similar function to deposits as the bank guarantees both the principal and a predetermined yield. The deposit guarantee issued by the government in late 1997 is also deemed to cover certain trust accounts.

9 For example, each financial regulator has issued accounting standards for each financial industry under its authority. In addition, they issued accounting guidelines each year to direct year-end closing of financial institutions. This standard setting practice has caused lack of comparability across financial industries. Further, the financial statements of financial institutions have lacked transparency and consistency over the years, since the year-end closing guidelines not only changed from year to year but also allowed accounting practices that differ from generally accepted accounting principles. Financial Supervisory Commission (FSC)/the Securities and Futures Commission (December 11, 1998: 6).

10 Long-term loans were defined as those with maturities of between one and ten years.

11 Bank for International Settlements (January 1998). The ratio fell to about 40 percent at the end of 1997.

12 BOK (1998: 7). At the end of 1997, short-term assets covered only 25 percent of short-term liabilities in merchant banks and 55 percent in commercial banks. The contracting foreign currency liquidity of the merchant banks was crucial to the buildup of the crisis.

13 Letters of Intent submitted by the government of Korea are available at the IMF website <http://www.imf.org/external/pubs/ft/op/opasia/index.htm>.

14 According to the FSC, one of the major goals of corporate restructuring is to regain stability of the financial system by preventing build-up of additional bad loans. FSC (December 1999: 5).

15 The kerb market refers to the unorganized money market in Korea, which is primarily outside government control and is represented by, for example, the *kye* system – essentially credit cooperatives organized by ordinary citizens and operated in an informal, club-like manner for saving and borrowing purposes. Euh and Baker (1990: 15).

16 For Korea's central banking system and the independence of the BOK, see Ko (1998).

17 These three special banks include the credit and banking sector of National Agricultural Cooperative Federation for agricultural and forestry loans, that of National Federation of Fisheries Cooperatives and its member cooperatives for fishery loans, and that of National Livestock Cooperatives Federation for livestock loans.

18 According to a World Bank report, such entry restrictions were preferred to high capital standards to encourage prudent behavior because this provided governments with a more discretionary tool to influence the behavior of the banks. World Bank (1993: 215).

19 Accordingly, the Securities and Exchange Commission, former regulator of the securities market, and the Insurance Supervisory Commission, former regulator of the insurance market, were dissolved.

20 Accordingly, the then four supervisory agencies, the Banking Supervisory Authority, Securities Supervisory Board, Insurance Supervisory Board, and Korea Non-bank Supervisory Authority were consolidated into the FSS.

21 Regulatory arbitrage consists of those financial transactions designed specifically to reduce costs or capture profit opportunities created by differential regulations or laws. See Section 10.3 Insufficient Regulatory and Supervisory Arrangements.

22 The Foreign Exchange Management Act was enacted on December 31, 1961 in order to unify previous laws and regulations regarding foreign-exchange control and to administer foreign-exchange policy more effectively. See Lee and Gallaway (1982: 246, 248). This act transferred the power of formulating foreign-exchange policy into the MOFE.

23 According to the MOFE, the reason for maintaining restrictions on nonresident local currency funding is to minimize the potential risk of speculative attacks. Ministry of Finance and Economy (November, 1999).

24 These acts were enacted, for the most part, by reference to Japanese bankruptcy laws. In general terms, the Corporate Reorganization Act has its roots in chapter 11 of the US Federal Bankruptcy Code, while the other two acts, the Bankruptcy Act and the Composition Act are based on German and Austrian laws, respectively.

25 The government introduced, effective January 1997, a deposit insurance scheme funded by low premiums contributed by banks.

26 For the progress of financial sector restructuring in Korea, see FSS (2000); FSC/FSS (2001).

27 See BOK (1998: 18–22); Ministry of Finance and Economy (1998: 22–4).

28 See Yi (1998: 1–20); Rough (1998: 37–43); Yoon and Gilligan (2000: 34).

29 For a list of ABS deals in Korea, see Giddy (2001: Supplement 3: Deals Illustrating Evolution of the ABS Market's Role in Korea) and Yoon and Gilligan (2000: 34–5). The issuing amount of ABSs in Korea was 6.8 trillion won in 1999, 49.4 trillion won in 2000, and 50.9 trillion won in 2001.

30 FSC, *Update on Progress of Strengthening Prudential Supervision and Regulation*, Press Release (December 15, 1998: 2).

31 These standards are the BIS capital adequacy ratio for banks and merchant banks, the operational net capital ratio to the securities companies, and payment capacity insufficiency ratio to the insurance companies.

32 The appraisal system of supervisory authority for supervision purpose is different from that of credit rating institutions whose objective is to provide information to their potential customers as investors.

Bibliography

Arner D. (1998) "An analysis of international support packages in the Mexican and Asian financial crises," *Journal of Business Law*, 42: 380.

Asia Development Bank (1998) *Executive Summary: The Role of Law and Legal Institutions in Asian Economic Development 1960–95*. Available Online, <http://www.adb.org/Publications/Online/role_of_law.PDF>.

Bank for International Settlements (January 1998) *The Maturity, Sectoral and Nationality Distribution of International Bank Lending: First Half 1997* (Monetary and Economic Department).

——(1997) *Payment Systems in Korea*.

Bank of Korea (BOK) (2001) *Financial System in Korea*.

——(December 1998a) *Bank Restructuring in Korea*.

——(July 1998b) *Financial Crisis in Korea: Why It Happened and How It can be Overcome*.

Baliño, T.J.T. and Ubide, A. (1999) "The Korean financial crisis of 1997–A strategy of financial sector reform," Working Paper No. WP99/28, International Monetary Fund.

Bhattacharya, A.K. and Fabozzi, F.J. (1996) "The expanding frontiers of asset securitization" in A.K. Bhattacharya and F.J. Fabozzi (eds), *Asset-Backed Securities*, New York: McGraw-Hill.

Bisignano, J. (1999) "Precarious credit equilibria: Reflections on the Asian financial crisis," Working Paper No. 64, Basel: Bank for International Settlements.

Blay, S. and Clark, E. (1993) *Australian Law of Financial Institutions*.

Borensztein, E. and Lee, J.W. (1999) "Credit allocation and financial crisis in Korea," Working Paper No. WP99/20, Washington, DC: International Monetary Fund.

Choi, D.Y. (2001) "The second stage foreign exchange liberalization and future policy directions," Policy Report No. 2001.01, Seoul: Korea Economic Research Institute.

Euh, Y.D. and Baker, J.C. (1990) *The Korean Banking System and Foreign Influence*, London; New York: Routledge

Financial Supervisory Commission (FSC) – (December 1999) *Corporate Restructuring—Performance and Future Plan*.

——(December 31, 1998a) *Korean Government Signs MOU with Newbridge Capital*.

——(December 17, 1998b) *Features about the New Cho Hung Bank*.

——(December 15, 1998c) *Update on Progress of Strengthening Prudential Supervision and Regulation*.

——(September 28, 1998d) *Progress in Financial and Corporate Restructuring and Future Tasks*.

——(September 2, 1998e) *Financial Restructuring in Korea – Progress to Date and Future Plans*.

——and Financial Supervisory Service (FSC/FSS) (2001) *Financial Reform & Supervision in Korea*. Available Online, <http://www.fss.or.kr/data/emglish/brochure2001.pdf> (accessed on July 11, 2001).

——and Securities and Futures Commission (December 11, 1998) *Reform of Accounting Standards in Korea*.

Financial Supervisory Service (2000) *Financial Supervisory System in Korea.* Available Online, <http://www.fss.or.kr/data/emglish/2001_publication.pdf> (accessed on June 1, 2001).

Giddy, I.H. (2001) "Financial institution risk management: the impact of securitization," Paper presented at Seminar on "Risk Management in Financial Institutions," Sogang University, Seoul.

Government of Korea, Letter of Intents submitted to IMF. Available Online, <http://www.imf.org/ external/pubs/ft/op/opasia/index.htm> (accessed on June 1, 1999).

Ko, D.W. (1998) "Korea's central banking system and independence of the Bank of Korea," *Korean Journal of International and Comparative Law*, 26: 143.

Lane, T., Ghosh, A.R., Hamann, J., Phillips, S., Schulze-Ghattas, M., and Tsikata, T. (January 1999) *Preliminary Copy: IMF-Supported Program in Indonesia, Korea and Thailand: A Preliminary Assessment*, Washington, DC: International Monetary Fund.

Lee, T.H. and Gallaway, Jr, W.H. (1982) "Foreign exchange controls in Korea and their impact upon international commercial transactions" in Chan-Jin Kim (ed.), *Business Laws in Korea: Investment, Taxation, and Industrial Property*, Seoul: Panmun.

Ministry of Finance and Economy (March 27, 1999) *Foreign Exchange Liberalization.*

——(November 1998) *The Year in Review: Korea's Reform Progress.*

Park, W.A. (1996) "Financial liberalization: the Korean experience" in T. Ito and A.O. Krueger (eds), *Financial Deregulation and Integration in East Asia*, Chicago: University of Chicago Press.

Rough, C. (1998) "Securitization in Korea" in *The Asia Law Guide to Securitization*, Asia Law and Practice.

Samsung Economic Research Institute (ed.) (December 31, 1998), *One Year after the IMF Bailout and the Changes in Korean Economy*, Seoul: Samsung Economic Research Institute (in Korean).

Yi, J.G. (1998) "Securitization in Korea," Paper presented at 1998 Annual Seminar of Korea International Trade Law Association, Seoul: Korea.

Yoon, E.S. and Gilligan, P.B. (2000) "Investment grade Korea revives securitization," *International Financial Law Review*, 19(2): 34.

11 Dynamic prospects for Korean banks' monitoring of business groups

Byung S. Min

11.1 Introduction

While it is not always the first best solution, an effective monitoring mechanism is important to ensure economic efficiency and to resolve potential conflicts between parties/entities, particularly in the absence of established (shared understanding based) long-term interactions. Banks' corporation monitoring in Korea, *ex ante* as well as *ex post*, is crucial to understand efficient capital allocation, business investment, and the agency problems because the economy has been dominated by debt-financing firms and/or business groups.[1]

The main objectives of this chapter are to examine economic restructuring following the 1997 financial crisis and to assess the development of a dynamic relationship between banks and business groups (*chaebols*). We take note of Diamond's famous question regarding who monitors banks as well as the role of government in Korea, and hence the dynamic assessment will be in the nexus of bank–corporation–government relationship.

The following section describes the bank–business groups relationship prior to the crisis, focusing on the principal transaction banking (PTB) system. In Section 11.3, the short-run impacts of the financial crisis on this relationship, in conjunction with constraints of the effectiveness of this *ex ante* change, will be discussed. Section 11.4 will analyse possible scenarios of this relationship in the long term. Historical experiences of the main industrial countries indicate that the relationship between banks and corporations has continuously changed to reflect the changing business environment. The analysis of these *ex post* long-run scenarios in this chapter is based on short-run constraining factors as well as determinant factors. The final section contains the conclusion.

11.2 Banks' failure in monitoring prior to the crisis

The bank–business groups relationship prior to the crisis was a hybrid one, and banks failed to monitor business groups. Instead, the role of government was relatively important. The emphasis on banks' intermediary role *vis-à-vis* competitiveness of the banking sector was the rationale for government intervention. While the introduction of the PTB system renders this *ex ante* relationship similar to the Japanese main bank system, this system was not effective in monitoring, due mainly to PTB's negligence and lack of feasibility. The relationship was similar to the Anglo-American system in terms of ownership structure and *ex post* banks' monitoring of *chaebols*. However, this Anglo-American type of capital market also did not effectively monitor *chaebols* due mainly to government intervention.

The Korean government intervened in two important ways in bank–business group relationship. One was the introduction of the PTB system, which aimed to link these two sectors under the industry policy regime, and the other was direct intervention in the banks' business management including personnel. The PTB system introduced in 1974 linked banks with business groups in the context of credit control (Nam 1996).[2] Major monitoring measures included correcting biased lending towards business groups, improving the corporate financial structure, and encouraging corporations to be listed publically. In addition, the PTBs were required to monitor *chaebols*' new investments (new establishments, purchasing, mergers), asset investment, financial structure, and inefficient business diversification since 1982 when the Banking Act was revised.

The performance of this PTB system was not satisfactory although it was justified by the shallowness of the capital market. In contrast with the main bank system, the Korean government sought to use this PTB system as a policy measure through its influence in capital allocation. Each PTB was not the major source of financing for individual groups although aggregate bank loans were an important investment source. Mutual ownership between them was small. PTBs could not create and/or share corporate information and there was no dispatching of their staff to *chaebols* to influence business decisions.[3] Banks did not want to lose their major customers, or business group. Consequently, there was little incentive for *chaebols* to cooperative with PTBs. Banks also had no incentives to achieve the objectives of this PTB system.

Adverse effects of this failure in the monitoring of *chaebols* were severe, despite the fact that these business groups had led Korean growth over the last two and a half decades. This malfunctioning monitoring mechanism, coupled with low (real) interest-rate policy and poor internal governance system, facilitated *chaebols*' high indebtedness. Debt–equity ratios of business groups have remained high due to inefficient and speculative investment (Krugman 1998, Lee 1998).[4] This indebtedness increased the instability of the economy before the crisis. Subsequently, instability and bankruptcies in corporate sectors during the crisis created a vicious circle, as these caused snow-balling non-performing loans and a credit crunch for the banks (Figure 11.1).[5]

11.3 The crisis, reforms, and changing relationship

11.3.1 Modified London approach for restructuring

Although there were institutional settings to reorganize and improve the formal insolvency procedures, the Korean government initially relied on the modified London approach that emphasized the role of the government-guided banks in

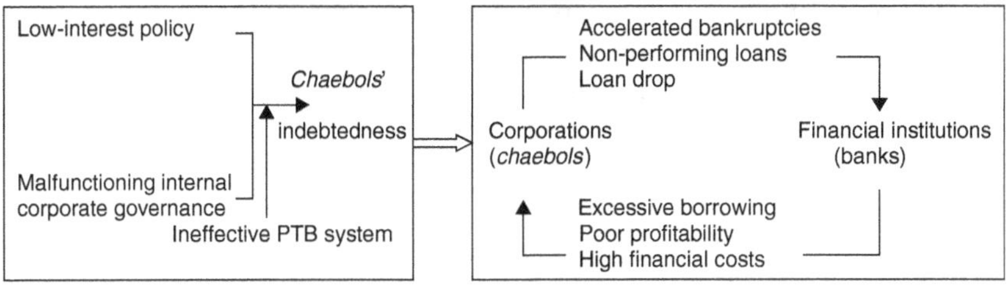

Figure 11.1 Vicious circle of bank–business groups.

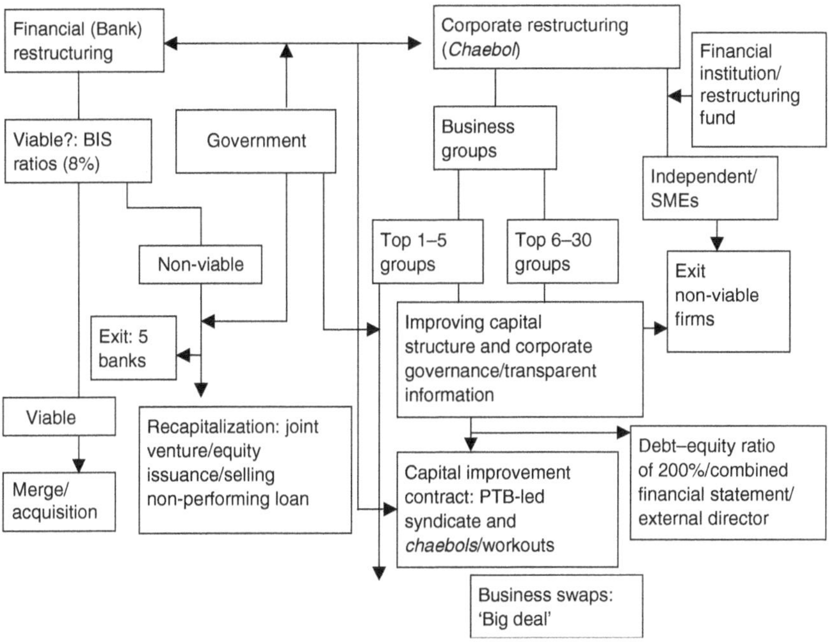

Figure 11.2 Bank–corporate restructuring in Korea.

restructuring business groups (Figure 11.2). Aiming at this, the government tried to restore banking industry first by recapitalizing and rehabilitating weak but viable financial institutions. In this process, more than 155 trillion won (around $125 billion: 125W/$) were injected by end of January 2002. Five non-viable banks were ordered to exit market and merged megacity banks such as Kookmin bank newly emerged. Second, prudential regulation and supervision needed to be strengthened via establishing a unified Financial Supervisory Commission (FSC) and requiring the recommended BIS (bank for internal settlements) capital equity, with accompanying improvement in accounting and disclosure rules. Justification of this modified London approach, *vis-à-vis* direct government-led centralized and market-led decentralized approaches, include inefficient bankruptcy law for corporate restructuring and domination of the economy by large firms.

Various measures for corporate (business groups) restructuring were introduced such as improving the corporate financial structure, the corporate governance mechanism, transparent/reliable information, and increased exit threat for poorly performing firms. The top thirty largest *chaebols* are required to drop their debt–equity ratio by 200 per cent by the end of 1999 and to remove mutual debt payment guarantees among subsidiaries by March 2000 (the Fair Trade Law), and to prepare combined financial statements for subsidiaries (Figure 11.2).[6] Introduction of external directors and strengthening minority shareholders' role in monitoring was to improve the internal governance mechanism. Effective bankruptcy procedures was set up via revising the existing bankruptcy law in order to speed up debt-resolution processes in order to ensure that non-viable firms would not continue to absorb credit, more importantly to create appropriate incentives for creditors (banks) to reach out-of-court settlements.

In sum, important implications of this restructuring for the bank–corporation relationship include capital injection from the government, restructuring strategy, and changing corporate governance structure associated with revision of statutes.

11.3.2 Ownership issue

Before the crisis, most commercial banks were virtually privatized and controlling shareholders' (such as founders and their kin) *de facto* ownership via interlocking shareholder were crucial to understand the ownership structure. The crisis provided new factors to be considered. Four important factors affected the ownership structure of bank and *chaebol* following the crisis and restructuring: reforms in the banking and real sectors, as well as the crisis impacts on economic growth (Figure 11.3).

First, the Korean government ownership of banks has increased in the process of recapitalization of the financial institution. The government injected capital of 64 trillion won initially, and then added to it later, resulting in more than 155 trillion won by the end of January 2002. Second, *chaebols*' restructuring by PTB-led syndicates has changed the corporate ownership structure. The debt–equity swap, coupled with deferral and deduction of debts (principal and/or interest rates), has been one of the major policy measures for the workouts because of its relative

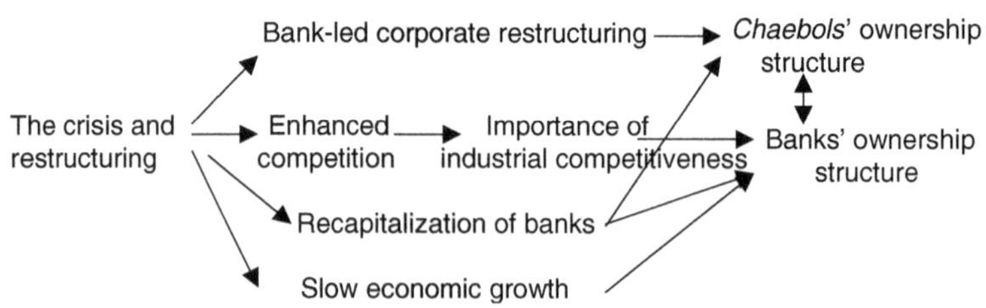

Figure 11.3 Restructuring and ownership issue.

flexibility and speed *vis-à-vis* the formal insolvency procedures. These swaps have increased the corporate equity ratio as well as the banks' BIS ratios.[7] The high indebtedness of *chaebols*, having around (exchange rate adjusted) 520 per cent of debt–equity ratio, implies this swap programme can significantly increase PTB-led syndicates' ownership of *chaebols*. Third, enhanced competition following the financial market liberalization has necessetated industrial competitiveness of the banking sector. Banks should compete with foreign banks and need to provide new products including derivatives. This competition will be facilitated by competition with NBFIs (non-bank financial institutions) as business scopes become deregulated. Finally, slow economic growth following the crisis has affected the macroeconomic environment in the relationship. Consequently, discussion arises on commercial industry's bank ownership as well as on the *chaebol* ownership structure as an option to increase efficiency arises.

11.3.3 Monitoring issue

The immediate impacts of the crisis include banks' enhanced role in *chaebol* restructuring and the increase in the *ex ante* banks' monitoring of *chaebols*, whereby the gravity of governance has shifted more towards the Japanese system (Figure 11.4).[8] The ownership and contractual effects of bank-led restructuring has facilitated this shift (Min 1999a,c).[9] Debt–equity swaps in the process of workouts indicate that the role of banks in monitoring corporations will rise. The PTB-led syndicates are required by contract (Capital Structure Improvement Contract) with groups to check *chaebols*' restructuring progress monthly as well as quarterly. Figure 11.4 thus indicates that the *ex ante* role of PTB-led syndicates in monitoring *chaebols* has increased. Figure 11.4 also shows that *chaebols* rely on PTB-led syndicates and (other) banks following the crisis will decrease due to government force to reduce their debt–equity ratios.

However, the short-term *ex post* effectiveness of this enhanced monitoring of *chaebols* will be constrained by pending challenges, such as snowballing non-performing loans and uncertainty, lack of incentive and shirking due to government intervention, poor feasibility due to limited, skilled human capital, and

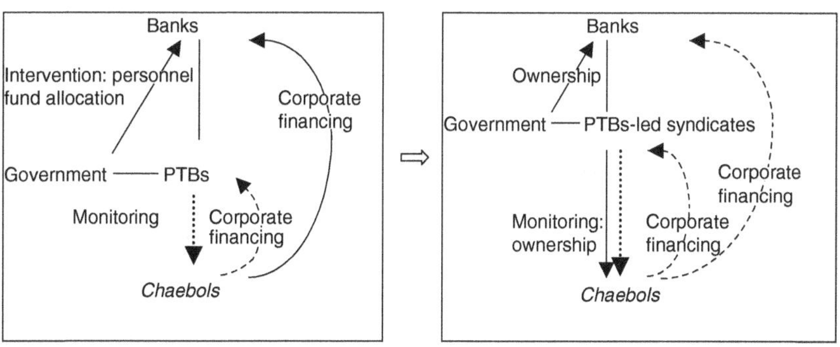

Figure 11.4 Bank–*chaebol* relationship prior to and following the crisis.

malfunctioning corporate governance (Min 1999b). In addition, diversification of corporate financing will promote an arm's length relationship.

In sum, PTB-led *chaebol* restructuring has shifted the gravity of the banks' monitoring role more towards the Japanese main bank system. This shift was facilitated by the ownership and contractual effect of bank-led workouts, as well as the new macro business environment following the crisis, wherein *ex post* effectiveness of the monitoring system has yet to be proven.

11.4 Scenarios for the changing relationship in the medium and the long run

The historical experience of developed countries indicates that the relationship between banks and corporations is evolutionary and also reflects the particular socio-cultural background. Neither the Anglo-American type of market monitoring nor the Japanese–German type of bank-oriented monitoring is regarded as an ultimate ideal system. The following analyses of long-term relationships between banks and business groups in Korea are based on the relative importance of current constraints, as well as the determinant factors following the crisis.

11.4.1 Back to the past: centralized system and government monitoring

This scenario implies strong government intervention in the bank–*chaebol* relationship, as was seen in the earlier stage of the development period (Figure 11.5). Figure 11.5 shows that (1) the long-term relationship moved towards the government-led centralized system; while (2) the short-run effects of bank-led

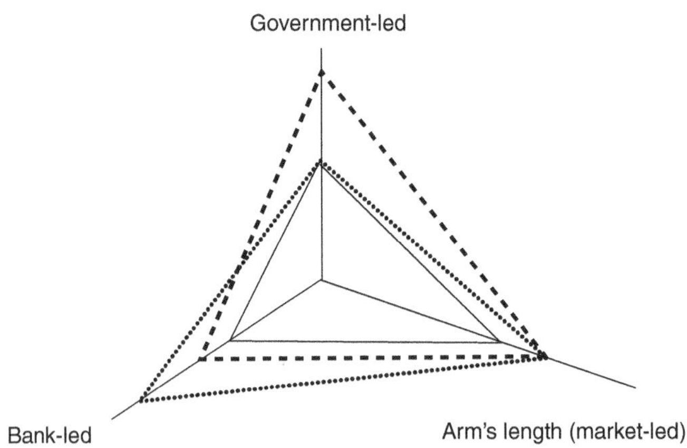

Figure 11.5 Chaebol monitoring under the centralized system.

Notes
—— Relationship prior to the crisis; ... Short-term relationship following the crisis; --- Long-term relationship.

restructuring have shifted the gravity more towards the Japanese system; (3) extension of market-led factors was due mainly to the liberalization of foreign investment in the equity market and measures to improve transparent information, which are essential to the development of the equity market; and (4) government intervention following the crisis increased through two channels, that is, increased bank ownership and direct intervention in *chaebol* restructuring.

Enhanced government ownership of banks in the process of recapitalization renationalized banks. The contract (Capital Structure Improvement Contract) for the program of *chaebol* restructuring between the PTB-led syndicates and *chaebols* was a product of the government intervention. The government intervened in the selection of fifty-five non-viable corporations in June 1998 and the business swap among the top five *chaebols*, or the 'Big Deal'.

Because of its publicity and for monetary policy, government involvement in the banking system is globally accepted. Rapid financial deregulation without prudential supervision can cause a financial crisis, although deregulation is a necessary condition for efficiency. Minimal government control during the crisis, in order to prevent a credit crunch and protection of depositors, is also justified.

However, long lasting direct intervention in Korea will create costs. First, credibility of government policy is a concern. Privatization of the banking sector has been scheduled since the early 1980s. Second, there is no countervailing power against government control and no mechanism to monitor government failure. X-inefficiency and moral hazard in the public sector is a rationale for the privatization (Min 1998). Less-regulated financial institutions such as NBFIs and later-established banks who were less regulated performed better. Third, while government ownership prevented economic power concentration of *chaebols* in the banking sector, managerial inefficiency of banks *vis-à-vis* private controlling will hinder competitiveness of the banking industry (Lee 1998). As the importance of productivity of the banking industry increases, the rationale of government ownership and direct control will decrease. Currently the government plans to privatize the nationalized banks.[10]

11.4.2 Relationship-oriented system and banks' monitoring

This system is similar to the Japanese main bank system and is a solution for the short-run impact of the crisis. According to the contract theory, the bank is the principal to monitor corporations (the agent). Resolving asymmetric information between corporations and banks is a major potential advantage of this system, whereas potential moral hazard from the lender, as well as disturbing non-viable corporate restructuring through cross lending, are potential dangers. As a result, the Japanese main bank system has turned more towards the Anglo-American system. Globalization of business in banks has diluted its close relationship with domestic corporations in Japan (Fukao 1995).

The shift in monitoring and ownership by banks towards the bank-oriented system following the crisis are major factors for the prediction of this solution.

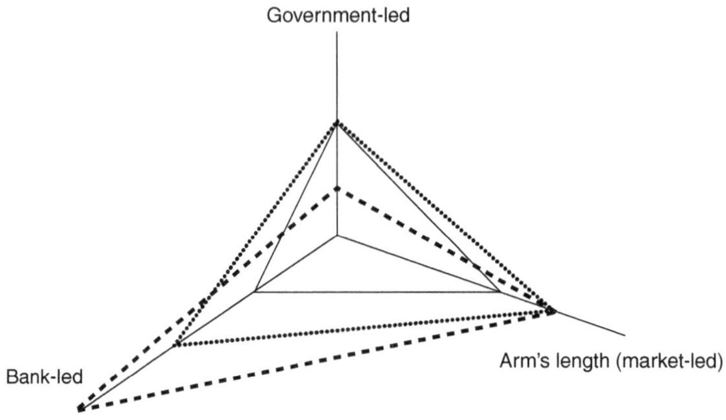

Figure 11.6 *Chaebol* monitoring under the relationship-oriented system.

Notes
—— Relationship prior to the crisis; ... Short-term relationship following the crisis; --- Long-term relationship.

Figure 11.6 shows this relationship oriented system prior to and following the economic crisis.

Important presumptions for this scenario are: (1) a permanent freer mutual ownership, (2) a successful PTB system and banks' capability to monitor business groups' business, and (3) diversified corporate financing. Freer ownership of banks by commercial industry is in particular an essential condition for this option. In contrast with the cases in Japan and Germany, Korean Banking Law tightly restricts commercial industry's ownership of banks. While most NBFIs were controlled by the top five *chaebols*, ownership of city banks (local banks) is limited by a maximum of 4 (15 per cent) with some exceptions.[11]

Commercial industry's ownership of banks has been controversial in Korea. Argument for allowing commercial industry's bank ownership is based on the industrial competitiveness of the banking sector. As competition increases between countries as well as between banks and NBFIs, the competitiveness of the banking sector as an industry is essential. The productivity of Korean banks, proxied by net profit per employee, was around $28,000 in 1995, which was 30 per cent of the average G-7 countries (Chang 1997). Profitability, represented by rate of return to asset, was around 50 per cent of the average of G-7 countries. The poor performance of Korean banks was attributed to accumulated non-performing loans and managerial inefficiency, which in turn was due to moral hazard from government intervention and regulated interest policy under the notion of 'picking the winner' policy.

While the commercial industry has a better business strategy and managerial know-how, *chaebols*' bank ownership has been restricted to prevent economic power concentration. However, it is controversial whether the absence of a large shareholder and participation from commercial industry's capital are the reasons for poor performance in the banking sector. One empirical study indicates that the value of financial institutions, proxied by modified Tobin's Q, had a negative relationship with the size of the largest shareholder (Park 1997). Public opinion on the adverse effects of economic power concentration by business groups following the crisis has also deteriorated in Korea.

Incidents of distorted capital flows towards the owners of NBFIs provide evidence for the argument against *chaebols*' ownership of bank.[12] Closer relationships through banks' ownership of *chaebol* increases instability of the economy and creates domino effects when an economy recesses, which have been seen in Japan and Malaysia. Corporate bankruptcies during restructuring have also increased non-performing loans to banks in Korea (Min 1999a,c).

Another constraint of this evolution is banks' capability to lead *chaebols*, as in the cases of Germany and Japan. Business groups have been more popular than banks to graduate students in Korea. In contrast with the banking sector, severe intra competition between managers in the subsidiaries of the group have produced business experts. Complicated intra financial linkage and cross-trade among subsidiaries of groups are also major hurdles to the banks' lead over *chaebols*.

Diversification of corporate financing is another issue. The more diversified the financing sources, the less incentive to own banks, given poor profitability of the banking industry. While equity financing began in 1980s, banks have been the major source of corporate financing. The share of direct financing between 1979 and 1997 was not important as the share of equity was 3–8 per cent and the corporate bond was 5–13 per cent (Bank of Korea).

However, the shares of banks in total corporate financing have decreased from 15 per cent in 1995 to 13 per cent in 1997 and to 0.2 per cent in 1998 (Bank of Korea). The shares of banks, *vis-à-vis* NBFIs, for the thirty largest business groups decreased from 72.5 per cent in 1988 to 40.1 per cent in 1995. Meanwhile, the share of NBFIs and the equity market has increased. This diversification tends to be facilitated by restructuring programmes following the crisis, such as liberalization of the capital market and development of the equity market. In this case, however, banks may want to increase long-term business relationship with *chaebols* as major customers.

11.4.3 Arm's length relationship and market monitoring

An arm's length relationship is the Anglo-American type of market-based system. While banks create corporate information, capital market monitorings such as active M&As are major threats to poorly performing managers. An active capital market mechanism ensures business performance and increases the wealth of shareholders. However, managers' myopic business attitudes and subsequent lack of long-term profitable investment is a potential disadvantage of this system. As a result, closer relationships between bank and commercial industry have been suggested (United States Department of the Treasury 1991). Figure 11.7 illustrates this market-led system prior to and following the economic crisis.

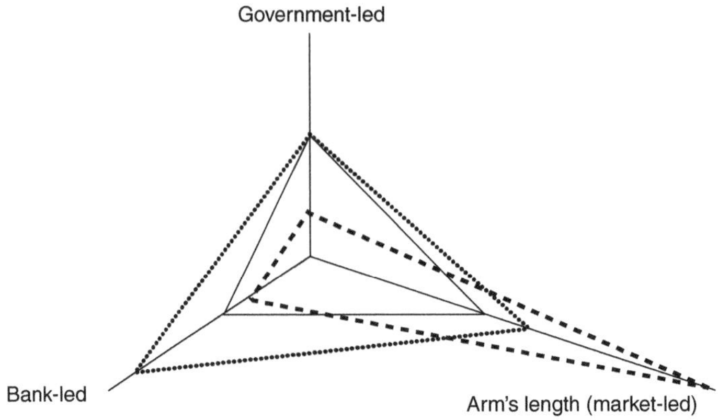

Figure 11.7 *Chaebol* monitoring under the market-led system.

Notes
—— Relationship prior to the crisis; ... Short-term relationship following the crisis; --- Long-term relationship.

Table 11.1 Trend of M&As in crisis ailing Asian countries (US$100 million)

	1991–95 (annual average)	*1996*	*1997*	*1998*
Korea	4	7	14	63
Thailand	13	21	14	18
Philippines	12	27	28	22
Indonesia	29	27	43	17
Malaysia	8	45	24	17
Total	67	126	123	138

Source: UNCTAD, readapted from Maekyung Newspaper (31 April 1999).

Note
Estimation at end of February 1999.

Because of corporate restructuring following the crisis and allowing hostile M&A, the number of M&As in Korea has increased dramatically (Table 11.1). There were 63 in 1998, which was 570 per cent of the total number in 1991–96, and 250 per cent of the total number in 1991–97. This significant change in Korea was the most conspicuous in the crisis ailing Asian capital market.

However, constraints to the evolution of the market-based monitoring system should be considered. The traditional Anglo-American type of arm's length relationship is based on weak ownership linkages between these sectors. On the contrary, as described in the previous section, government ownership in the banking sector and banks' *chaebol* ownership following the crisis have increased significantly.

The shallowness of capital markets is another major concern (Table 11.2). The occurrence of 'Fire Sales' following the crisis was the main reason for the sharp

Table 11.2 Sizes of equity markets in selected countries (1997, billion $ US)

	GDP: A	*Number of listed company*	*Total transaction: B*	*B/A (%)*
USA	8,111	9,091	12,884	159
Japan	4,192	3,140	2,217	53
UK	1,288	2,513	1,996	155
Germany	2,100	2,696	825	39
Korea	477	776	42	9

Source: Stock, July 1998, Korean Stock Exchange; Major Statistics of Korean Economy, 1999, National Statistical Office, Seoul Korea.

increase in M&As. Weak information-related infrastructure such as absence of a credit rating agency and reliable public information, as well as the weak role of institutional investors, has caused asymmetric information and an inefficient capital market. Inefficient monitoring from the capital market implies that there is no substitution for banks' monitoring in this scenario.

11.5 Conclusion

The Korean government adopted the modified London approach for the restructuring following the crisis. While restructuring measures include vitalizing the market force, the relationship between banks and business groups has shifted more towards the Japanese bank-led system and subsequently the *ex ante* required banks' business group monitoring has increased, due mainly to the ownership and contractual effects of recapitalized bank-led *chaebol* restructuring.

However, *ex post* effectiveness of banks' business group monitoring from this short-term shift will be constrained by challenging issues, such as snow-balling non-performing loans and business uncertainties in the banking sector, limited feasibility, and lack of incentives to monitor. Other factors affecting corporate–bank relationship include degree of diversification of corporate financing, coupled with capital market development and financial market liberalization, an improved corporate governance mechanism, and *ad hoc* change in government's bank ownership and banks' business group ownership given the cultural factors. While stylized scenarios of this business group monitoring are divided into government-led centralized, bank-led relationship orientation, and market-led arm's length, actual evolution of this mechanism in Korea depends on the relative importance of the current constraining factors, as well as the various mid- to long-term determining factors discussed in this chapter.

Notes

1 Non-bank financial institutions (NBFIs) have become more important in terms of saving and lending since the 1970s. This rapid growth was attributable to more-favourable

interest rates and less-regulated business activities, allowing freer entry of new firms than in the banking sector (Chang 1997). This chapter focuses on banks whose role in corporate restructuring has been dramatically enhanced following the crisis.

2 Under the administrative guidance of the government, large, nation-wide, commercial banks agreed to designate the bank with which the principal company of a group had major business relationships as the PTB for all the groups' subsidiaries.

3 For example, issuance of corporate bonds in Korea is currently decided by the Merchant Banking Corporation (MBC) whose judgement is based on credit rates of the corporation from two individual credit rating companies.

4 In 1997, the share of the thirty largest groups' debt (357 trillion won) accounted for 36 per cent of total corporate debts.

5 Estimated non-performing loans have increased from 7.5 per cent (69 trillion won) of total loans in 1997 to 12.4 per cent (125 trillion won) in 1998 (Financial Supervisory Commission 1998).

6 In fact, this Korean government's requirement of combined financial statement (F/S) is unique in the world. Corporations request that this combined F/S should gradually be substituted for a consolidated F/S that is accepted worldwide.

7 As of mid-1999, seventy-seven corporations were selected for workouts and the consequent amount of debt–equity swaps and issuance of convertible bonds reached around 3.5 trillion won, which accounted for 39 per cent of total financial subsidies for all the target firms.

8 In addition, bank restructuring *per se* could differentiate between bank–*chaebol* relationship, depending on the level of risk of individual *chaebols* and/or its subsidiaries (BOK 1999).

9 Improving corporate governance will raise internal prudential supervision. External directors are required in the corporate sector. Enhanced small shareholder's right is aimed at supervising poorly performing chief executive officers (CEO). However, external directors' lack of independence from the CEO is a major constraint in this Anglo-American type of internal governance system in Korea.

10 In July 1999, Jeil Bank, one of the major city banks, was sold to a foreign investor (New Bridge Capital). Seoul Bank, another major city bank, is also to be sold to a foreign investor.

11 For example, foreign ownership and ownership in joint banks and business converted banks are exceptional.

12 The share of the thirty largest groups in NBFIs' loan in the 1990s has continuously increased from 36.6 per cent in 1991 to 38.4 per cent in 1998. Rate of returns on equity of security companies owned by the thirty largest groups was generally lower than those owned by other commercial industry and financial institutions (Park 1997).

Bibliography

Bank of Korea, *Corporate Financial Statement Analysis*, various issues.

——, *Monthly Bulletin*, various issues.

Chang, K.-S. (1994) *Corporate Competitiveness and Governance Structure*, Seoul: Korea Institute of Finance.

——(1997) 'Trend and impact of asymmetric regulation between bank and nonbank financial institutions', Bank of Korea.

Financial Supervisory Commission (1998) 'Direction of financial and corporate restructuring', unpublished paper.

Flath, D. (1993) 'Shareholding in the Keiretsu, Japanese financial Groups', *Review of Economics and Statistics*, 75: 249–57.

Fukao, Mitsuhiro (1995) *Financial Intergration, Corporate Governance, and the Performance of Multinational Companies*, Washington, DC: The Brookings Institution.

Grosse, R. (1992) 'The debt/equity swap in Latin America-in whose interest?', *Journal of International Financial Management and Accounting*, 4(1): 13–39.

Krugman, P. (1998) 'What happened to Asia', mimeo, MIT, January.

Lee, J. (1998) 'Causes for business failures: understanding the 1997 Korean crisis', *Journal of Asian Economics*, 9(4): 637–51.

Lee, Young Ki (1996) *Corporate Governance*, Seoul: Korea Development Institute.

Min, Byung S. (1998) 'Imperfect competition, protection and X-efficiency in Korean manufacturing', *Asian Economic Review*, 40(2): 259–75.

——(1999a) 'The financial crisis impact on bank-business group relationship in Korea: some corporate governance context', *Economic Papers*, 18(3): 59–72.

——(1999b) 'Competition effects of import discipline in Korea', *Journal of the Asia Pacific Economy*, 4(2): 298–316.

——(1999c) 'South Korea's financial crisis: what have we learned?', *ASEAN Economic Bulletin*, 16(2): 175–89.

Nam, Sang-Woo (1996) 'The principal transactions bank systems in Korea and a search for a new bank-business relationship', in T. Ito and A.O. Krueger (eds), *Financial Deregulation and Integration in East Asia*, National Bureau of Economic Research, The University of Chicago Press.

Park, K.-S. (1997) 'Study on ownership and management for the financial institution', Policy Research Report No. 97.01, Korea Institute of Finance.

United States Department of the Treasury (1991) *Modernising the Financial System.*

12 The Korean steel industry after the economic crisis[1]

Challenges and opportunities

Kwang Soo Park and MoonJoong Tcha

12.1 Introduction

Korea was a typically less developed economy based on agriculture until the early 1960s. It had almost all the problems that poor developing countries might have: high population density, very low levels of income, scarce natural resources and low economic growth rates. However, it has achieved extremely rapid growth since the Korean government promulgated its first Five Year Economic Development Plan in 1962. Annual increase of GDP reached on average 7.5 per cent from 1963 to 1999, and was regarded as a model case of 'making a miracle' (Lucas 1993). The remarkable growth of the Korean economy was accompanied by the rapid development of the Korean steel industry. As shown in Figure 12.1, the domestic consumption of crude steel increased from 0.3 million tonnes in 1962 to 39.9 million tonnes in 1999, while production increased from 0.1 to 41 million tonnes for the same period. However, the future of the Korean steel industry does not look so rosy as it did in the the past. The domestic steel market is expected to be satiated. Business environments in the Korean steel industry have undergone a lot of changes. The world steel industry has been becoming much more competitive. Globalization and the IT (information technology) revolution have been changing the traditional transaction patterns. Environmental requirements have continued to have a major impact on the industry. Technological developments in the steel industry have been taking place faster than ever.

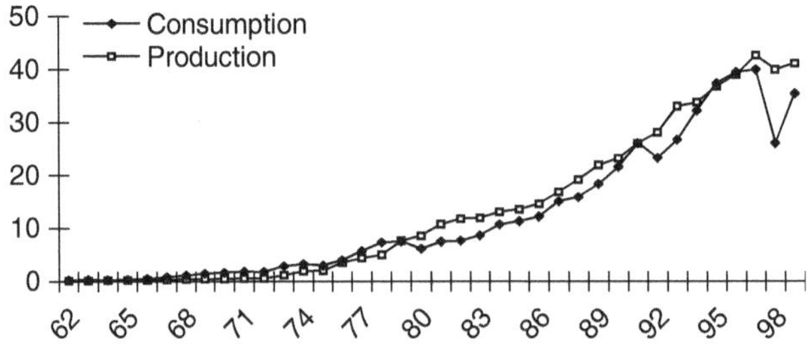

Figure 12.1 Crude steel consumption and production in Korea, thousand tonnes.
Source: Korean Iron & Steel Association, various years.

This chapter will identify the various challenges that the Korean steel industry is facing and will discuss whether the Korean steel industry can achieve a sustainable growth in the future and what the industry should do to overcome the challenges. The chapter consists of four parts. The next section will briefly describe the history of the Korean steel industry. Section 12.3 will investigate new challenges to the Korean steel industry and Section 12.4 will discuss the Korean steel industry's strategies to overcome the challenges. Section 12.5 will summarize.

12.2 The development of the Korean steel industry

Since the early 1960s, the Korean economy has recorded a sustained high growth, except for two years, 1980 and 1998, when output temporarily declined. There has been a general consensus that such a sustained rapid growth was primarily due to the adoption of an export-oriented industrialization policy. The modern steel industry in Korea was a core product of the government's policy of industrialization that attempted to create 'artificial' comparative advantage in heavy and chemical industries in the 1970s. The Korean steel industry's history can be divided into three stages.

12.2.1 The premature stage (before the POSCO's operation)

The history of the modern steel industry in Korea could date back to the period of Japanese occupation. In 1941, Japan built two (then) modern steel mills in southern Korea. However, Korea's steel making remained at the primitive stage in terms of capacity, technology, productivity, and product mix until POSCO, which is now a symbol of industrialization as well as the steel industry, was established.

As the Korean government promulgated its first Five Year Economic Development Plan in 1962, the economy entered a path of rapid industrialization and economic growth. Domestic steel demand increased rapidly as industrialization accelerated. As shown in Table 12.1, apparent consumption of finished steel increased to 1.8 million tonnes in 1972 from 0.3 million tonnes in 1962. The rapid increase in the demand for steel could not be met with outdated and small-scale steel production, which led to the increase in imports. The import of steel rose almost eightfold in ten years: from 0.3 million tonnes in 1963 to 2.1 million tonnes in 1972, which resulted in the increase in the import dependency ratio

Table 12.1 Korea's crude steel supply/demand (1963–72), million tonnes (%)

	1963	*1968*	*1972*	*Average annual growth rate (1963–72)*
Consumption (A)	0.4	1.1	1.8	19.8
Export	0.1	0.0	0.9	28.5
Import (B)	0.3	0.7	2.1	23.6
Production	0.1	0.4	0.6	16.9
B/A (%)	85.4	66.9	115.2	—

Source: Korean Iron & Steel Association.

from 85 to 115 for the same period. With the Korean government's ambition to build up the country as heavy industry oriented, it was expected that the amount of steel import would increase dramatically. As well as the rapid increase in imports, another serious problem in this period was the large imbalance in production capacities between rolling, steel making, and iron making because there was no modern integrated steel mill. There also existed substantial differences between the product items supplied and those demanded. To deal with these problems, the government strongly promoted the establishment of a large-scale integrated steel mill and founded POSCO as a state-run entity in 1968.

12.2.2 *The take-off period (1973–95)*

The second stage could be called the take-off period. The period covers from 1973 to 1995. In July 1973, POSCO started the operation of the Pohang Works, the first integrated steel mill in Korea. Since then, the Korean steel industry has been developing dramatically. POSCO's successful adoption of the most up-to-date technology in ordinary steel making substantially enhanced the nation's iron and steel production capability in terms of scale and integrated steel making technology and product mix. The expansion of mini-mills was just as remarkable in the 1990s and total electric arc furnace (EAF) capacity jumped up steadily from 8.3 million tonnes in 1990 to 17.5 million tonnes in 1995. However, a rapid growth in EAF capacity brought about the problem of overcapacity.

The rapid economic growth and the development of the heavy and chemical industries in this period were associated with the strong growth of domestic demand for steel products. Apparent consumption of finished steel rose from 3.2 million tonnes in 1973 to 37.3 million tonnes in 1995, recording an annual average growth rate of 12.4 per cent for the period. Production increased from 1.2 tonnes in 1973 to 36.8 million tonnes in 1995, at an annual growth rate of 17.0 per cent. The increased rate of production exceeded that of consumption, thus lowering the import dependency rate to 27.1 per cent in 1995 (Table 12.2).

12.2.3 *The maturing stage (after 1995)*

The Korean steel industry seems to have entered the maturing period from the mid-1990s onwards, as the rate at which domestic demand increases has become stagnant. Domestic consumption of finished steel was recorded at 40 million tonnes in

Table 12.2 Korea's crude steel supply/demand (1973–95), million tonnes (%)

	1973	*1980*	*1990*	*1995*	*Average annual growth rate (1973–95)*
Consumption (A)	2.9	6.1	21.5	37.3	12.4
Export	1.1	5.3	7.6	9.6	10.6
Import (B)	2.7	2.8	5.6	10.1	6.2
Production	1.2	8.6	23.1	36.8	17.0
B/A (%)	93.1	45.9	26.0	27.1	—

Source: Korean Iron & Steel Association.

Table 12.3 Recent crude steel demand/supply, million tonnes (%)

	1995	*1996*	*1997*	*1998*	*1999*
GDP growth rate (%)	8.9	6.8	5.0	−6.7	10.7
Consumption	37.3	39.4	39.9	26.0	35.4
	(15.9)	(5.6)	(1.3)	(−34.8)	(36.1)
Exports	9.6	10.3	11.6	17.5	13.9
	(−4.2)	(8.3)	(11.7)	(51.7)	(−20.6)
Imports	10.1	10.8	8.1	3.7	8.3
	(19.9)	(7.3)	(−25.3)	(−54.8)	(126.8)
Production	36.8	38.9	42.6	39.9	41.0
	(9.0)	(5.8)	(9.4)	(−6.2)	(2.9)

Source: Korean Iron & Steel Association.

Note
Figures in parentheses are change rates to the previous year.

1996. However, the rate at which consumption increased was relatively low, at 5.6 per cent, in that year, which was considerably lower than the previous year's 15.9 per cent, due to the economic slowdown. In 1997, when the economy was hit by the financial crisis, the rate at which apparent consumption increased fell to 1.6 per cent. When the crisis was deepening and the economy recorded a negative growth, the consumption of steel also recorded a negative growth rate of −34.8 per cent in 1998 (Table 12.3). It has been argued that the dominant cause of the Korean economic crisis that erupted in late 1997 was the near depletion of foreign currency reserves. However, it has also been pointed out that the latent background of the crisis lay in more fundamental factors, that is, structural weaknesses of the Korean economy. A series of bankruptcies of *chaebols* including the Hanbo, Sammi, Jinro, Haitai, and Kia Groups that took place around 1997 also had a critical effect on the Korean steel market as many of them were significant producers of steel as well as consumers.

The Korean steel industry experienced the first decline in crude steel production in 1998 since its start up, due to the response to the reduction of demand and bankruptcy of some firms. However, the decline was relatively moderate, compared to that in consumption. The Korean steel industry's competitive advantages played a significant role even in the economic crisis, enabling the industry to expedite trade as an effective means of preventing what, otherwise, would have caused a much sharper decline in steel output.

The Korean economy has recovered faster than expected since the first quarter of 1999, which led to the steep increase in the domestic demand for steel. Apparent consumption of finished steel increased by 36 per cent in 1999. However, such a rapid growth might be just a reaction against the previous year's deep fall, as it was still lower than the pre-crisis level of consumption.

12.2.4 The Korean steel industry's position in the world

The standings of the Korean steel industry in the world are summarized in Table 12.4. In 1970, Korea's crude steel production was 0.5 million tonnes and its share in the world production was a mere 0.1 per cent. In 1998, the production

Table 12.4 The Korean steel industry development, million tonnes

	1970	*1980*	*1990*	*1998*
Crude steel production				
World	595.4	715.6	770.1	775.0
Korea	0.5	8.6	23.1	40.0
Share (%)	0.1	1.2	3.0	5.2
Ranking	35th	18th	7th	6th
Crude steel consumption				
World	588.4	722.6	773.6	789.0
Korea	1.0	6.1	21.5	26.0
Share (%)	0.2	0.8	2.8	3.3
Ranking	38th	19th	8th	7th
Steel products export				
World	90.4	140.9	169.3	227.0
Korea	0.1	4.5	7.2	16.8
Share (%)	0.1	3.2	4.3	7.4
Ranking	36th	8th	8th	4th

Source: International Iron & Steel Institute (IISI), various years.

Table 12.5 Crude steel output of major steel companies, million tonnes

	1991		*1993*		*1995*		*1998*	
	Output	*Rank*	*Output*	*Rank*	*Output*	*Rank*	*Output*	*Rank*
POSCO	19.1	3	22.5	2	23.4	2	25.6	1
Nippon Steel	28.6	1	25.8	1	27.8	1	24.1	2
Usinor	22.8	2	17.6	3	15.5	4	16.4	5
British Steel	12.9	4	12.3	4	15.7	3	16.3	6
USX	9.6	10	10.0	8	12.1	6	10.2	10

Source: IISI 1998.

share soared up to 5.2 per cent. In crude steel consumption, Korea's share rose from 0.2 per cent in 1970 to 3.3 per cent in 1998. The Korean steel industry ranked sixth and seventh in the world in terms of crude steel production and consumption, respectively, in 1998. It is also notable that POSCO became the world's largest steel producer in 1998 by producing 25.6 million tonnes of crude steel, as shown in Table 12.5. This was in part due to the downsizing of production after restructuring by Nippon Steel. However, at the same time, it is also owing to the fact that POSCO has been continuously increasing its production efficiency as well as production capacity.

12.3 Challenges to the Korean steel industry

12.3.1 The end of a rapid growth period

As discussed in the previous section, the successful development of the Korean steel industry relied largely on a high economic growth. However, in the years ahead, it may be difficult for the Korean steel industry to experience such a favourable environment, because the Korean economy is likely to enter a path of slow and stable growth after a few years of adjustment. It is projected to grow at an annual average rate of 5.1 per cent for the period of 2000–10.[2]

In addition to the slow economic growth, the intensity of steel use (= (steel consumption in thousand tonnes/GDP in million dollars) ×100) in Korea is expected to be lowered in the near future. Figure 12.2 displays Korea's intensity of steel use, which has continuously increased with minor fluctuations. The intensity of steel use peaked in 1995, fell to the mid-1980s level when the economy was in the middle of the crisis in 1998 and then rebounded in 1999. However, the slope of the trend line is getting flatter, and it will reach the final peak around 2005.[3]

The intensity of steel use trend is closely related to the activities of major steel consuming industries and the proportion of steel in each product in Korea. The proportion of the GDP produced by the major steel consuming industries, such as automotive, construction, and shipbuilding, recorded an 18.6 per cent rise in 1996 and then showed a declining trend as seen in Figure 12.3. In addition to the shocks incurred by the economic crisis, the Korean economy has shown various signals that its consumption and production structures moved to the more matured economy where consumption and production are oriented towards service. Therefore, even when the economy emerges from the crisis, the share curve would be flat and then start to decline in the near future. From Figures 12.2 and 12.3, we can find that the intensity of steel use has a similar trend to that of the proportion of the GDP produced by the major steel consuming industries.

Recent projection of production activities in Korea reports that, as seen in Table 12.6, most industries are expected to grow at lower rates than the expected GDP growth in the future. Considering this, we can conclude that the domestic demand for steel in Korea will not grow as fast as before.

The decrease of the proportion of the GDP produced by these major industries or the decrease of the intensity of steel use does not necessarily imply that the (absolute amount of) demand for steel would decrease, as both of them are relative terms. Figure 12.4 shows that the three major industries have been continuously increasing their production until the recent past, and that the rate of increase in construction

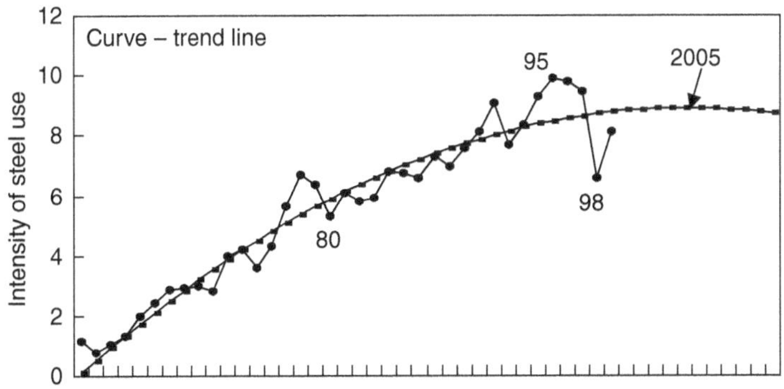

Figure 12.2 The intensity of steel use in Korea.

Source: Authors' calculation.

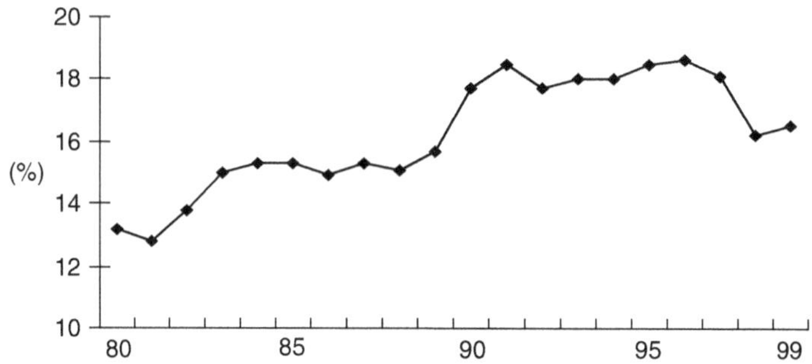

Figure 12.3 Proportion of GDP produced by the major steel consuming industries in Korea.

Source: The Bank of Korea, various years.

Table 12.6 Projection of production activities by industry

	Unit	*1997*	*2006*	*2010*	*Average annual growth rate, % (1997–2010)*
Fabricated metal		135	154	166	1.61
Machinery	1990 = 100	159	210	260	3.86
Appliances		168	272	363	6.09
Automobile	1,000 vehicles	3,011	3,585	3,913	2.04
Shipbuilding	1,000 G/T	7,450	8,554	8,309	0.84
Construction area	Mil. m^2	113	107	95	−1.35

Source: Hanyang University 1999.

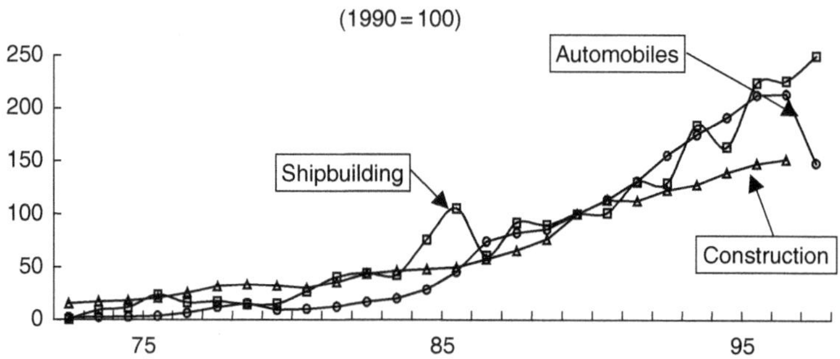

Figure 12.4 Production index movements of major steel consuming industries.

Sources: The Korea Automakers Association, the Korean Shipbuilder's Association, the Bank of Korea.

then stagnated and that of automotive manufacturing fell as they experienced the economic crisis. Also some sectors in Table 12.6 are forecast to increase their production activities at least up to the year 2010. Therefore, we cannot exclude the possibility that the demand for steel will substantially increase for the time being as some steel consuming sectors will increase their activities. However, the theories of

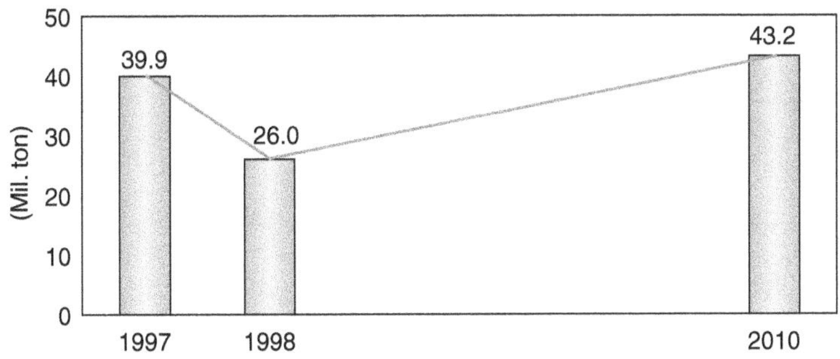

Figure 12.5 Domestic steel demand outlook.

Source: *POSRI*, 2000.

intensity of steel use indicate that substitution of materials happens in the process of development, where the direction is usually steel-saving. Considering that about 60–70 per cent of its steel product is consumed domestically, the rapid maturation of the domestic steel market implies that the Korean steel industry is to face difficulties in digesting its products.

Actually, the domestic demand for steel is expected to be 43.2 million tonnes in 2010, which is greater than 41.0 million tonnes in 1999, not to speak of 39.9 million tonnes in 1997, as summarized in Figure 12.5. These figures imply that an average annual growth rate of domestic steel demand from 1997 to 2010 would be as low as 0.6 per cent. With such a low rate of increase, it naturally follows that the excess capacity of production might be a serious problem.

12.3.2 Overcapacity

Until the mid-1980s, the Korean steel industry was regarded as the most efficient in terms of operating rate. Operation rate (crude steel production/annual production capacity) has been higher than 100. However, a steep and continuous increase in production capacity of steel caused the overcapacity, especially in some selected products such as cold-rolled (CR) coil, section and pipe as shown in Table 12.7. This overcapacity problem resulted mainly from the large expansion of EAF in the 1990s. The overcapacity implies low operating rate, which increases the burden of fixed costs and, in turn, weakens price competitiveness. A weakened price competitiveness will result in a decrease in demand, which in turn induces a further lowered level of operation. As a result, the industry gets caught in a vicious cycle.

12.3.3 Weakened cost competitiveness and low productivity

The Korean steel industry has been efficient and gained competitiveness based on low costs. Sometimes it is criticized that the competitiveness is due to low wages and a high level of government subsidy. This critique might have been true previously as a relatively high level of subsidy (3.2–33.2 per cent of total investment funding) was provided to the Pohang Works, and overall wage level was quite low

Table 12.7 Production capacity and demand by products, thousand tonnes

	CR coil	*Section*	*Reinforcing bars*	*Pipe*
Capacity (A)	14,652	6,302	10,773	5,635
Total demand (B)	10,895	3,780	8,805	3,415
B/A (%)	134	167	122	165

Source: Korean Iron & Steel Association 1998.

Table 12.8 The unit cost of CR coil

	Korea	*US*	*Japan*	*UK*	*German*	*Brazil*	*China*
Cost (US$/ton)	358	482	480	457	407	377	385
Korea = 100	100	135	134	128	114	105	108

Source: WSD 1999.

in Korea until the mid-1980s. However, this argument does not apply any more. For example, in establishing POSCO's four works in Kwanyang, only 1.6 per cent of the total investment funding was subsidized for only one of the works while the others completely relied on internal fundings such as loans and their own profits (Park and Shin 1999). In spite of experiencing militant labour movements in the mid-1980s, the wage level in Korea never became lower than other East Asian Tigers, which eroded competitiveness based on a lower wage. The relatively lower prices of products these days are rather attributed to efficient management, well-trained man power, shortened construction periods, relatively new facilities, and high rates of operation. According to the World Steel Dynamics (WSD), Korea's production cost of CR coil was US$358 per ton in 1998, which was lower by about 30 per cent than the United States and Japan, as shown in Table 12.8. However, the difference in costs will dwindle gradually since the advanced countries are recovering their competitiveness through restructuring, and newly emerging countries have advantage in labour cost and facilities. Just as many industries in Korea have recently experienced, the Korean steel industry is also in fear of being 'caught in a nut cracker'.

Another problem regarding the price competitiveness of the POSCO comes from the operation of mini-mills (EAF). The Korean steel industry, which is represented by POSCO, has a strong cost competitive edge in the world of integrated steel mills but most EAF companies in Korea still have much lower labour productivity than major advanced companies, as seen in Table 12.9.

12.3.4 The technology gap

The Korean steel companies' active R&D investments in the 1990s have narrowed the technology gap between the Korean steel producers and the advanced

Table 12.9 The comparison of productivity by EAF mills, tonnes, million won

	Korea (A)	*Korea (B)*	*Korea (C)*	*Nucor*	*Tokyo*
Prod. per employee	1,266	1,000	1,652	1,215	3,001
Sales per employee	620	594	870	807	1,070

Source: Annual report of each company.

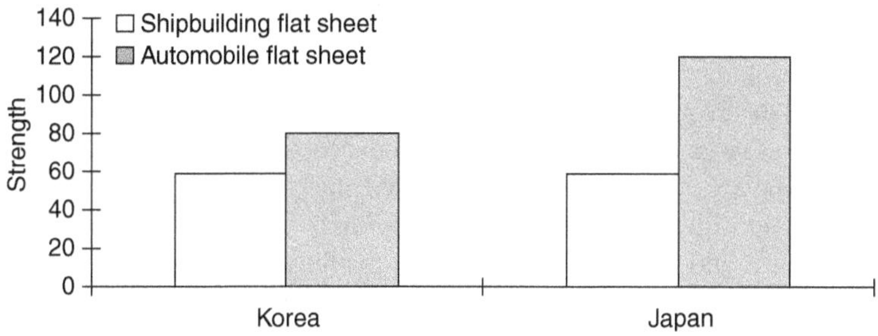

Figure 12.6 Quality comparison between Korea and Japan, kg/mm^2.

Source: Korean Iron & Steel Association.

steel mills in major developed countries. However, there still remains a significant technology gap in such areas as facilities, engineering, and product technologies, which lead to the difference in the quality of products. As an example, Figure 12.6 shows that the quality of the Korean flat sheet steel for an automobile is much lower than that of Japan's.

12.3.5 Changes in business environments

12.3.5.1 The era of global competition

The 1990s witnessed market deregulation and liberalization becoming a global phenomenon. The emergence of the WTO and its implementation of free trade doctrine has broken down the barriers of protection and accelerated the trend of globalization. Globalization is causing changes in the pattern of steel transactions too. Major industries, such as automotive and home appliance manufacturing, are already responding to globalization trends, developing new structures. In order to survive this period of Mega Competition, companies in these industries are seeking to decrease their average cost through the realization of the economy of scale and capital. They have shifted their business structures from local to global and established their value chain based on decentralization. In turn, those companies are expecting their steel suppliers to provide them with quality products and services stably on an international and global level. For instance, General Motors (GM) was reported to have made the biggest volume of steel purchase in its history in 1999. Drawing up a four-year contract with forty steel companies, GM is to buy 19.8 million tonnes of steel that is worth US$11.7 billion. The size and length of the deal by GM demonstrates the importance of developing new markets and new customers for the integrated steel markets.[4]

12.3.5.2 Regionalism

It has to be pointed out that, accompanied by the trend of globalization discussed earlier, there has been a consistent movement towards regionalization, which seems fairly contradictory. While the talks to achieve the free trade regime have been proceeding, we simultaneously observed the formation of economic blocs such as the evolution (devolution?) of the EC to the EMU, the emergence of the NAFTA, and the frequent talks to develop the ASEAN or APEC to the organization for more intensive (and discriminatory) economic cooperation. It implies that steel producers, who are not in the bloc, should exert their efforts to penetrate into this regional market with more difficult trade conditions. The frequent abuse of anti-dumping claims and the imposition of countervailing duties by developed countries are other obstacles inflicted by regionalism, and that is what the Korean steel producers should overcome.

12.3.5.3 Substitution between materials

Although the steel industry has greatly improved its competitive position as a major input of various products in the past decade, it still faces tremendous challenges in maintaining or increasing its share in the major steel using industries. Tilton (1983) found that while substitution between materials (including steel) does not take place significantly in the short run, however, various reasons such as technological advance, costs, environmental concerns, and government regulations would make the substitution more likely to happen in the long run. When substitution between materials occurs, this is usually away from steel. For example, environmental concerns are so mounting up over the world these days that automobile manufacturers are looking for alternative materials to steel. Automobile manufacturers are of the opinion that aluminium enables them to reduce the weight of their products considerably, which will make automobiles more environment-friendly by reducing fuel consumption. According to the automobile industry, the reduction of one tonne in the weight of a vehicle results in the reduction of toxic gases emitted by about 20 tonnes throughout the life of the vehicle.[5] It is reported that GM is planning to buy a large volume of aluminium from Alcan Aluminium to substitute steel. Therefore steel may lose its position as the most important material for the production of automobiles, and the same phenomenon may happen in other industries as well.

12.3.5.4 Introduction of e-commerce and conversion of buyers' market

The global wave of the IT revolution is surging over the conventional markets into cyber markets. E-commerce will accelerate the emergence of a more centralized global marketplace for steel. It will streamline the supply chain, give customers real-time information about mills' operations, speed up the transactions, and cut down the search and transaction cost. In the new business world where IT will play a key role, the buyers will have more power than ever in transactions as the buyers will have easy access to all the information relevant to their business. This change implies that the steel industry should cope with this new pattern of market environment by reorganizing their business structures and entering into e-selling. It is a possible scenario that steel producers in developed countries will have the edge of competition in this new market as they are steps ahead in developing and using internet-based transactions.

12.4 Future directions to opportunities

It is still controversial whether the rapid recovery of the Korean economy from the crisis is due to the fundamental restructuring of the economy or due to the favourable global conditions and economic prosperity led by major developed economies. However, as discussed earlier, the temporary downturn of the demand for steel seems reasonably well recovered, at least apparently. The more significant task for the current Korean steel industry is, therefore, not to overcome the reduction of demand by the crisis but to consider longer term challenges and obstacles. In previous sections, we have briefly examined prevailing environmental changes and challenges for the Korean steel industry that should be critical to its further success. If the Korean steel industry successfully copes with these threats, it will have another chance for further development. Otherwise, it will be driven to despair. The following chart (Figure 12.7) identifies challenging factors and summarizes strategies to overcome and convert them into opportunities. The next section discusses this in detail.

12.4.1 Continuous restructuring and shift towards higher-quality products

This strategy includes the following three sub-strategies: (i) persistent rationalization of inefficient and excess facilities, (ii) control of additional domestic capacity considering the limits of increase in steel demand, and (iii) management policy shift from volume-oriented growth to value-based growth.

POSCO has continued streamlining its operation. It suspended construction of No. 2 mini-mill at the Kwangyang steel complex taking its profitability and

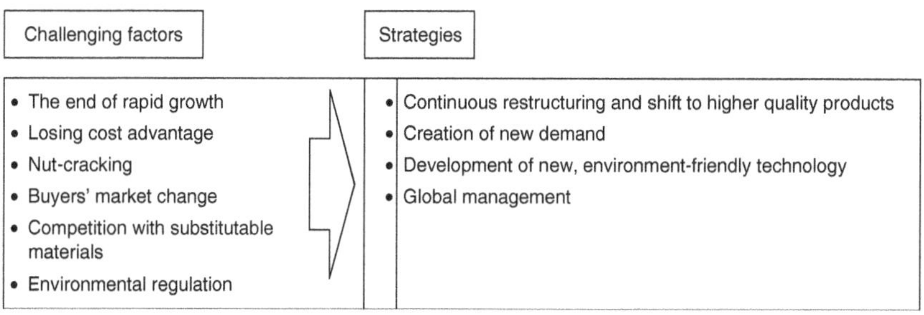

Figure 12.7 Challenges and strategies.

efficiency into consideration. Also, POSCO started operation of No. 5 blast furnace at Kwangyang a year after its completion of the construction work. POSCO explained that the operation of this new blast furnace after a year's gap is not to increase production and profit but to reduce the import of scrap and stabilize the world scrap price as well.

The Korean steel industry is undergoing the substantial restructuring. Hyundai subsidiary Inchon Iron and Steel (IIS) took over Sammi Specialty Steel on 4 May 2000. IIS had already merged Kwangwon Industries. Hanbo Steel was taken over by the consortium led by Nabors Capital and Third Avenue Fund of the US Kia Steel is on workout. If the restructuring is completed successfully, the Korean steel industry will have another chance for further development based on the economies of scale and better management.

12.4.2 Accelerating efforts to increase demand

Three sub-strategies should be pursued to maintain or create new demand: (i) enhancement of efforts to maintain current sales position in the existing markets, (ii) establishment of strategic partnerships throughout the value chain with steel using industries and material suppliers, and (iii) creation of new demand and exploitation of overseas markets.

This strategy is again very actively driven by the representative steel producer of Korea, POSCO. Under the banner of 'Co-survival with Customers', POSCO aims to realize a win–win relationship with its consumers (steel consuming industries) by securing a global marketing capability and establishing strategic alliances with them and with steel producing companies as well. Therefore, globalization through strategic alliance and business networking is not a slogan but an ongoing, concrete process. To achieve this vision, POSCO declared to carry out extensive internal business restructuring and management innovation. Furthermore, the company's organizations and functions are being reoriented to better serve the customers' needs.

The substitution between materials in general is away from steel as discussed, however, it is still possible to create new demand for steel, which is exemplified by POSCO's case. The company is actively engaged in market development activities to increase the demand for steel houses, steel cans, and steel furniture, by partnering with the rest of the steel companies and with other related industries.

12.4.3 Technology

Survival in the borderless competition in the globalized market would be critically influenced by the technology which includes: (i) development and commercialization of innovative technologies, (ii) development of new technology to reduce costs, and (iii) development of Green Technology to cope with mounting environmental concerns.

It is observed that the Korean steel industry has recognized the importance of technology and has exerted considerable efforts to develop and adopt the appropriate technology. For example, as a part of such efforts, POSCO operated

COREX facilities and continues to experiment on new steel making technologies. Other efforts include innovating new products, continuing to make strip casting practical for large-scale production, and developing next-generation technologies such as FINEX, which are under test-running. According to the continuous investment in R&D and adoption of new technology, the proportion of 'high-quality' steel produced rose from 26.2 per cent in 1992 to 33.7 per cent in 1997, and as of 1997, new product developments had risen to a cumulative 671 cases (Park and Shin 1999).

12.4.4 Global management

Global management includes three sub-strategies: (i) implementation and operation of a GPM (global professional management) to establish a transparent decision-making process and advanced ownership-governance structure, (ii) global management based on digital economy, and (iii) introduction of e-business.

It has been pointed out that Korean firms did not actively adjust to the new management environments. Therefore, it is of utmost importance for the Korean steel industry to innovate and adopt new management paradigms. In Korea, major moves towards e-business were initiated by large trading companies, which already have strong distribution networks all over the world. A recent report pointed out that the rate of increasing internet usage is highest in Korea. Established firms are preparing an intermediate function between the steel manufacturers and the customers.

12.5 Conclusion

The Korean economy has achieved a remarkable growth since the early 1970s, which, in turn, led to a successful development of the Korean steel industry. Both the economy and the steel industry seem to have overcome the economic crisis rather successfully. However, in the mid- or long-term, domestic steel demand will cease to show the high rate of growth, overcapacity will emerge as a structural problem, and user industries will mature rapidly.

To overcome these challenges, restructuring should be continuously pursued to enhance efficiency. Such efforts to rationalize management and improve efficiency will enable the Korean steel industry to secure stable growth and competitiveness even under unprecedentedly competitive circumstances. Also, the movement to produce an increasing proportion of higher-quality and value-added steel is vitally important to the industry's future. The Korean steel companies should strengthen their production and sales structure so as to maintain profitability and competitiveness, by successfully coping with the changes in the business environment. In the twenty-first century, information management will also be the key factor to survive fast ongoing changes.

The Korean steel companies have to create value continuously through speeding up work processes and eliminating inefficiency. However, some of these challenges apply to other steel companies over the world as well as the Korean steel industry. Therefore, through the exchange of workers, ideas, information, and techniques with other steel companies in the world, the Korean steel industry should prepare for future changes and, if need be, cooperate with them to overcome the challenges.

Notes

1 This chapter was prepared for the Conference of Asian Studies Association of Australia, July 2000. We are grateful to Yo Woong Kim, Management Director the of POSCO Research Institute, and Chung-sok Suh, Director of the Korea-Australasia Research Centre, the University of New South Wales, for their helpful comments and support. We also thank participants of the conference. The views expressed here are those of the authors and do not reflect those of the POSCO Research Institute.
2 KDI, Mid- and Long-Run Outlook of the Korean Economy 1999:11.
3 The inversed U-shape intensity of use has been analysed by many researchers. For example, see Tcha (1998) among others.
4 *New Steel*, April 1999: 2.
5 *Steel Times International*, January 1999.

Bibliography

Cyert, R.M. and Fruehan, R.J. (1996) 'Meeting the challenge: US industry faces the 21st century, the basic steel industry', Office of Technology Policy, US Department of Commerce.

Hanyang University (1999) 'Long-run projection for the Korean steel supply and demand (1999–2010)', Hanyang University, Korea.

Hogan, William T. (1998) 'Role of the Korean steel industry in Asia', Korea Iron and Steel Association.

International Iron & Steel Institute (IISI) (various years) *Steel Statistical Yearbook.*

Kang, Jongsoon (1994) 'Dynamic comparative advantage and sources of international competitiveness in the Korean steel industry', PhD dissertation, Australian National University.

Korea Development Institute (1999) *Mid- and Long-run Outlook of the Korean Economy*, Korea.

Korean Iron & Steel Association (various years) *Korean Steel Statistical Yearbook.*

Lucas, Robert Jr (1993) 'Making a miracle', *Econometrica*, 61(2): 251–72.

Park, Youngho and Shin, Hyungon (1999) 'POSCO's growth strategies: past experiences & strategic imperatives for the future', Paper presented at the Panel 'Strategic Review of Steel Companies before the XXI Century' of the 40th Annual ILAFA Congress.

POSRI (2000) 'Challenges and opportunities in the steel industry in new millennium', *POSRI*, Korea.

Tcha, MoonJoong (1998) 'Intensity of steel use and environments in Southeast Asia', ch. 3 in Y. Wu (ed.), *The Economics of the East Asian Steel Industry*, London: Ashgate.

The Bank of Korea (various years) *Statistical Yearbook of Korea*, Korea.

Tilton, John (1983) *Material Substitution: Lessons from Tin-Using Industries*, Washington DC: Resources for the Future.

World Steel Dynamics (WSD) (1999) *Steel Strategist #25*, Washington DC: WSD.

13 Restructuring of the public enterprise after the crisis

The case of deposit insurance fund

Sang-Moon Hahm

13.1 Introduction

To enhance macroeconomic and financial stability, the Korean government enacted the Depositor Protection Act in December 1995, and established the Korea Deposit Insurance Corporation (KDIC) accordingly in June 1996. The primary aim of the KDIC is the protection of depositors. Deposit insurance acts as the guarantor of deposits in case financial institutions become insolvent and thus unable to pay back depositors. Through protecting depositors, it reduces the incidence of bank runs, which, in turn, promotes the stability of the financial system.

The deposit insurance system has only been in operation for a relatively short period of time in Korea. Yet, with the foreign-exchange crisis in the second half of 1997 through 1998, KDIC has played a major role in financial industry restructuring through supporting the resolution of failed financial institutions.

This chapter studies the issues concerning fund management aspects for the KDIC. More specifically, it examines the current financial status of the Korean deposit insurance fund, the optimal size of the deposit insurance fund, a design of the deposit insurance system to minimize any excessive risk taking, and investment strategies to enhance the fund stability.

This chapter finds that the Korean deposit insurance fund is not viable with the negative balance of 49 trillion won (about US$40 billion) as of 31 December 2000. Furthermore, its liabilities are expected to increase by 19.1 trillion won from 2001 through 2006 due to interest payment. It is quite evident that the KDIC has no hope of making a full redemption by itself. The government is obliged to share the loss with the KDIC. An immediate resolution of loss-sharing between the government and the KDIC is needed to enhance the stability of the deposit insurance system in Korea.

As a basic strategy for deposit insurance fund management, it is recommended that the KDIC adopt a target zone with feedback. If the fund's reserve ratio stays within the target zone, KDIC should charge positive premiums to member financial institutions. If the fund's reserve ratio falls below the lower bound of the target zone, KDIC should charge higher premiums until the reserve ratio is within the target zone. If the reserve ratio rises above the upper boundary, then KDIC should rebate money back to financial institutions. Every three to five years, the overall performance of the deposit insurance fund should be reviewed and the centre of the target zone could be adjusted upward or downward.

To minimize excessive risk taking, it is recommended that the KDIC adopt a risk-based premium system. That is, a deposit insurance premium structure should reflect the different risks that stronger vs weaker financial institutions impose on the KDIC. To this end, deposit insurance premiums may be based on CAMELS ratings as well as some market signals, for example, subordinated debt spreads for large financial institutions and value of equities traded on the formal exchanges for other listed institutions.

To implement investment activities coherently, it is recommended that the KDIC set up a general treasury policy, which should provide a framework for governance of treasury activities undertaken on behalf of the KDIC. It should indicate who authorizes the president of KDIC to engage in treasury activity and what are the limitations of the president. It should also specify any delegation of authority for treasury activity and the extent of any such delegations. The treasury policy should also specify the duties and responsibilities pertaining to governance of treasury of the KDIC Policy Committee (KDIC's Board of Directors) and the KDIC management.

It is also recommended that special arrangements be established with the Bank of Korea (BOK) and the Ministry of Finance and Economy (MOFE) so that the KDIC could buy and sell the BOK's Monetary Stabilization Bonds (MSBs) and MOFE bonds without affecting the market interest rates. To achieve this, the government should consider creating non-marketable securities of which prices would precisely follow MSBs and MOFE bonds at the market. Once these arrangements are in place, the KDIC could sell and buy MSBs and MOFE bonds at the existing market interests without incurring any transaction costs. Thus, when the need arises for selling a large amount of these securities, KDIC could liquidate them without adversely affecting the domestic financial market.

Finally, it is recommended that the KDIC reinsure a portion of deposit insurance funds using domestic and foreign financial market instruments to hedge against catastrophic losses resulting from mega bank failures and/or financial crises. Examples of financial instruments to hedge against catastrophic losses are as follows: stock index options, US Treasury Securities, US Treasury Bonds (or Euro Dollar) Futures Contracts, and US Treasury bond (or Euro Dollar) Futures Options.

The organization of this chapter is as follows. Section 13.2 discusses the legal foundations of the Korean deposit insurance system. This section examines the aspects of the Depositor Protection Act on the sources and the uses of the deposit insurance fund. Section 13.3 discusses the current financial status of the Korean deposit insurance fund. This section briefly reviews the amount of financial assistance provided for restructuring the financial industry. This section also indicates the amount of Deposit Insurance Fund (DIF) bonds issued and their redemption schedule.

Section 13.4 discusses the experiences of the deposit insurance systems in advanced countries, the United States in particular, and their efforts to reform.

This section includes recommendations for the KDIC. Section 13.5 discusses issues concerning the KDIC's corporate investment strategies. In particular, this section emphasizes the need for using domestic and global financial instruments to hedge against catastrophic losses arising from financial crises. Concluding remarks are given in Section 13.6.

13.2 The legal foundations of the Korean deposit insurance system

Korea Deposit Insurance Corporation insured only bank deposits in January 1997 while the separate funds for each respective non-bank financial institution remained in place. The Depositor Protection Act was revised later in 1997 to consolidate the various deposit insurance funds under KDIC's management starting April 1998. Thus, insured deposits include not only those of banks, but of the deposits held in securities companies, insurance companies, merchant banks, mutual savings and finance companies, and credit unions.

In Korea, the MOFE, the Financial Supervisory Commission (FSC), the Financial Supervisory Service (FSS), the BOK, and the KDIC are responsible for implementing and executing financial policies and for supervision of financial institutions. MOFE is in charge of overall financial policy-making and coordination. It also has the right to amend related acts and presidential decrees through the National Assembly and the president of Korea, respectively, while BOK manages and enforces monetary policies. FSC has the right to enforce financial policies and supervise the operation of financial institutions through FSS. Under the direction of FSC, FSS supervises the insured financial institutions and enforces policies on financial stability as well as the resolution of insolvent institutions.

With recent amendments of the Depositor Protection Act and enactment of the Public Fund Management Act, the KDIC has the authority to require the member financial institutions and their holding companies (if applicable) to submit their financial information. It also has the authority to request the FSC to conduct examinations of the insured financial institutions. The KDIC may examine an insolvent financial institution in order to determine the most appropriate resolution methods for the institution. Also, if the financial institution is found to be in danger of default, the KDIC may request the FSC to take appropriate actions.

According to the Depositor Protection Act, the KDIC insures six different types of financial institutions: banks, securities companies, insurance companies, merchant banks, mutual savings and finance companies, and credit unions. In Korea, it is mandatory for financial institutions in these categories to be members of the KDIC. In the case of banks, commercial and regional banks approved under the Banking Act, domestic branches of foreign banks, and all specialized banks including the Korea Development Bank are insured. All securities companies excluding the KOSDAQ Stock Market Inc. are insured while the same applies for all insurance companies except reinsurance and guarantee insurance companies. All merchant banks, mutual savings and finance companies, and credit unions approved by FSC under their respective laws are insured as well.

The KDIC guarantees insured deposits if an insured financial institution fails according to Article 2 of the Depositor Protection Act. More specifically, the principal and interest of insured deposits are protected by the KDIC up to 50 million Korean won, about US$ 40,000. The interest will be paid only if the sum of the principal and the interest is less than 50 million won. Furthermore, the contractually provided rate or the rate calculated by the KDIC (set by the Policy Committee based on the market average of domestic time deposits with one-year maturity), whichever is lower, will be used to calculate the actual interest to be paid on such claim.

13.2.1 Deposit insurance fund

As indicated, the deposit insurance system aims to protect depositors and maintain the stability of the financial system with respect to situations in which a financial institution is unable to pay its depositors due to bankruptcy or insolvency. In order for the deposit insurance system to work, the Depositor Protection Act allows KDIC to establish the deposit insurance fund (Article 24, section 1 of the Depositor Protection Act).

13.2.2 Sources of funds

For normal revenue sources, the Depositor Protection Act lists membership fees, insurance premiums, and operating revenues (Article 24, section 2). For contingent funding sources, the act indicates the following: (1) borrowings from the government, the BOK and insured financial institutions, (2) DIF bonds issuance, and (3) state properties transferred from the government, subject to approval by the National Assembly (Article 24, section 2 and Article 16, section 2).

As for the types of premium system, the Depositor Protection Act does not specify whether it should be flat or risk-based. Currently, a flat rate premium system is chosen. Yet, according to Article 30 of the act, a presidential decree can change the types of premium system. According to Article 20, the premium for an individual institution is to be the multiple of the average outstanding amount of insured deposits and a prescribed premium rate that differs across the types of financial institutions. Article 30 of the act also specifies the maximum premium rate to be 5/1,000 (see Table 13.1).

Insured banks must remit premium payments to KDIC within one month following the end of each quarter. Insured non-bank financial institutions must remit premium payments to the KDIC within three months following the end of the year. The annual premium rate for each financial institution is determined considering the financial status of each financial industry, and it should not exceed the legal limit (0.5 per cent) of premium rates. Currently the insurance premium rate is flat. That is, premium rates are not risk based, across each sector.

The Depositor Protection Act also states that one time membership fees be collected within one month from the date of commencing business. According to the act, the maximum is 1 per cent of paid-in capital for banks, securities companies,

Table 13.1 Deposit insurance premium rates (as of 5 August 2000)

Insured financial institutions	*Formula*
Banks	Quarterly premium = quarterly average balance of deposits × 10/10,000 × 1/4
Securities companies	Annual premium = annual average balance of deposit × 20/10,000
Insurance companies	Annual premium = amount as stated in Article 16 section 3 × 30/10,000
Merchant banks	Annual premium = annual average balance of deposits × 30/10,000
Mutual savings and finance companies	Annual premium = annual average balance of deposits × 30/10,000
Credit cooperatives	Annual premium = annual average balance of deposits × 30/10,000

Table 13.2 Deposit insurance membership fees (one time)

Banks	*1/100*
Securities companies	1/100
Insurance companies	1/100
Merchant banks	5/100
Mutual savings and finance companies	5/100
Credit cooperatives	1/100

Note
A financial institution is required to contribute its one-time membership fee to the KDIC. An amount calculated by multiplying its paid-in capital by the relevant rates in the table within one month from the date of commencing business.

insurance companies, and credit cooperatives; for merchant banks and mutual savings and finance companies, the maximum is 10 per cent of paid-in capital. The power to set a specific amount of entrance fee is delegated to a presidential decree, a choice of which is detailed in Table 13.2.

Article 25 of the act limits the opportunity set for portfolio management to sovereign bonds, public bonds, and deposits in insured institutions. It allows certain discretion by delegating to the management of the KDIC the power of designating acceptable securities for investment.

Besides deposit insurance premium revenues and one-time membership contributions, there are additional sources of funds for KDIC according to the Depositor Insurance Act. If needed, the KDIC may fund through the issuance and sale of the DIF bonds. The government may guarantee payment of the principal and interest of DIF bonds with an approval of the National Assembly.

For additional funding needs, the KDIC may borrow from the government, the BOK, and member financial institutions. The government guarantees any borrowings from the BOK for the principal and interest. The KDIC may borrow funds from insured financial institutions, the Federation of Mutual Savings and

Finance Companies, Korea Securities Finance Corporation, Export-Import Bank, and the Federation of National Credit Unions. All borrowings require the prior approval of the Ministry of Finance and Economy.

The government may also transfer state properties such as stocks of state-run enterprises to the KDIC without any redemption requirements. Finally, any funds recovered are also sources of funds. Funds, initially used for resolving failed financial institutions and for deposit payoffs, can be recovered through the sale of assets and securities purchased by the KDIC during the resolution processes. Through dividends received from bankruptcy proceedings, the KDIC may also recover funds used in liquidating financial institutions.

13.2.3 Uses of funds

The KDIC may use funds to make insurance claim payments (deposit payoffs) to pay back the principal and interest on DIF bonds, and to pay back the principal and interest on borrowings from member financial institutions. The KDIC may purchase depositor's rights as the receiver of the failed financial institution and provide financial assistance to failed/failing financial institutions. The KDIC may also use funds to cover its operating expenses. Whenever the KDIC decides to make insurance payments, advance payments, or purchase depositor's rights, it must notify the depositors through public notices regarding the time and procedure of such payments.

13.3 Financial status of the Deposit Insurance Fund

13.3.1 Sources of funds

As of 31 December 2000, the size of the DIF was 96.6 trillion won. It consists of insurance premium revenue (1.7 trillion won), contributions from insured financial institutions (0.08 trillion won), funding through the issuance and sale of DIF bonds (52.4 trillion won), borrowings from government (7.6 trillion won), borrowings from financial institutions (19.8 trillion won), and recovery of funds (12.2 trillion won).

13.3.2 Uses of funds

The DIF has been used largely for two purposes: financial industry restructuring and operating expenses of the KDIC. As of 31 December 2000, the support for financial restructuring amounted to 78.0 trillion won (about US$63 billion). It comprises mostly equity participation (36.1 trillion won), purchase of assets (2.0 trillion won), open assistance (12.2 trillion won), and assumptions of deposits, insurance claim payoffs, and loans to offset losses arising from contract transfers (27.7 trillion won). The financial restructuring support of 78.0 trillion won is distributed to banks (44.0 trillion won), securities companies (4.9 trillion won), insurance companies (10.8 trillion won), merchant banking corporations (16.8 trillion won), mutual savings and finance companies (4.0 trillion won), and credit cooperatives (1.7 trillion won) (see Table 13.3).

Table 13.3 Financial assistance for financial industry restructuring (as of 31 December 2000; hundred million won)

	Equity participation	*Open assistance*	*Insurance payoffs*	*Purchase of distressed assets*	*Loans*	*Total*
Banks	2,08,834 (16)	1,05,067 (6)	—	82,888 (8)	—	3,96,789 (18)
Securities co.	49,000 (2)	—	144 (4)	—	—	49,144 (6)
Insurance co.	88,197 (8)	1,67,327 (9)	—	3,447 (4)	—	1,07,971 (16)
Merchant banks	15,029 (7)	—	1,40,268 (18)	—	12,917 (14)	1,68,214 (29)
Mutual savings and finance	101 (2)	179 (7)	35,477 (57)	—	4,649 (15)	40,406 (73)
Credit unions	—	—	16,599 (157)	—	367 (39)	16,966 (181)
Total	3,61,162 (35)	1,21,573 (22)	1,92,488 (236)	86,335 (12)	17,933 (68)	7,79,490 (323)

The total operating expenses of the KDIC for the year 2000 amount to 15.2 trillion won. It comprises mostly interest payments on DIF bonds and borrowings from financial institutions (9.7 trillion won) and paying back the borrowings (principal) from financial institutions (5.3 trillion won). Note that insurance premium revenues and membership fees from insured financial institutions are used for operating expenses of the KDIC. The rest of the fund is used for financial restructuring.

13.3.3 Deposit insurance fund bonds: current status and redemption schedule

Among the most relevant liabilities of the DIF are its bonds. As of 31 December 2000, the total amount of DIF bonds outstanding is 52.4 trillion won, and they account for 64.2 per cent of total DIF liabilities. They are to be redeemed between 2001 and 2006. The principal amount to be matured in 2001 is 1.5 trillion won. The principal amount to be matured in 2005 is the largest, 18.3 trillion won.

As for the interest on the outstanding DIF bonds, the government has agreed to lend the amount to the KDIC with zero interest for three years. The total amount of interest on the DIF bonds for the years between 2001 and 2006 is expected to be 16.4 trillion won. As of 31 December 2000, 8.2 trillion won of interest payment has been made (see Table 13.4).

13.3.4 Overall financial status of the deposit insurance fund

According to the DIF balance sheet (see Table 13.5) as of 31 December 2000, the total liability (81.57 trillion won) exceeds the total asset (32.33 trillion won) by

Table 13.4 DIF bond redemption schedule (trillion won)

	1998	*1999*	*2000*	*2001*	*2002*	*2003*	*2004*	*2005*	*2006*	*Total*
Principal	—	—	—	1.5	4.7	9.7	13.4	18.3	4.9	52.4
Interest	1.1	2.8	4.3	5.1	4.7	4.0	2.7	1.3	0.3	26.3
Total	1.1	2.8	4.3	6.6	9.4	13.7	16.1	19.6	5.2	78.7

Table 13.5 Balance sheet of the DIF (as of 31 December 2000; billion won)

Assets	*Amount*	*Liabilities*	*Amount*
Liquid assets	5,444	Short-term liabilities	19,577
Cash and bank deposits	472	Borrowings from financial institutions	14,078
Marketable securities	2,911		
Short-term loans	11,292	DIF bonds	1,464
(Allowance for bad debts)	(9,790)	Other	4,035
Other assets	556		
Fixed assets	26,878	Long-term liabilities	61,989
Equity participation	19,251	DIF bonds	50,977
Long-term loans	8,518	Premium on debentures	1,011
(Allowance for bad debts)	(15,073)	(Discount on debentures)	(56)
Purchase of distressed asset	1,991	Long-term borrowings	8,023
Off-setting account of		Other	2,034
liabilities and guarantees	12,191	Total liabilities	81,566
		Fund balance	Δ49,243
Total assets	32,323	Total liabilities and reserves	32,323

49.24 trillion won. The fund records tremendous negative balance. Out of the 82 trillion won liabilities, long-term liabilities account for 76 per cent (62 trillion won). The total liability at the end of 2000 increased from that at the end of 1999 (56.41 trillion won) by 25.16 trillion won. This increase resulted mostly from an increase in borrowing from financial institutions (8.24 trillion won), an increase in issuing DIF bonds for financial industry restructuring (8.94 trillion won), and an increase in borrowing from the government to cover interest payments (3.95 trillion won).

According to the DIF profit and loss statement for the year 2000 (see Table 13.6), the amount of fund income (5.83 trillion won) is much smaller than that of expenses (23.66 trillion won). Thus, the realized loss for the year 2000 was 17.83 trillion won (about US$14.4 billion), a huge loss. The major sources of the losses resulted from the valuation loss from equity participation (4.91 trillion won, 20.8 per cent of the total expense), loss provisions (6.93 trillion won, 29.3 per cent of the total), and the DIF bond interest payment (4.34 trillion won, 18.3 per cent of the total).

Table 13.6 Profit and loss statement of the DIF (as of 31 December 2000; billion won)

Income	*Amount*	*Expenses*	*Amount*
		Operating expenses	30
Revenue from the fund (insurance premiums and membership fees collected)	1,035	Expenses from resolutions	11,100
		Interest on borrowings	760
		Interest on DIF bonds	4,338
Revenue from fund management	799	Open assistance	3,928
		Other	2,074
Interest revenue	172		
Revenue from resolution	627		
Other revenue	3,992	Other expenses	12,528
		Losses on valuation of equity participation	4,914
		Loss provisions	6,834
		Other	780
Total income	5,826	Total expenses	23,658
		Net loss	Δ17,832

13.3.5 Assessment

The DIF is definitely not viable with the negative balance of 49 trillion won (about US$40 billion) as of 31 December 2000. Furthermore, its liabilities are anticipated to increase by 19.1 trillion won from 2001 through 2006 due to interest payment. The premium revenue in 2000 was 0.5 trillion won; it is expected to reach 0.8 trillion won in 2001 as the government increased the premium rate by 100 per cent on 5 August 2000. Even with the 100 per cent increase in the premium rate, the KDIC has no hope of making a full redemption by itself. The government is obliged to share the loss with KDIC as deposit insurance enhances macroeconomic and financial stability. A loss-sharing rule between the government and the KDIC must be resolved as soon as possible for the stability of the Korean Deposit Insurance System (KDIS).

13.4 An approach to deposit insurance reform

13.4.1 Goals of insurance fund management

According to Blinder and Wescott (2001), a publicly funded deposit insurance system should neither subsidize nor tax the insured financial institutions in principle. That is, deposit insurance should be implemented on a breakeven basis for normal operations. Furthermore, a deposit insurance system should minimize the risk to the taxpayer in cases where a tremendous adverse shock overwhelms the insurance funds and makes the economy and the financial system so weak that it becomes unwise to burden the financial institutions too heavily. The macroeconomic externality can justify some taxpayer exposure in extreme cases. These do not seem controversial to the students of deposit insurance. Thus, keeping the fund solvent and sufficiently liquid to meet the normal expenses and losses should be the primary goal of insurance fund management.

13.4.2 A target approach

To render the goal of maintaining solvency practical, we need to specify normal losses to the fund. Computing normal losses requires the knowledge of loss profile or loss distribution. If explicit loss distribution is available, we can apply one of the advanced risk management methodologies such as VaR (Value at Risk). We first choose the confidence level, then, define value at risk or expected normal losses as the losses corresponding to the confidence level. A fund is solvent when it is large enough to absorb the losses. Given the loss profile, the size of normal loss needs to be sufficiently large to cover most contingencies. Otherwise, the deposit insurance system would not be credible. For example, one may consider that 99 per cent of loss contingencies should fall into the normal loss range. Once the level of normal loss is chosen, then we may find the corresponding target level for an adequate fund size. In practice countries typically adopt a rule for adequate fund size without specifying the level of normal losses.

Nonetheless, concepts on normal losses and optimal target for the fund are missing in both the legal framework and practices in Korea. Without such, premium rates are determined on an *ad hoc* basis. This implies that the KDIC manages its DIF with no consideration of long-term viability.

The Federal Deposit Insurance Corporation (FDIC), as well as the Canada Deposit Insurance Corporation (CDIC), has adopted the target approach as basic strategies for sound fund management. That is, a target for the fund size is set first. Then, insurance premiums are set to maintain the target. In the United States, the Federal Deposit Insurance Corporation Improvement Act of 1991 (FDICIA) required the FDIC to maintain each fund at a designated reserve ratio (DRR), the ratio of mandated reserves to insured deposits, of 1.25 per cent. When a fund's reserve ratio falls below the DRR, the FDIC must raise premiums sufficiently to bring the reserve ratio back to the DRR within a year or must charge at least 23 basis points of the insured deposits until the reserve ratio meets the DRR.

However, no analytical rationale exists for the selection of 1.25. Instead, the FDIC indicates that the choice was made because 1.25 represented the approximate historical average ratio for the insurance fund when the concept was originally introduced in 1980 (see FDIC 2000). But, whether this is a right interpretation is still questioned.[1] The CDIC system is more advanced in this regard because at least they have an analytical framework to derive a target. As explained, their formula for the target is basically to calculate expected loss for the fund.

The target approach is currently facing more serious criticisms. The first concerns the target being a ceiling. This feature of FDIC fund management has never been seriously discussed in the past, since the fund size remained below the target due to the severe bank failures in the 1980s. Now that the fund has reached its target in the late 1990s, the FDIC is in a situation in which most of its member banks are not paying premiums. The circumstance has raised concerns over the free rider and moral hazard problem. The second concerns volatile premiums that are likely to rise substantially in an economic downturn. According to the FDICIA, if losses from bank failures reduce the fund below 1.25 per cent DRR, the FDIC imposes *ex post* higher premiums of at least 23 basis points during periods of financial distress. A better system might be less procyclical.

13.4.3 A target zone with feedback

To solve such problems, Blinder and Wescott (2001) have indicated the following. Deposit insurance should be conceived as selling insurance products to the financial institutions and it ought to charge actuarially fair premiums for that service. In that sense, deposit insurance premiums are regarded as user fees. There should always be a positive cost of insuring each marginal dollar of insured deposits. On the other hand, if the deposit insurance system is designed to neither tax nor subsidize the financial system in the long run, then the deposit insurance should strive to operate on an approximate break-even basis. This implies elements of a mutual insurance arrangement. To reconcile these two concepts, the deposit insurance should always charge positive marginal cost for the insurance it provides. To avoid an unnecessary build up of the fund, the deposit insurance should rebate money back to the financial institution in proportion to past premiums paid.

The deposit insurance system needs a feedback mechanism to adjust the average premium up or down in line with loss experience using a rebating system. The funds should be able to adjust to changed loss experiences over time. There should be a target zone so that the first deviations in the fund's balance away from the DRR should not require any premium adjustments. If the fund were to build up reserves beyond the upper bound, the system would then begin to rebate funds back to the financial institutions. If the balance were to drop below the lower bound, a temporary surcharge should kick in. Every three to five years, the overall performance of the DIF could be reviewed and the DRR could be adjusted upward or downward.

13.4.4 Inadequate pricing of risk

In general, insurance can distort incentives, that is, insurance can create moral hazard when it is not properly priced. The deposit insurance system should be designed to minimize excessive risk-taking. The deposit insurance system should not favour one type of financial institution over another, nor one type of deposit over another. Financial institutions, depositors, and borrowers should respond to market signals with minimal interference from the deposit insurance system.

Insurers generally price their product to reflect their risk of loss. If the pricing deviates from expected loss, managers tend to take excessive risks. Without risk-based pricing, safe banks unnecessarily subsidize risky banks. The premiums that financial institutions pay should reflect the expected costs they impose on the insurance fund. Financial institutions with stronger balance sheets (e.g. financial institutions with more capital or safer assets) are more likely to survive even an adverse macro shock and hence are less likely to cause a loss to the deposit insurance system. Thus, the risk-based premium system, which reflects expected loss, should be adopted.

13.4.5 CAMELS plus market signals

As is the case in the United States, deposit insurance premiums could be based on the five-category CAMELS rating. CAMELS is an acronym for component ratings assigned in a bank examination: Capital, Asset Quality, Management, Earnings, Liquidity, and Sensitivity to market risk. Then a schedule of deposit insurance premiums reflecting the greater risks of insuring deposits of lower-rated banks would have to be designed. The CAMELS rating is just one example. One might look at the spreads (over Treasuries, say) of banks' subordinated debentures for those large banks that have subordinated debt outstanding. The best market indicator would be the interest rate on that debt. Bond prices correlate better with banking problems than do equity prices according to Berger, Davies, and Flannery (2000). Yet, deposit insurance should not ignore the information contained in equity prices as long as there is a reasonable amount of trading. For small banks that do not have any securities actively traded in the market, there may be no realistic way to use market data to supplement supervisory information.

13.4.6 Recommendations for the KDIC

We recommend that the KDIC adopt a target zone with feedback as a basic strategy for fund management. For example, the centre of the target zone may be 2 per cent of insured deposits;[2] the upper bound of the zone may be 2.25 per cent and the lower bound of the zone may be 1.75 per cent. In this example, when the fund's reserve ratio stays within the target zone, the KDIC should charge positive premiums to financial institutions. When the fund's reserve ratio falls below 1.75 per cent, the KDIC should charge higher premiums until the size of the DIF becomes 2 per cent of insured deposits. When the funds reserve ratio rises above 2.25 per cent, the KDIC should rebate money back to financial institutions in proportion to past premiums paid until the reserve ratio becomes 2 per cent. Every three to five years, the overall performance of the DIF should be reviewed and the centre of the target zone could be adjusted upward or downward.

To minimize excessive risk-taking, the KDIC should adopt a risk-based premium system. Deposit insurance premiums should be based on CAMELS ratings as well as subordinated debt spreads for large financial institutions and equities traded on the formal exchanges for other listed institutions.

13.5 Investment management

13.5.1 Basic strategy

When the current government-led financial restructuring is complete and the DIF starts to accumulate, the role of the KDIC corporate investment becomes more important. To enhance the efficiency of the corporate investment process, the Office of KDIC Fund Management should incorporate the domestic and global economic trend analyses of the Financial Analysis Department and the risk profiles of individual financial institutions of the Risk Management Department before any investment decision is made.

As is the case in the FDIC, a formal interdepartmental head meeting should be convened at regular intervals to exchange information. In the event of market conditions or cash flow projections requiring a reassessment of investment strategies between regularly scheduled meetings, the head of the Department of Fund Management should determine whether an interim meeting should be held.

13.5.2 Establishing general treasury policy

For implementing KDIC investment activities coherently, it is also necessary to set up a general treasury policy, which should provide a framework for governance of treasury activities undertaken. It should indicate who authorized the president of the KDIC to engage in treasury activity and what are the limitations of the president. It should also specify any delegation of authority for treasury activity and the extent of any such delegations. The treasury policy should also specify the duties and responsibilities pertaining to governance of treasury of the KDIC Policy Committee and the KDIC management.

13.5.3 Short-term liquidity and long-term growth considerations

To satisfy short-term liquidity needs, the KDIC may continue to use the Money Market Deposit Accounts of member financial institutions and the obligations of the government and the BOK. To enhance fund growth, the KDIC may use BOK issued MSBs, the government bonds, or the government guaranteed bonds.

13.5.4 Fund stability consideration

To hedge against catastrophic losses resulting from mega bank failures and/or financial crises, the KDIC may consider reinsuring a portion of its funds using domestic and foreign financial market instruments.

13.5.5 Establishing special transactions mechanisms with the MOFE and BOK

By establishing special arrangements with the BOK and MOFE, the KDIC could buy and sell MSBs and MOFE bonds without affecting the market interest rates.

To achieve this, the government should consider creating non-marketable securities whose prices would precisely follow MSBs and MOFE bonds at the market. Once these arrangements are in place, the KDIC could sell and buy MSBs and MOFE bonds at the existing market interests without incurring any transactions costs. Thus, when the need arises, the KDIC could liquidate these securities without adversely affecting the financial market. Furthermore, since the purchasing and selling of these securities would not entail any transactions costs, the KDIC could economize on human resources.

13.5.6 Investment objectives

13.5.6.1 Operational principles

As a general rule, the KDIC should attempt to hold all investments to maturity, including securities designated for long-term growth needs, securities designated for short-term liquidity needs, and securities designated for hedging needs against catastrophic losses arising from mega bank failures and/or financial crises. Portions of each portfolio may be designated for short-term liquidity needs, long-term growth needs, and hedging needs. Discouraged investment practices include security day trading and frequent full-scale restructuring of investment portfolios. When purchases and sales are required to meet corporate funding needs, an investment portfolio's securities designated for liquidity needs shall be sold first, then the securities designated for long-term growth, and finally the securities designated for hedging needs.

13.5.7 Investment guidelines

13.5.7.1 Counter party risk considerations

The KDIC is exposed to the risk of transaction counter parties defaulting for investment product transaction obligations. To manage this exposure, counter parties must meet the credit rating standards throughout the life of the transaction. In the event that a debt issue is downgraded below acceptable credit rating, the KDIC should take steps to reduce holdings, while ensuring minimized exposure. Portfolio limits are applied to aggregate counterpart exposure for investment transactions. The credit ratings of counter parties assigned by the credit rating agencies as well as KDIC's knowledge of member institutions determine the acceptability of a counterpart's credit. Where there is a difference between two ratings, the lower credit rating should apply.

As a reference the CDIC has the following guidelines for acceptable investment. For investment up to one year, the counter parties must meet the minimum criteria of Standard and Poor's (S&P) rating of A1 and Moody's rating of P1 for short-term investment and S&P rating of A and Moody's rating of A2 for long-term investment. For investment of over one year and less than five years, the counter parties must meet the minimum criteria of S&P rating of AA- and Moody's rating of Aa3 for long-term investment. For investment up to one year, the counter parties must meet the minimum criteria of S&P rating of A1 and Moody's rating of P1 for short-term investment and S&P rating of A and Moody's rating of A2 for long-term investment. From time to time, the head of the KDIC Fund Management Department may establish certain limitations on any of the security types by investment portfolio.

13.5.8 Maturity considerations

Currently the terms to maturity of KDIC investments are less than a year on average, reflecting KDIC's high liquidity needs. When the government-led financial restructuring is completed and the DIF starts to accumulate, it is recommended to increase the average duration of KDIC's long-term investment portfolio. As a reference, as of 31 August 2000, the FDIC's maturity structure of its investment portfolio has a peak in 2001 (about 15 per cent of the total) and steadily declining thereafter until 2010 (about 3 per cent of the total). FDIC's investment with less than two-year maturity consists of about 27 per cent of the total. The weighted average of maturity is about 4.25 years as of 31 August 2000.

13.5.9 Liquidity considerations

Each investment portfolio should have reserves for adequate maintenance of liquidity so that the KDIC could meet anticipated and some level of unanticipated cash flow requirements. As indicated, currently KDIC's investment is characterized as highly liquid. In the future the share of investment to maintain liquidity should be reduced. As a reference, the share of FDIC's reserves for maintaining adequate liquidity is about 25 per cent. To be more specific, the share of FDIC's investment in Securities Designated Available for Sale is about 23.5 per cent of the total as of 31 August 2000.

13.5.10 Investment for enhancing fund stability

The KDIC may consider the following financial instruments to hedge against catastrophic losses arising due to financial crises: stock index options, US Treasury Securities, US Treasury Bonds (or Eurodollar) Futures Contracts, and US Treasury Bond (or Eurodollar) Futures Options. Note that these investment instruments are not currently permitted according to the Depositor Protection Act. In the remainder of this section, I will discuss the pros and cons of using such investment instruments.

13.5.11 Investing in domestic stock index options

If a financial crisis breaks out, the nation's bankruptcy rate would increase. As a result, the size of non-performing loans held by financial institutions would increase. This in turn would increase the probability of deposit insurance payouts, and the need for funds to cover deposit insurance. The financial crisis would worsen the financial positions of financial institutions, which would dampen the stock prices of financial institutions. The rise in the nation's bankruptcy rate due to the outbreak of the financial crisis would also reduce the stock prices in general.

To the extent that there is a positive correlation between the stock prices of financial institutions and general stock prices, the KDIC may purchase put options on Korea Stock Price Index (KOSPI) stock price index to meet the additional demand for DIFs. When the stock price index decreases below a certain point, which is the strike price of the put option, the payoff of the owner of the put option becomes positive and the size of the payoff is proportional to the difference between the actual stock price index and the strike price. Note that this approach will essentially use funds in the domestic capital market to raise funds to meet the increased demand for DIFs (unless of course the KDIC engages in the put option contract with foreign investors). Thus, it could further depress the already depressed domestic financial market due to the financial crisis.

13.5.12 Investing in US (or other advanced country's) treasury securities

If a financial crisis breaks out in Korea, the Korean won would depreciate sharply against the US dollar. In this case, if the KDIC has already held a sizable amount of US Treasury bills, it may meet the surge in demand for DIF due to the financial crisis by selling the US treasury bills. Unlike the previous approach of investing in put stock index options, this approach will use foreign funds to finance the additional demand for deposit insurance. Furthermore, converting US Treasury bonds into Korean won constitutes foreign capital inflow, which will reduce the domestic interest rate and relieve the depressed domestic financial market. However, there is an unwanted side effect to this approach. By holding US or other foreign countries' Treasury securities, KDIC's asset portfolio may be susceptible to foreign monetary policy shock.

13.5.13 Investing in US treasury bond futures or Eurodollar futures

Investment in futures contracts will achieve essentially the same objectives as investment in actual securities. Yet, investment in futures contracts allows the KDIC to commit fewer funds for hedging against catastrophic losses from financial crises than investment in actual US or other foreign Treasury securities. Furthermore, transacting actual securities in the financial market entails higher transaction costs. Finally, investing in futures contracts makes KDIC not to be susceptible to future unexpected changes in US or other foreign countries' monetary policy.

13.5.14 Investing in options on interest rate futures

Investment in options on interest rate futures such as US Treasury bond futures options (options to enter US Treasury bond futures contracts) or Eurodollar futures options (options to enter Eurodollar futures contracts) may allow the KDIC not to be susceptible to adverse future US or other foreign countries' monetary shock. Yet, since investing in options gives KDIC a right to exercise, it would allow foreign monetary shocks to positively affect KDIC's asset portfolio.

13.6 Concluding remarks

The government is in the deposit insurance business mainly to enhance macroeconomic and financial stability. Deposit insurance contributes to stability by preventing bank runs. Such macroeconomic externality justifies some tax payer exposure in extreme cases including the 1997–98 foreign-exchange crisis. As indicated, the Korean DIF is not viable. As of 31 December 2000, the fund balance is 49 trillion Korean won (about US$40 billion) on the negative side. The government is obliged to share the loss with the KDIC. A loss-sharing rule between the government and the KDIC should be resolved as soon as possible to enhance the stability of the deposit insurance system in Korea.

Even though it is not a fund management issue, I would like to emphasize that the FSC and KDIC should take supervisory action (prompt corrective action) effectively and efficiently when an insured financial institution is classified as not adequately capitalized. Prompt action reduces the likelihood that a failing financial institution will engage in risky and potentially expensive gambles for redemption if it is permitted to continue conducting business. Corrective action may include termination of insurance membership, regulartory sanction on financial institutions, and special on-site examination. Such supervisory action would also help resolve the problems of the insured financial institution with the least possible long-term loss to the DIF.

Notes

1 For example, see Kenneth Thomas (2000). He questions the correctness of the interpretation on the grounds that 1.25 cannot be obtained when computing the historical average for the period.

2 If the size of a loss is typically less than 20 per cent of insured deposits and the probability of a financial institution failure is 10 per cent, then 2 per cent reserve ratio should cover most financial institution failures. See DTT, KDI, and KIF (2001) for a rationale and further details.

Bibliography

Berger, A.N., Davies, S.M., and Flannery, M.J. (2000) 'Comparing market and supervisory assessments of bank performance: who knows what then?', *Journal of Money, Credit, and Banking*, 32: 641–67.

Blinder, Alan S. and Wescott, Robert F. (2001) *Reform of Deposit Insurance: A Report to the FDIC*, Washington, DC: Federal Deposit Insurance Corporation.

Deloitte Touche Tohmatsu, Korea Development Institute, and Korea Institute of Finance (2001) *Institutional Strengthening of Korea Deposit Insurance Corporation*, Seoul, Korea: Korea Deposit Insurance Corporation.

Federal Deposit Insurance Corporation (2001) *Keeping the Promise: Recommendation for Deposit Insurance Reform*, Washington, DC: Federal Deposit Insurance Corporation.

——(2000) *Deposit Insurance Options Paper*, Washington, DC.

Korea Deposit Insurance Corporation, *Annual Report* 2000, Seoul, Korea.

Thomas, Kenneth (2000) *Statement before the FDIC Roundtable on Deposit Insurance Reform*, Washington, DC: Federal Deposit Insurance Corporation.

14 The rise and fall of real estate trust institutions in Korea[1]

Jinu Kim, Sang-Young Lee, and Denny McGeorge

14.1 Introduction

After the currency crisis in 1997 and the subsequent financial crisis in 1998, there was a serious credit crunch in Korea. One of the consequences was that the two main Real Estate Trust companies, Korea Real Estate Trust Company (KORET), and Hankook Real Estate Trust Company (HRET), almost went into bankruptcy. Many projects handled by these companies were put on hold. In September 1998, the Finance Supervisory Commission found the operations of KORET and HRET to be insolvent. Poor management was cited as a major contributory factor. As a result of this, the Finance Supervisory Commission prohibited new Land Development Trust operations of the two Real Estate Trust companies for six months. In March 1999, the lenders to these Real Estate Trust companies accepted a delay in the repayment of their loans and interest. The Finance Supervisory Commission extended this delay for a further six months. Eventually, HRET went into bankruptcy in February 2001.

If both KORET and HRET had gone into bankruptcy, the financial institutions would have had to underwrite insolvent loans of 1.3 trillion won (about US$1.1 billion). About 150 apartment complex projects would have been stopped, and more than 30,000 buyers, supposed to move into the apartments constructed by these Real Estate Trust companies, would have been affected. In the light of these circumstances, the combined forces of the financial institutions and the real estate industry decided to restructure the two Real Estate Trust companies.

The Finance Supervisory Commission and the Ministry of Finance and Economy prepared a plan that included the transfer of good projects from the two insolvent companies to a new company – Saengbo Real Estate Trust Company (SRET) – which started operations in 1999. The Finance Supervisory Commission and the Ministry of Finance and Economy considered that all related companies including the parent companies and the financial institutions should share the burden, as they had common liabilities for the insolvency of the Real Estate Trust companies. The parent companies of the Real Estate Trust companies had not properly controlled their affiliated Real Estate Trust companies. The lenders had lent based on corporate guarantees of the parent companies rather than the feasibility of the projects, resulting in excessive loans being made to the Real Estate Trust companies.

On the face of it, the crisis of the Real Estate Trust companies in Korea was due to the currency crisis at the end of 1997 and the credit crunch that followed. The crisis, however, was not only the result of a temporary credit crunch, but also of internal problems in the Real Estate Trust companies. These structural problems can be viewed in comparison to foreign real estate trust institutions, such as the Australian Listed Property Trust (LPT) and the US Real Estate Investment Trust (REIT).

This chapter analyses the experiences and problems of the real estate trust institutions in Korea and concludes by proposing a Listed Real Estate Investment Trust in Korea (K-REIT), which would stabilise the real estate trust institutions and minimise further damage to the economy. Furthermore, this strategy would provide an investment medium in the Korean real estate market for international investors.

14.2 Evolution and characteristics of the real estate trust institutions in Korea

In the 1960s and 1970s, fast economic growth expedited real estate development in Korea. This development worsened the inequality of income distribution and wealth, because a few of the large business groups (*chaebols*) and landowners owned the greater part of the real estate and capital. Because of this, the Korean government determined to regulate the real estate market, and to levy heavy taxes on real estate capital gains. The government established a number of policies in order to prevent speculation in the real estate market following the skyrocketing prices of real estate in the 1990s due to the boom of the late 1980s.

The core policy was the 'Public Concept of Land' developed in 1989. This concept proposed a set of strong and fundamental measures, the Urban Residential Land Limit Charge, the Land Development Charge, and the Land Value Increment Tax. The objective of these laws was to regulate land use in order to satisfy public welfare, even though private ownership was recognised (Park *et al.* 1998).[2] When this policy was introduced, the government needed a regulatory mechanism to ensure that there was an efficient use of land. The new mechanism – the Real Estate Trust company – was introduced to prevent real estate market speculation and to lessen the public development burden through private investment in the developing land market.

A second objective of introducing Real Estate Trust companies was to improve the competitive advantage of local firms when Korean construction and real estate markets were opened up for international competition. Otherwise, foreign real estate companies with powerful capital and financial know-how could easily erode the market share of Korean real estate related companies. Hence, the government introduced real estate trust institutions in 1990, and permitted the formation of the Real Estate Trust companies (KORET and HRET) in 1991 (Jung and Choi 1996).

From the onset, the government controlled the real estate trust business by licensing. The requirements of a licence for real estate trust business were, basically, expertise combined with adequate capital, together with a stated intention to work in the public interest. Expertise was defined as an ability to carry out real estate trust business and employ professional staff. Adequate capital was simply the requirement to be a large company that had the credibility to operate a real estate trust business without incurring failure. At the beginning (in 1991), the minimum capital of a Real Estate Trust company was 500 million won (about US$417,000). This was increased to 10 billion won (about US$8.3 million) in 1998.

Among the licence requirements, the most important one was the public interest. To satisfy the requirement for acting in the public interests, an applicant (parent company) for a Real Estate Trust company had to be one of the following: (1) a government enterprise or government-funded enterprise; (2) a company that could be audited directly or indirectly by the National Assembly or the Board of Audit and Inspection; and (3) a company that was government controlled, either directly or indirectly, in the process of licence, product development, public offer, and the articles of association (Sohn 1998).

Table 14.1 presents a summary of Real Estate Trust companies established in Korea. Currently there are six Real Estate Trust companies, KORET, HRET, Korea Real Estate Investment Trust Company (KREIT), Jooeun Real Estate Trust Company (JRET), Daehan Real Estate Investment Trust Company (DREIT),[3] and SRET. All Real Estate Trust companies except SRET are companies affiliated with government agencies. KORET, HRET, and KREIT were established by government enterprises. JRET and DREIT were established by the Housing and Commercial Bank (government-funded enterprise) and the Korea Housing Financial Cooperative (association controlled by the government) respectively. The government only allowed the public companies to establish the Real Estate Trust companies to safeguard public interests and to minimise the negative side-effects of speculation in the real estate market. However, after the Korean economic crisis, the government allowed the private insurance companies to establish SRET.[4] It was expected that the private funds and the advanced management skills of private companies would revitalise the real estate market.

14.3 Scope of real estate trust business

There are two types of trust – a money trust and a real estate trust – depending on the type of entrusted property. By regulation, Real Estate Trusts can only deal with real estate up until 2000.[5] The landowners entrust their real estate to the Real Estate Trust companies, which develop, manage, and/or dispose the entrusted real estate. They arrange loans from financial institutions for landowners (beneficiary) with entrusted real estates as collateral. Because the Real Estate Trust companies cannot raise the funds by themselves, they rely on borrowing from outside when they need additional funds.

There are four major real estate trust categories: Management Trusts, Disposal Trusts, Land Development Trusts, and Collateral Trusts. A Management Trust is a vehicle where the trustee (Real Estate Trust company) manages the entrusted real estate for a beneficiary. A Disposal Trust is designed to dispose of the real estate safely and quickly for a beneficiary. A Collateral Trust is a vehicle that allows a beneficiary to use real estate as collateral for finance.[6] A Land

Table 14.1 A summary of the Real Estate Trust companies establishment

	KORET	*HRET*	*KREIT*	*JRET*	*DREIT*	*SRET*
Parent company	Korea Asset Management Corporation	Korea Appraisal Board	Korea Land Corporation	Housing & Commercial Bank	Military Mutual Aid Association	Three Life Insurance Companies
Establishment capital (US$)	1991.4.13 KW177 bil. (147.5 mil.)	1991.4.13 KW63 bil. (52.5 mil.)	1996.4.4 KW180 bil. (150 mil.)	1996.12.3 KW10 bil. (8.3 mil.)	1997.12.15 KW10 bil. (8.3 mil.)	1998.12.8 KW10 bil. (8.3 mil.)
Shareholders of the parent company (%)	Govt: 38.5 KDB: 30.8 Others: 30.7	Govt: 49.4 KDB: 30.6 Others: 20.0	Govt: 92.9 KDB: 7.1	Govt: 16.1 ESOP: 7.8 Etc.: 76.1	MMAA: 100	Private shareholders

Source: Sohn (1998).

Notes
KDB: Korea Development Bank; Others, financial institutions; ESOP: Employee Stock Ownership Plan; MIMAA: Military Mutual Aid Association.

Development Trust is designed to develop entrusted land for a beneficiary. The Real Estate Trust companies develop the entrusted land as a housing complex or land subdivision, and then return profits to beneficiaries after sale or lease of the developed real estate. Land Development Trusts can be classified into two types: for sale and for lease. The former distributes profits to beneficiaries after selling the developed real estate in lots. The latter returns the developed real estate and rental incomes to beneficiaries after leasing.

When they were initially established, Real Estate Trust companies operated as Management Trusts and Disposal Trusts. Land Development Trusts and Collateral Trusts were then introduced in November 1992 and February 1993, respectively. From January 1994 public land owned by the central government could be entrusted to Real Estate Trust companies. In 1999, public land owned by the local governments was included in Land Development Trust business. In the beginning, the Real Estate Trust companies concentrated on Management Trusts, Disposal Trusts, and related businesses only. Later however they focused on Land Development Trust business.

Figure 14.1 shows the basic elements and structure of Land Development Trusts. As all participants – beneficiary, trustee, constructor, financial institution, and end users – were satisfied with Land Development Trust business, it became the main business of the Real Estate Trust companies. For the beneficiaries (landowners), the vacant or underdeveloped lands could be developed without their own funds by the Real Estate Trust companies who could manage the constructors and other related parties effectively. For the trustees (Real Estate Trust companies), large-scale and short-term Land Development Trust business provided more profitable than other trust businesses, because its fee was bigger than

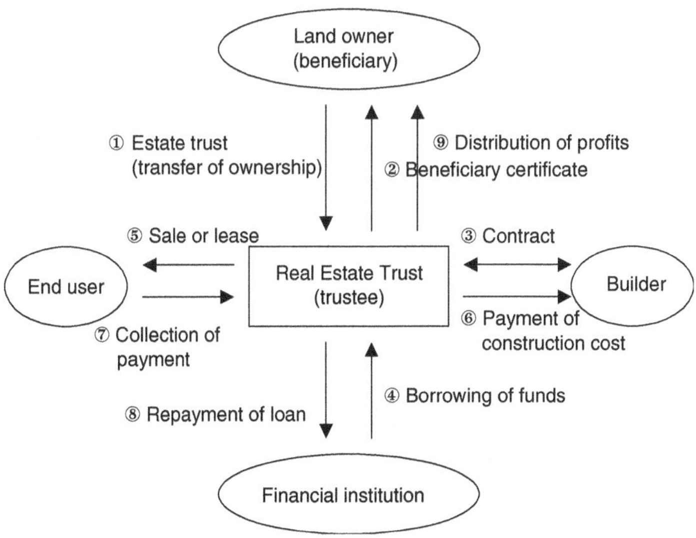

Figure 14.1 Basic elements of the Land Development Trust.

that of other trust businesses.[7] For the constructors, the Land Development Trust was a useful financing vehicle. Financial institutions regarded the Real Estate Trust companies as creditable borrowers for the following reasons. First, a Land Development Trust project could continue even though the constructor went into bankruptcy. Second, the Real Estate Trust companies were backed up by the creditability of the parent companies. Third, the financial institutions could, in the worst case, recover the loans by selling the land. End users (buyers) also regarded Land Development Trust projects as safe, because the Real Estate Trust company was the project manager.

14.4 Performance of the Real Estate Trust companies

Until recently, the Real Estate Trust companies in Korea concentrated their business on Land Development and Collateral Trusts. The portion of Management and Disposal Trusts to the total amount of the entrusted real estate was less than 10 per cent in 1997. In 1992, the total number of real estate trusts was 33 cases, and total amount of entrusted real estate was 18.6 billion won (US$15.5 million). In 1997, the year of the Korean economic crisis, the total number reached 394 cases, and total amount was 3.7 trillion won (US$3.1 billion). In 1997, Land Development Trusts accounted for 36.3 per cent of total amount of entrusted real estate.

As Table 14.2 shows, the total amount of entrusted real estate increased after the economic crisis. In 1998, the total number and amount of entrusted real estate reached 711 cases and 8.3 trillion won (US$6.9 billion). This was due to the increase of Guarantee Trust business that started in 1998.[8] Collateral Trusts, 81 cases (54.4 per cent of total real estate trust) and 2.2 trillion won (US$1.8 billion) (75.1 per cent of total real estate trust) was the second largest. The next was the Land Development Trust, with 26 cases (17.4 per cent) and 171.5 billion won (US$142.9 million). However, the number of cancelled trust businesses reached 96 cases amounting to 1.4 trillion won (US$1.2 billion) in 1998.

Since 1995, Land Development Trusts have doubled or tripled every year. From 1992 to 1997, there were 284 cases of Land Development Trusts with a total amount of 2.2 trillion won (US$1.8 billion). After the economic crisis, the number of Land Development Trusts decreased from 165 cases in 1997 to 26 cases in 1998. There were 223 cases of sale type in Land Development Trusts and 87 cases of lease type, between 1993 and 1998. The number of sale types was three times the lease type cases. However, the number of sale types decreased dramatically in 1998, while the number of lease types increased. There were 131 cases of apartments (42.3 per cent) and 55 cases of shopping centres (17.7 per cent). If residential and commercial complex buildings were regarded as apartments, the number of apartments became 156 cases (Korea Institute of Finance 1999).

There were 171 projects (55.2 per cent) with project cost (except land prices) of more than 20 billion won (US$16.7 million). This means that more than half of all Land Development Trust projects were large-scale developments. Twenty cases had project costs of more than 100 billion won (US$83.3 million). In particular, 19 cases of more than 100 billion won were sale-type trusts. In summary,

Table 14.2 Total entrusted real estate by trust business (million won (US$ million))

	1992		1993		1994		1995		1996		1997		1998	
	No.	*Amount*	*No.*	*Amount*	*No.*	*Amount*	*No.*	*Amount*	*No.*	*Amount*	*No.*	*Amount*	*No.*	*Amount*
Land Development Trust	—	—	4	11,419 (9.5)	8	26,365 (22.0)	25	203,001 (169.2)	72	599,719 (499.8)	165	1,352,342 (1,127.0)	26	171,549 (143.0)
Management Trust	6	2,719 (2.3)	33	54,228 (45.2)	43	47,305 (39.4)	52	165,332 (137.8)	69	225,457 (187.9)	15	125,645 (104.7)	28	411,209 (342.7)
Disposal Trust	9	15,925 (13.3)	11	85,395 (71.2)	24	42,659 (35.6)	43	28,843 (24.0)	69	371,016 (309.2)	108	181,881 (151.6)	14	143,180 (119.3)
Collateral Trust	—	—	26	12,923 (10.8)	87	128,222 (106.9)	75	144,854 (120.7)	16	60,907 (50.8)	64	2,069,401 (1,724.5)	81	2,187,321 (1,822.8)
Guarantee Trust	—	—	—	—	—	—	—	—	—	—	—	—	406	5,432,867 (4,527.4)
Consulting service etc.	18	—	44	—	84	—	78	—	59	—	42	—	156	—
Total	33	18,644 (15.6)	118	163,965 (136.7)	246	244,551 (203.9)	273	542,030 (451.7)	285	1,257,099 (1,047.7)	394	3,729,269 (3,107.8)	711	8,346,126 (6,955.2)

Source: Korea Institute of Finance (1999).

the majority of Land Development Trusts were short-term, large-scale, and sale-type apartment development projects (Korea Institute of Finance 1999).

As the demand for Real Estate Trusts increased, the profitability rapidly improved. According to the trust system in Korea, the performance of the Real Estate Trusts was assessed not by trust account, but by company account. The operating incomes of the Real Estate Trust companies' accounts were increased from 1.6 billion won (US$1.3 million) in 1993 to 56.6 billion won (US$47.2 million) in 1998. In 1991, the operating incomes from consultation were the main source of total incomes. After 1995, most operating incomes were generated from Land Development Trusts. Between 1993 and 1998, 71 per cent of total operating incomes were generated from Land Development Trusts. However, after the Korean economic crisis, the operation incomes from Land Development Trust decreased while the operating incomes from Collateral Trust rapidly increased (Korea Institute of Finance 1999).

The total net income of the Real Estate Trust companies was negative in 1991. But after the rapid improvement, it increased to 8.6 billion won (US$7.2 million) in 1997. Return on assets was negative until 1993. From 1994, return on assets turned positive (12.3 per cent) and was 17.8 per cent in 1995. From 1996 to 1997, return on assets decreased, because of the new Real Estate Trust companies (KREIT and DREIT). However, return on assets increased in 1998 for the following reasons. First, the moratorium on interest payments without the closure of insolvent trusts lessened the financial costs for the Real Estate Trust companies. Second, the operating incomes from Collateral Trusts were increased. Return on equity increased from 15.2 per cent in 1994 to 23.3 per cent in 1995. This means that the Real Estate Trust companies gained enormous profits before the economic crisis (Korea Institute of Finance 1999).

However, the forementioned outcome of the operating income, return on asset, and return on equity resulted from the separation of company and trust accounts. When a company account includes the short-term loans of trust accounts, return on asset and return on equity would decrease on a large scale. Since 1998, the government changed the accounting standard of Real Estate Trust companies, and company account must now include the short-term loans of trust accounts. The total net losses of six Real Estate Trust companies amounted to 105.7 billion won (US$88.1 million) in 1998, and 386.1 billion won (US$321.8 million) in 2000.

14.5 Finance and operation

The Real Estate Trust Code 11 of the Ministry of Finance and Economy (1991) states that Real Estate Trust companies are able to finance the project funds using the following methods: (1) loans from banks and insurance companies; (2) loans from trust companies; (3) loans from various funds; (4) entrusted funds and trustee's own funds; (5) loans from construction companies; (6) business funds such as sale or lease deposit; (7) advanced funds of real estate development; and (8) other methods approved by the Finance Supervisory Commission. The Real Estate Trust companies were not allowed to raise funds through issuing shares or receiving money trusts up until year 2000. As a result, financing of the Real Estate Trust companies

Table 14.3 Amount of financing by financial institutions (billion won (US$ million))

	1993	*1994*	*1995*	*1996*	*1997*	*Total*
Commercial bank	2.2 (1.8)	5.7 (4.8)	42.4 (35.3)	24.6 (20.5)	419.3 (349.4)	494.2 (20.8%) (411.8)
Merchant bank	—	43.5 (36.3)	69.8 (58.2)	433.8 (361.5)	1,157.2 (964.3)	1,704.3 (71.6%) (1,420.3)
Others	0.6 (0.5)	0.1 (0.1)	1.6 (1.3)	5.1 (4.3)	173.8 (144.8)	181.2 (7.6%) (151.0)
Total	2.8 (2.3)	49.3 (41.2)	113.8 (94.8)	463.5 (386.3)	1,750.3 (1,458.5)	2,379.7 (100%) (1,983.1)

Source: Korea Institute of Finance (1999).

depended on borrowing from financial institutions. The Real Estate Trust companies principally financed funds from merchant banks. In this case, finance was arranged through discount on short-term (three to six months) Commercial Paper (CP) of the Real Estate Trust companies. As Table 14.3 shows, the total amount of debts for the period from 1993 to 1997, in the Real Estate Trust companies, was 2,379.7 billion won (US$1,983 million). The main sources of financing were commercial banks – 494.2 billion won (US$412 million) (20.8 per cent), and merchant banks – 1,704.3 billion won (US$1,420 million) (71.6 per cent). The amount of debts reached 2.8 trillion won (US$2.3 billion) at the end of 1998.

The reasons why the Real Estate Trust companies preferred to finance the short-term loans from merchant banks were as follows. First, the interest rate was around 12–13 per cent through the CP discount from the merchant banks, while the interest rate of trust loans was around 14–15 per cent before the Korean economic crisis. Second, because Land Development Trusts that needed financing were capable of repaying debts with the advanced deposits, the Real Estate Trust companies preferred short-term loans. Third, the Real Estate Trust companies could arrange financing only with the credit backed by the parent companies and the stability of the real estate trust institutions, because the Real Estate Trust companies cannot provide entrusted real estate as collateral (Sohn 1998).

Management Trusts, Disposal Trusts, and Collateral Trusts did not need financing due to the nature of trust business. But, Land Development Trust businesses require the greatest amount of financing in terms of development projects. Hence, the debts of the Real Estate Trust companies should be separated into individual trust accounts. This in turn means that the Real Estate Trust companies should arrange financing only with the value of entrusted real estate and the viability of the projects. However, the Real Estate Trust companies borrowed the loans through company accounts with company credit.

14.6 Evaluation of the Real Estate Trust companies

The Real Estate Trust companies were growing rapidly until the Korean economic crisis, and profitability was very high. During this growth period, the Real Estate Trust companies carried out various social functions. First, the Real Estate

Trust companies contributed to the revitalisation and efficient use of land. They functioned as a private agent for real estate development, while public agents generally would not be accepted as developers in the Korean real estate market. Second, the Real Estate Trust companies enhanced the competitiveness of local developers in the real estate market. The Real Estate Trust companies improved the transparency of real estate business and the new financing methods. Third, the Real Estate Trust companies contributed to the housing supply through Land Development Trusts for apartments. They also played the role of intermediates between landowners and constructors coordinating the conflict of interests, and sharing loss and risk (Sohn 1998).

Nevertheless, the Real Estate Trust companies were in financial difficulties after the Korean economic crisis. First, the domestic credit crunch following the currency crisis, made it impossible for the Real Estate Trust companies to finance the necessary funds. Whilst new loans were suspended, and the pressure of repayment increased, the interest rate rose to around 35 per cent. Due to this credit crunch, the Real Estate Trust companies that borrowed short-term loans, encountered very difficult situations. Second, because of the interruption of financing, the projects of Land Development Trusts were suspended. As a result, the values of projects were reduced, and the projects became worthless. The bankruptcy of constructors worsened the loss of the projects. Third, due to asset deflation after the credit crunch, the profitability of Land Development Trusts was forecasted unfavourably. Hence, one of the Real Estate Trust companies went into bankruptcy.

Although those financial difficulties were generated by the external elements, the fundamental causes were basic structural problems in the Real Estate Trust companies themselves. The structural problems of the Real Estate Trust companies were as follows:

1 The Real Estate Trust companies were controlled by the public administration and were not managed according to market principles. The public entities backed by the government agencies were primarily used as credibility for finance from financial institutions. Despite the code of separate trust accounts, the Real Estate Trust companies borrowed the funds with the company credit and payment guarantee by the parent companies. Therefore, during the period of credit crunch, not only the projects in trusts, but also the Real Estate Trust companies as a whole went into a risky situation.
2 The Real Estate Trust companies were prohibited from financing through issuing shares or receiving money in customers' accounts. Although beneficiary certificates that guaranteed dividends from entrusted real estate were issued, the certificates were illiquid. Therefore, the entrusted land was the only equity capital of the Land Development Trust and the remainder was loans. This business structure of Real Estate Trust exposed the Real Estate Trust companies to liquidity and interest risks. There was no securitisation of real estate to hedge these risks.
3 As the Real Estate Trust companies tried to satisfy mainly the parent companies' interests, there were conflicts of interests between the Real Estate

Trust (trustee) and landowners (beneficiaries), and between the Real Estate Trusts and financial institutions. Although the principles of separate trust accounts and sharing risks were instituted, the Real Estate Trust companies actually did not follow those principles. There was no system to control the Real Estate Trust companies by landowners and financial institutions against conflict of interest. Although the Real Estate Trust companies were able to manage real estate in the long term, they concentrated on Land Development Trusts of high profit and short-term sale-type projects. The Real Estate Trust companies therefore focused mainly on high-risk and high-return projects.

4 The government, which should supervise the Real Estate Trust companies, was blamed for their mismanagement. The government not only neglected the structural problems before the economic crisis, but also left the disease untreated after the suspension of Land Development Trust projects. As a result of this policy, things went from bad to worse. When the values of the projects decreased, it was more difficult for the government to restructure the Real Estate Trust companies. The Real Estate Trust companies were regarded as financial companies by regulation, but they had a combined function of financing and construction for entrusted property. Therefore, the supervision system was confused. Whilst the Ministry of Finance and Economy took charge of permission, mergers and acquisitions (M&A), dissolution, and liquidation of the Real Estate Trust companies, the Finance Supervisory Commission took charge of general business. As the Real Estate Trust companies were affiliates of the government agencies, the government supervised them as the affiliates. For example, while the parent companies of two Real Estate Trust companies (KORET and JRET) were under the supervision of the Finance Supervisory Commission, those of three Real Estate Trust companies (HRET, KREIT, and DREIT) were under the supervision of the Ministry of Construction and Transportation. This overlapping of supervision mechanisms caused confusion in policy for the Real Estate Trust companies. Currently, the Ministry of Construction and Transportation, the Ministry of Finance and Economy, and the Finance Supervisory Commission control the Real Estate Trust companies and the parent companies. This complexity of control mechanism needs simplification.

14.7 Conclusions: the introduction of listed real estate investment trust (K-REIT)

Although the Real Estate Trust companies were introduced as real estate trust institutions, they actually functioned not as real estate trusts but as real estate development companies. The Real Estate Trust companies developed real estate with loans from the financial institutions. The Real Estate Trust companies had the same business mechanism as the construction companies that were affiliates of *chaebols*, the characteristics of which were guarantee of repayment and short-term capital gains in real estate development business. On the other hand, the

Real Estate Trust companies as financial institutions supplied the funds to risky land development businesses. Hence, after the Korean economic crisis, the Real Estate Trust companies encountered the crisis of bankruptcy due to undertaking hazardous and high-risk development projects.

Recently, the government and the lenders tried to restructure the Real Estate Trust companies in order to solve the forementioned problems. Certainly, restructuring of the insolvent Real Estate Trust companies (KORET and HRET) was an urgent problem. However, the restructuring had been delayed and eventually failed as HRET went into bankruptcy. There were two major reasons for this failure. First, it has not yet been decided how the participants of the projects should share the burdens of bad trusts. Second, a valuation method for individual projects has not yet been decided. These problems have delayed the restructuring of the Real Estate Trust companies. Unanswered questions include whether the projects should continue or not, and who should be the project owner. For the former, the priority order among the participants – landowners (beneficiary), Real Estate Trust company (trustee), parent companies, and financial institutions – should be decided according to one's stake in the project. If buyers and subcontractors are already involved financially, then these secondary participants should be included in this priority order. For the latter problem, it is necessary to decide on a valuation method that estimates the value of the project on the basis of land price, input value, and future cash flow. The Resolution Trust Corporation (RTC) in the United States developed the method of Derived Investment Value (DIV) in the disposal process of the insolvency problems of Savings and Loan Associations (S&L) (FDIC 1998). The Real Estate Trust in Korea needs a valuation method for its disputed projects such as DIV.

Once these problems have been solved, the government should restructure the Real Estate Trust companies using methods similar to those used in restructuring other financial institutions. The good trust accounts should be distinguished from the bad ones, and the former should be continued. The government should prevent the Real Estate Trust companies from bankruptcy through bad account liquidation or by handing over to the Korea Asset Management Corporation.

Moreover, the government and related industries should determine how to improve the real estate trust institution and management, separate from the restructuring process. First, the focus of public welfare should be changed to market principles. After the Korean economic crisis, the Real Estate Trust companies could not do business like government agencies any more, and the financial institutions could not lend funds solely on the collateral of real estate. Instead, market principles should be applied, and money lending based on the profitability of the project should be implemented. This trend would change how the real estate trust institutions do business. The securitisation of real estate such as project finance, money trust, issuing certificate note, and financing through Special Purpose Company (SPC) should be considered.[9]

Furthermore, the government should consider introducing the K-REIT, on lines similar to the REIT in the United States or the LPT in Australia, in order to revitalise the troubled Land Development Trusts. The K-REIT would not only strengthen the liquidity of the assets, but also prevent moral hazard through corporate governance. The Real Estate Trust companies have a serious problem of improper disclosure or corporate governance.[10] In April 2001, the Korean government introduced the K-REIT.

In terms of listing the Real Estate Trust, the information on the Real Estate Trust companies' business should be disclosed. After listing, corporate governance should be established in order to guarantee profitability and security. In the LPT, the corporate governance was institutionalised together with the disclosure requirements. Managers can be retired by vote of the unit holders in the event that they fail to meet their obligations. Most transactions between the manager and the trust should be governed by disclosure requirements and requires ratification by unit holders as well as the trustee, in the case of major investment or capital expenditure decisions (Kim 1998). This mechanism should be incorporated into the K-REIT.

Finally, the government should allow tax benefits to the new institution (K-REIT). In the case of trust business in Korea, the amount of tax evasion was smaller than that of other businesses, because of reporting the correct business incomes to the tax office. Because the tax benefits are the determining factors of real estate investment, they should be given to the trust business (Lee 1998). The government removed double taxation in the K-REIT, as is the case with the existing mutual funds. The capital gains tax in the K-REIT should be reviewed so as to be levied in the case of more than 30 per cent transaction gains for some periods, in a similar fashion to the United States. These tax benefits are desirable in order to establish the new institution in Korea.

It is debatable whether the heavy taxes on real estate in Korea should be cut or not. In 1995, the ratio of tax liability of real estate to total tax revenue in the holding stage was 4.3 per cent, while the ratio in the transactional stage amounted to 11.6 per cent (Ro 1998). When the SPC was introduced in Korea in 1998,[11] there were tax benefits of real estate transactions. But, it was really difficult for the local government to allow the tax reduction on real estate transactions, because they faced a fiscal difficulty after the Korean economic crises. The government allowed the tax reduction on real estate transactions in the K-REIT.

However, the K-REIT is not necessarily the only solution. One thing that is clear is that the real estate industry in Korea is at a watershed and has a unique opportunity to put in place fundamental structural changes that will encourage the internationalisation of the industry. For this to happen it is essential that there is greater transparency of procedures and accountability for actions amongst the major players.

Notes

1 The chapter was originally published in the *Journal of Construction Research* (*JCR*), No. 1, Vol. 1, March 2000.

2 After the Korean economic crisis in 1997, the implementation of 'Public Concept of Land' policy was repealed.

3 Military Mutual Aid Association took over the DREIT from the Korea Housing Financial Cooperative in 2001. Formerly, it was the Housing Cooperative Real Estate Trust Company (HCRET).

4 SRET is a private company established by three insurance companies. (Equity capital ratio: Kyobo 0.5, Samsung 0.4, Heungkook, 0.1.)

5 The ABS law introduced in 2000 permitted the RET to issue ABS. Also the K-REIT's, law introduced in 2001 permitted the RET to manage K-REIT.
6 Collateral Trust has advantages of cost, management, and disposal in comparison with the fixed collateral of financial institutions (Korea Institute of Finance 1999).
7 During the construction period, the fee of Land Development Trust is up to 5 per cent of the value of entrusted real estate plus construction cost. After the construction, the fee is up to 10 per cent of annual rental incomes or 5 per cent of sale price (KREIT 1997).
8 Guarantee Trust is the specific business of DREIT, in which the land component of the project is entrusted for the guarantee of sales by DREIT.
9 The SPC was allowed in 1999.
10 There is no disclosure requirement of financing in the Real Estate Trust company (Lee 1998).
11 Korea and Japan enforced the SPC law at the same time in September 1998. The difference between the two countries is as follows. While Japan allows a stock company to be listed in the stock exchange market, Korea allows only a limited company to be listed. Hence, the SPC in Japan could function as a listed real estate investment vehicle (J-REIT), and the SPC in Korea could only liquidate bad debts and real estate.

Bibliography

FDIC (1998) 'Managing the crisis: the FDIC and RTC experience 1980–94'.

Jung, Hee-nam and Choi, Soo (1996) 'Land development trust: policy alternatives to promote', Korea Research Institute for Human Settlement (in Korean).

Kim, Jinu (1998) 'Recession of Australian property market and property securitization', chapter 7 in S. Hong (ed.) (1998), *Asset Deflation and Real Estate Securitization*, Seoul: Construction and Economy Research Institute of Korea (in Korean).

Korea Institute of Finance (1999) *The Revitalization of the RET Financing*, Korean.

Korea Real Estate Trust Association (2000) *The Report of the RET Financing*, Korean.

KREIT (1997) 'Manual of *land development trusts*' business'.

Lee, Min-sung (1998) 'The problems and alternatives of *land development trust* finance – central to *land development trust's* note', *The Journal of Real Estate Analysis*, 4, The Association of Real Estate Analysis (in Korean).

Lee, Sang-young *et al.* (1999) 'A study on the institutionalization of the real estate investment company in Korea', Construction & Economy Research Institute of Korea (in Korean).

Lee, So-han (1998) 'The introduction of REIT', in S. Hong (ed.), *Asset Deflation and Real Estate Securitization*, Seoul: Construction and Economy Research Institute of Korea (in Korean).

MOFE (1991) 'The operating principles of the RET business' (in Korean).

Park, Hun-joo *et al.* (1998) 'A study on the comprehensive evaluation for the public concept in land', Korea Research Institute for Human Settlement (in Korean).

Ro, Young-hoon (1998) 'Recent trends in real estate market and tax policies on real estate', Korea Institute of Public Finance, *Monthly Public Finance Forum*, No. 33 (in Korean).

SBC Warburg Dillon Read (1998) 'A comparison of the Australian LPT and United States REIT models'.

Sohn, Jin-su (1998) 'The status and alternatives of the RET institution', in S. Hong (ed.), *Asset Deflation and Real Estate Securitization*, Seoul: Construction and Economy Research Institute of Korea (in Korean).

15 Asia crisis postmortem[1]

Where did the money go and did the United States benefit?

Eric van Wincoop and Kei-Mu Yi

In the crisis years of 1997–98, the hardest-hit Asian countries experienced net capital outflows of more than $80 billion. Almost all of the outflows originated as banking flows. The majority went first to offshore centre banks and then to banks in Europe. Much of the capital eventually reached the United States, but in the form of foreign direct investment or portfolio investment rather than banking flows. An equilibrium analysis of supply- and demand-side channels suggests that the overall effect of the crisis on US GDP was positive but small.

The recent currency crises in Asia have raised important questions about the sensitivity of economies in industrialized countries to financial turmoil in emerging markets. In late 1997 and in 1998, Indonesia, Korea, Malaysia, the Philippines, and Thailand experienced net capital outflows of more than $80 billion, plunging them from 'growth-miracle' status into their worst recessions in decades. The GDP growth rates in Korea and Malaysia in 1998 were −5.8 and −7.5 per cent, respectively, and in Indonesia and Thailand the rates were worse at −10 per cent. By comparison, the GDP growth in the United States was a healthy 4.3 per cent that year.

These contrasting experiences are puzzling at first glance, because it was widely believed that the downturn in Asia would have a negative effect on the US economy.[2] Recessions in the crisis countries, according to this logic, in conjunction with sharply depreciated currencies, would reduce the countries' demand for US exports. In addition, the depreciated currencies would lead to a surge in US imports from these countries. Hence, through these international trade channels, the Asia crisis was expected to contribute negatively to US growth. The US net export deficit did, in fact, increase, contributing −1.2 percentage points to US GDP growth in 1998. However, the increase in the deficit was more than offset by increased spending on consumer goods and producers' durable equipment, so that employment and production rose. Quarter by quarter, US GDP growth in 1998 consistently exceeded projections.

In our view, this apparently surprising immunity of the US economy to the Asia crisis reflects the fact that the original way of thinking about the crisis was flawed. First, it focused only on demand-side channels and ignored the supply side. Second, the depreciation of the Asian currencies against the dollar and the recessions in the crisis countries represented endogenous responses to a large and sharp reallocation of capital out of the Asia crisis region. From the point of view of the United States, this reallocation of capital is the appropriate starting point – rather than the depreciations and recessions – for considering the implications of the crisis.

What, then, precipitated the large and sharp reallocation of capital out of Asia? We believe that increased expectations of private sector bankruptcies and currency depreciations are likely forces. These expectations could have been grounded in fundamental information about conditions in the private sector. They could also have been influenced by non-fundamental forces such as rational or irrational herding behaviour. As we indicate later, it is immaterial to our framework whether the change in expectations was driven by fundamentals or non-fundamentals. In either case, there was a large decline in demand for Asian assets. A large capital outflow occurred, and all the macroeconomic consequences for the United States ensued from this outflow.

The reallocation of capital toward the United States generated the forementioned negative trade effects on the country's GDP. But the capital inflows also created a positive effect by financing a rise in US spending, directly through increased financing for liquidity-constrained firms and consumers as well as indirectly through a drop in interest rates. The capital inflows also led to an appreciating dollar, which made imported inputs cheaper. These cheaper inputs generated a positive effect on GDP similar to that of a positive productivity shock.[3]

As the crisis proceeded and US growth remained strong, a new scenario along the lines sketched previously – with capital inflows to the United States as the centerpiece – became increasingly popular.[4] Yet surprisingly little quantitative research has examined this scenario. This chapter aims to fill that gap at least partially. Specifically, we begin by attempting to document the trail of capital out of Asia and into the United States.[5] We then discuss and quantify the implications for short-run US GDP growth of the direct and indirect reallocation of capital from Asia to the United States. Our quantification employs an 'equilibrium' approach in which both supply- and demand-side channels are calculated.

It is not difficult to document the 'beginning' and the 'end' of the money trail insofar as it involves the Asian countries and the United States. Capital outflows from Indonesia, Korea, Malaysia, the Philippines, and Thailand from the start of the crisis in February 1997 to the end of 1998 amounted to more than $80 billion. The US current account deficit in 1998 was $221 billion, which represented an increase of $77 billion from 1997, financed by a rise in capital inflows.

It *is* difficult, however, to document the precise money trail from these Asian countries to the United States. In particular, it is hard to ascertain in exactly what form (banking, portfolio, or direct investment flows) and from exactly which countries the funds entered. We assume that the initial 'round' of bilateral international money flows arises directly from the crisis, but subsequent rounds of flows could be due to other causes. Also, the net errors and omissions component of the US balance of payments is typically large and, more importantly, it tends to spike during crises. At times, the change in errors and omissions is often large enough to cancel out even the largest change in reported capital flows.

Nevertheless, using Bank for International Settlements (BIS) data and data drawn from the US Treasury Department's Treasury International Capital (TIC) system, we can follow the trail to a certain extent. Accordingly, we find that banking flows were the major source of the outflows, and that these outflows were dispersed all over the world, to such places as Japan, Europe, the United States, and to offshore banking centres. The majority of the flows went to the offshore centres. Our findings also suggest that most of the offshore centres funneled their funds to European banks. Although the trail runs cold from there, we conclude that banks clearly played an important role at the beginning of the reallocation process and that the money clearly came to the United States in a roundabout fashion.

To analyze the impact of the crisis on short-run US GDP growth, we consider three channels. The first is the trade channel, which has a negative impact on growth. The second is a domestic demand channel, in which capital inflows finance an increase in domestic demand. The counterpart to the two demand channels is our third channel: the supply channel. The appreciation of the dollar against the Asian currencies leads to a decrease in prices of imported inputs. We provide evidence consistent with each of these channels and quantify their impact on US GDP growth. We find that the net effect of the Asia crisis on US growth was small but positive – +0.2 percentage points – confirming the newer wisdom.

15.1 The outflow of capital from the Asia crisis countries

The sharp and sudden net capital outflow from the 'Asia-4' crisis countries of Indonesia, Korea, the Philippines, and Thailand is evident in Figure 15.1.[6] These countries experienced positive net capital inflows throughout the 1990s. Then, in March 1997, a sharp outflow began. In the six quarters from March 1997 through April 1998, the countries experienced a net outflow of $77.9 billion. By

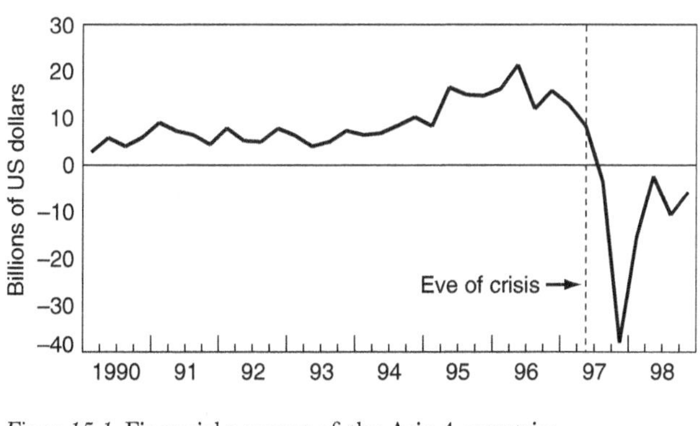

Figure 15.1 Financial account of the Asia-4 countries.

Source: See Appendix 15.1.

Note

The financial account is net capital – that is, the net sum of direct, portfolio, and other investment balances.

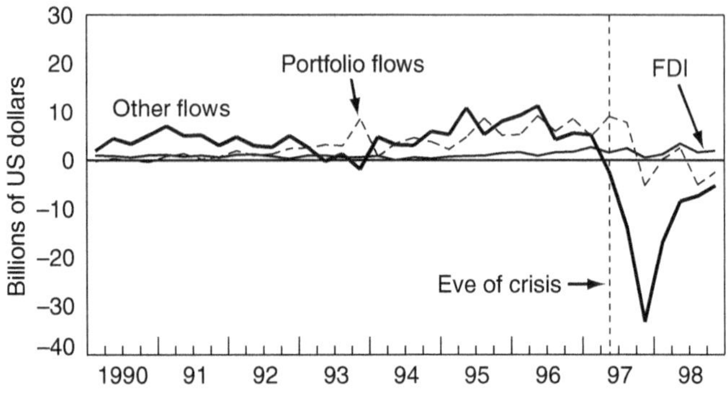

Figure 15.2 Breakdown of the Asia-4 countries' financial account.

Source: See Appendix 15.1.

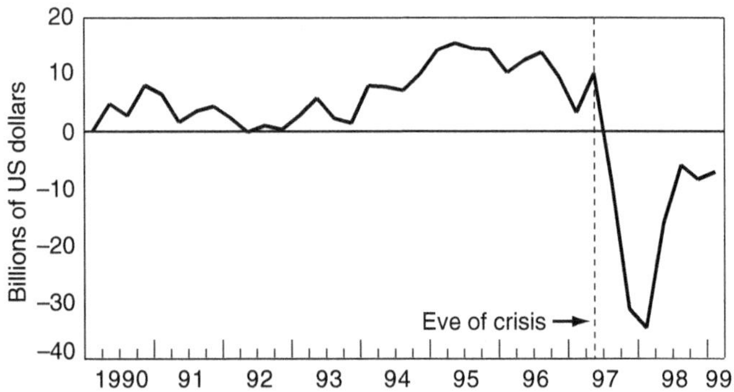

Figure 15.3 BIS reporting banks' net lending to the Asia-4 countries.

Source: See Appendix 15.1.

contrast, in the six quarters prior to the crisis, the Asia-4 countries experienced a cumulative net *inflow* of $86.8 billion. Even today, three years after the beginning of the crisis, these countries continue to experience net capital outflows.

If we divide the financial account (we use this term and capital account interchangeably) into portfolio flows, foreign direct investment (FDI) flows, and 'other' flows, we see that the bulk of outflows since the onset of the crisis consisted of other flows (Figure 15.2).[7] Indeed, other flows accounted for more than 100 per cent of the total net outflows, with a cumulative outflow of $84.9 billion from March 1997 through April 1998. During this period, $46.2 billion – equivalent to 59.3 per cent of the total outflows – represented Asia-4 bank flows.

Figure 15.3 suggests that the counter-parties to the capital flows involving the Asia-4 countries were almost surely BIS reporting banks, a group that includes banks from most of the Organization for Economic Cooperation and Development countries as well as several offshore centres in the Caribbean, Hong Kong, and elsewhere.[8] Figure 15.3 shows exchange-rate-adjusted net lending flows from the

BIS reporting banks to the Asia-4. The increase in net lending in the years preceding the crisis, as well as the sharp reduction in net lending by these banks after February 1997, closely mirrors the overall capital inflows and outflows from the Asia-4 depicted in Figures 15.1 and 15.2.[9] The cumulative net lending flows from March 1997 through April 1998 equal a net outflow of $105.3 billion. This amount is equal to about one-third of the total stock of claims against these countries in February 1997. Taken together, Figures 15.2 and 15.3 suggest that most of the capital outflows involved banks on both sides – Asia-4 banks on the one hand and BIS reporting country banks on the other hand.

Which countries were the largest sources of the reduction in net bank lending to the Asia-4? There are two ways to address this question. One way views countries as locations, the other views them as representing nationalities. For example, a Swiss bank subsidiary operating in the United States would count as a US bank based on geography and a Swiss bank based on nationality. The two ways are complementary because the geographic approach is consistent with balance-of-payments data on capital flows, while the nationality approach helps control for the fact that many cross-border banking flows involve borrowing and lending by banks with their subsidiaries in other countries. This is especially true for banks that have branches or subsidiaries in offshore centres.

We begin by examining the geographic approach (Figure 15.4). Here, net bank lending flows to the Asia-4 are reported by location of the BIS reporting bank. Figure 15.4 focuses on four regions: Japan, the 'Europe-7' countries, the United States and its international banking facilities (IBFs), and the offshore centres. Europe-7 comprises France, Germany, Italy, the Netherlands, Spain, Switzerland, and the United Kingdom. Although banks in all four regions reduced their net lending to the Asia-4, the reductions by banks in Japan, the Europe-7, and the United States typically were in the order of several billion dollars per quarter. The figure clearly shows that the majority of outflows from the Asia-4 was accounted for by the offshore centres: $54.3 billion of the total net outflow of $105.3 billion.

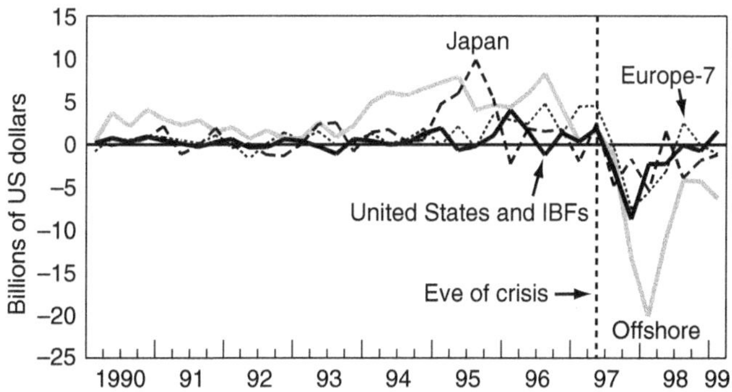

Figure 15.4 Net bank lending to the Asia-4 countries by location of BIS reporting bank.

Source: See Appendix 15.1.

Note
IBFs are international banking facilities.

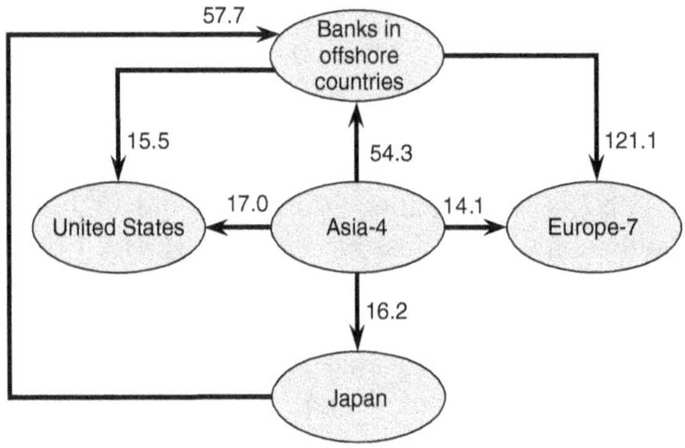

Exhibit 15.1 Net lending of BIS country banks: June 1997 to December 1998, billions of US dollars.

Source: BIS.

Notes
The flows out of the Asia-4 correspond to an increase in net liabilities *vis-à-vis* the Asia-4 of BIS reporting banks in the offshore countries, the United States, the Europe-7, and Japan. The flows of the offshore countries *vis-à-vis* the United States, the Europe-7, and Japan correspond to net lending by banks in the offshore countries to both banks and non-banks in the United States, the Europe-7, and Japan.

Because the economies of the offshore centres are relatively small, we presume that most of their inflows must generate corresponding outflows. To a large extent, one can therefore view these centres as 'pass-through stations'.[10] Exhibit 15.1 depicts this in the form of a flow process. It presents net cumulative bank lending of BIS reporting countries over the March 1997–April 1998 period. Banks in offshore centres experienced $112 billion in net inflows from the Asia-4 and Japan between June 1997 and December 1998. Most of this money went to banks in the Europe-7, which experienced a $121.1 billion net inflow from the offshore centres.

What is also striking is the small amount of banking inflows to the United States originating directly from the Asia-4 or mediated through the offshore centres. The funds associated with the Asia-4 capital outflow could have reached the US banks via more indirect channels, such as through Europe or even from Japan by way of the offshore centres and Europe. Once the flows become so indirect, however, it is difficult to follow the original source of the funds. This phenomenon is apparent already in Exhibit 15.1. More funds entered the offshore centres from Japan than from the Asia-4, so we cannot conclude that the funds exiting the offshore centres are directly connected to the Asia-4 outflows. This exiting offshore money could also be the result of net capital outflows from Japan connected to its own economic downturn.

Of the $105.3 billion reduction in lending, $98.5 billion represented declines in claims on the Asia-4 (Table 15.1, top row). Hence, we find that most of the adjustment is on the claims side. We also find that, even though a not-insignificant share of the BIS bank loans was denominated in domestic currencies, the

Table 15.1 Change in assets and liabilities of BIS reporting banks *vis-à-vis* the Asia-4 countries: June 1997 to December 1998

	Assets	*Liabilities*	*Net claims*
Geographic breakdown			
Cumulative exchange-rate-adjusted flows	−98.5	6.8	−105.3
Change in stocks			
All BIS countries	−99.4	6.9	−106.3
Offshore countries	−51.3	2.8	−54.1
United States	−14.9	2.1	−17.1
Europe-7	−11.4	2.6	−14.0
Japan	−18.4	−0.8	−17.6
Nationality breakdown			
Change in stocks			
All nationalities	−79.7	—	—
United States	−7.6	—	—
Europe-6	−11.2	—	—
Japan	−28.6	—	—
Other non-offshore			
BIS nationalities	−7.0	—	—
Other nationalities	−25.3	—	—

Source: BIS.

Notes
The geographic breakdown refers to all banks located in BIS reporting countries. The nationality breakdown refers to all banks located in non-offshore BIS reporting countries, plus the foreign affiliates of these banks if they have the nationality of one of the non-offshore BIS reporting countries. This means that banks in offshore countries with nationalities other than those of the non-offshore BIS countries are not included in the nationality breakdown, even though they are included in the geographic breakdown. This accounts for the small discrepancy between the totals based on the geographic and nationality breakdowns. The nationality data are available only for claims. Europe-7 includes France, Germany, Italy, the Netherlands, Spain, Switzerland, and the United Kingdom. Europe-6 excludes Switzerland. Banks of Swiss nationality in Switzerland are included in the total for the nationality breakdown, but are not included in the European nationality subcategory.

exchange-rate-adjusted flows are almost identical to the change in the stock of claims less liabilities (Table 15.1, second row). The reduction in stocks was $106.3 billion and the reduction in claims was $99.4 billion. These two findings are useful, because they suggest that comparisons can be made between the geographic-based and nationality-based data. The nationality-based data are available only for claims and not liabilities, and they are available only for stocks of claims rather than for exchange-rate-adjusted flows.

A summary of bank lending to the Asia-4 by nationality can be found in the bottom panel of Table 15.1. Time series of both the geographic and nationality data are presented in Figure 15.5 as well. First, note that the total reduction in assets based on the nationality data ($79.7 billion) is $19.7 billion less than that based on the geographic breakdown. The reason is that the nationality data exclude banks in the offshore centres with nationalities other than those of the non-offshore BIS countries. Examples are banks of Hong Kong or Saudi Arabian nationality operating in Hong Kong. Of the $79.7 billion reduction in assets that

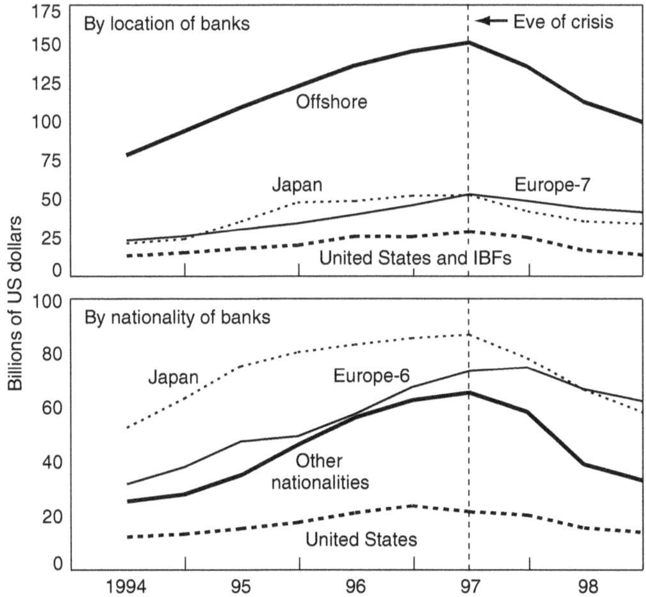

Figure 15.5 Source of BIS reporting banks' claims on the Asia-4 countries.

Source: See Appendix 15.1.

Note
IBFs are international banking facilities.

can be assigned to nationalities, only $47.4 billion involves the United States, the 'Europe-6' countries (the Europe-7 excluding Switzerland), and Japan. Banks whose nationalities are the same as that of one of the smaller non-offshore BIS countries account for an additional $7 billion.[11] This leaves $25.3 billion that is accounted for by banks of other nationalities operating in the BIS countries, such as Thai and Korean banks in the United States. Therefore, a total of $45 billion in outflows from the Asia-4 to banks located in BIS countries ($19.7 billion plus $25.3 billion) involves nationalities other than those of the non-offshore BIS countries. This amount is almost half of the total outflows from the Asia-4. Only $7.6 billion is associated with banks of US nationality.

We note parenthetically that the Asia-4 current account was initially buffered against the large capital outflows by International Monetary Fund (IMF) credit and a rundown of reserves (Figure 15.6). It is worthwhile to recall that from a balance-of-payments perspective, a rundown of central bank foreign-exchange reserves is a net official capital inflow, which is about half of the rise in reserves in Figure 15.6. The other half is associated with the increase in IMF credit. The figure shows that the full current account adjustment did not take place until January 1998.

To summarize, banks played a large role in the immediate outflows from Asia, most of which went to offshore centre banks. These banks, in turn, played a large

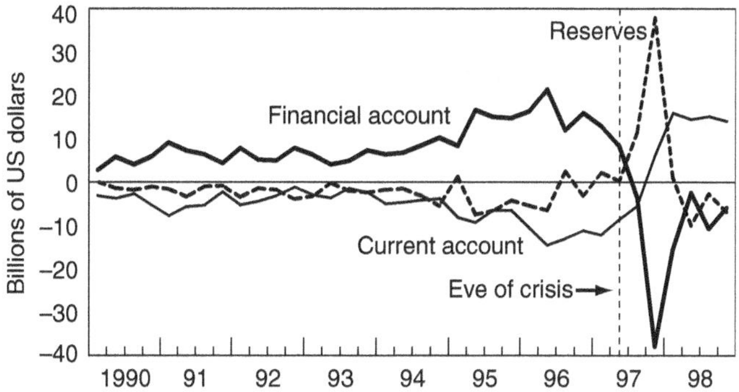

Figure 15.6 Asia-4 current account vs the financial account.

Source: See Appendix 15.1.

Note
The financial account is net capital inflows – that is, the net sum of direct, portfolio, and other investment balances.

role in funneling the outflows to banks in Europe. Once the money reached Europe, it became part of a vast pool of capital, rendering the trail difficult to follow from there. Consequently, we now focus on how the capital flows entered the United States.

15.2 Capital flows to the United States in the wake of the crisis

Turning our attention from Asia-4 outflows to US inflows, we examine the seasonally adjusted quarterly current account balances of Japan, the Europe-7, the Asia-4, and the United States (Figure 15.7). Here we see that the United States experienced a large, \$31.3 billion deterioration of its quarterly current account from February 1997 to April 1998. By comparison, the Asia-4 current account improved by \$19.7 billion during this period. If we include Malaysia, the improvement was \$26 billion. Japan also experienced an improvement in its current account.

Figure 15.7 gives the impression that most, if not all, of the capital outflows from Asia went to the United States. However, this impression is not completely warranted. Since 1991, the US current account has been trending downward, while the Europe-7 current account has been trending upward. Because US GDP growth rates throughout this period have been higher than European growth rates, it is entirely possible that these trends would have continued in the absence of the crisis. Accordingly, we fit a simple linear-time trend to the two current accounts using data from January 1990 to February 1997. Extrapolating forward, we find that the actual Europe-7 current account decreased by \$22 billion relative to trend between February 1997 and April 1998. The actual US current account decreased by \$25 billion relative to trend during this period. Hence, relative to

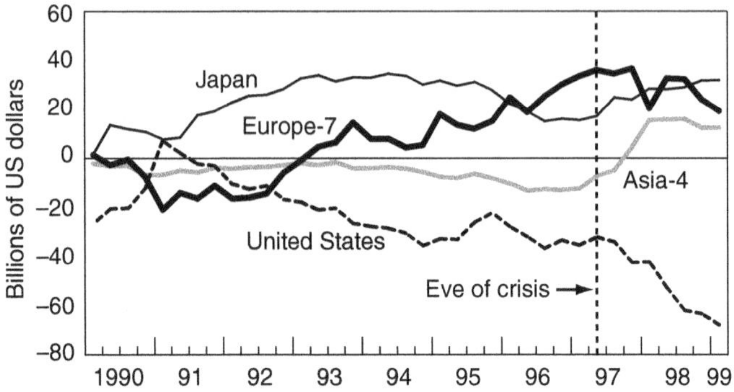

Figure 15.7 Current accounts.

Source: See Appendix 15.1.

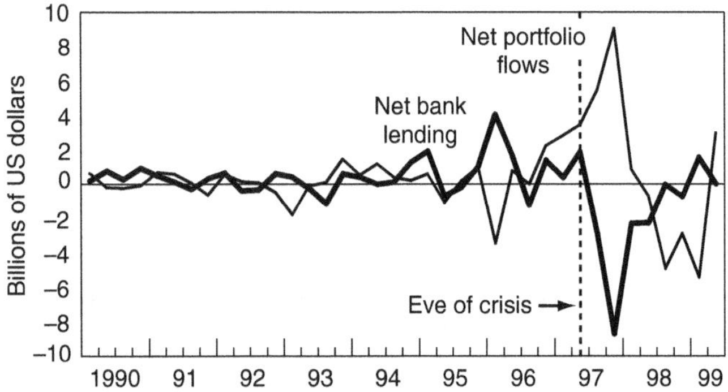

Figure 15.8 Net lending by the United States to the Asia-4 countries.

Source: See Appendix 15.1.

trend, both regions' current accounts deteriorated by similar magnitudes. This evidence, coupled with the evidence presented earlier, suggests that both the United States and Europe experienced substantial capital inflows connected to the Asia crisis.[12]

We also showed earlier that very little of the Asia crisis capital flows to the United States took the form of direct flows from the Asia-4 to the United States. This point is illustrated in Figure 15.8. US banks' net lending to the Asia-4 fell by about $10 billion from February 1997 to April 1997, but the reduction in net lending was relatively short-lived, as negative net lending was less than $2 billion from January 1998 onward. By comparison, total net US capital inflows averaged $68 billion per quarter between March 1997 and April 1998. Figure 15.8 also depicts net portfolio flows during this period. These flows include both long-term portfolio flows and changes in the holdings of US Treasury bills by the Asian countries. Interestingly, the portfolio flows move in the opposite direction of the bank flows. The net portfolio outflow from the United States to the Asia-4 in the

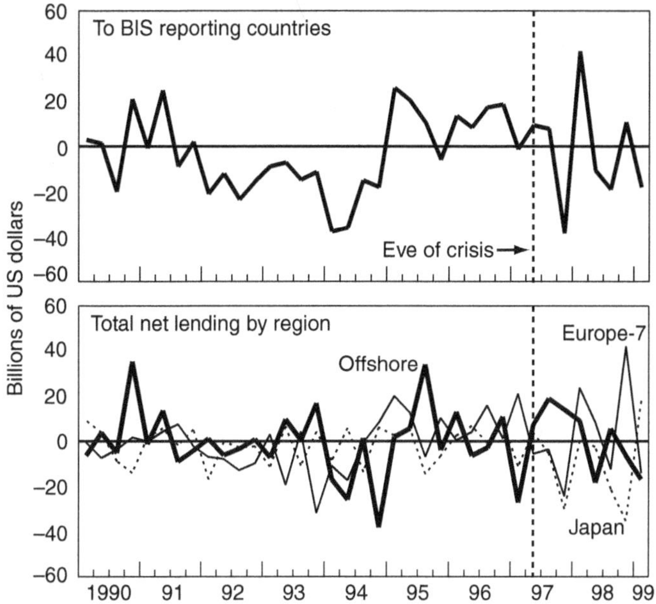

Figure 15.9 Net lending by US banks.

Source: See Appendix 15.1.

midst of the crisis, at the end of 1997, is likely the result of the sale of Treasury securities by central banks in the Asian countries.

Our evidence, then, indicates that there were large capital flows to the United States (and Europe) as a result of the Asia crisis, but it also shows that the flows reached the United States in a roundabout fashion, going through several countries before eventually winding up there. To the extent that these flows were intermediated through banks, we would expect to see a surge in net flows to US banks (or, equivalently, a decrease in net external lending by US banks). As we see from the top panel of Figure 15.9, this was not the case. Although inflows to the United States increased by about $40 billion in April 1997, there was an equally large outflow in January 1998. The cumulative net inflow over the entire March 1997–April 1998 period was only $8.4 billion. The bottom panel of Figure 15.9 breaks down net lending by region (Europe-7, offshore, and Japan). Although there was an increase in net flows from Japan to US banks from the beginning of the crisis, there was also a similarly large increase in net flows from US banks to Europe.

Hence, while BIS banks accounted for virtually all of the net outflows from Asia, we also know that the net capital flows into the United States were not intermediated through US banks. Other intermediation channels existed. European banks, for example, could have shifted lending from Asia to local institutions, which then could have used the money for FDI or portfolio investment in the United States. Indeed, cumulative net inflows to the United States from

March 1997 through April 1998 associated with FDI and portfolio investment totaled $326.9 billion. Of course, given the large US current account deficits, much of these flows would have occurred anyway.

A key difficulty with using the US balance-of-payments data is that errors and omissions (the statistical discrepancy) were very large and volatile after the crisis. Between February 1997 and April 1998, cumulative errors and omissions were −$92.6 billion, implying that net capital inflows were $92.6 billion less than what was actually reported during this period.[13] Also, from 1997 to 1998, the current account deficit increased by $76.7 billion, but reported capital inflows decreased by $70.8 billion. Put differently, net errors and omissions rose by $152.7 billion between 1997 and 1998; this suggests that actual capital inflows rose by $152.7 billion more than reported.

Changes in net errors and omissions were also very important in many of the key quarters (Figure 15.10). For example, in April 1997, the United States experienced a net capital inflow of $114 billion, which represented an increase of about $40 billion from the previous quarter. The current account deficit was $41 billion, representing a $4 billion decrease from the March 1997 deficit. Errors and omissions, then, were −$73 billion, representing a change of −$44 billion relative to the previous quarter. This suggests that the increase in US capital inflows in April 1997 might not have occurred. Similarly, the data show a sharp drop in capital inflows in January 1998, but this drop is again offset by a movement in errors and omissions in the opposite direction. There are several other episodes – for example, during the Mexican crisis in 1994 and 1995 – in which changes in errors and omissions were the opposite of changes in the financial account. It is therefore difficult to infer much from the US capital flows data.

Finally, we consider the possibility that the United States functioned as a 'safe haven' during this period. In this scenario, foreign investors shifted their

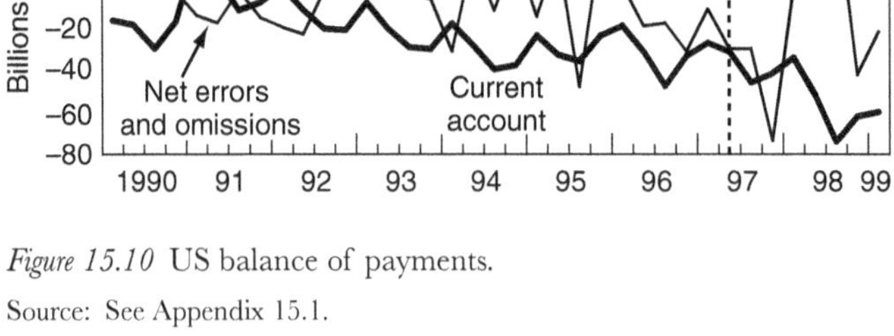

Figure 15.10 US balance of payments.

Source: See Appendix 15.1.

Note
The financial account is net capital inflows – that is, the net sum of direct, portfolio, and other investment balances.

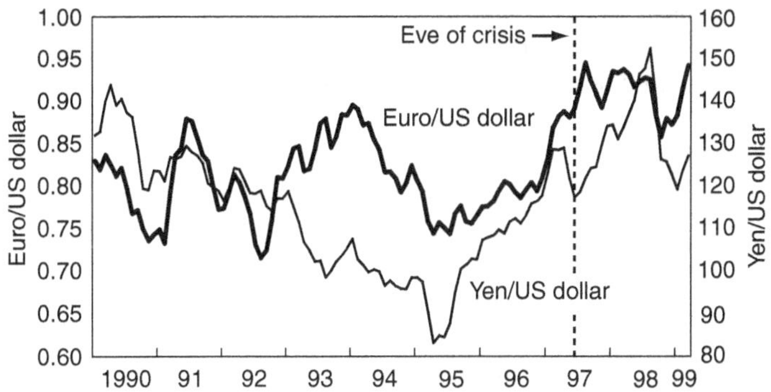

Figure 15.11 Euro/US dollar and yen/US dollar real exchange rates.

Source: See Appendix 15.1.

capital – including capital from other industrialized countries – *en masse* to the United States during the crisis. In that case, we would expect a real dollar appreciation against the currencies of other industrialized countries. Real exchange rates vs the dollar and the yen are presented in Figure 15.11.[14] The dollar did appreciate against the yen, but the appreciation was short-lived and, by the end of 1998, the dollar's yen value had fallen to pre-Asia crisis levels. The euro/dollar rate was fairly stable during the first five quarters after the crisis. This evidence suggests that there was no significant safe-haven effect in response to the Asia crisis. It is also consistent with our earlier evidence indicating that both the United States and Europe experienced large capital inflows connected to the crisis.

15.3 Did US GDP increase?

Having documented, to the extent possible, capital flows from Asia and into the United States, we turn to the consequences of those flows for the US economy. As we noted earlier, there are at least three important channels through which the crisis in the Asian emerging markets could have affected US GDP:

- the net export demand channel (negative),
- the domestic demand channel (positive), and
- the supply channel (positive).

The three effects are interrelated because the total demand for US goods (net exports plus domestic demand) must equal supply. Appendix 15.2 presents two simple models that include these three channels. One is a partial-equilibrium model of the United States, the other is a two-country model of the United States and Asia. We briefly describe the intuition behind these models. Assume for simplicity that the world consists of two countries: the United States and Asia, with investors holding financial assets in both countries. Then, increased expectations of private sector bankruptcies, a sharp local currency depreciation, and/or a stock market collapse cause them to shift their capital from Asia to the United States. These expectations could be driven by deteriorating fundamentals in Asia or they could be self-fulfilling and not based on fundamentals at all. Either way, the changed expectations lead to a fall in desired holdings of Asian assets.[15]

The capital outflows from Asia lead to a depreciation of Asian currencies – that is, an appreciation of the dollar. Asia's output declines because there is less financing of its economic activity. Both the dollar appreciation and the decline in Asian output lead to lower US net exports. At the same time, the capital inflow to the United States lowers US interest rates, which leads to an increase in US domestic demand by stimulating consumption and investment.[16] In equilibrium, the total effect on demand for US goods (the sum of lower net exports and higher domestic demand) is equal to the effect on the supply of those goods. The dollar appreciation leads to lower prices of imported inputs, which increases output supply in a manner analogous to the way an increase in productivity raises supply. Because the effect on output supply is positive, the total effect on demand is also positive.

Our interpretation of the crisis differs from the standard scenarios because of the central role assigned to the (net) capital outflows. The outflows are what leads to the currency depreciation and recession in Asia. In the standard scenarios, the currency depreciation and recession occur first, and the net capital outflow is just the passive counterpart to the recession-induced improvement in the current account surplus.

In our scenario, the declining future fundamentals or non-fundamentals that give rise to the increased expectations of default, sharp currency depreciations, and/or stock market collapses have no effect other than their impact on desired net capital flows. It is possible that these declining forces could also have had a direct negative effect on current domestic demand in the Asian countries, independent of the decline in demand resulting from the cutoff of foreign inflows.[17] When Asian domestic demand declines in this way, we show in Appendix 15.2 that our findings of reduced output in Asia, higher output in the United States, a dollar appreciation, and lower US interest rates are reinforced. This additional transmission channel, in other words, does not overturn the implications of our basic scenario. However, we also show that the decline in Asian domestic demand leads Asian real interest rates to fall relative to US real interest rates, a finding that is inconsistent with the evidence. We therefore conclude that our basic 'capital flow' scenario, which implies a rise in Asian interest rates, is more empirically relevant.

15.4 Evidence on the three channels

We now examine several macroeconomic indicators that provide evidence on the three channels. Together, Figures 15.12–15.18 show that the evidence is broadly in line with the models.

The negative trade (net exports) channel is illustrated in Figures 15.12 and 15.13. Figure 15.12 presents the real exchange rate of the dollar against a GDP-weighted average of the Asia-4. We use GDP deflators as proxies for the price levels. The figure shows a 40 per cent real appreciation of the dollar from February 1997 to

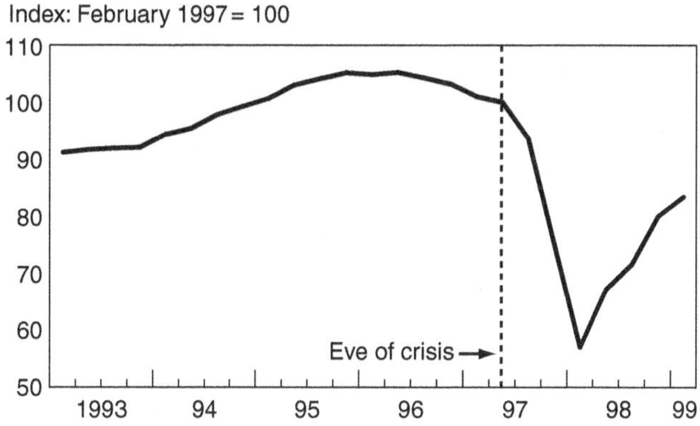

Figure 15.12 US dollar/Asia-4 GDP-weighted real exchange rate.

Source: See Appendix 15.1.

Notes
The real exchange rate is the GDP deflator of Asian countries relative to the US GDP deflator, both in US dollars. GDP weights are 1994–96 average GDP shares.

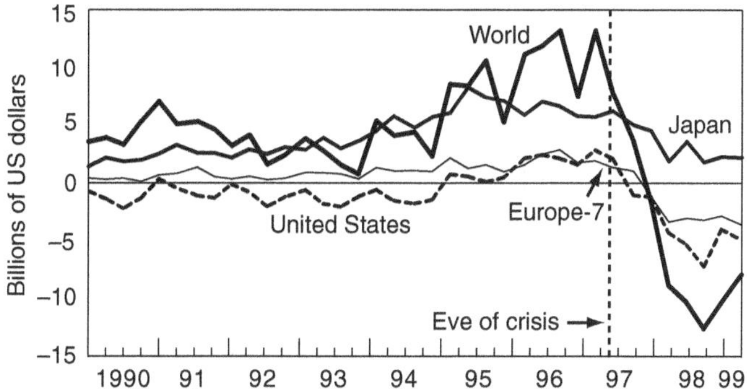

Figure 15.13 Net exports to the Asia-4 countries.

Source: See Appendix 15.1.

January 1998. Together with the immediate and sharp recession in the Asia-4 following the crisis, the appreciation led to a large drop in net exports to the Asia-4 economies. Figure 15.13 shows that US merchandise net exports to the Asia-4 fell from about \$3 billion per quarter before the crisis to −\$6 billion per quarter soon after it. Summing over the four quarters preceding the crisis (March 1996 – February 1997) and over 1998, we find that net exports fell by about \$30 billion after the onset of the crisis. For a broader group of 'Asia-8' countries – which also includes mainland China, Hong Kong, Malaysia, and Singapore – US net merchandise exports fell by \$46 billion after the crisis. Figure 15.13 shows that the United States was not alone in the export decline: net exports from Japan and Europe to the Asia-4 also fell sharply following the crisis.

Evidence of the second channel's importance can be found in Figures 15.14–15.16. Figure 15.14 shows that real interest rates declined considerably

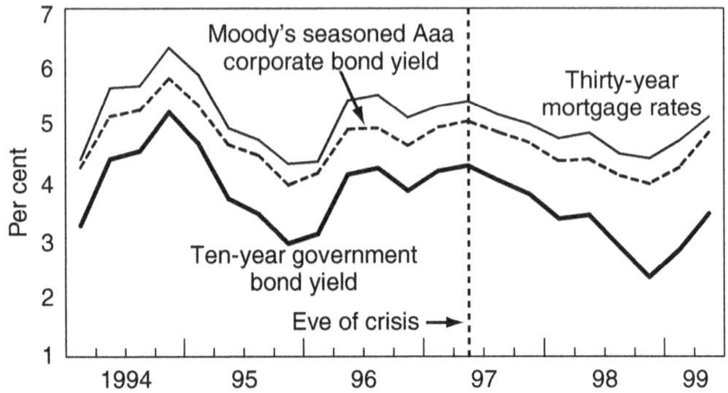

Figure 15.14 US interest rates less the core CPI.

Source: See Appendix 15.1.

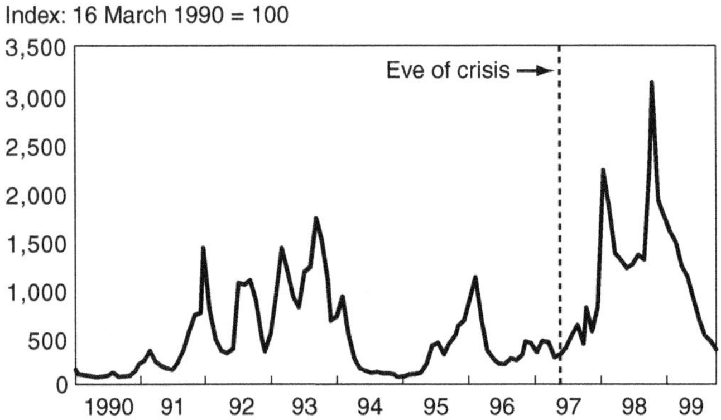

Figure 15.15 Number of US mortgage refinancings.

Source: See Appendix 15.1.

after the crisis.[18] The ten-year real government bond yield fell by close to 100 basis points from February 1997 to January 1998. The thirty-year mortgage yield and Moody's Aaa Seasoned Corporate Bond Yield fell by similar magnitudes. Interest rates slid even further toward the end of 1998, and the nominal thirty-year mortgage yield reached its lowest level in thirty years. This drop in mortgage rates led to a sharp increase in mortgage refinancings (Figure 15.15). A significant share of the mortgages refinanced during 1998 involved cash-outs, which increased the overall size of the mortgages.

Our framework implies that we would expect to see a drop in the contribution to GDP growth coming from net exports (the first channel) while we would expect to see a rise in the contribution from domestic demand. Figure 15.16 indicates that this is exactly what occurred. Although the GDP growth rate of 4 per cent in 1998 remained virtually unchanged from the 1997 growth rate, the contribution from domestic demand rose from about 4 per cent precrisis to about 5 per cent post

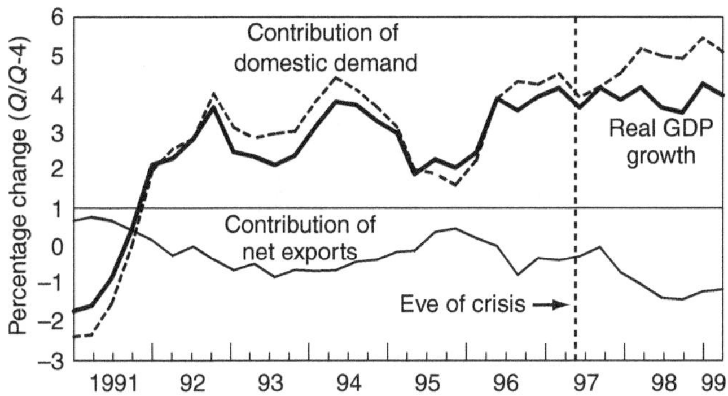

Figure 15.16 Composition of US growth.

Source: See Appendix 15.1.

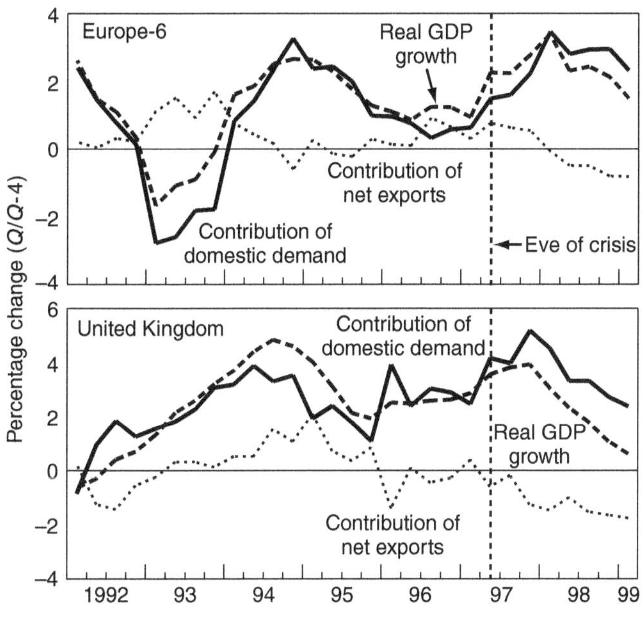

Figure 15.17 Composition of European growth.

Source: See Appendix 15.1.

crisis. At the same time, the contribution from net exports went from being slightly negative to about −1 per cent. Europe's response to the crisis was similar to the United States, as we see from Figure 15.17. Here, we have separated the United Kingdom from the Europe-6. The United Kingdom is a special case because significant fiscal consolidation and a tightening of monetary conditions dampened

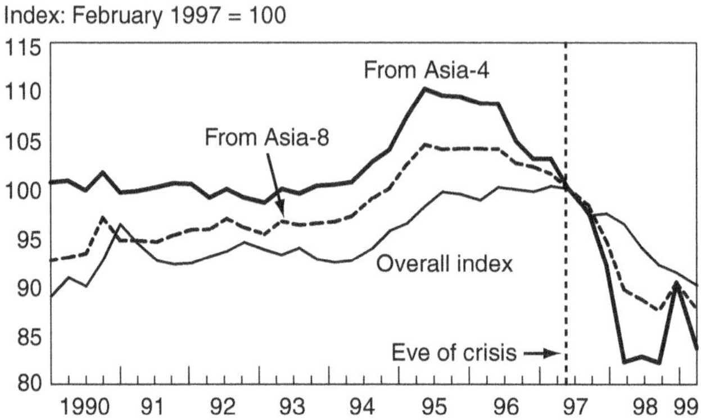

Figure 15.18 Real US import price indexes relative to the GDP deflator.

Source: See Appendix 15.1.

domestic demand growth. In the Europe-6, we see that the contribution of domestic demand growth rose from about 1 per cent precrisis to a level between 2 and 3 per cent postcrisis. At the same time, the contribution of net exports to GDP growth went from slightly below 1 per cent to slightly above −1 per cent.

The third channel depends on both the change in the relative price of imports (the reciprocal of the real exchange rate) and on the elasticity of supply with respect to the relative price of imports. Here, we provide evidence on the relative price of imports; in the next section, we derive the elasticity of supply. The import price index for total imports as well as for merchandise imports from the Asia-4 and the Asia-8 appears in Figure 15.18.[19] All import price indexes are shown relative to the US GDP deflator, and all are indexed to 100 in February 1997. The Asia-8 index represents a broader view of the impact of the Asia crisis on US import prices. The import price indexes show a sharp decrease for both sets of countries: from the precrisis period of March 1996–February 1997 to 1998, the relative import price index dropped by 18 per cent for the Asia-4 and by 12 per cent for the Asia-8.[20]

15.5 Quantifying the three channels

We now quantify the effect on GDP growth of each of the three channels. By doing so, we impose only minimal assumptions, in contrast to the strong structure imposed by the models in Appendix 15.2. We consider both the Asia-4 countries and the broader set of Asia-8 countries. By looking at the Asia-8, we can account for spillovers from the crisis to some important neighbouring countries. However, we do not consider indirect supply channels operating through oil or commodity prices. The recessions in the Asia-8 countries clearly had some negative effect on oil prices in 1998. These indirect channels would tend to raise the estimates of our supply channel effect.

We define the pre- and postcrisis periods as we did earlier: March 1996–February 1997 and January 1998–April 1998, respectively. It is not appropriate simply to compare 1997 with 1998 because the crisis had already started in 1997. It is also not appropriate to compare the four quarters before the crisis with the four quarters following the start of the crisis – March 1996 – February 1997 and March 1997 – February 1998, respectively – because the crisis did not take effect fully until 1998. As shown in Figure 15.13, it took two or three quarters for US and Europe-7 net exports to decline to their lower postcrisis levels. Also, as we noted, the effect of the capital outflows on the current account of the Asian countries was initially buffered by IMF credit and a drop in reserve assets. The full adjustment in the current account did not occur until January 1998.

We compute the trade effect without making any model-specific assumptions. We do not need to know the exact causes of the decline in net exports to the Asia crisis countries. Rather, we employ bilateral trade data to calculate how much the contribution of net exports to US GDP growth fell as a result of the crisis. We focus on merchandise trade because it accounted for 79 per cent of total US trade in 1998; it is also considerably more volatile than services trade. The contribution to real GDP growth of net exports can be written as

$$\frac{P_X X}{Y}\frac{\Delta X}{X} - \frac{P_M M}{Y}\frac{\Delta M}{M} = \frac{\Delta(P_X X - P_M M)}{Y} - \left(\frac{P_X X}{Y}\frac{\Delta P_X}{P_X} - \frac{P_M M}{Y}\frac{\Delta P_M}{P_M}\right) \tag{15.1}$$

where Y is nominal GDP, P_M and P_X are import and export price indexes *vis-à-vis* the Asian countries, and X and M are quantities of bilateral exports and imports. The first term on the lower part of the equation measures the change in the nominal trade balance relative to GDP. The second term measures the price effects. The price effects are subtracted from the nominal trade effect to get the overall real trade effect. We approximate the US export price index to the Asian countries by the overall US export price index. The import price index is approximated by using an import-weighted index of the Asian country export price indexes.

Supply is determined by the production of firms, which are assumed to maximize profits by choosing optimal levels of labour input and imported intermediate goods. This approach ensures that output is not determined only by demand. To facilitate our calculations of the supply effect, we make two auxiliary assumptions. First, we hold the capital stock constant. This assumption is not restrictive, because it merely reflects the fact that our analysis focuses on the short-term effects. Second, we assume that the real wage rate is constant. This assumption implies that the labour supply schedule is perfectly elastic. We argue in the following that this assumption is not essential to our main findings. As long as the labour supply schedule is not perfectly inelastic, we will obtain qualitatively similar results.

The details of the firms' profit-maximization problem that underlies our calculation are as follows. Maximize $P\tilde{Y} - WL - P_M M$, where $\tilde{Y}$, output; L, labour; K, capital, constant; M, imported intermediates and imported capital goods; P, price of gross output; W, nominal wage rate (W/P assumed constant); P_M, price of imported inputs; $\tilde{Y} = F\ (\phi(K,L),\ M)$ (production function); $\phi(K,L)$,

Cobb–Douglas index of K and L (labour share, α); $F(.,.)$, CES index with elasticity of substitution ε.

Firms maximize the difference between revenues (the value of output) and costs. The variable costs are labour costs and the costs of imported inputs. With no loss of generality, we aggregate the entire domestic production process; hence, we do not include domestic intermediate goods. Our goal is to quantify the effect of a decrease in imported input prices on supply.

After computing the first-order conditions for imported inputs and labour, the supply effect can be written as

$$\frac{\Delta GDP}{GDP} = \frac{\beta}{1-\beta}\,\frac{\alpha}{\alpha-1}\,\frac{\Delta(P_M/P)}{P_M/P} \tag{15.2}$$

where β is the share of imported inputs in total production costs in the precrisis period and α is the share of labour income in domestic value-added. P_M/P is the price of imported inputs relative to the price of output. Real *GDP* is equal to the total value of domestic output, minus imported inputs, measured at precrisis price levels. Notice that the supply effect is independent of the elasticity of substitution between imported inputs and domestic value-added. Notice also that as long as import prices fall, the supply effect is positive.[21]

We compute the change in the overall P_M/P as the merchandise import share from the Asia-4 or the Asia-8 multiplied by the percentage change of P_M/P for the Asia-4 or the Asia-8. In the Asia-8 case, the change in the overall P_M/P is about −2.3 per cent.[22] The labour income share of GDP in 1997 was 58 per cent, so we set α equal to 0.58. We set β equal to US imports of intermediate and capital goods in 1998 (about 60 per cent of total merchandise imports) divided by the sum of those imports and US GDP. This calculation yields approximately 0.06.

Although the net effect can be computed from the supply effect alone, it is still useful to know how the demand side breaks out into the net exports effect and domestic demand effect. We estimate the domestic demand effect as the residual – that is, we compute the effect as the difference between the supply effect and the net exports effect. It would be difficult to calculate the domestic demand effect directly. For example, we would have to know the size of the increase in capital flows to the United States that can be traced to the crisis, the effect of these inflows on the interest rate, and the elasticity of investment demand and savings demand with respect to the interest rate. To know the savings demand and investment demand elasticities, we would require a model of consumption behaviour and of investment behaviour, with the corresponding set of assumptions. Therefore, by treating the domestic demand effect as the residual, we avoid making the large number of assumptions necessary to calculate it.

The results of these computations are reported in Table 15.2. If we interpret the Asia crisis broadly as corresponding to developments in the Asia-8 countries, US GDP fell by 0.8 percentage points as a result of a drop in net exports to those countries, while it rose by 1.0 percentage points as a result of the increase in domestic demand. The net effect, which is also the supply effect, is +0.2 percentage points

Table 15.2 The growth effect of the Asia crisis (per cent)

	Asia-4	*Asia-8*
Trade effect	−0.5	−0.8
Domestic demand effect	0.6	1.0
Total effect	0.1	0.2

Source: Authors' calculations.

Notes
The table reports the contribution to GDP growth of lower trade and higher domestic demand as a result of the Asia crisis, as well as the total effect on GDP growth (which is also the supply effect). Results are reported based on one associating narrowly the Asia crisis with four countries: Indonesia, Korea, the Philippines, and Thailand, as well as with a broader set of eight countries that also includes mainland China, Hong Kong, Malaysia, and Singapore.

of GDP. The numbers are slightly smaller for the Asia-4. Our supply effect calculations suggest that the net effect of the Asia crisis is small, but positive.

These results do not change in a major way if labour supply is not perfectly elastic. In this case, the increased demand for labour (which results from lower prices of imported goods) leads to a rise in real wages. In the extreme case where labour supply is completely inelastic, the supply effect is zero. Although the lower prices of imported inputs lead to an increase in demand for the inputs, which raises gross output, domestic value-added remains unaltered because both the capital stock and labour input are unchanged. In general, when labour supply's elasticity is finite, the supply effect will be somewhere between 0 and 0.2 per cent.[23]

Our findings correspond well with Figure 15.16, which shows that real GDP growth remained virtually unchanged following the crisis. The negative effect from lower net exports was almost exactly offset by the rise in domestic demand. The increase in the contribution of domestic demand to GDP growth from the pre- to the postcrisis period was about 1 per cent. Hence, while mindful of the fact that we have calculated the domestic demand effect as a residual, we suggest that the Asia crisis could have accounted for all of the increase in US domestic demand.

There are other explanations for the increase in US domestic demand during the crisis. However, to the extent that these explanations involve developments specific to the United States, such as the rise in the US stock market, we believe that they are not very plausible.[24] If, for whatever reason, there is a substantial increase in domestic demand specific to the United States, we would have expected to see a rise in US real interest rates and a real dollar appreciation relative to other major currencies. We have seen neither of these developments. Real interest rates actually fell rather than rose. Moreover, we saw that the increase in the contribution of domestic demand to GDP growth in Europe was similar in magnitude to that for the United States.

It is possible that a worldwide event, such as the improved growth outlook, led to a rise in domestic demand on both sides of the Atlantic at the same time. This possibility also seems dubious, because the growth forecasts fell in Europe and in the United States after the crisis. The fact that the pickup in domestic demand took place soon after the crisis – and that it occurred both in Europe and in the United States – is highly suggestive of a causal link to the crisis.

15.6 Conclusion

In the 1990s, many emerging market countries facilitated foreign investor access to their financial markets by liberalizing controls on international capital flows. This action has been beneficial for the emerging markets as well as for investors from industrialized countries. However, because capital inflows can easily be reversed in a short period of time, there have also been risks associated with the increased exposure of foreign investors to these new markets. To date, much of the literature on the Asia crisis has focused on assessing the causes and consequences for the crisis countries. In this chapter, we have shifted the focus by examining the implications for industrialized countries – and for the United States in particular – of such economic turmoil.

Although the negative trade effects for industrialized economies were emphasized early in the crisis, it soon became clear that the trade channel was not the only transmission channel. By definition, a capital outflow from Asia is a capital inflow somewhere else. Capital inflows can finance an increase in domestic demand, which leads to an increase in GDP. One goal of this chapter, therefore, was to follow the trail of money out of Asia to ascertain its final destination. We have found it difficult to follow the trail very far, and to determine exactly how much of the funds ended up in the United States. We have also found that large errors and omissions in the US balance of payments complicate the documentation of capital inflows to the United States.

Nevertheless, several stylized facts have emerged:

- The Asia crisis countries experienced net capital outflows of more than $80 billion from the start of the crisis to the end of 1998.
- The counter-parties to the Asia outflows essentially were BIS reporting country banks.
- The majority of the outflows went to offshore centre banks, which funneled the capital to banks in Europe.
- Almost half of the outflows went to banks whose nationalities were not American, Japanese, or European.
- The United States and Europe were the final destinations for most of the outflows from the crisis countries and from Japan.
- Very little money reached the United States directly from the crisis countries or through the offshore centres.

These facts highlight the importance of banks as the initial propagation mechanisms of the Asia crisis as well as the 'roundaboutness' of the banking flows.

A second goal of this chapter was to analyse and quantify the short-run effect of the crisis on US GDP growth. We identified three channels through which US growth was affected. In the first channel, the recessions in the Asian countries and the depreciated Asian currencies imply fewer US exports and more US imports. In the second, the lower US interest rates that result from the increased inflows imply greater domestic demand. And in the third, dollar appreciation implies lower prices for imported intermediates and imported capital goods, which reduces the cost of production. In equilibrium, the sum of the first two demand channels equals the third: the supply channel. Our calculations suggest that the negative trade response is −0.8 per cent of GDP, while the positive supply response is +0.2 per cent of GDP. The domestic demand response, which we calculate as a residual, is about +1 per cent of GDP. The overall effect on the US economy in 1998, therefore, is about +0.2 per cent of GDP, or $15–20 billion. Going forward, we can expect these effects to move in the opposite direction as the Asian economies recover. If our findings are correct, however, a reversal of capital flows to the Asian countries will generate only a small net effect on US growth. Yet such a reversal could still generate large compositional effects on domestic demand and net exports.

Appendix 15.1

Figures

Figure 15.1 Sum across Korea, Thailand, Indonesia, and the Philippines (henceforth the 'Asia-4') of the financial account as reported by the IMF's International Financial Statistics (IFS) database. IFS had not yet reported the Korean financial account for April 1998, so we use McGraw-Hill's DRI Asia CEIC database.

Figure 15.2 Sum across Asia-4 of portfolio investment (liabilities–assets), direct investment abroad–direct investment in the reporting economy, and other investment (liabilities–assets), respectively, reported in IFS. Because of missing April 1998 Korean data, the CEIC database is used to complete the direct investment, portfolio investment, and other investment series.

Figure 15.3 Exchange-rate-adjusted flows and assets–liabilities (including non-bank) are from the BIS. The '*vis-à-vis*' area is Asia-4; the reporting area is the 'grand total' of BIS reporting countries.

Figure 15.4 Exchange-rate-adjusted flows and assets–liabilities (including non-bank) are from the BIS. The '*vis-à-vis*' area is Asia-4; the reporting areas are Japan, the offshore centres, and the United States and IBFs, as well as France, Germany, Italy, the Netherlands, Spain, Switzerland, and the United Kingdom (henceforth the 'Europe-7').

Figure 15.5 The top panel is the stock of total assets *vis-à-vis* Asia-4, with the geographic origin of a bank being the reporting area. The BIS is the source. The bottom panel is also the stock of total assets *vis-à-vis* Asia-4, but by nationality of ownership. The BIS' *Consolidated International Banking Statistics* is the source. Because of data unavailability, we exclude Switzerland from the Europe series in the bottom panel.

Figure 15.6 The financial account series is the same as in Figure 15.1. Other series: sum across Asia-4 of 'reserves and related items' and the current account as reported by the IFS. The IFS had not yet reported the Korean financial or current account for April 1998, so we use the Bank of Korea's External Economic Indicators Table P.F.2b for Korean current account data. For changes in reserve assets, we use the CEIC database for Korea for April 1998.

Figure 15.7 With some exceptions in the most recent quarters, current account balance data for France, Germany, the Netherlands, Spain, Switzerland, and the United Kingdom are from the BIS; Italian data are from Banca d'Italia; Indonesian, Japanese, Korean, Philippine, Thai, and US data are from the IFS. The exceptions are the Spanish current account for January 1999, which is from Bloomberg, and Korean data for April 1998 and January 1999, which are from J.P. Morgan International Data Watch, as is the Indonesian value for January 1999. Data from the BIS are converted to US dollars using period-average exchange rates. All series are seasonally adjusted using the X11 additive filter in Eviews 3.0.

Figure 15.8 The net bank lending series is the same as in Figure 15.4. The net portfolio flows series is derived from Treasury International Capital data. Long-term net sales by foreigners to US residents is calculated from the TIC's US Transactions with Foreigners in Long-Term Securities Table. Short-term Treasury obligations from the TIC's Liabilities to Foreigners Reported by Banks in the US Table are also included. Quarterly data are calculated using monthly sums.

Figure 15.9 These data are exchange-rate-adjusted flows, assets–liabilities (including non-bank), as reported by the BIS. The top panel is the United States and IBFs reporting *vis-à-vis* all BIS reporting countries; the bottom panel is the United States and IBFs reporting *vis-à-vis* Japan, the offshore centres, and Europe-7.

Figure 15.10 The US financial account, current account, and net errors and omissions are from the IFS.

Figure 15.11 Monthly averages of the daily BIS nominal exchange rate series for Europe and Japan are multiplied by the ratio of the US and European consumer price indexes (CPIs) and the ratio of the US and Japanese CPIs, respectively. The US CPI is from Haver Analytics' USECON database. The European and Japanese CPIs are from the BIS. All CPIs are indexed to 1995 = 100.

Figure 15.12 Quarterly average exchange rates for the Asia-4 are from the IFS. The GDP deflators are calculated using nominal and real GDP series from the CEIC database. After indexing all series to February 1997 = 100, we use a GDP-weighted (1994–96 average GDP shares) average of the real exchange rates to yield the Asia-4/US real exchange rate.

Figure 15.13 Data are from the IMF's Direction of Trade Statistics database. Asia-4 countries are the primary countries – that is, they report data on exports and imports – while secondary countries are the world, the United States, Japan, and Europe-7. To construct each series, we sum the quantity (net exports × −1) across the Asia-4 countries and across Europe-7.

Figure 15.14 Ten-year government bond yields are from the European Central Bank's Euro Area Statistics Monthly Data Table 3.2 and its website (http://www.ecb.int/stats/mb/eastats.htm). The Moody's Seasoned Aaa Corporate Bond Yield series and thirty-year mortgage rate series ('Contract rates on commitments: conventional thirty-year mortgages, FHLMC (per cent)') are both from USECON. All interest rates are quarterly averages of daily rates minus the Q/Q-4 growth rate of the CPI, excluding food and energy. The CPI series is from USECON.

Figure 15.15 This series is the refinancing index from the Mortgage Bankers Association's weekly survey. Data are seasonally adjusted, and weekly observations have been converted to monthly averages.

Figure 15.16 All data are from USECON. Contribution of domestic demand = (nominal DD(Q-4)/nominal GDP(Q-4))× real DD growth Q/Q-4. Nominal domestic demand is the sum of the C, I, and G (consumption, investment, and government) series. Real domestic demand is the sum of the CH, IH, and GH (1992 chain-weighted dollars of the C, I, and G series) series. Nominal GDP is simply the series GDP. The real GDP growth series is GDPH (seasonally adjusted, 1992 chain-weighted dollars). The contribution of net exports series is the difference between real GDP growth and contribution of domestic demand.

Figure 15.17 For the top panel, contribution of domestic demand = (sum nominal domestic demand(Q-4) across Europe-6/sum nominal GDP(Q-4) across Europe-6)×(Europe-6 real domestic demand growth (Q/Q-4)).

In the formula, the nominal domestic demand and nominal GDP series are from the BIS, where nominal domestic demand is reported in the local currency and nominal GDP is reported in dollars. Nominal domestic demand is converted to dollars (for the purpose of summing) using the period-average quarterly exchange rates from IFS. Real domestic demand growth for the individual Europe-6 countries of France, Germany, Italy, the Netherlands, Spain, and Switzerland is from the BIS. The BIS had not yet reported Italy's April 1998 real domestic demand growth, so we use Bloomberg (the original source is ISTAT). Europe-6 real domestic demand growth for each quarter is constructed as the weighted average (a country's weight is its nominal domestic demand four quarters ago) of the individual countries' real (Q/Q-4) domestic demand growth rates.

Europe-6 real GDP growth is calculated as the weighted average (a country's weight is its nominal GDP four quarters ago) of the individual countries' real (Q/Q-4) GDP growth rates. The nominal GDP data used in the weighting are the same as those used in the construction of contribution of domestic demand (see previously). The individual countries' real GDP data are from the BIS.

For the bottom panel, the United Kingdom's contribution of domestic demand = (nominal DD(Q-4)/nominal GDP(Q-4)) × real DD growth Q/Q-4. In this formula, the nominal domestic demand and nominal GDP series are from the BIS, where nominal domestic demand is reported in British pounds and nominal GDP is in US dollars. Nominal domestic demand is converted to dollars (for the purpose of summing) using IFS quarterly period-average exchange rates. Real domestic demand growth and UK real GDP growth are from the BIS.

In both panels, contribution of the net exports series is the difference between real GDP growth and contribution of domestic demand.

Figure 15.18 US import price indexes from the Asian countries are approximated using export price indexes of the Asian countries (from Oxford Economics) in dollar terms. Indexes are deflated using the US GDP deflator. After we calculate real import price indexes for the eight Asian countries, 1995 US import shares yield weighted averages for Asia-4 and Asia-8.

Appendix 15.2

Two models

Here we present two models that deliver the implications discussed in the text. The first is a partial-equilibrium model for the United States, the second is a two-country general-equilibrium model for the United States and Asia. The first has a goods–market equilibrium condition and a balance-of-payments equilibrium condition:

$$Y(\overset{+}{RER}) = DD(\overset{-}{r}, \overset{+}{Y}) + NX(\overset{-}{RER}, \overset{-}{Y}), \tag{15.A1}$$

$$NX(\overset{-}{RER}, \overset{-}{Y}) + KA(\overset{+}{r}, \overset{+}{\gamma}) = 0. \tag{15.A2}$$

$Y\,(RER)$ is output supply. It is a positive function of the real exchange rate: a real appreciation (a rise in *RER*) lowers the relative price of imported goods, which stimulates production. On the right-hand side of the goods – market equilibrium equation (15.A1) is total demand for US goods, which is the sum of domestic demand (*DD*) and net exports (*NX*). Domestic demand is a positive function of income Y and a negative function of the real interest rate r. Net exports fall in response to both a real appreciation and a rise in domestic income, which raises imports.

The second equation (15.A2) represents balance-of-payments equilibrium: the sum of net exports and net capital inflows (*KA*) must be zero. A rise in the real interest rate raises capital inflows. Capital flows also depend on the shift parameter, γ, which represents a desire by investors to reallocate their capital to the United States based on concerns of increased risks of default in Asia as well as increased probabilities of currency depreciations and stock market collapses. In our framework, it does not matter whether these concerns are based on fundamentals, are rational self-fulfilling beliefs, or are irrational altogether.

It is easily verifiable from these two equations that an increase in γ, which leads to a shift of capital to the United States, implies a real dollar appreciation, a drop in the real interest rate, and a rise in output.

The second model extends the first to a general-equilibrium model for the United States and Asia:

$$Y(R\overset{+}{E}R) = DD\,(\overset{-}{r}, \overset{+}{Y}) + NX(R\overset{-}{E}R, \overset{-}{Y}, \overset{+}{Y}^{*}), \tag{15.A3}$$

$$Y(R\overset{-}{E}R) = DD^{*}(\overset{-}{r}^{*}, \overset{+}{Y}^{*}) - NX(R\overset{-}{E}R, \overset{-}{Y}, \overset{+}{Y}^{*}), \tag{15.A4}$$

$$NX(R\overset{-}{E}R, \overset{-}{Y}, \overset{+}{Y}^{*}) + KA(r\overset{+}{-}r^{*}, \overset{+}{\gamma}) = 0. \tag{15.A5}$$

Asia is indicated by *. This model adds a goods–market equilibrium condition for Asia and makes US net exports also a function of income in Asia. Moreover, net capital flows now depend on the interest rate differential. It is easily verifiable that an increase in γ has the same implications for the United States as in the first model. Now the model also has implications for the Asian economy: its real interest rate rises and its output falls.[25]

We can extend the two-country model to include a shift parameter, θ, in the Asia domestic demand function. A decrease in θ corresponds to a decrease in government purchases or to a decrease in consumption or investment demand resulting from, say, increased pessimism about future macroeconomic prospects. θ captures the idea that other forces could lead to a reallocation of capital from Asia to the United States independent of changes in γ. It is easily verifiable that a decrease in θ has the same implications for the United States: a lower interest rate, a real dollar appreciation, and a rise in output. These implications, therefore, reinforce the effect of a rise in γ. We believe that the latter effect was more likely to be important in the Asia crisis, because a rise in γ leads to higher Asian interest rates, consistent with the evidence, while a fall in θ results in the opposite.

Notes

1 The views expressed are those of the authors and do not necessarily reflect the position of the Federal Reserve Bank of New York or the Federal Reserve System. The authors thank Barbara Berman, Melissa Fiorelli, Chris Gorband, Dan Kinney, Sydney Ludvigson, Therese Melfo, Don Morgan, Dick Peach, Monica Posen, Russ Scholl, Charles Steindel, two anonymous referees, and participants at the Bank for International Settlements' Autumn 1999 Meeting of Central Bank Economists. Scott Nicholson and Stefan Papaioannou provided outstanding research assistance. An earlier version of this chapter appeared in the *BIS Conference Papers*, 'International financial markets and the implications for monetary and financial stability', March 2000.

2 A reasonable consensus was reported in the *New York Times*: 'Many forecasters estimate that the Asian crisis will in time shave half a percentage point from the nation's economic growth' (30 January 1998). For example, between September and November, J.P. Morgan revised its forecast of the net export contribution to GDP growth in 1998 from −0.1 to −0.6 percentage points. Most forecasts of the impact of the crisis were based only on international trade channels.

3 We therefore believe that the demand-oriented Mundell–Fleming type of model is not sufficient for considering the implications of the crisis.

4 The first hints that market forecasters were aware of the positive effects of the crisis through lower interest rates came as early as January 1998. See, for example, J.P. Morgan's 'US Economic Outlook' (16 January) or *New York Times* (30 January).

In addition, Jeffrey Frankel, then at the Council of Economic Advisors, indicated in a 17 November 1999 speech at the Institute of International Finance that the negative effect of the crisis through trade could be mitigated 'if one takes into account that the likely effect would be interest rates lower than they otherwise would be, thereby replacing demand lost in the trade sector with output in producers' durable equipment, construction, and consumer durables'. However, Frankel also pointed out that at the time 'many of the estimates of the East Asian crisis are just the effect on US net exports'. Even analysts who understood the positive effects through lower interest rates generally still considered the overall effects of the crisis to be negative. Only as 1998 proceeded did it become increasingly clear that the US economy did not suffer a negative hit from the crisis in Asia.

5 Related research includes Ito (1999), Bonti *et al.* (1999), and Fornari and Levy (1999). These studies, however, tend to focus on the flows/stocks of financial assets into or out of emerging Asia. None of them attempts to trace the flow of capital from emerging Asia to the United States during the recent currency crisis.

6 Although Malaysia is often included as one of the crisis countries, we do not include it in our main calculations because of incomplete data, particularly in terms of the breakdown of the financial account into portfolio investment, FDI, and other investment. For 1998, however, we know that Malaysia experienced at least a $5 billion net outflow of short-term capital alone. We include Malaysia in a broader set of eight Asian countries when we consider the effect of the crisis on US growth.

7 Direct investment refers to international flows of 'equity capital, reinvested earnings, and other capital associated with various intercompany transactions between affiliated enterprises' (International Monetary Fund 1999). It generally refers to greenfield investment and to mergers and acquisitions. Portfolio investment refers to international flows of equity (except equity counted as direct investment) and debt securities of any maturity. 'Other' investment involves bank and non-bank intermediaries on either side of the transaction.

8 The offshore centres include the Bahamas, Bahrain, the Cayman Islands, Hong Kong, the Netherlands, Antilles, and Singapore.

9 The only difference of note is that in January 1998 the extent of the capital outflow from the Asia-4 was less than it was in the previous quarter, while the reduction in net lending by BIS reporting banks was slightly larger.

10 In other words, we assume that these countries typically have small current accounts and small net changes in central bank reserves. This is a reasonable assumption for all of the offshore centres except Hong Kong and Singapore. Total net cumulative external lending of the offshore centres was $29 billion during this period. However, this amount is a relatively small fraction of the gross flows in and out of the centres. By contrast, during the crisis, the gross flows of the Asia crisis countries were similar in magnitude to the net flows.

11 Data for Switzerland were not available.

12 Applying a linear trend to Japan as well, we find that the country's current account surplus increased by $12 billion relative to trend in this period. This increase is less than one-half of the increase in the Asia-4 and Malaysian current accounts. Hence, it seems clear that most of the decrease in the Europe-7 and US current accounts can be attributed to the emerging market crisis in Asia.

13 The figure assumes that all the errors occur because of misreporting of the capital account data. In other words, we assume that the current account data are represented accurately.

14 Real exchange rates are normalized to equal nominal exchange rates for the average of 1995.

15 See, for example, Corsetti *et al.* (1999) for a 'fundamentals'-based explanation of the Asia crisis and Radelet and Sachs (1998) for a self-fulfilling-expectations explanation. In our framework, it does not matter for the US economy whether or not the expectations are driven by fundamentals. However, the source of the changed expectations does matter, of course, for the Asian countries, particularly from a policy standpoint.

16 Empirical documentation of the textbook linkages from lower interest rates to higher consumption and investment is not widespread. Campbell and Mankiw (1989), for example, conclude that there is virtually no link between real interest rates and consumption. However, evidence of such linkages does exist. See Barro and Sala-i-Martin (1990) for evidence that ties interest rates to investment. See Mankiw (1985) and Beaudry and van Wincoop (1996) for evidence that ties interest rates to consumption.

17 An expected drop in future income could similarly lower consumption.

18 We subtract the Q/Q-4 core inflation rate from nominal interest rates as a proxy for inflation expectations. Core inflation rates are considered a good indicator of long-term inflation trends. Inflation survey data are available only up to one year ahead.

19 We have proxied the US import price index from each Asian country by each country's overall export price index, expressed in US dollars.

20 These figures are consistent with those reported in Barth and Dinmore (1999).

21 It therefore might seem that we have 'rigged' our approach to guarantee a positive net impact of the crisis on the United States. This assumption is incorrect for several reasons. First, it is possible (although not probable) that the crisis in Asia could have led to higher US import prices, to the extent that financing difficulties severely disrupted Asian production. If higher prices induced by lower production more than offset the effects of exchange rate depreciation, US import prices could have risen. Second, it is hard to see how lower import prices could have a negative effect on supply, just as it is hard to see how lower oil prices or higher productivity would lower supply. Third, as discussed later, our estimates of the supply effect and the net exports effect imply a domestic demand effect that is consistent with what is observed in the data.

22 We approximate P with the GDP deflator, as in Figure 15.12. This is not exactly correct, because P is the price of value-added plus imported inputs, not just value-added. But it is a close approximation, as β is quite small.

23 As noted earlier, we abstract from indirect supply effects, such as those resulting from oil prices. If the decline in oil prices in 1998 is entirely attributable to declining demand in the Asia-8 countries, then the supply effect would be considerably larger, close to 1 percentage point of GDP. In addition, as noted earlier, supply also could have been affected through the profits channel. Although corporate profits rose somewhat following the crisis, it is hard to say how much this rise could have affected the supply effect.

24 Although European stock markets appreciated as well, these markets are much smaller in scale – in total and in per capita – than the US stock markets.

25 The model is very similar to the flexible-price model in Abel and Bernanke (1995). One difference is that we include an additional supply-side channel from imported inputs to output.

Bibliography

Abel, A. and Bernanke, B. (1995) *Macroeconomics*, 2nd edn. New York: Addison-Wesley.

Barro, Robert J. and Sala-i-Martin, X. (1990) 'World real interest rates', in Olivier Blanchard and Stanley Fischer (eds), *NBER Macroeconomics Annual 1990*, Cambridge: MIT Press.

Barth, M. and Dinmore, T. (1999) 'Trade prices and volumes in East Asia through the crisis', Board of Governors of the Federal Reserve System International Finance Discussion Paper No. 643, August.

Beaudry, P. and Wincoop, E. (1996) 'The intertemporal elasticity of substitution: an exploration using a US panel of state data', *Economica*, 63(251): 494–512.

Bonti, Rudi *et al.* (1999) 'Supervisory lessons to be drawn from the Asian crisis', Basel Committee on Banking Supervision Working Paper No. 2, June.

Campbell, John Y. and Mankiw, N.G. (1989) 'Consumption, income, and interest rates: reinterpreting the time series evidence', in Olivier Blanchard and Stanley Fischer (eds), *NBER Macroeconomics Annual 1989*, Cambridge: MIT Press.

Corsetti, G., Pesenti, P., and Roubini, N. (1999) 'What caused the Asian currency and financial crisis?', *Japan and the World Economy*, 11(3): 305–73.

Fornari, F. and Aviram Levy, A. (1999) 'Global liquidity in the 1990s: geographical allocation and long-run determinants', unpublished paper, Banca d'Italia, October.

International Monetary Fund (IMF) (various years) International Financial Statistics.

Ito, Takatoshi (1999) 'Capital flows in Asia', NBER Working Paper No. 7134, May.

Mankiw, N. Gregory (1985) 'Consumer durables and the real interest rate', *Review of Economics and Statistics*, 67(73): 353–62.

Radelet, S. and Sachs, J.D. (1998) 'The East Asian financial crisis: diagnosis, remedies, prospects', Brookings Papers on Economic Activity No. 1: 1–90.

16 Interpreting some empirical facts of business cycles and stock returns in Korea[1]

David Deok-Ki Kim

16.1 Introduction

Economists have long been interested in the relationship between real economic activity and the financial markets. Nevertheless, this long-held line of inquiry has not yielded any definitive answers to conventional questions such as 'Was the stock market crash responsible for the latest recession?' Numerous studies attempted to find the link between the two sides of the economy empirically or theoretically. Pioneered by Fisher (1907), many authors have been interested in the link between the financial market variables and real economic activity.[2] Another line of research that has received as much attention in the 1980s and 1990s was to find the stylized facts of an economy over business cycles and growth, in the spirit of Kaldor (1957). Since the seminal contribution by Hodrick and Prescott (1997), a number of studies attempted to empirically document these stylized facts, mostly for the US and European economies. For the East Asian economies, Kim and Choi (1997) document stylized features for Korea and Kim (1999) presents some evidence on the empirical properties of South East Asian business cycles.

Economists have also called it a puzzle that the excess returns from common stocks exceed returns from relatively riskless assets by a large magnitude, simply because the standard equilibrium models could not account for this empirical observation. Indeed, this has been a robust phenomenon in international data for most developed economies, and attracted a considerable amount of theoretical research for a plausible explanation.

This chapter explores the two strands of empirical facts; that is, the stylized facts of business cycles and the equity premium puzzle in the context of Korea and Japan. In presenting business cycle facts, the definition suggested by Lucas (1977) and the empirical methodology proposed by Hodrick and Prescott (1997) are employed. In investigating the existence of the equity premium puzzle, the theory pioneered by Merton (1973) and the methodology proposed by Campbell (1996) are employed, both of which are based on the inter-temporal consumption-based asset pricing model (C-ICAPM). While the chapter documents some business cycle properties for Korea in line with Kim and Choi (1997), the major aim of the chapter is to examine the data from real sectors and financial markets, with the purpose of exploring whether there are any puzzling features in the data that require an interpretation in the context of historical episodes.

In the sections that follow, this chapter discusses each of these empirical issues for Korea, which will then be compared with the evidence for Japan. Japan was chosen as a reference country due to the high level of financial and physical trades between the two countries as well as similar industrial compositions.

The recent economic crisis in Korea has yielded a great deal of interest and debates from both economists and policy analysts as to what went wrong in the precrisis period.[3] While many arguments were given, one of the primary arguments about the causes of the crisis focused on the financial (more precisely, credit) markets. Economists pointed to the role of financial intermediaries in Korea, in relation to the government's implicit guarantees of the loans to major corporations and inadequate risk management by banks. However, no explicit attention was given to the stock market in Korea, although the bulk of capital outflow during the financial crisis occurred in the stock market. It is to be noted that in terms of market capitalization and liquidity, the Korean stock market was the third largest emerging market and the fifteenth largest market in the world as of 1996.

16.2 Equity premium puzzle: theoretical background

In this section, the asset pricing theory underlying the equity premium puzzle is briefly outlined. This simple theory is then used to compute the excess equity returns over bills. Consider a representative agent who maximizes the expected time-separable power utility that increases with consumption, C, subject to a sequence of lifetime budget constraints comprising lifetime income and a given level of initial wealth.

$$\text{Max } E_0 \sum_{j=0}^{\infty} \delta^j \frac{C_{t+j}^{1-\gamma}}{1-\gamma},$$

where E_0 is the expectation formed at time 0, δ is the rate of time preference, and γ is the coefficient measuring the risk perception held by the representative agent. Solving this intertemporal problem yields the following bond pricing formula:

$$1 = E_t[(1 + R_{i,t+1})\delta(C_{t+1}/C_t)^{-\gamma}] \tag{16.1}$$

Note that E_t is the expectation conditional on information available at time t, R_i is the yield on a one-period bond i, C is the consumption, γ is the coefficient of relative risk aversion, and δ is the subjective rate of time preference. The joint conditional distribution of asset returns and consumption is assumed to be lognormal and homoskedastic.

It can be shown (see Campbell (1996) for derivation) that the log risk premium is defined as

$$E_t[r_{i,t+1} - r_{f,t+1}] + \sigma_i^2/2 = \gamma\sigma_{ic} \tag{16.2}$$

where r is the log gross real return, $\log(1 + R)$, on a risky asset i and a riskless asset f, and $\sigma_i^2/2$ is a Jensen's inequality adjustment.

Rewriting the equation, to remove the adjustment term, we get:

$$\log E_t[(1 + R_{i,t+1})/(1 + R_{f,t+1})] = \gamma\sigma_{ic} \tag{16.3}$$

This implies that the log risk premium can be determined by the coefficient of relative risk aversion (RRA) times covariance with consumption growth. This equation is employed to provide the theoretical basis for computing the empirical excess return.

16.3 Data and methodology

16.3.1 Business cycle

The dataset used in this study covers a broad spectrum of macroeconomic time series for Korea and Japan including financial and monetary variables: GDP, consumption (C), investment (I), government consumption (G), labour productivity, employment, the price level, financial markets indicators, and monetary aggregates. All data are quarterly, and taken from the following sources: International Financial Statistics (IFS) on CD-ROM, the Bank of Korea, National Statistical Office (NSO) of Korea, and the *Main Economic Indicators* (MEI) published by the OECD.[4]

Data for output, consumption, government spending, and investment are all expressed in real terms by the GDP deflator. The deflated variables are then transformed into natural logarithms. While there is no universal definition[5] of business cycle, the following decomposition is not rare:

$$y_t = \tau_t + c_t + e_t,$$

where a series for output, y, can be decomposed into 'trend' (τ), 'cycle' (c), and 'noise' (e).

Therefore, before documenting business cycle facts, one needs to remove the trend component (τ) from the data. A widely adopted procedure in business cycle literature is to use the Hodrick–Prescott (HP) filter, due to Hodrick and Prescott (1997), to extract the 'business cycle' or 'cyclical components' from the data. This filter is consistent with the business cycle definitions characterized by Lucas (1977).[6] The business cycle components obtained after filtering indicate fluctuations around the growth path with a frequency of 3–8 years (see Cooley and Prescott 1995).

16.3.2 Equity premium

The quarterly data used in this section are taken from the following sources: the Emerging Markets Data Base (EMDB) on CD-ROM published by the International Finance Corporation (IFC), Morgan Stanley Capital International (MSCI), and the Korean Stock Exchange (KSE). The measures of stock prices, dividends, and yields are defined and transformed in the following way.

Stock returns defined here are gross returns measured in local currency units. For Korea, two measures of stock returns are used. The first is to use the total return index taken from the EMDB, which computes stock price and total return indices both in local and US currencies from emerging markets for international investors. The data on total return index in local currency (TRLC) will be used for analysis. The IFC Global Index in which TRLC is a subset covers 70–75 per cent of total exchange market capitalization and is adjusted for corporate cross-holding and government ownership, but does not take foreign investment restrictions into account.[7]

The annualized percentage gross stock return can then be computed as follows.[8]

$$SR1 = [(TRLC_t - TRLC_{t-1})/TRLC_{t-1}] \times 400 \quad (16.4)$$
$$SR1' = (\ln TRLC_t - \ln TRLC_{t-1}) \times 400 \quad (16.4)'$$

An alternative measure of total stock return is to compute the *ex post* return as

$$SR2 = (P_{t+1} + D_t - P_t)/P_t \quad (16.5)$$

as used for annual data by Mehra and Prescott (1985).

Implementing this method using quarterly data requires a slight modification. For stock prices, KOSPI is used which is a market value weighted Laspeyres index for all listed common stocks. Unlike the IFC Global Index, this is the most comprehensive measure and works as a benchmark for local investors, although this data is likely to be more noisy.

To compute the *ex post* annualized percentage return, the following formula is used:

$$SR3 = [(KOSPI_{t+1} + DYMA_t - KOSPI_t)/KOSPI_t] \times 400 \quad (16.5)'$$

where $DYMA_t = [\Sigma_{j=0}^{3} DY_{t-j}/4]/4$ simple moving average of quarterly data on dividend yields (DY), assuming the dividend growth rate is constant within a year.

Stock returns on Japanese shares are computed using the MSCI gross return index. Many researchers use the MSCI data in analyzing the equity markets in developed countries (see, e.g.: Harvey 1995, Campbell 1999). To compute the stock returns for Japan, the formulas (16.4) and (16.4)′ are used.

The best proxy for the short-term riskless return would be the three-month or ninety-day treasury bills or notes. Unfortunately, these short-term debt instruments are not well traded in Japan and Korea although the long-term bonds are readily available. To qualify as a proxy for these, it should satisfy two things. First, it should be relatively default free, and second, it should generate a reasonable rate of return.

For Korea, the short-term money market rate (MM) included in the IFS is used to represent the returns on short-term debt instruments. Commercial Papers (CP) (91 days) are widely traded and were initially considered but ruled out due to its higher risk structure and much smaller sample period. The data period for the MM compiled by the IFS and used for computation of bill returns in this chapter is April 1976–April 1996.

For Japan, the rate on the lending rate on short-term loans and collateral is used to represent the return on short-term debt instruments. The data period covers January 1970–April 1996. For the notations used in this chapter and details on computation, see Appendix 16.1 at the end of the chapter.

16.4 Interpreting the evidence

16.4.1 Business cycles

Tables 16.1 and 16.2 show the cyclical properties of the major economic variables in Korea and Japan. Business cycle characteristics of the data are documented by

Table 16.1 Descriptive statistics for cyclical components of quarterly series for Korea, 1975/1980–96

Series	*Sample*	*Std. dev.*	*Cross-correlations of output* ($Corr(X_t +_k Y_t)$)												
			−6	*−5*	*−4*	*−3*	*−2*	*−1*	*0*	*1*	*2*	*3*	*4*	*5*	*6*
Real GDP	75:1 -	3.50	−0.21	0.08	0.43	0.01	0.03	0.36	1	0.36	0.03	0.01	0.43	0.08	−0.21
C (Non-durable)	75:1 -	2.77	−0.38	0.04	0.24	−0.14	−0.25	0.27	0.72	0.14	−0.14	0.22	0.48	0.03	−0.18
C (Durables)	75:1 -	8.88	−0.09	0.04	0.13	0.41	0.39	0.44	0.50	0.50	0.35	0.21	0.17	0.13	−0.06
I (Gross fixed)	75:1 -	11.2	−0.25	0.00	0.35	−0.02	0.06	0.37	0.81	0.28	0.15	0.22	0.46	0.05	−0.07
I (Equip. and machine)	80:1 -	7.63	−0.17	0.04	0.05	0.06	0.03	0.34	0.27	0.39	0.21	0.21	−0.13	0.12	−0.08
I (Non-residential bldg)	75:1 -	14.20	0.04	−0.15	−0.20	0.26	0.23	0.14	0.13	0.49	0.38	0.16	0.06	0.33	0.16
G (G. consumption)	75:1 -	6.31	−0.07	−0.10	−0.01	0.05	0.06	−0.02	−0.08	−0.03	−0.04	−0.00	0.03	0.05	0.00
Employed persons	75:1 -	4.20	−0.17	−0.19	0.31	0.27	−0.19	−0.24	0.42	0.35	−0.20	−0.34	0.25	0.26	−0.22
Hours worked	75:1 -	1.17	0.24	0.15	0.26	0.12	0.12	0.01	0.08	−0.02	−0.17	−0.27	−0.18	−0.15	−0.23
Wage (earnings)	75:1 -	3.33	−0.30	−0.18	−0.12	−0.02	−0.13	0.01	0.12	0.09	−0.03	0.05	0.20	0.24	0.08
Cap. utilization	75:1 -	4.09	0.13	0.26	0.31	0.39	0.52	0.57	0.53	0.37	0.23	0.10	0.01	−0.06	−0.15
Labour productivity	75:1 -	3.60	−0.28	0.03	0.33	0.06	−0.01	0.34	0.95	0.35	0.09	0.18	0.47	0.12	−0.13
Export	75:1 -	10.37	0.13	0.02	−0.11	0.22	0.22	0.12	−0.07	0.21	0.12	0.01	−0.16	0.14	0.06
Import	75:1 -	9.48	−0.34	−0.23	−0.21	−0.09	−0.09	0.10	0.15	0.34	0.22	0.22	0.16	0.35	0.23
Real interest rate	76:4 -	5.20	0.07	0.04	0.20	0.22	0.05	0.02	−0.14	0.01	−0.09	−0.40	−0.23	−0.22	−0.18
Stock price	75:1 -	17.58	0.15	0.15	0.15	0.25	0.27	0.22	0.19	0.17	0.11	−0.01	−0.03	−0.05	−0.02
Price (IPD)	75:1 -	4.66	−0.22	−0.15	−0.21	−0.38	−0.52	−0.29	−0.26	−0.35	−0.37	−0.03	0.13	0.00	0.02
Export price	75:1 -	4.99	−0.22	−0.19	−0.18	−0.19	−0.13	−0.00	0.12	0.13	0.16	0.20	0.21	0.21	0.19
Import price	75:1 -	5.87	−0.29	−0.39	−0.42	−0.40	−0.44	−0.41	−0.28	−0.16	−0.03	0.10	0.16	0.26	0.29
Exchange rate (won/$)	75:1 -	5.01	0.05	0.03	0.03	−0.23	−0.35	−0.40	−0.40	−0.43	−0.46	−0.37	−0.23	−0.16	−0.14
Money supply (M2)	75:1 -	2.73	−0.14	0.05	0.15	0.06	0.10	0.23	0.26	0.08	0.02	−0.01	−0.03	−0.17	−0.18

Table 16.2 Descriptive statistics for cyclical components of quarterly series for Japan, 1960–96

Series	*Sample*	*Std. dev.*	*Cross-correlations of output* ($Corr(X_t +_k Y_t)$)												
			−6	*−5*	*−4*	*−3*	*−2*	*−1*	*0*	*1*	*2*	*3*	*4*	*5*	*6*
Real GDP	60:1 -	1.70	−0.19	−0.06	0.09	0.29	0.50	0.72	1.00	0.72	0.50	0.29	0.09	−0.06	−0.19
C (Non-durable)	60:1 -	1.27	−0.19	−0.16	−0.07	0.07	0.15	0.24	0.40	0.32	0.31	0.27	0.16	0.10	0.05
C (durable)	60:1 -	2.25	−0.21	−0.15	−0.07	0.05	0.11	0.23	0.36	0.38	0.29	0.22	0.19	0.15	0.02
I (fixed private)	60:1 -	3.63	−0.16	−0.10	0.01	0.16	0.31	0.46	0.61	0.54	0.47	0.37	0.24	0.08	−0.01
I (Equipment and machinery)	60:1 -	6.12	−0.07	−0.03	0.04	0.13	0.26	0.38	0.50	0.50	0.47	0.37	0.22	0.07	−0.05
I (Nonres. buildings)	60:1 -	5.97	−0.05	−0.05	0.01	0.13	0.18	0.19	0.29	0.21	0.11	0.07	−0.02	−0.12	−0.14
Inventory	60:1 -	6.10	−0.13	−0.13	−0.06	0.05	0.21	0.36	0.47	0.47	0.43	0.32	0.17	0.02	−0.11
G (G. consumption)	60:1 -	1.26	0.10	0.10	0.15	0.13	0.09	0.07	0.05	−0.03	−0.04	−0.11	−0.18	−0.15	−0.10
Employment	60:1 -	0.64	−0.09	−0.10	−0.06	−0.01	0.15	0.21	0.23	0.21	0.26	0.24	0.17	0.07	0.02
Wage	60:1 -	2.04	0.01	−0.06	−0.04	−0.06	−0.06	−0.06	0.01	0.01	0.06	0.09	0.06	0.05	0.02
Hours worked	60:1 -	1.14	0.12	0.18	0.25	0.33	0.38	0.37	0.38	0.23	0.12	−0.04	−0.14	−0.28	−0.30
Labour productivity	60:1 -	1.65	−0.28	−0.19	−0.08	0.08	0.25	0.49	0.77	0.58	0.43	0.33	0.19	0.13	0.01
Export	60:1 -	7.60	0.14	0.14	0.10	0.07	0.04	−0.04	−0.09	−0.13	−0.11	−0.08	−0.02	0.03	0.04
Import	60:1 -	11.94	0.07	0.08	0.06	0.05	0.05	0.00	−0.04	−0.07	−0.07	−0.06	−0.04	−0.02	−0.01
Stock prices	60:1 -	11.34	−0.01	0.07	0.12	0.18	0.24	0.25	0.18	0.09	−0.02	−0.11	−0.19	−0.20	−0.19
Price (IPD)	60:1 -	1.74	−0.10	−0.15	−0.21	−0.25	−0.24	−0.19	−0.13	−0.10	−0.03	0.00	0.04	0.01	−0.02
Export prices	60:1 -	5.32	0.06	0.03	−0.03	−0.07	−0.10	−0.15	−0.19	−0.18	−0.12	−0.06	0.04	0.11	0.13
Import prices	60:1 -	11.21	0.14	0.13	0.10	0.06	0.01	−0.08	−0.17	−0.22	−0.24	−0.23	−0.17	−0.07	0.00
Exchange rate (¥/$)	60:1 -	7.95	0.19	0.23	0.25	0.22	0.18	0.08	0.00	−0.03	−0.04	−0.05	−0.02	0.05	0.04
M2 + CD	60:1 -	1.86	−0.17	−0.09	0.00	0.08	0.16	0.21	0.20	0.17	0.13	0.08	0.04	0.02	0.03

computing the estimates of the 'variability', measured by the standard deviation or variance, 'co-movement' measured by the contemporaneous correlations, and 'cyclical nature' measured by the cross-correlations with output.[9] A widely documented feature in the business cycle study for developed economies is that consumption is smooth and pro-cyclical while investment is very volatile and strongly pro-cyclical. The standard deviations of the non-durable consumption in both Korea and Japan are less than those of output, and the contemporaneous correlations with output are all positive. Investment is much more volatile than output while showing a strongly positive contemporaneous relationship with the output. This confirms the findings documented in previous work for other industrialized countries.

The cyclical property of government consumption appears to be country specific. It is weakly and negatively correlated with output in Japan while a weakly negative relationship is found for Korea. Considering that it is acyclical in the United States and weakly and negatively correlated in Australia, one cannot get a consistent finding on this. Employment appears to be pro-cyclical as expected a priori. However, the degree of volatility differs across countries. A consistent finding in work for the industrialized countries is that employment responds with a slight lag. Korean data on employment is an outlier in the sense that it fluctuates as much as output while the opposite is true for other countries. There is no consistency in the cyclical properties of the wage. Wages appear to be negatively correlated with the future output in both Korea and Japan. While wages appear to be acyclical in most developed countries, it appears to be counter-cyclical in Korea since the 1980s, although it is found to be pro-cyclical over the full sample. The counter-cyclical wages in Korea reflect the increase in wages growth in excess of productivity growth, which led to deterioration in the competitiveness of manufacturing products.

The cross-correlations of output with other variables are useful in identifying leading, coincident, and lagging indicators of business cycles. For Korea, stock price, export, capacity utilization, M2, real interest rate, price of imports, and the level of exports appear to be leading the cycles. This indicates that the Korean economy has been largely dependent on export over the decades. In particular, stock price appears to be a highly persistent indicator of future output level at forecasting horizons exceeding six quarters. This is extraordinary as the stock price fails to predict future output level exceeding four quarters from today in other countries studied (see, e.g. Harvey 1989 and Harvey 1993). Coincident indicators in Korea are consumption, investment, employment, labour productivity, and the wage rates while import and construction investment appear to be lagging indicators.

For Japan, stock price, exchange rate, and M2 are found to be the main leading indicators. The yen/US$ rate is leading the cycle in Japan by two to six quarters, which implies that the cyclical nature of output in Japan has been largely affected by this bilateral exchange rate. What distinguishes the Japanese leading indicators from those of Korea is that the information contained in the stock price cannot predict the future output level four quarters ahead, a finding also found for most developed economies. Overall, except for the labour market evidence, the business cycle statistics for Korea appear to be qualitatively consistent with the findings for Japan, the United States, and Australia.

Table 16.3 Market capitalization relative to GDP for Korea and Japan

Country	*Index source*	*Date*	*Market cap. (V_i) (billion of US$)*	*V_i/GDP_i (%)*	*No. of firms in the index*
Korea	IFC Global	1996	73.1	79.1	162
Japan	MSCI	1993	1,652	39.7	N/A

Note
The market capitalization reported here is only for those stocks included in the indices, which would include those between 60–75 per cent of the total market capitalization.

Table 16.4 Summary statistics for stock returns in Korea and Japan

Country	*Sample*	*Annualized mean (%)*		*Annualized Std. dev. (%)*		*Autocorr.*
		Arithmetic	*Geometric*	*Arithmetic*	*Geometric*	
Korea	76:1 -	19.04	15.38	27.03	25.47	0.20
	80:1 -	15.53	12.18	26.31	24.70	0.19
Japan	70:1 -	16.65	14.29	21.14	20.13	0.36
	80:1 -	15.57	13.27	21.19	20.06	0.33

16.4.2 *Stock market*

Table 16.3 reports the market capitalization in Korea and Japan. According to the IFC Global index in 1996, the market capitalization in Korea was approximately 79 per cent as a percentage of its GDP and US$73 billion. The market capitalization in Japan, however, was well in excess of US$1,650 billion in 1993. In terms of market capitalization, Korea is less than one-twentieth of that in Japan even under the conservative assumption that the market capitalization in Japan has not grown since 1993.

Table 16.4 reports average stock returns in Korea and Japan for the period to the fourth quarter of 1996. For the full sample, the average return is higher in Korea but when one considers a return in the post-1980 period, the Japanese stock return appears to be slightly higher than its Korean counterpart. The Korean stock returns are also found to be more volatile. The level of persistence in stock returns is captured by the first-order autocorrelation coefficient. By this measure, Japanese stock returns appear to be more persistent. The high volatility and low autocorrelation imply that predicting stock returns in Korea is a very difficult exercise.

Turning to the bill returns in Korea and Japan, Table 16.5 reports that average bill returns in Korea are very high, two to three times those of Japan. These returns are *ex post* nominal returns in which the inflationary expectations were realized, implying higher expectation of the changes in the price level in Korea.

Table 16.6 provides summary statistics on consumption and dividend in Korea and Japan. The average consumption growth in Korea is almost twice that of Japan, and in particular, the consumption growth in Korea is positively correlated with dividend growth while these features are not observed in the Japanese data. This implies that consumption data contains some useful information that can be

Table 16.5 Summary statistics for bill returns in Korea and Japan

Country	*Sample*	*Mean (%)*	*Std. dev. (%)*	*Autocorr.*
Korea	76:4 -	14.13	3.87	0.93
	80:1 -	13.26	3.59	0.86
Japan	70:1 -	6.58	1.60	0.95
	80:1 -	5.96	1.57	0.94

Table 16.6 Summary statistics for consumption and dividend growth

Country	*Sample*	*Consumption* (Δc)			*Dividend* (Δd)			*Corr.*
		Mean	*S.D.*	$\rho 1$	*Mean*	*S.D.*	$\rho 1$	(Δc, Δd)
Korea	76:1 -	6.94	6.78	−0.15	−10.15	32.29	−0.02	0.15
	80:1 -	6.52	3.28	0.07	−14.62	32.38	0.00	0.20
Japan	70:1 -	3.66	2.28	−0.16	−5.00	20.52	0.27	−0.16
	80:1 -	2.94	1.46	−0.12	−4.12	22.20	0.24	−0.09

Table 16.7 The equity premium puzzle in the Korean and Japanese data

	Sample	$\mu(er)$	$\sigma(er)$	$\sigma(\Delta c)$	ρ *(corr.)* (*er*, Δc)	*Covariance* (*er*, Δc)	*RRA 1*	*RRA 2*
Korea	76:4 -	3.72	25.84	5.32	−0.034	−4.61	−80.78	2.71
	80:1 -	2.11	25.22	3.28	−0.095	−7.87	−26.79	2.55
Japan	70:2 -	6.83	21.60	2.35	0.100	5.09	134.12	13.44

Note

The estimates for the Japanese data are taken from Campbell (1999), which covers the sample period February 1970–February 1996. The data period for Korea runs through December 1996.

used to forecast dividend growth in Korea. Table 16.7 reveals what the data say about the equity premium puzzle in Korea and Japan. The table reports the average excess log return on stock over bills, standard deviations of the excess log return and consumption growth, the correlation and covariance of the excess log return and consumption growth, and also estimates of the relative risk aversion coefficient.

The estimate of equity premium over bills in Korea is much lower than that in Japan while the volatility is higher. Not only is the volatility of stock returns higher in Korea but the volatility of consumption is also high. This implies that risks implicit in holding the stock in Korea is higher than in Japan but the reward for bearing these risks is low in Korea. Moreover, consumption pattern in Korea appears to be susceptible to shocks that may hit the economy. This has an important welfare implication for short-term economic fluctuations as this can lead to erratic reactions in consumption without room for gradual consumption adjustment.

At any point in time, however, the correlation of consumption and excess return is found to be low. This seems an interesting phenomenon because, as in Table 16.6, the consumption growth is positively correlated with the growth in dividend yields. It implies that short-term consumption decisions are not affected by the excess returns on stocks. A plausible interpretation is that financial investors face a higher degree of risk in the market, in which environment the economic agents are reluctant to materialize any short-term capital gains from holding stock into increased consumption.

What is however puzzling is that despite such a risk perception held by investors in Korea, the excess return over bills was surprisingly low. This can be partially answered by computing the RRA coefficients implied in the asset-pricing model. Two risk aversion coefficients are computed. The estimates of RRA1 reported in Table 16.7 indicate that investors in the stock market in Korea are risk-seeking. This behaviour is not significantly altered even if the risk aversion coefficient is recomputed assuming a perfect correlation between the stock return and consumption growth. The RRA2 computed in this manner is 2.71 for the entire sample and 2.55 for the later sample period. As these estimates are point estimates, allowing for standard errors of estimates, it would be difficult to reject the hypothesis that the true risk aversion coefficient is close to zero.

Campbell (1999) examined eleven industrialized countries to see whether or not the equity premium puzzle was a robust international phenomenon. None of the countries Campbell examined shows a feature of very low excess return and negative risk aversion simultaneously unlike Korea. Korea would have been an outlier if included among this group of countries considered by Campbell (1999).

Another possible interpretation is that there had been some economic catastrophe that depressed, if not destroyed, almost all stock market value, which is very unlikely in reality. In the industrialized countries, a good example of this catastrophe that was a disaster for stockholders but did not adversely affect holders of short-term debt instruments is the Great Depression. For the peso problem to be a plausible candidate as an explanation for the Korean evidence, a sequence of the catastrophes must have occurred almost continuously over the last two decades, which is hardly convincing. Although the peso problem[10] may be inherent in historical economic and financial data such as exchange rates, there is no reason to believe that the peso problem is a problem only found in Korea. Hence the peso problem *per se* is very unlikely to be considered a plausible explanation for the Korean evidence.

Moreover, this could mean that the stock market and the market for short-term debt instruments are viewed differently by both market participants and investors. One can potentially relate this concept to the risk-seeking behaviour of the Korean financial investors. But the remaining puzzle is the implication that taking a risk in the short-term money market is highly rewarded while, taking a higher level of risk in the organized exchange is not adequately compensated. That is, during the sample period, both financial investors and borrowers in Korea seem to have shown a strong preference for hoarding short-term debt instrument or money market over stock market.

This could imply a segregation of financial markets in Korea. It is highly probable that investors and corporate borrowers have quite different perceptions of the stock market relative to money market. The explanation of market segregation is potentially very important, as one needs to look into the institutional as well as the market structure to provide a full and plausible theoretical explanation for this kind of behaviour.

There is much work to be done in order to properly model the financial returns in Korea and this would require a careful modeling of institutional regimes and microeconomic behaviour of market participants, which would be an ongoing research project.

16.5 Concluding remarks

A variety of symptoms can foreshadow economically difficult times ahead. It is often difficult to distinguish symptoms of a short-term nature from those that are long-term. While a country can enjoy high growth coupled with strong productivity growth, a country is more likely to be prone to a serious economic instability, if abnormal and persistent characteristics in the financial markets are long left ignored, however it might appear to be unrelated to the 'economic fundamentals' in the eye of the policy makers.

This chapter attempted to document some historical properties of business cycles and stock returns in Korea relative to Japan using selected time-series data. Throughout this chapter, a dichotomy of 'real sectors' vs 'financial sectors' was maintained because this chapter was not an attempt to provide a theoretical linkage between the real activity and financial markets. Some stylized facts were presented in relation to the cyclical behaviour of macroeconomic time series in both Korea and Japan. These facts were then compared with those found in the work for other industrialized countries. What distinguishes Korea from other countries such as Japan and other industrialized countries in terms of the characteristics of the historical time-series data is the puzzling behaviour of equity returns over the comparable bill returns.

While the phenomenon of high equity premium over bill returns has been termed a 'puzzle' by theoretical economists, this phenomenon has appeared to be a robust 'normal' feature in the international financial data. This has been at least a feature of markets in the industrialized countries. The Korean data, however, reveal quite the opposite. The *ex post* real return of the bills has often outperformed that of the equity, contradicting the conventional wisdom and anecdotes found in the finance literature. This chapter provides some interpretations and implications of the Korean evidence in financial returns. Peso problem, risky attitude, and market segregation were all considered as possible explanations.

While explaining this 'puzzling' phenomenon using a theoretical model should be left for future research, a feasible starting point in this line of research would be to consider the market segregation from a micro-structural perspective.[11] This chapter provides a preliminary but empirical basis for interpreting the empirical evidence in connection with the recent financial crisis in Korea. Empirically examining the asset market along with business cycle properties yields very important welfare implications of macroeconomic fluctuations. In an economic environment, where consumption growth is strong but unstable, and heavy preference towards short-term money market is prevalent, any external shock to the economy is almost certain to have a serious welfare cost of short-term fluctuations.

This chapter concludes with the interpretation that this may have been a long-held but largely ignored symptom that could lead to serious economic instability such as the recent financial crisis experienced by Korea. This is an important welfare implication that policy makers should take into account when policy trade-offs between growth and macroeconomic stability lie ahead.

Appendix 16.1

Filtering the data for business cycle analysis

To extract the business cycle components from the time-series data, the data filtering method suggested by Hodrick and Prescott (1997) is used.

The HP-filter is based on the following minimization problem:

$$\min_{\{g_t\}} \left\{ \sum_{t=1}^{T} c_t^2 + \lambda \sum_{t=2}^{T-1} [(g_{t+1} - g_t) - (g_t - g_{t-1})]^2 \right\}$$

where the cyclical or 'business cycle' component $\{c_t\}$ of a log time series $\{y_t\}$ is defined as deviations from the growth component $\{g_t\}: c_t = y_t - g_t$.

The value for the smoothing parameter, λ, is set at 1,600, which is well accepted for quarterly data series.

Computing the equity premium (see also the notes for Table 16.7)

The average excess log return is the left-hand side of equation (16.3) multiplied by 400 to express it in annualized percentage point. Annualized standard deviation of the excess log stock return can then be computed by multiplying the quarterly return by 200. The notations and computation details are as follows. The average excess log return on stock over bills adjusted for the variance of this excess return is

$$\mu(\text{er}) = [\,\overline{r_i - r_f} + \sigma^2(r_i - r_f)/2] \times 400$$

where r_i the log return on stock $[= \log(1 + R_i)]$; r_f the log return on bills $[= \log(1 + R_f)]$; σ the variance of the excess return, $r_i - r_f$.

Also, the following notations are used in Tables 16.1–16.7. $\sigma(\text{er})$ is the standard deviation of the excess return; $\sigma(\Delta c)$ the standard deviation of the log real consumption growth rate, times 200 in quarterly data; $\rho(\text{er}, \Delta c)$ correlation between the excess log stock return and consumption growth; $\text{Cov}(\text{er}, \Delta c)$ covariance between the log stock return and consumption growth: $\sigma(\text{er}) \times \sigma(\Delta c) \times \rho(\text{er}, \Delta c)$.

Relative risk aversion (RRA) coefficients are computed as follows. RRA1 is $100 \times \mu(\text{er})/\text{cov}(\text{er}, \Delta c)$, a measure of risk aversion computed from equation (16.3). RRA2 is $100 \times \mu(\text{er})/\sigma(\text{er})\ \sigma(\Delta c)$, a measure of risk aversion computed assuming perfect correlation between stock returns and consumption growth (see Mehra and Prescott (1985)).

Notes

1 An earlier version of this research was presented to the Biennial Conference of the Korean Studies Association of Australia and at the University of New South Wales. I wish to thank the conference and seminar participants for their comments. I am also grateful to Professor John Campbell for making his data appendix available. I wish to thank the editors of this book for their encouragement and generosity. Any errors are my own.

2 See, for example, Stock and Watson (1989), Harvey (1989), Bernanke (1990), Chen (1991), Estrella and Hardouvelis (1991), and Plosser and Rouwenhorst (1994), for the United States and other OECD nations, and Lowe (1992) and Kim (1998) for Australia.

3 High debt to equity ratio, overexposure to short-term debt denominated in US dollars and Japanese yen, structural imbalances due to the government's emphasis on growth rather than on profitability, moral hazard, and inappropriate government policies were all blamed.

4 Quarterly series of national accounts data are available from both the IFS and the Bank of Korea website. Monetary and financial series are available from the Bank Of Korea website. Quarterly series of labour market data are available from the NSO website.

5 There are two broad definitions of business cycles: classical and growth. To qualify for the classical cycles, there should be an absolute decline in the level of output for at least two consecutive quarters, for example, see Burns and Mitchell (1946). The growth cycle does not require an absolute decline in output but a decline below growth or the trend path. For many East Asian countries in which persistent and high growths were a norm, growth cycles would be more of interest to policy makers and business firms. However, the recent financial crisis in Korea resulted in absolute declines in the level of output, hence being a classical recession.

6 The HP Filter is consistent with the 'growth cycles', not the classical cycles.

7 The methodology is quite similar to that of Morgan Stanley's MSCI (see The IFC Indexes: Methodology, Definitions and Practices 1997).

8 Note that the geometric mean will always be less than or equal to the arithmetic mean. (see, e.g., Harvey 1995, Bekaert and Harvey 1995, Goetzmann and Jorion 1997).

9 Due to the space constraint, standard errors for the point estimates were not reported in the tables.

10 A peso problem is basically a sample problem due to infrequent important events such as war and regime breakdown or shifts.

11 I am grateful to Drs Glenn Otto, Graham Voss, and Lance Fisher for providing their insights concerning this issue.

Bibliography

Bank of Korea (1988) 'Korean financial system: history in stock market', The Bank of Korea Home Page. Available Online, <http://www.bok.or.kr>.

Bekaert, G. and Harvey, C. (1995) 'Time-varying world market integration', *Journal of Finance*, 50(2): 403–44.

Bernanke, B.S. (1990) 'On the predictive power of interest rates and interest rate spreads', *New England Economic Review* (Nov/Dec): 51–68.

Burns, A.F. and Mitchell, W.C. (1946) *Measuring Business Cycles*, New York: National Bureau of Economic Research.

Campbell, J. (1996) 'Consumption and the stock market: interpreting international experience', *Swedish Economic Policy Review*, 3: 251–99.

——(1999) 'Asset prices, consumption, and the business cycle', in J. Taylor and M. Woodford (eds), *Handbook of Macroeconomics*, Amsterdam: North-Holland.

Campbell, J., Lo, A., and Mackinlay, C. (1995) *The Econometrics of Financial Markets*, Princeton University Press.

Chen, Nai-fu (1991) 'Financial investment opportunities and the macroeconomy', *Journal of Finance*, 46: 529–44.

Cooley, T. and Prescott, E. (1995), 'Economic growth and business cycles', in T. Cooley (ed.), *Frontiers of Business Cycle Research*, New Jersey: Princeton University Press.

Estrella, A. and Hardouvelis, G.A. (1991) 'The term structure as a predictor of real economic activity', *Journal of Finance*, 46(2): 555–76.

Fisher, I. (1907) *The Rate of Interest*, New York: Macmillan.

Fisher, L.A., Otto, G., and Voss, G. (1996) 'Australian business cycle facts', *Australian Economic Papers*, 35(67): 300–20.

Goetzmann, W. and Jorion, P. (1997) 'Re-emerging markets', National Bureau of Economic Research Working Paper No. 5906, Cambridge.

Harvey, C.R. (1989) 'Forecasts of economic growth from the bond and stock markets', *Financial Analysts Journal*, 45: 38–45.

——(1995) 'Predictable risk and returns in emerging markets', *Review of Financial Studies*, 8(3): 773–816.

Hodrick, R.J. and Prescott, E.C. (1997) 'Postwar US business cycles: an empirical investigation', *Journal of Money, Credit, and Banking*, 29(1): 1–16.

Hu, Z. (1993) 'The yield curve and real activity', *IMF Staff Papers*, 40(4), December: 781–806.

Kaldor, N. (1957) 'A model of economic growth', *Economic Journal*, 67: 591–624.

Kim, D. (1998) 'The term structure of interest rates in a simple stochastic growth model: evidence from Australian data', Working Paper Series in Economics No. 98.02, University of Sydney.

——(1999) 'International business cycles in South East Asia and Japan: an empirical investigation', paper presented at *The 1999 Australasian Meeting of the Econometric Society* held at University of Technology, Sydney.

Kim, K. and Choi, Y. (1997) 'Business cycles in Korea: is there any stylized feature?', *Journal of Economic Studies*, 24: 275–93.

Lowe, P. (1992) 'The term structure of interest rates, real activity and inflation', Reserve Bank of Australia Discussion Paper No. 9204.

Lucas, R.E., Jr (1977) 'Understanding business cycles' in K. Brunner and A.H. Meltzer (eds), *Carnegie-Rochester Conference Series on Public Policy*, 5: 7–29.

Mehra, R. and Prescott, E. (1985) 'The equity premium puzzle', *Journal of Monetary Economics*, 15: 145–61.

Merton, R. (1973) 'An international capital asset pricing model', *Econometrica*, 41: 867–87.

Plosser, C.I. and Rouwenhorst, K.G. (1994) 'International term structures and real economic growth', *Journal of Monetary Economics*, 33: 133–55.

Stock, J.H. and Watson, M.W. (1989) 'New Indexes of coincident and leading indicators' in Olivier J. Blanchard and Stanley Fischer (eds), *NBER Macroeconomics Annual*, Cambridge: MIT Press, 4: 351–93.

17 The role of FDI in the recovery of the financial crisis in Korea

The bilateral economic relationship between Korea and Australia under APEC

Hyung-Min Kim

17.1 Introduction

International trade has served the world economy in many profitable ways. Many of the economies in the world have enjoyed rapidly increasing economic growth through promoting trade activities and developing more extensive trade patterns. However, the world economic order has seen the emergence of a new tendency, 'regionalism', which 'discriminates' in favour of intra-regionally-driven members and against non-members. Realising that discriminatory regionalism is a main cause of reduction in global welfare, the economies in the Asia-Pacific region came together to develop the idea of the Asia-Pacific Economic Cooperation (APEC).

Despite the progress of the APEC process over time, increasing concern over the uncertainty of the success of the process has remained. A major cause of the concern is the economic disparities among the member economies which have led to the realisation of the importance of reducing the economic and technological gap, and the creating of the Economic and Technical Cooperation (Ecotech) agenda to promote more extensive cooperation. In this context, promotion of technology flows in the region is a main agenda item. However, the economic diversity has necessitated the development of a new channel to maximise potential gains for both developed and developing economies.

The evolution of APEC has seen the acceleration of bilateral economic relationships between member economies. One significant relationship which has rapidly emerged is bilateral economic ties between the Republic of Korea (hereafter, Korea) and Australia. The period of financial crisis in Korea has provided opportunities to restructure its economic patterns and to realise the significance of foreign direct investment (FDI) in sustaining its economic growth. At the same time, it also has provided opportunities for the bilateral economic relationship between Korea and Australia to realise mutual benefits by increasing bilateral investment and developing a strategic approach to technology cooperation in advanced industrial sectors.

17.2 The evolution of APEC

17.2.1 The establishment of APEC

Decades of dedicated regional discussions have achieved significant contributions in defining a new approach to regional economic cooperation within the special constraints of a politically and economically diverse region (Garnaut 1999: 35). The two main arguments have focused on the ways in which economic regionalism can be compatible with and support a multilateral trade regime. The first is that grouping national economies into several blocs reduces the number of actors in collaborative efforts to manage the global economy, thereby facilitating international cooperation (Hellmann and Pyle 1997: 162). The second is the notion of 'open regionalism', which is fully supportive of and complementary to the multilateral system. The call for strengthening the multinational trading system and stimulating open and free trade and investment in the world economic order has inspired the economies in the Asia-Pacific region to form APEC a new regional forum.

APEC is now a 21-member organisation. The region is now one of the most diverse and the fastest growing economic regions in the world, including major economies such as the United States, Japan, and China. The Asia-Pacific region is a huge market containing three sub-regional groups (ASEAN, CER, and NAFTA), with a total population of 2.5 billion, and incorporating about half of world output and almost half of world trade. In particular, the intra-regional exports among member economies show remarkable interdependence in sharing outflows of trade, most of them reaching above 70 per cent of total exports (see Table 17.1).

17.2.2 The development of arrangements in APEC

APEC has matured in various ways and now incorporates three main meetings (Leaders', Ministerial, and Senior Officials'), and is effectively divided into sections such as Working groups, Committees, and Eminent Persons Group (EPG). Each year since its formation, APEC has rapidly evolved towards a freer environment for trade and investment in the region, taking a significant step forward. One of the most significant steps taken by member countries was the symbolic and historical gathering of all the APEC leaders, except the leader of Malaysia, in Seattle in 1993. At this summit, the leaders issued a vision statement in which they pledged to support an expanding world economy and an open multilateral trading system (Ching 1995: 36). After Seattle, the second summit was held in Bogor in Indonesia in 1994. At this meeting, another milestone in the development of the APEC process was an agreement on the specific target dates of 'Vision 2010' for developed economies, and for developing economies, 'Vision 2020' with regards to free and open trade and investment in the region. To achieve the goals, a clear guidance of the 'Action Agenda' was announced and confirmed at the next summit in Osaka, Japan in 1995. The Osaka Action Agenda (OAA) includes two major categories – the trade and investment liberalisation programme, the trade facilitation programme, and the programme for 'Ecotech'. At the Manila meeting in 1996, the leaders of the APEC member economies declared that APEC work has shifted from 'Vision' to 'Action' under the rubric of 'the Manila Action Plan for APEC' (MAPA) (Omura 1997: 21).

Table 17.1 APEC member statistics, 1999

APEC member economies	*Population*			*GDP*			*Exports to APEC* ratio (%)*
	(Millions)	*Ratio (%)*		*US$ (billions)*	*Ratio (%)*		
		APEC	*World*		*APEC*	*World*	
Australia	18.9	0.8	0.30	365.1	2.2	1.25	75.6
Brunei	0.3	0.0	0.01	4.9	0.0	0.02	76.5
Canada	30.3	1.2	0.48	603.8	3.7	2.06	90.3
Chile	14.8	0.6	0.24	72.9	0.4	0.25	53.6
China	1,248.1	49.8	19.93	960.9	5.9	3.28	73.9
Chinese Taipei	21.9	0.9	0.35	261.6	1.6	0.89	78.1
Hong Kong	6.7	0.3	0.11	166.0	1.0	0.57	76.3
Indonesia	204.0	8.3	3.26	103.1	0.6	0.35	76.0
Japan	126.5	5.1	2.02	3,806.0	23.3	12.00	74.5
Korea	46.4	1.9	0.74	310.1	1.9	1.06	66.5
Malaysia	22.2	0.9	0.35	73.3	0.4	0.25	78.2
Mexico	95.8	3.8	1.53	424.5	2.6	1.45	89.5
New Zealand	3.8	0.2	0.06	52.7	0.3	0.18	70.9
Peru	24.8	1.0	0.40	62.8	0.4	0.21	49.7
PNG	4.3	0.2	0.07	0.0	0.0	0.01	72.8
Philippines	75.2	3.0	1.20	65.1	0.4	0.22	79.4
Russia	147.1	5.9	2.35	276.5	1.7	0.94	19.9
Singapore	3.8	0.2	0.06	84.4	0.5	0.29	76.9
Thailand	61.5	2.5	0.98	116.9	0.7	0.40	70.6
United States	270.0	10.8	4.31	8,511.0	52.1	29.08	61.2
Vietnam	78.1	3.1	1.25	24.6	0.2	0.08	70.9

Source: APEC Economic Outlook 1999: 2, 94.

Note
* The figures are as of 1996.

Moreover, MAPA included the Individual Action Plans (IAPs) for each member economy, encouraging sincere implementation of trade liberalisation and investment facilitation. The APEC member economies are a diverse group at various levels of economic development and structure. IAPs have invited the individual member economies to work towards the same goal of trade liberalisation and investment facilitation at an individually appropriate pace.

As well as the ongoing process for the ultimate goal of APEC, in 1997 another demand was forced during the preparation for the fifth Leader's Meeting in Vancouver, Canada. In other words, this was the so-called financial crisis that occurred in Thailand in 1997 and spread to Indonesia and Korea, destabilising the Asian and world financial market (Ahn 1999: 14). A high priority was to provide relief to the crisis-hit member economies, and the financial ministers of the member economies played a significant role for APEC. Meanwhile, Early Voluntary Sectoral Liberalisation (EVSL) was launched with the endorsement of fifteen sectors. Given the spread of the economic crisis to other regions, a further challenge was forced the following year in Kuala Lumpur, Malaysia of overcoming and sustaining the continuing crisis in the region. This resulted in a lack of concrete outcomes from EVSL. As a consequence, the seventh Summit hosted in New Zealand in 1999 identified four goals: (1) to achieve further substantive progress towards trade and investment liberalisation and facilitation; (2) to shape a credible response to the economic crisis; (3) to reinforce the capacity of institutions and human resources in the region to deal with the economic challenge they face; and (4) to build broader support for APEC among the wider community (Ahn 1999: 16). With the rapidly progressing stage of overcoming the economic hurdles in the crisis-affected member economies, it is anticipated that continuous support will be given to the previously initiated APEC arrangements to sustain the process for freer trade and investment in the region.

17.3 The Ecotech agenda

17.3.1 The creation of the Ecotech agenda

One major hurdle in pursuing further implementation of the APEC process was the increasing gap in the level of infrastructure between the developed and developing member economies. The member economies have come to the realisation that throughout the development of APEC arrangements, developed member economies have overemphasised the lifting of trade and investment impediments, which existed mainly in the developing members, and devoted too few efforts to promoting economic and technology cooperation (Omura 1997: 149). Finally, it has been perceived that concerted efforts to reduce economic and infrastructure disparities between developed and developing APEC economies will provide a more significant contribution to the promotion of equitable development in the region, rather than achieving this by further reduction of trade barriers. Given the strong call for the development of a balanced programme, combining economic and technical cooperation with efforts to reduce economic disparities among APEC economies was given a high priority at the third Summit in Osaka, leading to the creation of 'Ecotech'. At the next Summit in Manila, the Declaration of a Framework of Principles for Economic Cooperation and Development articulated a new model of development cooperation as follows:

> the principles of mutual respect and equality, mutual benefit and assistance, and consensus building underpinning APEC economic and technical cooperation forcefully shifts the nature of economic cooperation from the 'old style donor-donee' relationship that characterised past foreign aid relationships. Instead, the APEC relationship points toward joint responsibilities and 'pooling' of resources, expertise and technology for commonly agreed activities.
>
> (Omura 1997: 18)

The declaration included the following three characteristics: (1) economic and technical cooperation in APEC must be result-oriented with explicit objectives, milestones, and performance criteria; (2) cooperation can be implemented by combining government actions with private/business activities to achieve sustainable growth and equitable development in the region, and (3) the cooperation must create shared benefits among APEC economies, based on voluntary contributions and complementary capabilities of the economies (Omura 1997: 18). These characteristics indicate that the effectiveness of the economic and technical cooperation among APEC member economies is limited without the participation of a private sector. The vitality of private flows in the APEC process can be reflected in potential benefits such as financial assistance in more sophisticated joint activities among member economies. So far, some 320 joint activities, some 151 sub-activities, and some 220 projects have been extensively pursued by the member economies (Ro and Ahn 1997: 15). In the implementation of the projects, it is strongly anticipated that private participation will increase contributions to the building of more sophisticated complementarity among member economies. Through the partnership between the government and the business sector, it is highly likely that the Ecotech agenda will be a vehicle, leading member economies to widening, balancing and deepening mutual benefits that are more visible to both developing and developed economies.

17.3.2 The significance of FDI in the Ecotech agenda

There are several sub-regional agreements in the Asia-Pacific region, including NAFTA and ASEAN. The fact that thirteen member economies of APEC share sub-regional membership within the APEC region strongly suggests that the sub-regional promotion of trade and investment will stimulate the entire process of regional affairs of APEC. In particular, the trade share among member economies shows strong intra-regional economic dependence. As noticed in Table 17.2, the APEC member economies share almost 70 per cent on average of their total exports and imports among themselves. In addition, the average of intra-regional trade of the three regional arrangements within APEC is over 70 per cent, with ASEAN being the highest with 74 per cent. This large trade expansion among member economies of the sub-regional arrangements within APEC strongly implies that the sub-regional arrangements will further build up economic confidence as the basis for potential gains from regional economic activities towards the APEC process.

Table 17.2 Trade matrix for major APEC sub-regions in 1998 (US$ billion)

	NIES3	*ASEAN7*	*CER*	*NAFTA*	*APEC*	*World*
Japan	63	46	9	130	272	388
China	49	10	3	41	135	184
NIES3	47	36	7	102	299	417
ASEAN7	41	70	9	73	245	333
CER	10	7	6	8	47	67
NAFTA	51	41	15	522	719	1,009
United States	48	39	14	233	416	680
Other APEC	2	1	1	11	24	93
APEC	263	213	50	887	1,740	2,490
World	344	265	71	1,207	2,373	5,487

Source: Okuda 2000: 33.

Since the establishment of the Ecotech agenda in the APEC process, it has become more compelling for the individual member economies to further endeavour to promote profit-creating and cost-saving trading patterns. One main area in this process is the fast development of intra-APEC flows of FDI, rising from US$965 billion of inward and outward FDI among APEC member economies during the 1980s, to US$1,737 billion during the four years from 1995 to 1998. The major players for outward investments were the United States and Japan. However, there has been a growing tendency in recent years that NIES3 become active investors, with the ratio of GDP equalling 22 per cent in 1998. In addition, it can be noticed that Newly Industrialized Economies (NIE3's) (Korea, Taiwan, and Hong Kong) NIES3's outward investment for the period 1995–98 recorded US$ 128 billion, which exceeded Japan's figure of US$98 billion. The presence of FDI in ASEAN was large, and the balance to GDP ratio recorded as much as 34 per cent in 1998. Another noticeable fact is that in the 1990s, inward investments increased drastically in China, indicating the significance of an FDI host of APEC capital (see Table 17.3).

The pursuit of stronger economic and technical cooperation in the region is one of the distinguishing characteristics of APEC, compared to other regional or international forums or organizations (Elek 1997: 68). In this context, the increasing intra-regional FDI in the APEC region has a profound meaning for developing APEC economies since it not only provides a source of finance to develop their

Table 17.3 Flow and estimated balance of FDI in APEC (US$ billion)

	Flow			*Estimated balance, end of 1998*	*Balance/ GDP (98, %)*
	*1980–89**	*1990–94**	*1995–98**		
Inward					
Japan	2	7	7	11	0
China	15	80	164	198	20
NIES3	20	22	35	51	7
ASEAN5	39	75	98	144	34
ANZ	48	36	43	77	18
NAFTA	395	256	540	792	8
United States	331	194	451	647	7
APEC21	524	486	927	1,316	2
Outward					
Japan	144	131	97	215	6
China	4	12	9	17	2
NIES3	28	75	128	166	22
ASEAN5	4	19	38	45	10
ANZ	28	17	17	35	8
NAFTA	233	321	510	750	8
United States	188	290	435	646	7
APEC21	441	578	810	1,238	2

Source: Okuda 2000: 10.

Note

* Total flow during the indicated period. The stock of inward and outward FDI of each sample economy was calculated by summing up the annual respective flows allowing for a depreciation rate.

industries, but also typically involves the transfer of technology and management expertise, which is widely perceived to have spillover benefits (BIE 1995: 24). For the active economies in the APEC region, it has been deeply perceived that reduction of the technological gap between developed and developing member economies provides an environment more conducive to profit-sharing in performing the activities. The APEC Eminent Person Group also observed that the flow of new technology among the member economies stimulates economic development, intensifies scientific and technological capabilities, stimulates trade and investment liberalisation, and alleviates disparities among APEC economies (Omura 1997: 116). Through the establishment of the Ecotech agenda, the member economies have embarked on technical cooperation, taking a closer step to the success of the trade and investment liberalisation and facilitation (TILF) process. Moreover, through freer flows of technology, it is most likely that further progress will follow, and that more active cooperation will be carried out. The flow of technology has developed in many ways. Historically, one commonly used form to increase technological flow is through technology transfer, and this form is still widely practised in more sophisticated ways. The channel between private sectors will be mainly discussed in this study since it is through this channel that the most complicated technologies are transferred and sophisticated methods applied.

Technology transfer is both a dynamic and complex activity in the sense that it involves human interactions and entails a wide range of knowledge and long experience for successful performance (KITI 1991: 42). In transferring technology, one particular commonly used channel is the so-called 'North–South channel' (i.e. technology transferred from industrially advanced economies to less advanced ones). This channel has, however, created two main criticisms – (1) the technology transferred is often too modern in terms of technology absorption capability in host countries, and (2) most R&D activities are conducted in home countries, preventing the development of core technologies in host countries (Enos *et al.* 1997: 56). In other words, when technology is transferred to a less technologically advanced country, catching-up may be impossible since the difference in technological capability might be so great that the backward country cannot possibly apply or diffuse the advanced technology (Tho 1991: 33). In this regard, the compelling question in regard to technology transfer should be how rapidly and effectively the technology transfer process will occur, rather than whether advanced technologies will be transferred. One of the models that demonstrates the existing inefficiency of the North–South channel is the Yamashita's Black Box Model (Yamashita 1996: 29). More specifically, the model implies that the North–South channel has contributed insufficient technological transfer as well as managerial transfer to the process of production in host countries, leaving locals only simple tasks such as preliminary processing and assembling. However, the model does not describe the specific disadvantages that host countries have when the North–South channel is applied. As Figure 17.1 reveals, the egg is the technological capability of the home country transferring technology to the host country. The activities required to absorb imported technologies for the host country such as spinning out skilled workers, providing technical guidance to subcontractors, bringing in new capital goods and technology, introducing

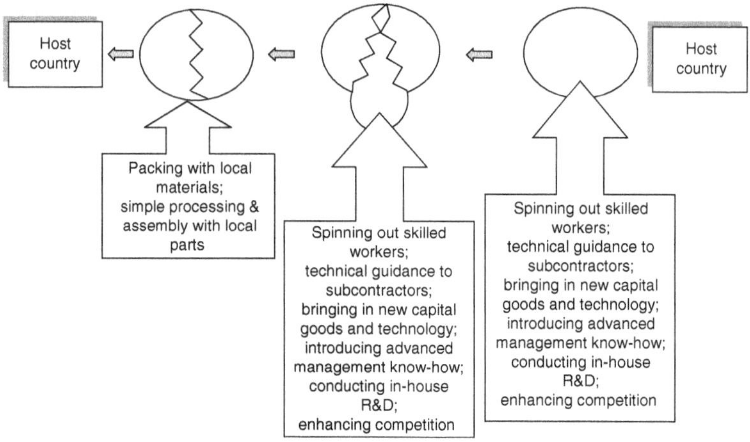

Figure 17.1 The egg without the yolk transferred from a home country to a host country.

advanced management know-how, conducting in-house R&D, and enhancing competition also need to be possessed by the host country since they are interrelated in accumulating the new technologies. However, in many cases, given the fear of losing access to new markets or distribution channels, the home country avoids sharing the key activities, using the imported components in which advanced technologies are applied.

Overall, the success of technology transfer requires interaction between the increase in technological inputs from the technology donor and technological progress from the technology recipient. Furthermore, the process of technology transfer should be coupled with proper demand based on sufficient technological capability, equipped with a supporting environment for both technology recipient and donor. Due to the large gap of technological capability between the two parties, it is, however, unfortunate that the existing patterns for technology transfer are lacking in most of the cases in the North–South channel.

APEC is a fast-developing and fast-changing organisation. For the dynamic economies in the region, the traditional 'catch-up' approach in technology transfer can no longer sustain growth that relies on leading-edge products and processes (Turpin and Spence 1996: 9). In addition, although the member economies have shown firm responses to the importance of promoting technology transfer in the region, in reality, there has been limited participation by developing member economies in the Ecotech projects since many of the projects have been divergent from the developing economies' actual requests (Ahn and Han 1998: 14). Here, there is a strong need for developing a new channel in transferring technology in more problem-solving and concrete-results-providing ways among the member economies. In the meantime, middle-sized economies have successfully absorbed advanced technologies with sufficient personnel who have received professional training previously, and have now acquired leading technologies in many industries.

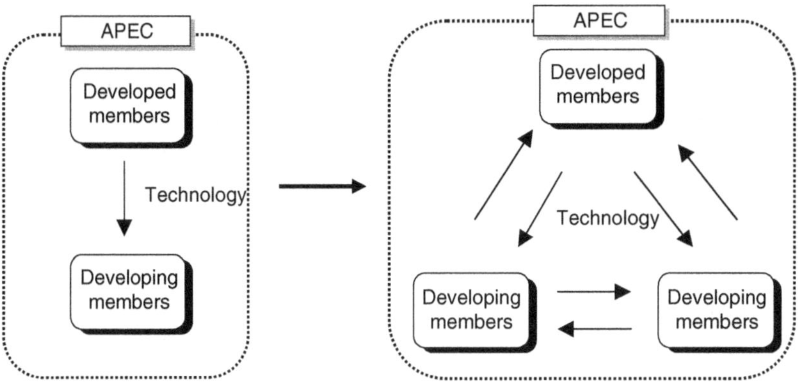

Figure 17.2 Paradigm of more vigorous technical cooperation in a new channel.

In this context, exchange of transfer of comparatively advanced technologies between middle-sized economies can be more beneficial due to the provision of a similar level of industrialisation equipped with sufficient infrastructure. In other words, instead of less technologically developed economies merely being receivers of intended technology, more economic benefits can be provided to both transferees and transferors by exchanging their comparatively advanced technologies between middle-sized economies. In doing so, it can be anticipated that more active participation in transferring technology, and more appropriate transfer of technology can be performed. This argument is supported by the concept of an 'optimal technological gap' stressed by Chen (1985 in Tho 1991: 32). When technology is transferred within a narrow level of technological gap, more active participation in technology transfer and better performance of appropriate transfer can be anticipated. As shown in Figure 17.2, it is highly probable that a new channel will bring more economic benefits to both participants. In addition, it is highly probable that structural development in technology transfer will provide a more balanced relationship between developed and developing member economies of APEC in persuading the ultimate goal of the liberalisation and facilitation process of trade and investment in the region.

17.4 The changing bilateral economic relationship between Korea and Australia

17.4.1 The increasing significance of FDI in sustaining the Korean economic growth

Korea's industrial structure has been transformed from concentration on a light and labour-intensive industry (1960s) to a heavy and capital-intensive industry (1970s–80s), and to a capital-intensive and high value-added technology-intensive industry (1990s) (Hong 1998: 24). The economic growth patterns of Korea have rapidly evolved and transformed, culminating in Korea becoming the eleventh trading country in the world. Meanwhile, the international competitiveness of the economy is a different story, with Korea ranked as the thirty-fifth competitive economy among the forty-five economies evaluated (IMD 1998). This implies that unbalanced efforts have been taken towards increasing trading volume and improving technological capability. In other words, Korea has been unsuccessful in attracting a large amount of FDI relative to the size of its economy. Korea acquired mature technologies mainly from the United States and Japan. Due to the heavily regulated inward FDI policy with a preference for foreign borrowing in Korea, the diminution of investment from the two has been encountered over the last decade. The main reason for this is the reserved public attitude towards FDI, caused by the fear of foreign domination. Albeit a temporary success, becoming the twenty-ninth member of the OECD realigned the Korean FDI regime with international norms and standards. However, the basic position towards FDI remained a passive one. In other words, the government allowed FDI into a number of business categories and activities, but was not interested in removing various impediments in promoting FDI in general (Kim 1999: 11).

Many economists have called the economic and financial crisis in Korea a necessary evil. Albeit belated, the Korean government finally came to the understanding that FDI plays a pivotal role in boosting the domestic economy and sustaining its long-term growth. In addition, as a recent research project conducted by the Korea Institute for International Economic Policy (KIEP) reveals, a lack of FDI or FDI-related debt in total debt increases the probability of currency crashes (Kim and Hwang 1998: 32). As can be seen in Table 17.4, further evidence indicates that countries like Malaysia could endure or overcome the recent economic crisis without being forced to resort to the IMF bail-out loans due to the dominant presence of multinationals (Kim and Hwang 1998: 25).

Given the clear understanding of the significance of promoting FDI in Korea, the government has taken more tangible actions such as allowing hostile cross-border Merger and Acquisitions (M&As), enacting the Foreign Investment Promotion Act, and ending most restrictions on foreign land ownership in 1998. In particular, as shown in Table 17.5, the enactment of the Foreign Investment Promotion Act indicates the government's commitment to achieving freer flows of FDI into Korea. This legislation covers almost all existing regulations, focusing on creating an investor-oriented policy environment by streamlining foreign investment procedures, expanding investment incentives and establishing an institutional framework for investor relations, including a one-stop service (Kim 1999: 12). Moreover, the Committee for Regulatory Reform was established under the

Table 17.4 Comparison of incoming FDI between Korea and Malaysia (US$ billion)

	1993	*1994*	*1995*	*1996*
Korea	0.6	0.8	1.8	2.3
Malaysia	5.0	4.3	4.1	4.7

Source: UNCTAD/ICC 1998.

Table 17.5 Major points of the 1998 investment promotion act in Korea

Objectives	*Measures*
Simplified procedures	• Streamline the investment notification system. • Expand the number of institutions accepting notifications and applications. • Abolish the notification requirement for the arrival of induced foreign capital and mandatory requirement of using a resident agent.
Transparent and liberalised regulations	• Reduce the number of provisions regulating FDI from 66 to 36. • Proclaim no restrictions on FDI in principle unless the preservation of national security, public order, public health, environment, or social morals are threatened. • Announce each year all laws and regulations relevant to investment.
Expanded incentive system	• Increase tax incentives-tax reduction and exemption periods. • Provide greater autonomous power to local governments in the fields of local tax and rent reduction and tax exemption. • Expand the number of high technology manufacturing and service industries where tax reductions are available for foreign investors from 265 in seven sectors to 516 in nine sectors. • Expand the rental period for national and local government activities to promote FDI by providing funds and public subsidies.
One-stop service system	• Establish the Korea Investment Service Centre to assist foreign investors with each other facet of the investment process. • Expedite approval or authorisation procedures by establishing a Comprehensive Process System; where, if the main points of a process package is approved, approval is then given and supplemental items are reviewed afterwards. • Introduce the Automatic Authorisation System where, if there is no response to an investment application for approval or authorisation within a given period, approval or authorisation shall be automatic.
Free Investment Zones	• Establish Free Investment Zones (FIZs) to induce large-scale FDI. • Give greater autonomy for designating, developing, and maintaining FIZs to local governments.

Source: Hong 1998: 16.

Prime Minister's Office in order to review the remaining regulations to deregulate them. Besides the deregulations, various benefits can be provided to foreign invested firms in Free Investment Zones (FIZs), such as tax benefits, infrastructure support, receive lower utilities rates (Kim 1999: 30).

In the immediate aftermath of the Korean financial crisis, the investment climate in Korea was decidedly negative. However, intensive efforts exerted by the government and the private sector to induce more foreign direct investment and technology transfer, along with the liberalisation and deregulation drive, resulted in a series of positive outcomes (Hong 1998: 40). As Table 17.6 shows, the recent trend (from July 1998 to November 1998) has shown a substantial month-to-month increase, implying that increasing numbers of foreign firms have taken advantage of the opportunity created by the economic and financial crisis in Korea. The Foreign Investment Promotion Act was enacted in November 1998. Having the largest expansion of the monthly growth in November, it can be noted

Table 17.6 The statistics of current incoming FDI in Korea (1996 – 98.11) (US$ million)

	1996	1997	1998							
			Jan.–Mar.	Apr.–Jun.	July	Aug	Sept.	Oct.	Nov.	Jan – Nov
Amount	3,203	6,971	572	1,889	1235	407	534	894	1,378	6,909
	(65.0)	(117.6)	(−73.1)	(−19.3)	(203.4)	(128.7)	(23.3)	(147.6)	(1,414)	(16.4)
Number of cases	968	1,055	309	370	100	96	145	88	117	1,227
	(11.0)	(9.0)	(20.7)	(45.1)	(16.3)	(5.5)	(79.0)	(2.3)	(54.0)	(31.8)

Source: KIEP 1998: 31

Note
The figures in the brackets are the increased and decreased rate compared to the previous year.

that the government's trust-building efforts to establish a freer environment for incoming FDI in Korea were well appreciated by foreign investors. Considering all of the trends, it is highly likely that FDI inflows into Korea will continue to increase in the future as long as the government continues to make progress in providing a FDI friendly environment.

17.4.2 The bilateral role for Korea and Australia under the Ecotech agenda

Since the 1960s, trade opportunities based on complementarity have driven the emerging bilateral economic relationship between Korea and Australia. Two-way trade between Korea and Australia has increased noticeably during the 1990s. This view is further reflected by the fact that Korea has overtaken New Zealand to become Australia's third largest export market in 1990, behind only Japan and the United States (Dupont 1992: 14). Within the following four years, Korea overtook the United States as Australia's second largest export market (EAAU 1999: 119). While this ranking has slipped as a consequence of the financial crisis in Korea in 1997, Korea is still the third largest export market for Australia after Japan and the United States, and fourth largest trading partner overall (Endres 2001). In 1998, the rapid increase of bilateral trade share between Korea and Australia led to Australia becoming Korea's sixth largest trading partner (Endres 2001).

The previous decade shows the growing trading volumes in the bilateral economic relationship. As can be seen in Figure 17.3, two-way trade flows between Korea and Australia have increased rapidly from 1989–90 to 2000–01, marking A$27 billion and A$92 billion in 1989–90 and 2000–01 respectively for Australia's exports to Korea, and A$12 billion and A$47 billion in 1989–90 and 2000–01, respectively for Korea's exports to Australia. Meanwhile, Australia has been a strong export destination for Korea throughout the 1990s, with the average growth rate of 15 per cent. Although the share of Australia's exports to Korea has fallen off during the years between 1996–97 and 1998–99 when Korea was hit by the financial crisis, the share has rebounded, recording the growth of approximately A$22 billion from A$25 billion in 1996–97 to A$47 billion in 2000–01. During these years, the average growth rate has been 18 per cent, and this rate is far

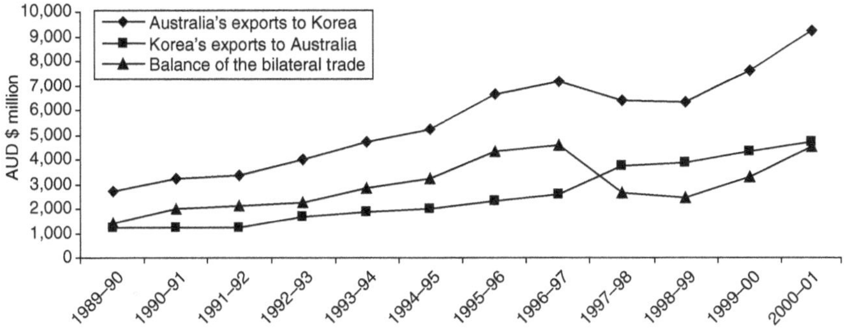

Figure 17.3 Bilateral trade share between Korea and Australia.

Sources: ABS 1999; ABS 2001, 5422.0.

greater than the average growth rate of Korea's exports to other major export markets such as Japan and China over the same period of time (EAAU 1999).

The trade complementarity between the Korean and Australian economies is primarily based on the differences wherein Korea imported raw materials, principally minerals and energy, and then processed and sold on domestic and international markets as finished products. In return, Australia purchased increasing volumes of Korean manufactured products, initially textiles, clothing and footwear, and later, automobiles (EAAU 1999: 119). This view is further emphasised when commodity-specific two-way trade is investigated. Australia's main export items to Korea are mainly natural resources such as crude materials, inedibles, lubricants, and related materials (see Table 17.7). Although the Korean domestic consumption for most of the items imported from Australia decreased during the financial year of 1997–98 due to the financial crisis in Korea, the overall Korean import volumes from Australia has not dropped severely, and took only one year to regain the share of Australian exports in the Korean market. One of the changing patterns of the Australian export flows to Korea is that Australia has taken a larger Korean domestic market share in manufactured goods, and machinery and transport equipment. In particular, the growth rate of Australia's exports in manufactured goods, and machinery and transport equipment to Korea from the financial year of 1989–90 to the year prior to the financial crisis in Korea, 1995–96, is 160 and 990 per cent, respectively. This is far greater than those of the items such as food and live animals, and crude materials. It can be said that Korea has come to the realisation that mutual benefits can be further created from extended complementarity in the two-way trade share.

With regard to Korean exports to the Australian market, the total Korean exports to Australia have increased without any fluctuation throughout the 1990s. Three of the largest Korean exporting items to Australia from the financial year of 1989–90 to 1998–99 are manufactured goods classified chiefly by material, machinery and transport equipment, and miscellaneous manufactured articles. The annual growth

Table 17.7 Australia's merchandise exports to Korea (A$ million)

SITC code & commodity	*1989–90*	*1990–91*	*1991–92*	*1992–93*	*1993–94*	*1994–95*	*1995–96*	*1996–97*	*1997–98*	*1998–99*
Food and live animals	289	391	357	262	224	278	243	483	252	324
Crude materials, inedible, except fuels	789	873	1,015	1,096	1,037	1,145	1,077	1,029	1,146	1,417
Mineral fuels, lubricants and related materials	526	608	722	946	998	1,005	1,101	1,196	1,420	1,333
Chemical and related products	54	47	53	66	90	100	99	110	105	106
Manufactured goods classified chiefly by material	467	585	540	539	704	730	746	727	606	747
Machinery and transport equipment	41	106	111	163	254	383	406	408	412	259
Miscellaneous manufactured articles	45	54	65	78	85	85	102	111	102	79
Commodities and transactions not classified elsewhere in the SITC*	486	564	499	810	1,295	1,517	2,832	3,052	2,340	2,047
Total Australian exports to Korea	2,700	3,237	3,365	3,970	4,706	5,250	6,615	7,134	6,397	6,320

Source: ABS 1999, 5422.0.

Note
* Includes export commodities subject to a confidentiality restriction.

rate of these items has been consistently increasing. In particular, as can be seen in Table 17.8, the growth rate of machinery and transport equipment between the financial year of 1989–90 and 1998–99 is 510 per cent. This reflects the strong demand of Australian customers for Korean finished products.

Foreign Direct Investment plays a pivotal role in promoting economic growth between host and recipient country through various channels. Expected contributions from FDI in a bilateral relationship can be allocation of resources such as natural resources, capital, and technologies, and provision of market access and marketing channels in other countries. In the case of the bilateral relationship between Korea and Australia, as compared to the dynamic two-way trade flows, the industrial distribution of bilateral investment between the two countries is at a low level. As of March 2001, the cumulative total amount of Korea's investment in Australia reached US$889 million in 217 cases (Table 17.9). Remarkably, the amount of Korea's investment in Australia in the year that Korea was severely hit by the financial crisis, 1997, was more than US$150 million for the first time. This accounts for 18 per cent of the cumulative total of Korea's investment in Australia. Furthermore, the total amount of Korea's investment in Australia during the four years from 1997 to 2000 accounts for almost half of the cumulative total of Korea's investment in Australia since 1968. These figures show not only the significance of Australia as an attractive market for Korean investors, but also that the investment patterns in the bilateral relationship have been extended from investment only in resource-intensive industries to capital and technology-intensive industries. In addition, it can be said that the Korean government's endeavour to reduce the weight of dependency on foreign sources for securing natural resources through various diversification policies has provided a positive outcome, leading to Australia taking a larger share of the total of Korea's FDI abroad.

When Korea's investment in Australia is compared to Australia's investment in Korea, there is a remarkable imbalance in the amount of investment, that is, the two-way investment has been in favour in Australia. The imbalance of the cumulative total of Korea's investment in Australia and Australia's investment in Korea is US$492 million (see Table 17.10). Although there are differences in the economic structures of the two countries both should be encouraged to make joint efforts to develop further strategies in order to improve both economic ties and imbalances. In addition, together with the recent enactment of the Foreign Investment Promotion Act, the FDI environment in Korea has been more favourable than ever before.

Before the financial crisis occurred in Korea in early 1998, the Korean government had maintained a reserved attitude towards incoming FDI for various reasons, such as protection of the domestic market in particular industries. However, the financial crisis has led to the reduction of barriers that discouraged or prevented incoming FDI, and presented various initiatives for foreign investors. In other words, the Korean government has switched its policy on FDI from 'restriction and control' to 'promotion and assistance' (Kwon and Oh 2001: 5). As can be seen in Figure 17.4, the total FDI inflows in Korea reached US$15,541 million in 1999, with the number of cases reaching 2,086, which increased from the previous year at the growth rate of 49 per cent for the number of cases and

Table 17.8 Korea's merchandise exports to Australia (AUD $ million)

SITC code & commodity	*1989–90*	*1990–91*	*1991–92*	*1992–93*	*1993–94*	*1994–95*	*1995–96*	*1996–97*	*1997–98*	*1998–99*
Food and live animals	22	18	21	21	19	21	18	18	23	30
Crude materials, inedible, except fuels	9	7	8	7	8	12	13	7	8	10
Mineral fuels, lubricants and related materials	6	3	7	20	10	14	14	13	20	23
Chemical and related products	66	52	64	105	125	142	170	159	160	163
Manufactured goods classified chiefly by material	434	397	429	462	504	568	539	542	658	729
Machinery and transport equipment	360	457	402	813	960	1,014	1,322	1,543	1,973	1,838
Miscellaneous manufactured articles	257	252	230	219	177	160	154	134	148	153
Commodities and transactions not classified elsewhere in the SITC*	96	65	51	49	78	98	62	132	776	948
Total Korean exports to Australia	1,254	1,254	1,213	1,696	1,882	2,028	2,293	2,550	3,767	3,894

Source: ABS 1999, 5422.0.

Note
* Includes import commodities subject to a confidentiality restriction.

Table 17.9 Korea's investment in Australia (US$ million)

	1992	*1993*	*1994*	*1995*	*1996*	*1997*	*1998*	*1999*	*2000*	*The cumulative total*
No. of cases	5	3	18	20	29	36	18	15	11	217
Amount	16	32	18	59	51	158	132	22	105	889

Source: KOTRA 2001.

Table 17.10 Australia's investment in Korea (US$ million)

	1992	*1993*	*1994*	*1995*	*1996*	*1997*	*1998*	*1999*	*2000*	*The cumulative total*
No. of cases	1	5	2	12	3	8	11	10	18	95
Amount	0.07	10.3	0.5	6.9	3.2	5.7	3	276	79	397

Source: KOTRA 2001.

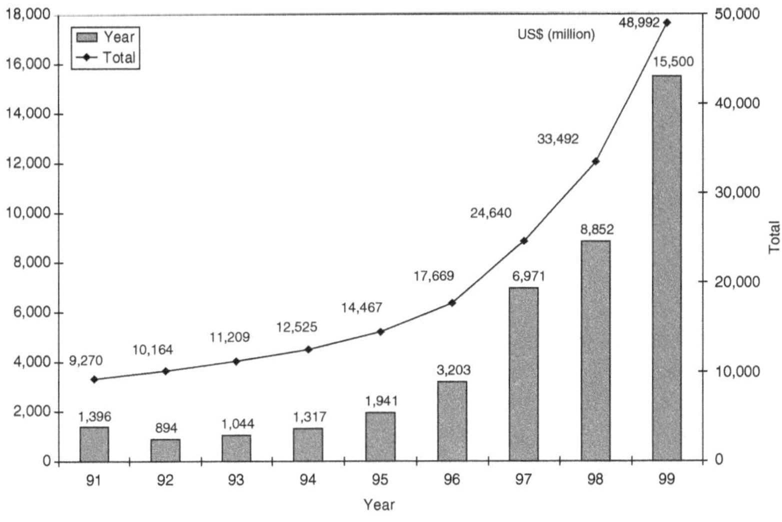

Figure 17.4 Total FDI inflows in Korea.

Source: MOCIE 2000: 2.

75.6 per cent for the amount. Furthermore, from the year that Korea started investing directly in overseas markets for the first time (1962) to the year prior to the financial crisis in Korea (1997), the cumulative total of the investment amount is US$246 million. It is remarkable that it took merely two years to double this amount, with the total amount of US$ 244 million from 1998 to 1999. This substantial increase implies that increasing numbers of foreign firms have taken advantage of the opportunity created by the economic and financial crisis in

Korea. Considering all of the trends, it is highly likely that FDI inflows into Korea will continue to increase in the future as long as the government continues to make progress in providing a FDI friendly environment.

As global competition intensifies, technology change and liberalisation of trade and capital movements have become key priorities for many countries in their industrial globalisation process. One phenomenon caused by the restructuring of industrialisation on a global scale during the last decade is the increasing number of cross-border business activities. One particular mechanism that has rapidly evolved in this globalisation process for industrial restructuring is cross-border M&As. In this context, Korea shows strong signs of becoming a more attractive market for M&As for foreign investors. The value of inward M&As between 1997 and 1999 increased substantially from US$0.64 billion to US$10.08 billion at the annual growth rate of 363 per cent. This remarkable growth strongly suggests that the government's effort to build a transparent and competitive industrial environment with a minimum of interference and regulatory stance has provided confidence for foreign investors in forming strategic relations with Korean counterparts. The case of Australia also shows a strong increase of the value of inward and outward cross-border M&As, implying high concentration of the internationalisation process in local firms. In this regard, in order to construct a more sophisticated bilateral relationship between Korea and Australia, there should be stronger mutual awareness of the significance of bilateral commitments to strategic technology cooperation models, such as cross-border M&As (Figure 17.5).

Realising that advancement of technology will provide the basis for economic growth in the twenty-first century, the governments of Korea and Australia have increasingly recognised the significance of bilateral technology cooperation in advanced technology industries such as information and communication technologies (ICT) sector. There is evidence of the bilateral cooperation in this sector such as the operation of the Code Division Multiple Access (CDMA) system by Korean firms in Sydney and Melbourne (The Korea Herald 1999: April 15). The two firms signed an agreement on export of their systems management expertise and dispatch of engineers to run operating and maintenance centres in two Australian cities (The Korea Herald 1999: April 15). This exchange of technology transfer presents opportunities to exploit the comparative advantages of each country. They include relatively high hardware capability and active involvement of large-scale businesses for Korea, a sufficient highly educated and skilled workforce; stable, developed and orderly legal, business and government environments, and well established competition policy for Australia. Korea and Australia now need a new competitive strategy to build a more sophisticated bilateral cooperation. The new strategy should be based on technology and innovation. The strategy must promote a competitive advantage based on differentiation of the two. To this end, stronger bilateral commitments to an efficient R&D strategy and active inducement of FDI in more sophisticated sectors for exchange of technology transfer between the two are required. With the spirit of the Ecotech agenda, Korea and Australia are undoubtedly of great importance to each other in creating potential gains from technical cooperation for further evolution of the bilateral economic relationship and APEC as a whole (Figure 17.6).

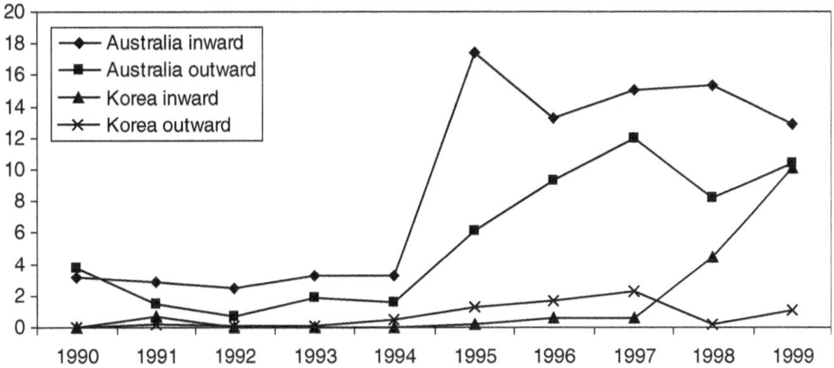

Figure 17.5 Inward and outward cross-border M&As in Korea and Australia (US$ billion).

Source: OECD 2001.

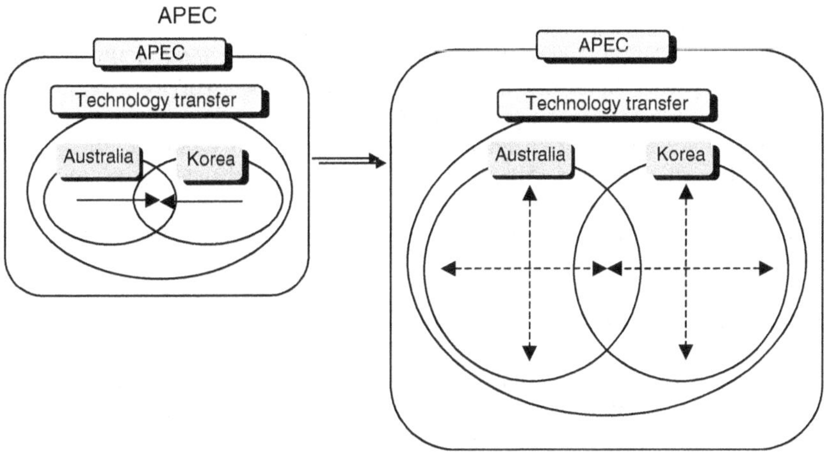

Figure 17.6 Paradigm of closer bilateral economic relationship on the evolution of APEC.

17.5 Conclusion

The world economy is faced with the need to cope with the changes towards 'regionalism' and 'globalism'. In order to strengthen the new world economy for the upcoming twenty-first century, the fruition of these changes cannot be delayed any further. Fortunately, the formation of APEC has clearly encouraged guidance of the changing world patterns towards an open and free environment for trade and investment. To this end, member economies have come to realise the significance of technical cooperation among member economies, and of initiating the Ecotech agenda for the achievement of the ultimate goal.

The Ecotech agenda needs to persuade member economies to further proceed with the process for free and open trade and investment in the region. One major area of the agenda is promoting technology transfer. Given the constant criticisms of inefficient results from the North–South channel, the development of a new channel to maximise the potential economic gains for both developed and developing member economies has been an urgent need. One of the suggested options to meet this need can be 'exchange of technology transfer'.

Based on a clear view that the Asia-Pacific region is the most important region to both Korea and Australia in economic terms, the two close economies share common interests in playing a leading role for the technical cooperation under the Ecotech agenda. Given the opportunities from the economic and financial crisis of Korea, it is suggested that both should encourage one another in exchanging technology transfer in technology-driven industries such as ICT industries, in order to enlarge mutual economic gains. In so doing, more vigorous and broad economic and technical cooperation in the APEC region will be unavoidable.

Bibliography

Ahn, Hyungdo (1999) *APEC After 10 years: Is APEC Sustainable?* KIEP Working Paper 99-08, Seoul: Korea Institute for International Economic Policy.

——and Han, Hongyul (1998) *APEC's Ecotech: Linking ODA and TILF*, KIEP Working Paper 99-08, Seoul: Korea Institute for International Economic Policy.

APEC Economic Outlook (1999), Singapore: APEC Secretariat.

——(1999), 'International merchandise trade', Australia, 5422.0, Canberra.

Australian Bureau of Statistics (ABS) (2001), 'International merchandise trade', Australia, 5422.0, Canberra.

Bureau of Industry Economics (BIE) (1995) 'Potential gains to Australia from APEC: open regionalism and the Bogor declaration', Occasional Paper 29, Canberra: Australian Government Publishing Service.

Chen, Edward K.Y. (1985) *The Newly Industrializing Countries as Exporters of Technology in Asia-Pacific*, Paper presented to the Sixth Meeting of the Association of Development Research and Training Institute of Asia and the Pacific (ADIPA), Bangkok, June.

Ching, Frank (1995) 'APEC mustn't lose momentum: lack of progress in Osaka would be a serious blow', *Far Eastern Economic Review*, 158(30): 36.

Dupont, Alan (1992) *Australia's Relations with the Republic of Korea: An Emerging Partnership*, Australia-Asia Paper No. 58, February, Griffith University.

East Asia Analytical Unit (EAAU) (1999) *Korea Rebuilds: From Crisis to Opportunity*, Canberra: Department of Foreign Affairs and Trade.

Elek, Andrew (ed.) (1997) *Building an Asia-Pacific Community: Development Cooperation within APEC*, Brisbane: The Foundation for Developing Cooperation.

Endres, James (2001) *The Asian Financial Crisis and Its Impact on Korea-Australia Economic Relations*, Australia-Korea Paper No. 4, Brisbane: Griffith University.

Enos, J.L. (1989) 'Transfer of Technology', *Asian-Pacific Economic Literature*, 3(1): 3–37

——, Lall, S., and Yun, M. (1997) 'Transfer of technology: an update', *Asian-Pacific Economic Literature*, 11(1): 56–66.

Garnaut, Ross (1999) *APEC Ideas and Reality: History and Prospects*, A Paper presented at the 25th Pacific Trade and Development Conference, Osaka, July 16–18, 1999.

Hellmann, Donald C. and Pyle, Kenneth B. (eds.) (1997) *From APEC to Xanadu: Creating a Viable Community in the Post-Cold War Pacific*, New York: M.E. Sharpe, Inc.

Hong, Yoo-Soo (1998) *Technology-Related FDI Climate in Korea*, KIEP Working Paper 98-15, Seoul: Korea Institute for International Economic Policy Islam.

International Institute for Management Development (IMD) (1998) *World Competitive Report*

——(1997) *World Competitive Report.*

Kim, June-Dong (1999) *Inward Foreign Direct Investment Regime and Some Evidences of Spillover Effects in Korea*, KIEP Working Paper 99.09, Seoul: Korea Institute for International Economic Policy.

——and Hwang, Sang-In (1998) *The Role of Foreign Direct Investment in Korea's Economic Development: Productivity Effects and Implications for the Currency Crisis*, KIEP Working Paper 98.04, Seoul: KIEP.

Korea Institute of Industry & Technology Information (KITI) (1991) *Technology Transfer among Developing Countries*, Seoul: Korea Institute of Industry & Technology Information.

Korea Institute for International Economic Policy (KIEP) (1998) *The Shortcut to Overcoming the Economic Crisis*, KIEP Working Paper 98.13, Seoul: KIEP.

Kwon, O. Yul and Oh, I. (2001) *Korean Direct Investment in Australia: Issues and Prospects*, Australia-Korea Paper No. 5, Brisbane: Australian Centre for Korean Studies.

Ministry of Commerce, Industry and Energy (MOCIE) (2000) *A Reference Report on Foreign Direct Investment*, Seoul.

Okuda, Satoru (ed.) (2000) *Industrial Linkage and Direct Investment in APEC*, APEC Study Centre publications in FY 1999/2000, Japan.

Omura, Keiji (ed.) (1997) *The View of Economic and Technology Cooperation in APEC*, APEC Study Centre: Institute of Developing Economies.

Organization for Economic Cooperation and Development (OECD) (2001) *New Patterns of Industrial Globalisation: Cross-border Mergers and Acquisitions and Strategic Alliances.*

Ro, Jaebong and Ahn, Hyungdo (1997) *APEC's Eco-Tech: Prospects and Issues*, Seoul: Korea Institute for International Economic Policy.

The Korea Herald, 'KTF, Hansol to export CDMA operating expertise to Australia', 15 April 1999.

Tho, Tran Van (1991) *Technology Transfer in the Asian Pacific region: Implications of Trends since the Mid-1980s*, JCER Discussion Paper No. 19, JCER and Obirin University.

Turpin, Tim, and Spence, Heather (1996) *Science and Technology, Collaboration and Development Among Asia-Pacific Economies*, Issue Paper No. 2, Melbourne: The Australian APEC Studies Centre.

United Nations Conference on Trade and Development (UNCTAD)/International Chamber of Commerce (ICC) (1998) *The Financial Crisis in Asian and Foreign Direct Investment.*

Yamashita, Shoichi (1996) *Technology Transfer for Upgrading the National Capabilities of Technology Absorption*, IDEC Research Paper Series No. 1, Hiroshima: IDEC Hiroshima University.

Electronic references

Korea Trade Investment Promotion Agency (KOTRA) (2001) 'Request for investment data'. E-mail (10 December 2001).

18 Korea's FTA policy

Background and current progress[1]

Inkyo Cheong

18.1 Introduction

Though Korea achieved economic growth through export-oriented growth policy, its reaction to a widening spread of regional trading blocs has been lukewarm due to domestic opposition to a market opening under regional trading agreements (RTAs). However, since the financial crisis began, the Korean government has been re-evaluating the potential gains to be made by removing trade barriers on a preferential basis, and has decided to pursue the establishment of preferential trading blocs.

A free trade agreement (FTA) eliminates tariffs and improves non-tariff barriers (NTBs), stimulating trade for member nations while limiting imports from non-member nations at the same time. In an effort to avoid the negative effects of exclusion from such agreements, to maintain economic reform and an open policy, and to actively cope with proliferating regionalism, the Korean government has decided to pursue FTAs with other nations.[2] Forming FTAs will enable Korea to create political allies, attract foreign investment, and establish overseas footholds, as well as allow Korean companies to secure foreign export markets and overcome discriminatory practices under other FTAs.

Following the introduction, Section 18.2 examines the background of Korea's FTA policy, since the financial crisis. Section 18.3 describes the FTAs that Korea is currently considering. There has been some criticism over Korea's pursuit of an FTA with Chile. This chapter argues in Section 18.4 that the government of Korea decided to negotiate the bilateral FTA with Chile after considerable discussions. Section 18.5 discusses the need for an FTA with Japan, emphasizing that, despite many obstacles, a Korea–Japan FTA is strategically significant and offers various economic benefits. To conclude, in Section 18.6, the author stresses that Korea's long-term FTA goal should be to establish an East Asian FTA, towards which the FTA with Japan would be the first step.

18.2 Background of Korea's FTA policy

One major reason for Korea's new thinking on regionalism is the trade diversion caused by the growth of RTAs. A WTO (1995) report discusses the causes of the rapid increase in the number of RTAs in the early 1990s. The report concluded that there was a growing trend of using regionalism as an insurance policy in the event of the failure of the Uruguay Round negotiations. An implication of that conclusion is that regional integration initiatives would be weakened as the multilateral trading system became firmly established. Yet following the inauguration of the WTO, regional trading blocs have continued to expand both in number and in scope.

Regionalism is one of the most dominant trends in the world economy today. There were only twenty-six new RTAs reported to GATT prior to 1969.[3] Following a weakening in the pace of regional integration in the 1980s, the number of RTAs exploded in the 1990s. Thirty-five additional RTAs were signed during the two years of 1995 and 1996, and seventeen such agreements were concluded in 1997 and 1998. This demonstrates that major trading countries view regionalism as a viable commercial strategy that complements multilateral trade agreements rather than simply a type of insurance policy taken against the potential shortcomings of multilateral trade liberalization (Figure 18.1).

In line with this increasing trend towards regional integration and to minimize the losses from it, Korea has altered its past position of opposing RTAs and is now cautiously investigating the possibility of establishing FTAs with major trading countries. Korea's decision to pursue FTAs was motivated not only by a fear of exclusion from the recent trend of growing regionalism, but also by the outbreak of the Asian financial crisis. Korea has opened most of its financial sectors to foreign investors and has implemented unilateral trade liberalization measures.

Korea's new trade policy is aimed at promptly adapting to the changing economic environment, as well as resolving the nation's economic difficulties. Consequently, the ultimate goal of this policy is to transform Korea into an 'open trading country', which makes a meaningful contribution to opening up the world economy at the international level. At the national level, the government remains

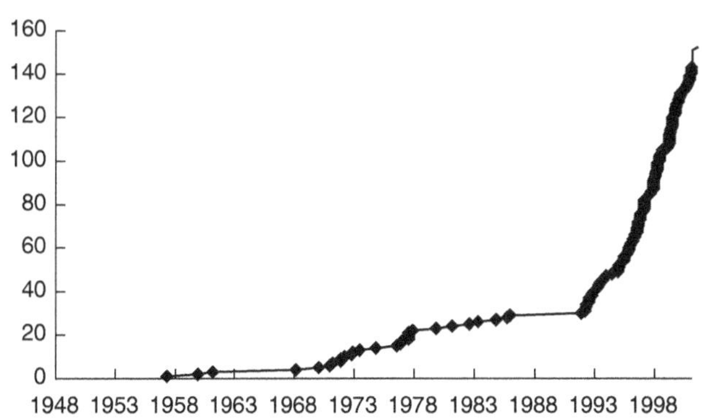

Figure 18.1 Annual changes in regional trade agreements.

Source: WTO homepage (www.wto.org)

Note

The above information only includes currently active RTAs reported to the GATT/WTO, and the number of RTAs is cumulative.

committed to opening its market through a parallel development of democracy and a market economy.

In addition, it is recognized that the supplier-oriented trade policy of the past must be changed into a consumer-oriented policy, which maximizes the convenience and benefits to the general public. In terms of cost-efficiency, the public's well-being is better served when the majority of consumers can be supplied with low-cost, high-quality goods rather than defending the interests of a minority of domestic producers. Therefore, the government must perform the role of opening up the domestic market, so that consumers can enjoy an abundance of low-cost, high-quality goods and services.

As part of its liberalization measures, the Korean government abolished the import diversification programme (IDP) at the end of June 1999. The IDP, introduced in early 1978, was a system of restricting imports from specific countries (targeting Japan) with which Korea was experiencing a serious trade deficit. The abolishment of the IDP can be regarded as one of Korea's most dramatic liberalization measures. Most Koreans have viewed this liberalization as beneficial, and there is a growing perception that the establishment of FTAs with major trading partners will bring greater welfare gains. Moreover, Korea has recognized the importance of stable export markets; it is thought that the current account deficit that preceded the financial crisis was the major cause of the loss of international confidence in the Korean economy that followed.

Another important background factor for the current trend towards regionalism can be found in trade policymakers' recognition of the need to upgrade Korea's economic system to meet international standards. The Korean government, with its policy goal of building an 'open trading country', is firmly committed to maintaining friendly trade relations with its trading partners, while also promoting strategic alliances in the form of FTAs and bilateral investment treaties (BITs).[4] Through such agreements, Korea seeks to establish alliances with its trading partners in order to secure the forward base in strategic regions and to upgrade its national competitiveness.

Though Korea has employed a relatively passive trade policy in the past, in the coming era of unlimited competition, Korea must be equipped with a more active and assertive trade policy in order to lay the foundation for national prosperity in the twenty-first century. Also, it is important to maintain friendly relations with trading partners, and to secure a stable export performance based on competitive domestic industries. In addition, Korea must attract additional foreign investment, not only for financial purposes but also for acquiring the advanced technology of foreign companies.

The establishment of FTAs helps to attract foreign investment and establish overseas footholds. The expansion of the domestic market through FTAs with major trading partners may give rise to new investment demand by parties interested in using Korea as a production base. The ability to attract foreign investment depends on the size of the domestic market as well as a favourable investment environment; if Korea establishes FTAs, foreign companies interested in exporting products to countries affiliated with Korea will invest in Korea to avoid tariffs.

In the process of overcoming the financial crisis, the Korean government realized that economic reform and an open policy can greatly influence foreign credit ratings and that continuous efforts are necessary for Korea to fully recover and play a pivotal role in the world economy. Although FTAs had long been considered elements of a closed trade policy that offered exclusive benefits to members, recently FTAs have come to be widely seen as channels for an open trade policy. Multilateral trading organizations such as the WTO and OECD now evaluate FTAs as having a positive influence on world trade liberalization, and this fact has played a part in the Korean government's decision to promote FTAs.

On the other hand, the need for measures to cope with the expansion of FTAs has also increased. In the past, Korea supported the superiority of the WTO multilateral trade system, adhering to its standpoint that regionalism should conform to a larger world trade system. At the first WTO Ministerial Conference in 1996, Korea pointed out the negative effects of regionalism and demanded tighter regulations against the expansion of regionalism. However, even after the launch of the WTO, RTAs continued to spread and currently nearly all countries with the exception of Korea, China and Taiwan are members of various RTAs. Members of RTAs rationalize their positions by asserting that further liberalization through regional trade agreements greatly contributes to a multilateral trade system, resulting in the creation of new trade opportunities. Thus, although various means of coping with the spread of regional trade agreements exist, the promotion of free trade itself, following the examples of other nations should be considered.

Free trade agreements help secure stable export markets and increase consumer welfare. While Korean companies have maintained a production system based on their comparative advantage in manufacturing technology, companies in other countries have made Korean products less competitive through advanced technology, in the case of developed countries, and low-wage price competitiveness, in the case of developing countries.[5] FTAs can improve Korea's production structure and strengthen exporting capabilities by enabling Korean companies to adopt advanced technology from foreign companies to integrate with Korea's production and marketing skills.

The new international order has shifted its emphasis from security and military-based power to economic power. The strong tendency to establish regional blocs through economic integration is being witnessed within and across all the continents. Regional integration has offered countries a way to resolve issues that would be more difficult to resolve in the wider multilateral context. To take an example, for the European Community, greater trade and economic integration was seen, above all, as a way of welding Europe's political future and making another continental war unthinkable. Also in the case of North American Free Trade Agreement (NAFTA), the degree of economic integration called for a deeper and more comprehensive regime of rules than could be achieved in the larger multilateral system.

Korea's pursuit of FTAs with major trading countries does not mean that it is necessarily downplaying the role or significance of the multilateral trade system. Rather it means that Korea is pursuing regional economic cooperation within the framework of the WTO, in line with the growing presence of other regional groups including the EU, NAFTA and ASEAN Free Trade Area (AFTA). The Korean government is also actively participating in the process of creating a new free trade framework such as the WTO New Round to counter the threat of emerging protectionism. Therefore, it plans to sign FTAs with its trade partners, starting with Chile. Korea and Chile reached an agreement on the basic principles of an FTA during the APEC summit meeting in November 1998. Currently, the FTA is still under negotiations.

18.3 Current progress of Korea's FTAs

18.3.1 Korea–Chile FTA

The basic direction of Korea's FTA policy was decided in a meeting of the Committee on International Economic Policy in November 1998. An FTA with Chile, currently under negotiations, would have priority and then sequential FTAs with similar small and medium-sized countries would be pursued after discussions with related government agencies and conducting studies on potential merits. Additional FTAs with major economies such as the United States, Japan and China would be decided upon after detailed in-depth analyses.

Korea and Chile agreed to begin official negotiations for a bilateral FTA at the Korea–Chile summit meeting held during the APEC Leaders' Meeting in Auckland in September 1999. Four rounds of negotiations were held from December 1999 to 2000, but a fifth round is being delayed due to differences on concessions in the agricultural sector. An agreement was reached at the bilateral summit meeting in Brunei in November 2000 to conclude negotiations as quickly as possible. Efforts to converge bilateral differences on agricultural concessions continued throughout 2001, with both countries airing their positions in a meeting between trade ministers in Santiago and agreeing to hold working meetings in the near future.[6]

Positions are sharply divided on the issue of concessions in the agricultural sector, mainly regarding the number of commodities for which tariffs will not be eliminated within ten years. Korea is demanding a flexible approach for highly sensitive items, while Chile wants all agricultural products to be liberalized within ten years after the conclusion of the FTA.[7] While an agreement was reached on areas of mutual exemption regarding anti-dumping measures, customs procedures, telecommunications, competition policy and dispute settlement, further negotiations on investment, product standards, rules of origin and safeguards are necessary.

18.3.2 Korea–Japan FTA

Although Japan is a major trading partner of Korea, second only to the United States, progress in the discussions of a bilateral FTA between the two countries has been slow. Anti-Japanese sentiments rising from historical antagonism, along with such thorny political, economic and social issues such as Korea's demand for a formal Japanese apology for past misdeeds, distortions in Japanese history textbooks, territorial disputes over Tokdo Island, and the issue of compensation for comfort women have aggravated fears over the bilateral FTA. In addition to these issues, Koreans are concerned about the possibility of economic subordination and growing trade deficit with Japan.

Official government reference to a bilateral FTA dates back to 1998. At a monthly meeting of the Federation of Korean Industries on 16 September 1998, the then Japanese ambassador to Korea, Ogura Kazuo, mentioned the need for a joint study on a Korea–Japan FTA in an address entitled 'Korea–Japan cooperation in the twenty-first century'. He also indicated the need to establish international regulations on anti-dumping and the opening of the rice market in order to cope with spreading globalization, as well as the need for expanded bilateral corporate alliances based on bilateral free trade. This was Japan's first official remark on the need to pursue an FTA between the two countries.[8]

The official government proposal for a joint study on a Korea–Japan FTA was made during Korean President Kim Dae-jung's state visit to Japan in October 1998. The Korean and Japanese governments appointed the Korea Institute for International Economic Policy (KIEP) and the Institute for Developing Economies (IDE) affiliated with the Japan External Trade Organization (JETRO) as joint research institutions. During his visit to Korea in March 1999, the Japanese Prime Minister Obuchi Keizo expressed his desire for strengthening bilateral relations beyond the scope of existing economic cooperation. Based on the results of a joint study, KIEP and IDE hosted the first symposium on a Korea–Japan FTA in Seoul in May 2000 (the second was conducted in Tokyo in September 2000).

During his September 2000 visit to Japan, President Kim proposed a Korea–Japan Business Forum (KJBF) to exchange views with the private sector, and proposed speedy negotiations for a BIT and expanded cooperation in the IT sector. Upon agreement, both countries set up a KJBF in the first half of 2001 and hosted the meetings in Seoul in September 2001 and in Tokyo in January 2002. In-depth consultations covered such comprehensive issues as the effects of a bilateral FTA on both countries' industries and ways of fostering an appropriate environment for a bilateral FTA. The January 2002 forum adopted a joint statement saying that governments of both countries should hasten to conclude a bilateral FTA.

Korea's President Kim and Prime Minister Koizumi of Japan held summit talks in March 2002 in Seoul, and agreed to continue probing the possibility of concluding an FTA through the introduction of a joint study group including government officials, industry representatives and academics.

18.3.3 FTAs with other nations

Korea is also currently studying FTAs with New Zealand and Thailand. At a meeting of trade ministers on 14 November 1998, Korea and Thailand agreed to initiate a joint study on the feasibility of an FTA that would facilitate bilateral trade and investment. An agreement on a joint study was reached at the eleventh Korea–Thailand Trade Commission Meeting in November 1999, with both governments designating the research institutions to conduct the study (Korea: KIEP, Thailand: Department of Business Economics under the Ministry of Commerce and Chulalongkorn National University). The joint study was conducted from November 1999 to March 2001, at the end of which the institutions exchanged their findings of positive results for an FTA between the two countries.

During her state visit to Korea in July 1999, New Zealand's Prime Minister Jennifer Shipley suggested pushing forward with discussions on a Korea–New Zealand

FTA. The two heads of state agreed to conduct a joint study on strengthening bilateral economic cooperation during President Kim's visit to New Zealand two months later. The designated research institutions in both countries (Korea: KIEP, New Zealand: New Zealand Institute for Economic Research (NZIER)) proceeded with the study. The two governments agreed to continue discussions on a bilateral FTA during Prime Minister Clark's visit to Korea in May, and a review meeting on the findings of the joint study was held in New Zealand in August 2001.

Although official discussions on a Korea–Singapore FTA have not yet taken place, the Singapore government has expressed an interest in concluding such an agreement. Michael Teo, Singapore's ambassador to Korea, sent a letter to Korea's Ministry of Foreign Affairs and Trade in 1999 expressing Singapore's desire to hold discussions on an FTA. At a summit meeting held during the APEC Leaders' Meeting in Auckland in September 1999, Prime Minister Goh Chok Tong of Singapore proposed a bilateral FTA to President Kim, a proposal which Singapore's Senior Minister Lee Kuan Yew reiterated in October of the same year. At that time, Korea maintained the position that an FTA with Chile held higher priority and did not actively review Singapore's proposal.

18.4 Why Korea chose Chile as its first FTA partner

The successful conclusion of the first FTA will be especially important to Korea since other potential FTAs will heavily depend on the first model. Prior to establishing FTAs with larger trade partners such as the United States, Japan, China and AFTA in the long term, Korea needs to pursue FTAs with smaller partners in the short term. The experience will help the government to minimize risks and possible losses, as well as to be better prepared for the operation and negotiation of FTAs. In this respect, Chile was considered to be the most appropriate partner for the following four reasons.

First, Chile's industrial structure, mainly concentrated on primary goods such as copper, wood and agricultural products, is highly complementary to Korea's industrial structure consisting of manufactured goods such as automobiles and electronics. Korea has few natural resources but has a large and well-trained workforce and well-developed technology. Chile is blessed with an abundance of natural resources and a strong agricultural base. Hence, the two economies, being dependent on different industries, can mutually benefit through strengthened economic cooperation. Moreover, being a small economy, the adjustment costs caused by an FTA are expected to be lower. This economic consideration increases the feasibility of a Korea–Chile FTA.

Second, Chile has accumulated over twenty years of experience in regional agreements with small and large economies. Chile has so far successfully concluded FTAs with Mexico, Canada, MERCOSUR (Common Market of South America), Peru, Venezuela, Ecuador and Columbia and is currently discussing the establishment of FTAs with Bolivia, Panama, Cuba and the EU. It has implemented drastic economic and institutional reforms under an economic opening process and is currently enjoying the full benefits of trade liberalization. Thus Chile can guide Korea in the course of the FTA negotiation with its know-how and group of skilled experts. Also, Chile's experience with operating a relatively liberalized economic market under FTAs will provide a useful example for Korea in adapting to a newly liberalized environment.

Third, the successful establishment of an FTA is highly dependent on the willingness and matched interests of the negotiating countries. Chile considers Korea as a model country for industrial development and as a foothold for gaining access to and luring foreign investment from the East Asian market. So, Chile has willingly accepted Korea's proposal of establishing a bilateral FTA and is strongly committed to ensuring a positive outcome to the negotiations.

Fourth, Chile can serve as a bridge toward the newly emerging Latin American market. Recognizing the importance of this market for Korean companies and the need to overcome its trade dependence on the United States and Japan, Korea has accelerated its advance to Latin America since the late 1980s. As a result, the percentage of exports to Latin American countries out of Korea's total exports increased from a mere 0.3 per cent in 1964 to 6 per cent in 1990, marking an annual average increase rate of nearly 50 per cent during the period 1990–95.

This sharp increase of exports is mainly due to the liberalization of tariff and non-tariff barriers and the increased demand for imports in Latin American countries resulting from political and economic stability and market opening since the early 1990s. Latin America has emerged as a newly developing region with its high growth potential. Moreover, with the establishment of NAFTA and other regional economic agreements such as MERCOSUR, CACM (Central America Common Market) and ANCOM (Andean Community), Latin America has been recognized as a new economic bloc with a big open market and increased competitiveness. Developed countries, such as the United States, EU and Japan, have already been trying to secure this market to take full advantage of first entry amid fierce competition.

In order to diversify Korea's export market and fully exploit the comparative advantage of Korean products such as electronics, textiles and automobiles, Korea also needs to take an aggressive export strategy towards this newly emerging continent. Chile, one of the most open economies having a multiple set of trade relations with other countries in Latin America, can be an ideal strategic partner for Korea to penetrate the Latin American trading bloc.

In this new era of economic interdependence, Korea also needs to protect and maximize its national interest by joining or creating trading blocs. The economic cooperation is expected to spill over to political and diplomatic cooperation, covering a wide range of issues such as security, environment, labour and cultural exchanges. In addition to economic aspects, Korea will enhance its political influence and diplomatic weight in international organizations and intergovernmental institutions. Chile and Korea share common principles of democracy and a free market economy, and there is a strong eagerness to expand commercial and political relations among the government leaders of both countries. So, the successful signing of a Korea–Chile FTA will provide the momentum to reinforce diplomatic ties between the two countries and serve as a catalytic force to intensify cooperation between the continents of East Asia and Latin America. Through the strategic alliance, the two regions are expected to emerge as key players in a newly established world order.

18.5 The need for a Korea–Japan FTA

Korea and Japan have decided to pursue FTAs with major trading partners in order to secure stable export markets, improve domestic trading rules, and strengthen industrial competitiveness. However, these are merely the general goals of pursuing FTAs and may not be sufficient in providing a logical basis for an FTA between Korea and Japan. Notwithstanding that an FTA with Japan has more political and historical obstacles than agreements with other countries, the objectives underlying the pursuit of a bilateral FTA are as follows: to form a strategic alliance and ease the excessive competition between the companies of the two countries; to jointly prepare against the rise of China and for Northeast Asian and East Asian economic integration; to strengthen international recognition; and to secure political stability in Northeast Asia.

What is Korea's motivation for concluding an FTA with Japan? First, among possible FTA candidates, Japan is the trading partner that can offer the most substantial increase in Korea's total exports. To date, the adverse effects of an FTA on the trading relations between Korea and Japan have been greatly emphasized. Despite the anticipated deterioration in its global trade balance with Japan, Korea should re-evaluate the positive impacts of an FTA with Japan, which will increase Korea's total exports and improve its global trade balance gradually.

Second, the opportunity costs of not having an FTA with Japan may be considerable. As widely known, Japan's manufacturing sector is more internationally competitive than Korea's. Overlapping investments and price competition in export markets can bring serious damage to both countries. The bilateral FTA can play an important role in establishing strategic joint ventures between companies of the two countries. If Japan proceeds with FTAs with Taiwan and ASEAN instead of Korea, the economic damage to Korea will be tremendous. In other words, Korea needs to contemplate whether it is able to sustain its current status without an FTA with Japan.

Finally, a Korea–Japan FTA is strategically significant. Discussions on a Korea–Japan FTA will be a driving force for other FTAs with the United States, China and ASEAN. If this FTA proceeds, China and the United States, who want to maintain their influence in Northeast Asia, may consider FTAs with Korea. Since 2001, talks on an East Asia free trade area (EAFTA) have been active. A realistic and subtle approach to accomplishing this FTA is to conclude a Korea–Japan FTA first and link it to Southeast Asia's AFTA. In short, a Korea–Japan FTA plays a critical role in generating interest in an FTA with Korea among Korea's trading partners.

A Korea–Japan FTA is expected to bring substantial economic gains to Japan. First of all, Korea charges higher tariffs than Japan generally, and the bilateral trade liberalization will allow Japanese firms to increase their exports to Korea.

While presenting the mutual benefits of a Korea–Japan FTA, Fukagawa (2000) evaluates Korea as one of the most appropriate FTA partners for Japan. A bilateral FTA could help foster more political stability on the Korean peninsula and allow Japan and Korea to enjoy greater economies of scale and larger inflows of foreign direct investment. Bilateral trade liberalization would also reduce overlapping investments, and strengthened financial cooperation could also expand Korea's use of capital in Japanese yen.

As for Japan, Korea is an ideal FTA partner since it can absorb Japan's various assets such as financial assets, technological assets and production know-how, more easily than other countries. Korea would be a strategic choice in converting Japan's full-set economy into a balanced economy of manufacturing and investment. Faced with an aging society, Japan needs to reorganize its industrial economic structure in haste. In order to avoid a labour shortage in the near future, Japan should relocate its production technology overseas and convert its industrial structure into a knowledge-based industry. Korea is a model partner in this aspect since it can absorb Japan's high technology at low cost and cooperate with Japanese companies. Considering Korea's positive social climate resulting from its reforms after the financial crisis, as well as reforms in economic policy, a bilateral FTA would provide Japan with the momentum to pursue much-needed reforms. These advantages give Korea the highest priority over Japan's other potential FTA partners, following the Japan–Singapore FTA (officially named the 'New Age Economic Partnership Agreement').

To elaborate further on the need for a Korea–Japan FTA, it should be pointed out that not only have shares of the world trade volume for both Korea and Japan been decreasing in recent years, but also trade between the two countries especially has declined after 1995. While there is no sign that the problem of overlapping and excessive investments will be resolved in the near future, excessive competition between Korean and Japanese companies for overseas markets continues to intensify. The competition for the US market can be clearly seen in the export similarity index (ESI)[9] in Table 18.1. The sustained ESI between Korea and Japan from 1995 to 1999 shows that Korea is not differentiating its products from Japanese goods, resulting in prolonged bilateral competition. The table also suggests that Korea's competition with China and Taiwan is increasing. According to the similarity index in industry structure, Korea is failing in reducing the gap with Japan in terms of competition, while facing increased competition with China and Taiwan.

If the competitiveness of Korea and Japan in the US market is examined by industry through revealed comparative advantage (RCA),[10] Korean products such as semiconductors, computers, automobiles, steel, textiles, musical instruments and rubber products have comparative advantage as of 2000. The comparative advantage of computers, automobiles, machinery, chemicals, steel and rubber products, and textiles, has improved since 1995, while the index for semiconductors, apparel, leather and plastic goods, musical instruments, and footwear has decreased (Table 18.2).

A study of the export competitiveness of Japanese products shows that semiconductors, computers, automobiles, machinery, precision machinery, musical

Table 18.1 ESI in the US market

	1995	*1997*	*1999*
Korea and Japan	0.61	0.62	0.62
Korea and China	0.51	0.50	0.56
Korea and Taiwan	0.71	0.73	0.74

Source: Park 2001.

Note
Use of two-digit SITC statistics.

Table 18.2 Changes in Korea's RCA by commodity

	1995	*2000*
Heavy and chemical industry		
Electric/electronic	2.55	2.45
(Semi-conductors)	5.57	4.73
(Computers)	2.10	2.66
Transportation equipment	0.52	0.89
(Automobiles)	0.79	1.33
Machinery	0.37	0.63
Precision machinery	0.37	0.31
Chemicals	0.21	0.24
Steel	1.36	1.58
Light industry		
Textiles	1.59	1.32
(Apparel)	1.41	1.15
(Fabrics)	3.12	3.17
Leather	1.77	0.82
Musical instruments	4.91	3.41
Plastic	0.87	0.77
Rubber	1.06	1.31
Footwear	1.31	0.28
Toys	0.52	0.37

Source: KOTIS Korea trade statistics, US trade statistics.

instruments, rubber goods and toys have comparative advantage. The comparative advantage of automobiles, machinery, musical instruments, rubber goods and toys has increased since 1995 but has decreased for semiconductors and computers (see Table 18.3).

The intensifying competition with Japan for export markets is worsening Korea's terms of trade. Korea's export structure is heavily dependent on a few selected commodities such as machinery, semiconductors and electric and electronic products, and therefore is volatile to world price fluctuations. As previously seen in Korea's RCA and Japan's ESI, rivalry with Japan combined with increasing competition from developing countries is weakening Korea's terms of trade (Figure 18.2).

For the last few decades, industries and related government agencies in both countries have held discussions on how to relieve the problem of excessive and

Table 18.3 Changes in Japan's RCA by commodity

	1995	*2000*
Heavy and chemical industry		
Electric/electronic	1.55	1.39
(Semi-conductors)	1.63	1.47
(Computers)	1.58	1.36
Transportation equipment	1.77	1.98
(Automobiles)	2.03	2.44
Machinery	1.68	1.86
Precision machinery	2.07	1.95
Chemicals	0.86	0.88
Steel	0.77	0.66
Light industry		
Textiles	0.08	0.08
(Apparel)	0.01	0.01
(Fabrics)	0.40	0.40
Leather	0.01	0.01
Musical instruments	1.89	2.30
Plastic	0.74	0.75
Rubber	1.08	1.44
Footwear	0.00	0.00
Toys	0.64	1.03

Source: KOTIS trade statistics, US trade statistics.

overlapping investments and how to avoid bilateral competition. However, trends in the ESI, RCA, and terms of trade of both countries show that the attempts have had little effect, proving that systematic mechanisms are necessary to alleviate these problems. Establishing an FTA that will influence the actions taken by companies may be more effective in inducing them to achieve structural adjustment.

Another rationale for concluding a Korea–Japan FTA is the need for joint action against the rapidly growing China. With the accession of China to the WTO at the Doha Ministerial Meeting in November 2001, China is in a position to gain increased international recognition as well as rapid economic growth. A Korea–Japan FTA may provide the means to cope with China's growing position on the international stage as well as the changing political order in Northeast and East Asia. A Korea–Japan FTA is expected to influence the struggle for leadership for Northeast Asian economic integration in the long run. After the Asian financial crisis, Japan tried to establish the Japanese yen as an international standard of currency in the East Asian region and to push forward with the establishment of an Asian Monetary Fund (AMF), but its attempts were thwarted by the objections of China, the United States, and the EU. Given the recent discussions on a Northeast Asia FTA consisting of Korea, China and Japan as well as an East Asia FTA, Korea and Japan may share a common interest in concluding a bilateral FTA first and then branching out to larger regional FTAs based on that experience.[11] Finally, a Korea–Japan FTA would strengthen the international status of both countries, and economic cooperation would considerably alleviate political and historical tension between them.

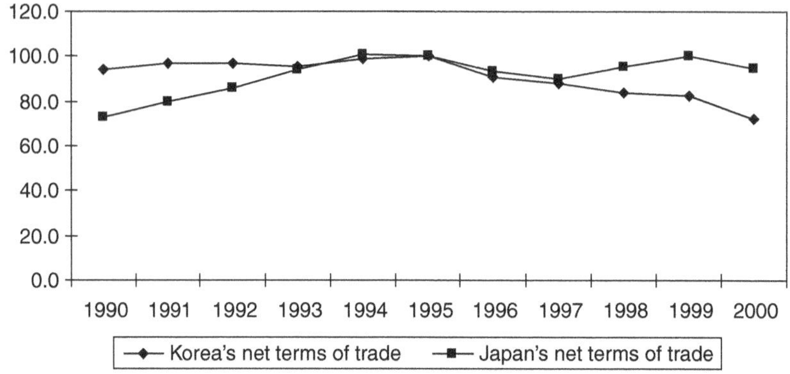

Figure 18.2 Korea and Japan's terms of trade (95 = 100).

Source: IMF 2001, *International Financial Statistics*; KOTIS 2001, *Major Trade Indicators.*

Note

Net terms of trade indicate the amount of products imported for one unit cost of export and is calculated by dividing the export unit cost index by the import unit cost index multiplied by 100.

18.6 Conclusion

Korea is in the process of FTA negotiations with Chile, and should expedite these negotiations to provide a feasible FTA environment internally and externally.[5] Furthermore, it should endeavor to seek a model FTA that provides a basis for negotiations to facilitate future FTAs. In the meanwhile, Korea should hasten FTA negotiations with Chile to lay the foundation for future FTAs.

In addition to the Korea–Chile FTA, Korea looked into the economic feasibility of an FTA with Japan in 1999 and came up with a positive prognosis. Korea's FTA with Japan is expected to yield substantial benefits by strengthening the strategic alliances among the firms of the two countries. A strategic alliance with Japan is especially critical, not only because of Japan's vast potential for providing investment capital but also because the combination of Japan's advanced technology with Korea's production capability will substantially enhance the competitiveness of domestic businesses. Moreover, an effective Korea–Japan partnership will mitigate Korea's trade imbalance with Japan.

Which country will be a good candidate for FTA partner after the FTA with Chile? Korea should pursue an FTA with Japan, regardless of the conclusion of the FTA with Chile (Cheong 2001b). Although the government of Korea maintains a sequential approach[12] for FTAs, a multi-track approach, that is, negotiating FTAs with multiple countries at the same time is advisable in order to maintain the momentum for FTA policies. Under the sequential approach, Korea will not have any FTA unless it concludes the first FTA negotiation with Chile. The majority of the public seems concerned about the negative effects of trade liberalization between the two countries, placing greater emphasis on the negative, rather than the positive, aspects. Many fear that competitive Japanese products will weaken Korea's industrial structure, pointing out that Korea's industrial competitiveness is weaker than Japan's, and that while Japan's average tariff rates range between 2 to 3 per cent, Korea's are much higher at 7 to 8 per cent.

However, the study by Cheong (2001a) indicates that Korea's industrial structure will not weaken as many people fear as long as Japan's high non-tariff barriers (NTBs) are mitigated, and a substantial amount of foreign direct investment flows into Korea. Instead, Korea would enjoy large mid- and long-term benefits under a bilateral FTA with Japan. Both Korean and Japanese companies have suffered from excessive competition in overseas markets mainly due to overlapping investments in their major industries. In order to alleviate this problem, the governments of the two countries have called for more bilateral industrial cooperation. However, a bilateral FTA would eliminate trade barriers and promote competition, leaving both Korean and Japanese companies with no choice but to pursue strategic alliances in order to survive. This can effectively eliminate overlapping investments and result in substantial long-term benefits.

Notes

1 The author appreciates fellow colleagues of Korea Institute for International Economic Policy (KIEP) and Korean trade policy makers for active discussion on Korea's FTA policy. The opinion provided in this paper is the author's personal ones.
2 RTAs can include all forms of preferential trading agreements, such as FTAs, customs unions, economic unions, etc. An FTA is the simplest form of RTA, in that it specifies tariff elimination among the member economies, without introducing common external tariffs.
3 The arrangement of preferential trading blocs must be reported to the GATT/WTO according to GATT XXIV, GATS V, and the Enabling Clause.
4 Korea signed the BIT agreement with Japan in March 2002, and is now negotiating a BIT with the United States.
5 Booz, Allen and Hamilton (1997) warned that Korea could be trapped in a 'nutcracker' – being caught between China's low costs and Japan's technical excellence. It states that 'Korea is too small to compete directly with either Japan or China over the long-term in its core industries', and thus, it suggests that Korea must leverage to the maximum extent possible the business and technical knowledge of the rest of the world.
6 Delegates of Korea and Chile met in Los Angeles in February 2002 and discussed the future negotiation schedules, including the fifth round negotiation, which was held in July 2002.
7 Although Chile maintains a position of complete liberalization, the country designated thirty-four items (wheat flour, sugar, oil seed, etc.) to be excluded from the liberalization scheme.
8 Discussions in the private sector for a Korea–Japan FTA were also underway. At a Korea–Japan meeting in Tokyo on 29 October 1998, participants agreed to conduct studies on a bilateral FTA and a free trade area consisting of the three Northeast Asian countries of China, Japan and Korea.
9 The export similarity index (ESI) illustrates the level of bilateral competition in a specific market. The make-up of export commodities is disparate when the index is nearer to 0 and similar when nearer to one.
10 Revealed comparative advantage (RCA) index allows for the comparison of competitiveness between countries with different-sized economies. It is calculated by dividing a country's share of exports in a given commodity category by the share in the world

exports of manufactured goods and is used to identify products in which a country does or does not have comparative advantage. If the index takes a value greater than one, then the share of a product in a country's exports is larger than the corresponding world share, therefore that country has a revealed comparative advantage in that product.

11 Discussions on a Northeast Asia FTA are currently underway between Korea, Japan and China for cooperation in industries such as steel. Although industrial cooperation is expected to strengthen regional economic cooperation, there are fears that without the introduction of an eligible institutional system such as an FTA, allowing preferential tariffs on certain commodities to only the three countries may violate multilateral trade rules.

12 A sequential approach is to conclude an FTA with Chile first before deciding on another partner with which to negotiate the next FTA.

Bibliography

Booz, Allen and Hamilton, Inc. (1997) *Revitalizing the Korean Economy towards the 21st Century*, Report for Vision Korea Committee, October.

Cheong, Inkyo (1995) *The Economic Effects of Asia-Pacific Economic Cooperation (APEC) and Asia-Based Free Trade Area (AF-11): A Computational General Equilibrium Approach*, PhD dissertation, Michigan State University.

——(1999) 'Keeping Korea's FTA policy consistent with APEC goals', *Journal of APEC Studies*, 1(1): 31–50.

——(2001a) 'The economic effects of a Korea–Japan FTA and policy implications', KIEP Policy Paper 01.04, Seoul: KIEP.

——(2001b) 'How to cope with the expansion of FTAs?', KIEP FTA Research Series, 01, Seoul: KIEP.

——(2002) *'Korea's FTA policy: current progress and desirable policy directions'*, KIEP Discussion Paper 02-02, Seoul: KIEP.

——and Wang, Yunjong (1999) 'Korea–US FTA: prospects and analysis', KIEP Working Paper 99.03, Seoul: KIEP.

——and Yoon, Jinna (2001) 'Korea–Chile FTA: background and economic effects', unpublished manuscript, KIEP.

Fukugawa, Y. (2000) 'Japan–Korea FTA as a new initiative in East Asia: beyond bitterness', Global Communications Platform from Japan No.00.05. Available Online, http://www.glocom.org/opinions/essays/200005_fukagawa_jp_kr_fta/index.html.

Igawa, Kazuhiro and Kim, Bonggil (2001) 'A note on possibilities about Japan–Korea free trade area: a theoretical and strategic approach', mimeo, Kobe, Japan: Kobe University.

International Monetary Fund (1997) *Direction of Trade Statistics Yearbook*, IMF Statistics Department, Washington, DC: IMF.

——(2001) *International Financial Statistics*, Washington, DC: IMF.

National Statistical Office (1999) *Quarterly Bulletin of International Statistics*, Seoul: National Statistical Office.

OECD (1999) *Financial Market Trends*, Paris: OECD.

Park, Soon-chan. (2001) 'Analysis of factors and changes in Korea's export competitiveness', *KIEP Internal Report*, Seoul: KIEP.

Ryou, Jai-Won and Lee, Honggue (1996) *Globalization of the Korean Economy: Challenges and Responses*, Seoul: Kon-Kuk University.

Sohn, Chan-Hyun and Yang, Junsok (1998) *Korea's Economic Reform Measures under the IMF Program*, Seoul: Korea Institute for International Economic Policy.

World Bank (1996) *World Development Report 1996*, Washington, DC: World Bank.

World Trade Organization (1995) *Regionalism and the World Trading System*, WTO Secretariat, Geneva: WTO.

Index

For Product Safety Concerns and Information please contact our EU representative GPSR@taylorandfrancis.com
Taylor & Francis Verlag GmbH, Kaufingerstraße 24, 80331 München, Germany

www.ingramcontent.com/pod-product-compliance
Lightning Source LLC
LaVergne TN
LVHW011110300926
849160LV00008B/329
* 9 7 8 1 1 3 8 8 1 0 6 8 6 *